Important Toolbars in E

Auditing toolbar

Remove Precedent Arrows   Remove Dependent Arrows   Trace Error   Show Info Window

Trace Precedents   Trace Dependents   Remove All Arrows   Attach Note

Drawing toolbar

Line   Ellipse   Freeform   Arrow   Filled Rectangle   Filled Arc   Create Button   Bring to Front   Group Objects   Reshape   Pattern

Rectangle   Arc   Text Box   Freehand   Filled Ellipse   Filled Freeform   Drawing Selection   Send to Back   Ungroup Objects   Drop Shadow

Query and Pivot toolbar

Pivot Table Field   Group   Show Detail   Refresh Data

Pivot Table Wizard   Ungroup   Hide Detail   Show Pages

For every kind of computer user, there is a SYBEX book.

All computer users learn in their own way. Some need straightforward and methodical explanations. Others are just too busy for this approach. But no matter what camp you fall into, SYBEX has a book that can help you get the most out of your computer and computer software while learning at your own pace.

Beginners generally want to start at the beginning. The **ABC's** series, with its step-by-step lessons in plain language, helps you build basic skills quickly. Or you might try our **Quick & Easy** series, the friendly, full-color guide.

The **Mastering** and **Understanding** series will tell you everything you need to know about a subject. They're perfect for intermediate and advanced computer users, yet they don't make the mistake of leaving beginners behind.

If you're a busy person and are already comfortable with computers, you can choose from two SYBEX series—**Up & Running** and **Running Start**. The **Up & Running** series gets you started in just 20 lessons. Or you can get two books in one, a step-by-step tutorial and an alphabetical reference, with our **Running Start** series.

Everyone who uses computer software can also use a computer software reference. SYBEX offers the gamut—from portable **Instant References** to comprehensive **Encyclopedias, Desktop References**, and **Bibles**.

SYBEX even offers special titles on subjects that don't neatly fit a category—like **Tips & Tricks**, the **Shareware Treasure Chests**, and a wide range of books for Macintosh computers and software.

SYBEX books are written by authors who are expert in their subjects. In fact, many make their living as professionals, consultants or teachers in the field of computer software. And their manuscripts are thoroughly reviewed by our technical and editorial staff for accuracy and ease-of-use.

So when you want answers about computers or any popular software package, just help yourself to SYBEX.

For a complete catalog of our publications, please write:

SYBEX Inc.
2021 Challenger Drive
Alameda, CA 94501
Tel: (510) 523-8233/(800) 227-2346 Telex: 336311
Fax: (510) 523-2373

SYBEX is committed to using natural resources wisely to preserve and improve our environment. As a leader in the computer book publishing industry, we are aware that over 40% of America's solid waste is paper. This is why we have been printing the text of books like this one on recycled paper since 1982.

This year our use of recycled paper will result in the saving of more than 15,300 trees. We will lower air pollution effluents by 54,000 pounds, save 6,300,000 gallons of water, and reduce landfill by 2,700 cubic yards.

In choosing a SYBEX book you are not only making a choice for the best in skills and information, you are also choosing to enhance the quality of life for all of us.

Mastering Excel 5 for Windows, Special Edition

Mastering Excel 5 for Windows™,
Special Edition

THOMAS CHESTER

San Francisco • Paris • Düsseldorf • Soest

SYBEX®

DEVELOPMENTAL EDITOR: Richard Mills
EDITOR: D. Robert
TECHNICAL EDITOR: Tanya Strub
BOOK DESIGNER: Suzanne Albertson
PRODUCTION ARTIST: Claudia Smelser, Alissa Feinberg
SCREEN GRAPHICS: John Corrigan, Aldo Bermudez
TYPESETTER: Ann Dunn
PROOFREADER/PRODUCTION COORDINATOR: Janet Boone
INDEXER: Ted Laux
COVER DESIGNER: Ingalls + Associates
COVER PHOTOGRAPHER: Mark Johann
Screen reproductions produced with Collage Complete.
Collage Complete is a trademark of Inner Media Inc.

Library of Congress Card Number: 93-87245
ISBN: 0-7821-1312-5

Manufactured in the United States of America
10 9 8 7 6 5 4 3 2 1

ACKNOWLEDGMENTS

I WISH to thank the talented people who helped make this book possible.

First and foremost, I would like to thank Julia Kelly, my associate at LEX Software Systems, who worked with me on this project from start to finish. Her skill and dedication were indispensable factors in the development of this book.

I am fortunate to have affiliated with a quality publisher like SYBEX, and particularly wish to thank Richard Mills and Doug Robert. You guys were a pleasure to work with.

The technical review was done by Tanya Strub, who did a great job under pressure.

There are many people at Microsoft who helped, directly and indirectly. Thank you to Corey Salka, Eric Michelman, Eric Wells, and Dan Williams. And thanks to Mike Conte for helping me out over the years.

I owe a lot to my associates at LEX Software Systems. I am proud to work with amazingly talented people like Chris Kinsman and Mark Nelson—this book would not have been possible without the two of you holding down the fort.

Karie, thanks for putting up with the long hours, and for your encouragement. Thanks to Kaitlin and Miles, the greatest kids around. (I told you I'd put your names here!)

Finally, I wish to thank my dad, a great writer and an all-around great guy.

Contents
AT A GLANCE

CONTENTS

PART FOUR   GRAPHICS AND CHARTS

PART FIVE DATABASE POWER

PART SEVEN **SOLVING REAL-WORLD PROBLEMS**

APPENDICES

INTRODUCTION:
What's New in Excel 5

SPREADSHEETS started out as electronic versions of hard copy accounting worksheets with one major purpose: simple row-and-column arithmetic. These programs have evolved dramatically over the past decade, and are one of the most widely used categories of software products. Excel has long been the leading graphical spreadsheet, and Microsoft has released a major upgrade with version 5.0.

What's New in Excel 5?

There are a lot of new features in Excel 5 that you will want to explore.

Everything Is a Workbook

Workbooks were first introduced in Excel 4. In Excel 5, workbooks are no longer an option. All Excel 5 worksheets reside in workbooks, with tabs used to navigate the sheets. See Chapter 2 for in-depth coverage of this key structural change.

Charting Overhaul

Many users will welcome the major overhaul of Excel's charting engine. Some of the key new features are:

- Simplified interface for creating, modifying, and customizing charts

- Drag and drop data onto a chart to add a data point or data series

- New Error Bars and Trendlines

- Flexible combination charts

See Chapters 14 and 15 for in-depth coverage of the new charting features.

Simplified Interface

The Excel interface has received a facelift. Several new interface features are covered in Chapter 1:

- Submenus, also known as cascading menus

- Tabbed dialog boxes

- Tear-off palettes

TipWizard

The new TipWizard, covered in Chapter 7, provides shortcuts for tasks that you perform, as you perform them.

In-Cell Editing

This feature will be welcome news to those with eye fatigue after squinting at the formula bar for hours on end. Chapter 3 explains how to edit cells in-place.

Format Individual Characters within a Cell

Excel has long provided a rich variety of cell formatting options. Now, you can format *individual characters* within a cell. See Chapter 5.

Database Management

Excel has always provided powerful database manipulation features, but a lot of learning was involved in order to harness this power. Excel 5's major overhaul of the database features is one of the most important improvements to Excel. Sorting and filtering have been vastly simplified. See Part 5 to learn about managing and analyzing data.

Pivot Tables

For many users, Pivot Tables will be the most important new feature in Excel 5. Pivot Tables provide a very flexible and powerful way for users to view and pivot data. If you are considering using Lotus Improv as an analytical tool, it will serve you well to explore Excel's Pivot Table before taking the Lotus plunge. See Chapter 17 for coverage of this powerful new feature.

Simplified Access to External Databases

A large percentage of Excel users, particularly those in the corporate environment, use Excel to access information stored in external database systems such as dBASE, Paradox, Foxpro, SQL Server, and Oracle. A new tool, Microsoft Query, has vastly simplified access to external databases. See Chapter 18 for a fast-track primer on Microsoft Query.

OLE 2 Support

Excel now supports the second version of the object linking and embedding specification (OLE 2). This means it will be easier to work with embedded objects from other applications, such as a word processor or graphics program, in your Excel documents. (See Chapter 25.)

Visual Basic, Applications Edition

Excel 5 is the first Microsoft application to adopt Microsoft's common macro language, which is based on their highly successful programming language, Visual Basic. This will be by far the biggest news for application developers. See Part 6 for an introduction to VBA.

How Excel Is Used in the Workplace

Excel is used for a wide variety of applications.

Basic Use

Even though Excel is a multifaceted tool, many people still use it as an electronic replacement for the hardcopy accountant's worksheet. In this capacity, Excel can be used to help automate financial statements, business forecasting, transaction registers, inventory control, accounts receivable, accounts payable—the list of potential applications is endless.

Financial Modeling

Financial models can be created that let you play *what-if*. By changing one or more variables, the model recalculates, and a new set of results can be presented in tabular and/or graphical format. Multi-level rollups can be performed automatically. For example, cost centers can roll up into departments, which roll up into divisions, which roll up into company summaries.

Scientific & Engineering

While spreadsheets are usually thought of as tools for business, Excel provides many statistical, analytical, and scientific functions. It is used in many scientific and engineering environments to crunch numbers and present findings.

Presentation Graphics

Excel is a powerful, flexible graphical presentation tool. Worksheets can include charts and graphs, and can be formatted for high-impact presentations.

Database Management

Excel is a highly adept data management tool. For many database requirements, users find that Excel's interface allows them to get up to speed very quickly in comparison to "real" database management programs. It is very easy to enter, edit, sort, and filter databases in Excel.

Database Front-End

Excel database manipulation is simple, yet spreadsheets inherently lack certain features found in actual database management programs. By using Excel as a database *front-end*, you can realize the best of both worlds. Excel is able to access data stored in a wide variety of database formats, and is an ideal tool to analyze and manipulate data, and to create high-impact reports and graphical presentations.

Custom Applications

Excel is a powerful application development tool. Many of the world's largest corporations have utilized Excel to create serious, large-scale custom applications. It is the first Microsoft product to include *Visual Basic, Applications Edition* (VBA), the language that will eventually drive all of Microsoft's programmable applications.

A Roadmap to This Book

The book is divided into seven parts.

Part One—Getting Started

This part of the book is important for beginners, but even veterans can learn about some important new features.

- Chapter 1 explains the elements of the Excel workspace, including new user-interface features such as tabbed dialog boxes and sub-menus.

- Learn about the new workbook interface in Chapter 2, and basic skills such as how to save your work.

- Chapter 3 is essential for novices. It explains how to enter and edit information, how to navigate the worksheet, and how to copy and move information.

Part Two—Basic Skills

Here is where you learn many of the most important basic skills.

- In Chapter 4, learn how to enter formulas and functions. You can also get a clear explanation of a topic that sometimes confuses new users—cell references.

- Chapter 5 covers the many different ways you can format cells.

- Learn about the nuances of printing in Chapter 6.

- Chapter 7 provides a number of productivity tips. You will probably learn some important skills, regardless of how much Excel experience you have.

Part Three—Tapping Excel's Power

This section of the book provides important insights on how to get the most out of Excel.

- Using names is vitally important, and Chapter 8 provides a thorough discussion of this topic.

- Chapter 9 provides a comprehensive discussion of the handful of worksheet functions considered essential for serious Excel users.

- Don't skip Chapter 10! Templates are an important topic, and this chapter explains not only how, but why.

- Chapter 11 explains how to audit, protect, and document workbooks and worksheets.

Part Four—Graphics and Charts

You might have a lot of fun in this part of the book.

- Chapter 12 shows you how to place graphics on worksheets, and how to format them.

- Learn all of the important charting skills in Chapters 13 and 14

Part Five—Database Power

This part of the book is vitally important, even if the problems you are trying to solve do not appear to be database problems.

- Chapters 15 and 16 show you how to work with internal databases (or "lists")—data that resides on a worksheet.

- Arguably, Pivot Tables are the most important new feature in Excel 5, and they are covered in depth in Chapter 17.

- Excel is a powerful tool for accessing external databases, and Chapter 18 explains how.

Part Six—Customizing Excel

Excel is easy to customize, so don't be put off if you are not a programmer.

- In Chapter 19, learn how to place controls, such as list boxes and option buttons, on worksheets. (It's easy!) You'll also learn how to create custom dialog boxes.

- Chapter 20 provides an introduction to macros, and shows you how to use the macro recorder effectively.

- Create a powerful, graphical custom application, start to finish, in Chapter 21.

Part Seven—Solving Real-World Problems

This part of the book covers many special skills to help you solve real problems.

- A vital topic, consolidation, is covered in Chapter 22.

- Chapter 23 shows how to use three important what-if features: Goal Seek, Solver, and Scenario Manager.

- Learn how to work with add-ins in Chapter 24, including View Manager, Report Manager, and the Analysis ToolPak.

- If you think OLE is just a buzzword, read Chapter 25 to learn how to employ this important (yet simple) technology. You will also learn how to import and export data, and how to transition from Lotus 1-2-3.

- Learn some key skills in Chapter 25, such as custom AutoFill, customizing toolbars, and array formulas.

Conventions Used in This Book

- Toolbar shortcuts are indicated with an icon in the left margin, as pictured here.

- Menu commands are expressed using the following convention: File ➤ Print.

- The plus sign is used to indicate when one key is held down while another key is pressed. For example, Alt+Tab means to hold down the Alt key and then press the Tab key.

- At the beginning of each chapter is a *Fast Track*, which provides quick coverage of the most important topics covered in the chapter.

PART ONE

Getting Started

The Excel Environment

fast **TRACK**

All Excel 5 files are workbooks.   **13**

- A workbook contains one or more sheets.
- When you open and save a file created with an earlier version of Excel, it is saved as a workbook with only one sheet in it.

**A worksheet consists of 16,384 rows and
256 columns.**   **15**

They are all available whether you use them or not.

To display or hide a toolbar   **15**

Choose View ➤ Toolbars, select checkboxes for the toolbars to display, and click OK.

THIS chapter provides the essential skills needed for working with workbooks, worksheets, and windows:

- *opening, closing, and saving workbooks*
- *managing worksheets within workbooks*
- *arranging and navigating windows*
- *controlling how things are displayed*

Workbooks

Unlike previous versions of Excel, *all* Excel 5 documents are workbooks. Think of a workbook as a binder. This binder contains one or more sheets, which can be thought of as pages within the binder. Workbooks can contain:

- worksheets (covered in this chapter)
- chart sheets (covered in Chapter 13)
- macro sheets, modules, and dialog sheets (covered in Part Six)

When you start Excel, a workbook named *Book1* is automatically displayed. Book1 is a new, unsaved workbook that is ready for input.

- Icons can be placed on the Program Manager desktop to start Excel *and* open a specific file—see Chapter 7, "Productivity Basics," to learn how.

The first time you run Excel, you are given the opportunity to take a guided tour. If you decline, you can later choose Help ➤ Quick Preview to get an interactive tour of the Excel environment.

NOTE   Because Excel 5 can be easily customized by the user, the screen you see when you first start up the program will probably not look exactly like the screen you might see on your coworkers' machines. Excel's default appearance is based on settings that were chosen when the program was installed; also, its startup appearance can be set from within the program—for example, you can instruct it to remember certain settings from session to session.

The Windows Interface

Excel runs under Microsoft Windows, and adheres to Windows interface standards. If you have used other Windows programs, you will see many familiar controls, such as the application controls, window controls, menu bar, and scroll bars (see Figure 1.1). These controls work the same way as other Windows programs. If you are new to Microsoft Windows, refer to the introduction for pointers on getting up to speed on the Windows interface.

FIGURE 1.1

The Excel Workspace

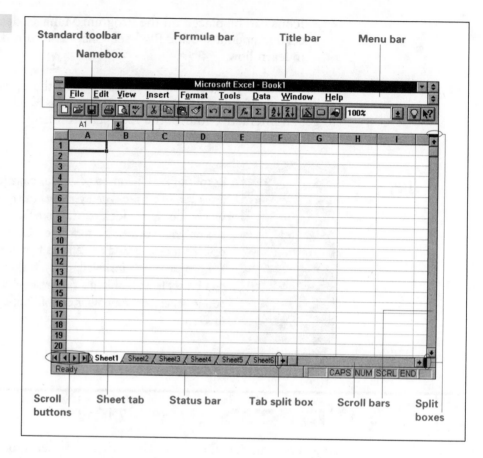

The Menu System

In Excel 5, the menus have been completely reorganized, and veterans will require some adjustment to the new structure (see Figure 1.1). The simplification of the menu system is achieved with *submenus* and *tabbed dialog boxes*. (Appendix A provides a cross-reference between the Excel 4 menu system and the Excel 5 menu system.)

If You Know One Windows Application...

Perhaps the most beneficial aspect of Microsoft Windows is its *common user interface*, often referred to as CUI. What this means is that some of the most often used commands, such as File ➤ New, File ➤ Open, File ➤ Close, File ➤ Save, Edit ➤ Copy, and Edit ➤ Paste, are similar, if not identical, from program to program. If you have used other Windows programs, these commands will be familiar to you when using Excel.

Submenus

An important improvement to the Excel interface is submenus, sometimes referred to as cascading menus. The submenu displays more choices which *cascade* to the right of the menu command when selected. You then choose a command located on the submenu. Commands that display submenus are indicated by the triangle symbol:

For example, the Format ➤ Row command, when selected, displays a submenu with several options from which you can select:

Keyboard Shortcuts

Many menu commands have keyboard shortcuts, which display to the right of the command. For example, Ctrl+C is the shortcut for the Edit ➤ Copy command , and F5 is the shortcut for Edit ➤ Go To, as you can see in the Edit menu:

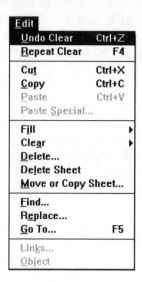

Commands with Checks

Some menu commands, such as View ➤ Status Bar, have a checkmark next to the command:

Such commands are toggles—the checkmark is an indicator specifying if the setting is toggled on or off.

- When checked, choosing the View ➤ Status Bar command hides the status bar and unchecks the command.

- When unchecked, choosing the View ➤ Status Bar command displays the status bar and checks the menu command.

Dimmed Menu Commands

A dimmed menu command is a command that is unavailable for one reason or another. For example, the Window ➤ Unhide command in the following menu is available only when a window is hidden; otherwise it is dimmed:

Quick Explanations of Menu Commands

The status bar (refer to Figure 1.1) displays a brief explanation for menu commands. The description is displayed when the command is *selected* but not *issued*. To select a command with the mouse, click on it but don't release the mouse button. An explanation of the selected command will display.

Which Commands Stop for Input?

Menu commands that display dialog boxes have an ellipsis (three dots) after the command. For example, the View ➤ Toolbars... command in the View menu pictured earlier displays a dialog box, whereas the View ➤ Formula Bar command takes immediate action.

There are exceptions to this interface convention. Some commands are immediate in certain situations and display a dialog box in others. An example is the File ➤ Save command. When saving a file that has never been saved, a dialog box is displayed. Otherwise the command acts immediately. Such commands do not include an ellipsis.

Tabbed Dialog Boxes

An important new feature used in Excel is the tabbed dialog box. Tabbed dialog boxes serve to group related dialog boxes under one roof. A good example is the dialog box displayed by the Format ➤ Cells command pictured in Figure 1.2.

FIGURE 1.2

A tabbed dialog box is like a stack of index cards

All of the cell formatting commands are grouped together in the Format ➤ Cells tabbed dialog box. The tabs on top of the dialog box are clicked with the mouse to display the desired dialog box. Tabbed dialog boxes remember which tab was last used—when you redisplay the dialog box, the last tab used is the active tab.

Workbooks

An Excel document is a *workbook*. Workbooks are containers for one or more *worksheets* (and other types of sheets, as you will later discover).

- Think of a workbook as a *binder*.
- Think of every worksheet as a *page* in the binder.

NOTE Whereas workbooks were an option in Excel 4, all Excel 5 documents are workbooks. Also, there is no longer a concept of bound and unbound worksheets. All worksheets in an Excel 5 workbook are automatically bound.

Upon starting up Excel, the first thing you typically see is a workbook named *Book1* (see Figure 1.1). Book1 is a new, unsaved workbook that is displayed by default.

Opening Worksheets Created in Earlier Versions of Excel

Worksheets that were created in earlier versions of Excel can be opened using the File ➤ Open command. When opened, the old worksheet automatically becomes a workbook containing just one worksheet. When you save the file, Excel asks if you want to convert to Excel 5 format. If you answer no, the file stays in the older format, though any formulas and formats you may have used that are new to Excel 5 will not be saved (Figure 1.3).

TIP If users within your organization are still using an older version of Excel, you can still transfer files back and forth. Just remember *not* to update the file to Excel 5 format. See Chapter 2 to learn about workbooks and worksheets.

FIGURE 1.3

When you save a file created in an earlier version of Excel, you will be asked if you want to save it in the previous version or update it to Excel 5 format

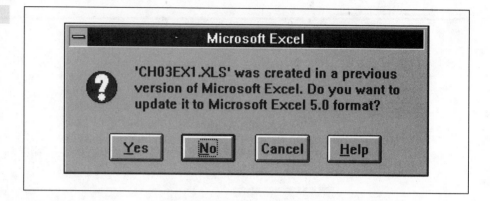

Worksheets within Workbooks

Worksheets are the pages within a workbook. A worksheet consists of a grid of *cells*, very similar to a hardcopy accounting worksheet. Cells, which are oriented in rows and columns, are used to store numbers, text, and formulas. Worksheets are not limited to numbers and text—they can also contain graphical objects, such as charts, arrows, and pictures.

By default, a workbook includes 16 worksheets, named *Sheet1* through *Sheet16*, though there is no limit other than available memory. Typically, you would store related worksheets in a single workbook to keep them together. For example, you might keep regional sales projections in one workbook, with information for each region stored on individual worksheets. Another worksheet within the same workbook might be used to consolidate the regions.

At the bottom of the workbook are tabs, which are used to activate the worksheets within that workbook (see Figure 1.1). Activating a worksheet is the equivalent of bringing the page to the front of the binder. See Chapter 2 for more information on worksheets.

Cells

Each worksheet is comprised of a tabular grid of *cells*. There are 16,384 rows of cells, numbered 1 through (you guessed it) 16,384 along the left margin of the worksheet. There are 256 columns labeled alphabetically as A through IV using a single-digit then a double-digit alphabetization scheme along the top margin of the worksheet. This means that every worksheet contains over 4,000,000 cells. Text, numbers, and formulas can be entered into cells.

Cell References

Cells are referred to using the column label followed by the row number. For example, the cell coordinate A2 would refer to column 1, row 2. In spreadsheet terminology, a cell's row and column coordinates are called the *cell reference*. See Chapter 4 to learn about cell references.

The Active Cell

When you select a cell by clicking it with the mouse, or moving to it using the keyboard, it becomes the *active cell*. The *Name Box*, on the left of the formula bar (see Figure 1.1), displays the reference of the active cell.

Toolbars

Toolbars provide shortcuts for many of the most common commands. There are many different toolbars, each of which contains several individual *tools*. The *Standard toolbar* is displayed by default (see Figure 1.1).

Displaying and Hiding Toolbars

The View ➤ Toolbars command displays the toolbar dialog box, which controls which toolbar or toolbars are displayed and allows them to be customized (see Figure 1.4). The toolbar names have checkboxes next to them—check the box to display the toolbar, or uncheck the box to hide the toolbar.

FIGURE 1.4

The View ➤ Toolbars
dialog box

> **TIP**
>
> A quick way to display the toolbar dialog box is to point at a toolbar, click the right mouse button, and choose Toolbars from the shortcut menu that appears.

Getting Pop-up Tool Explanations

The function of a tool is sometimes hard to determine by looking at the graphical toolface. The *Show ToolTips* setting (see Figure 1.4), when checked, causes the title of a tool to display when the tool is pointed at with the mouse. Regardless of the *Show ToolTips* setting, a brief explanation of the tool is displayed on the status bar when the tool is pointed at with the mouse.

Controlling the Size of the Tools

By default, tools are relatively small, and, depending on your monitor, it may be difficult to clearly discern the toolface. Choose the *Large Buttons* setting (see Figure 1.4) to display large tools.

Moving Toolbars

By default, toolbars are *docked* underneath the menu bar. To move a toolbar, point at the bar (i.e., without actually pointing at any single tool) and drag it to a different location on the Excel window. If the toolbar is dragged to the top, bottom, left, or right edge of the workspace, it is docked. If it is dragged anywhere inside the workspace, it is said to "float," as pictured in Figure 1.5.

FIGURE 1.5

A floating toolbar

One advantage of floating toolbars versus docked toolbars is you gain a larger workspace, though a floating bar will always obscure some part of the active worksheet.

Drop-down Palettes

 Some tools have an arrow button next to them. An example is the Border tool shown at left, found on the Formatting toolbar. You can click the arrow to display a drop-down palette of choices:

The palette can be torn away from the toolbar by grabbing the edge of the palette with the mouse, and dragging it away from the toolbar. After being torn away, the palette behaves just like a floating toolbar (except that you cannot dock it again—you must click its control box to close it instead).

What the Tools Do

Table 1.1 describes the functions of the tools on the *Standard* toolbar. Toolbars and tools can be customized—see Chapter 26 to learn how.

TABLE 1.1: Standard Toolbar Tools

TOOL	COMMAND EQUIVALENT	FUNCTION
	File ➤ New	Opens new workbook
	File ➤ Open	Opens existing workbook
	File ➤ Save	Saves active workbook
	File ➤ Print	Prints active workbook

TABLE 1.1: Standard Toolbar Tools (continued)

TOOL	COMMAND EQUIVALENT	FUNCTION
	File ➤ Print Preview	Previews what printed pages will look like
	Tools ➤ Spelling	Checks spelling
	Edit ➤ Cut	Moves selected cells
	Edit ➤ Copy	Copies selected cells
	Edit ➤ Paste	Pastes cut or copied cells
	n/a	Format Painter—Copies formatting between cells or objects (see Chapter 5)
	Insert ➤ Function ➤ Sum	AutoSum—Enters SUM function in selected cells (see Chapter 4)
	Insert ➤ Function	Starts FunctionWizard
	Edit ➤ Undo	Undoes last action
	Edit ➤ Repeat	Repeats last action
	Data ➤ Sort Ascending	Sorts selected cells in ascending order
	Data ➤ Sort Descending	Sorts selected cells in descending order

TABLE 1.1: Standard Toolbar Tools (continued)

TOOL	COMMAND EQUIVALENT	FUNCTION
	Insert ➤ Chart	Starts ChartWizard (see Chapter 14)
	n/a	Draws text box (see Chapter 13)
	View ➤ Toolbars ➤ Drawing	Displays Drawing toolbar
100%	View ➤ Zoom	Reduces/enlarges worksheet magnification
	n/a	Starts TipWizard
	Help	Displays Help pointer (see Help section in Chapter 1)

Charts and Graphics

Excel worksheets are not limited to numbers and text. Charts and other graphical objects can be placed on worksheets, allowing for the creation of high-impact graphical presentations.

 There are several ways to create charts, but the *ChartWizard* is the quickest and easiest method. The ChartWizard, accessed by clicking the ChartWizard tool shown at left, gives you a variety of basic chart types to work with, as shown in Figure 1.6.

- Charts are usually linked to data stored on worksheets, and change automatically when the data on the worksheet changes.

FIGURE 1.6

Chart types
available through
the ChartWizard

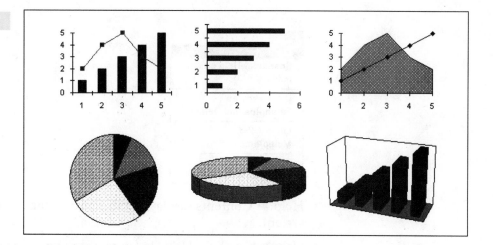

- Charts are usually linked to data stored on worksheets, and change automatically when the data on the worksheet changes.

- Excel is a capable drawing program in its own right. The drawing tools allow various objects to be drawn on worksheets (covered in Chapter 12).

- Graphics from other programs can be pasted onto a worksheet. See Chapters 12 and 25, to learn how to incorporate graphics from other programs.

- Many formatting options can be applied directly to cells, such as fonts, borders, and colors. See Chapter 5 to learn how to format cells.

Using Online Help

Excel's online help system is extensive, and there are a number of ways to access it, as explained in the following paragraphs.

The Help Menu

The Help menu provides several entry points into the online help system.

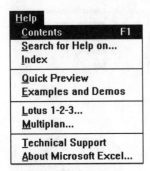

- Help ➤ Contents displays a table of contents for the online help system.

- Help ➤ Search for Help On lets you search for help on a certain topic.

- Help ➤ Index displays an index for online help.

- Help ➤ Quick Preview provides a tutorial-like preview of Excel.

- Help ➤ Examples and Demos accesses various samples of work-sheets and charts, in a tutorial format.

- Help ➤ Lotus 1-2-3 provides help for Lotus users.

- Help ➤ Multiplan diplays a dialog box that provides help for Multiplan users.

Getting Help on a Specific Menu Command

Help can be easily displayed for any menu command. Follow these steps:

1. Using the mouse, select the command *but don't release the mouse button*. (Or, using the keyboard, select the command without pressing Enter.)

2. Press F1.

Using the Help Tool

 Another way to get help is with the Help tool shown at left. It lets you get context-sensitive help by pointing and clicking on different areas of the workspace.

1. Click the Help tool. The mouse pointer will now have a large question mark next to it—it is now a *help pointer*, as seen below.

2. Point and click on the part of the window that you want help for. Excel will display a window with text explaining the use of the selected item.

3. To cancel the help pointer, click the Help tool again or else press Esc.

Getting Help for Dialog Boxes

Online help is available for every dialog box. Click the Help button in the dialog box, or else press F1 while the dialog box is displayed.

CHAPTER

2

Workbooks, Worksheets, and Windows

f a s t TRACK

THIS chapter provides the essential skills needed for working with workbooks, worksheets, and windows:

- *opening, closing, and saving workbooks*
- *managing worksheets within workbooks*
- *arranging and navigating windows*
- *controlling how things are displayed*

Workbooks

Unlike previous versions of Excel, *all* Excel 5 documents are workbooks. Think of a workbook as a binder. This binder contains one or more sheets, which can be thought of as pages within the binder. Workbooks can contain:

- worksheets (covered in this chapter)
- chart sheets (covered in Chapter 13)
- macro sheets, modules, and dialog box sheets (covered in Part Six)

When you start Excel, a workbook named *Book1* is automatically displayed. Book1 is a new, unsaved workbook that is ready for input.

NOTE

In earlier versions of Excel, the first action taken by many users after starting Excel was to close the automatic new worksheet. (Opening old documents is no doubt a more common activity than creating new ones.) In Excel 5, if the first thing you do is open an existing workbook, Book1 is closed automatically—no need to close it on your own.

Creating New Workbooks

Choose the File ➤ New command to create a new workbook. Each workbook that you create during an Excel session is automatically named using a sequential number, i.e., *Book1*, *Book2*, etc. The first time a workbook is saved, you can assign it a name of your choosing (within DOS file naming limitations).

TIP

You can create a new workbook by dragging a worksheet tab out of the workbook window and dropping it on the Excel desktop (resize the workbook window so that there is room on the Excel desktop to drop the sheet icon).

Opening Existing Workbooks

Choose the File ➤ Open command to open a workbook that has been previously saved to disk (see Figure 2.1). This dialog box is very similar to other File ➤ Open dialog boxes you may have used in other Windows programs. You can select the file from the list of files, or type in a file name.

Finding Workbooks

Click the Find File button in the File ➤ Open dialog box (see Figure 2.1) to search for a workbook based on name, location, title, subject, author, keywords, time created, or time last saved. More details on the Find File feature are in Chapter 11, "Auditing and Protecting Your Work."

Opening Files Read-Only

Check the *Read Only* setting if you want to open the file *without* the ability
to save changes. Opening a file read-only does not prevent you from making changes—it prevents you from *saving* the changes. The read-only option serves several useful purposes:

- You can open a workbook as read-only to avoid accidentally
  changing a file that you don't want to change.

- A read-only workbook may be shared by more than one user on a
  network; if opened as read-only, another user can still open it,
  change it, and save it.

- If another user on the network has a file open with write permis-
  sion (in other words, not read-only), you will still be allowed to
  open it as read-only.

TIP

What if you make changes to a read-only workbook, and want to save the changes? *Answer:* Choose the File ➤ Save As command to save it to a different file name.

Many Types of Files Can Be Opened

The *List Files of Type* list in the File ➤ Open dialog box determines which files are displayed in the File Name list box. It serves to filter the file names just as you can at the DOS prompt using an asterisk as a wildcard. See Chapter 25, "Working with Other Programs and Data," for more information on the types of files Excel is capable of working with.

Opening More Than One File at a Time

Mouse Approach The list box in the File ➤ Open dialog box is a multi-select list box. You can select more than one file by holding down the Ctrl or Shift keys while selecting from the list. When OK is clicked, all selected files are opened.

Keyboard Approach Type the file names in the *File Name* box, separated by spaces.

If the Workbook Is Stored on a Network Drive

If you are already logged on to a network, no problem—just open the file using one of the approaches discussed above.

If you are not already logged on to the network—that is, if your machine is physically connected but you haven't logged on, click the Network button, and a dialog box is displayed allowing you to make the network connection to the disk drive containing the workbook.

Opening Recently Used Files

Excel keeps track of the last four files used, and displays them on the bottom of the File menu:

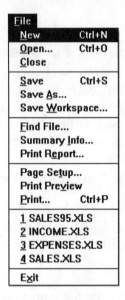

Choose the file name from the File menu to open it.

More Than One Workbook Can Be Open

As implied above, Excel supports what is known as the *multiple document interface*, or MDI. You may have more than one workbook open at a time. Each time you create a new file using File ➤ New, or open an existing file using File ➤ Open, another workbook is added to the workspace. The Window menu will list all open workbooks at the bottom, with a checkmark next to the *active* workbook. Select a different workbook from the Window menu to activate it.

Saving Your Work

 Once changes are made to a workbook, choose the File ➤ Save command to save it to disk. The first time you save a workbook, Excel displays the Save As dialog box (Figure 2.2) so you can give the file a name.

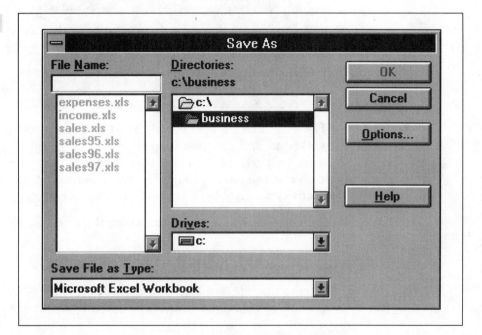

Subsequent File ➤ Save commands automatically use the current file name to save the file.

The file name is subject to DOS file name limitations.

Save As...

The File ➤ Save As command allows you to save a file under a different name. The command's dialog box is identical to the one displayed the first time you save a file (see Figure 2.2).

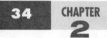

Creating Different Types of Files

The *Save File as Type* drop-down list lets you save the file in one of many different file formats. See Chapter 25, "Working with Other Programs and Data," to learn how to work with different types of files in Excel.

Options

Click the Options button in the File ➤ Save As dialog box to access a variety of save options:

The File Sharing options in this dialog box provide protection for the workbook, and are covered in Chapter 11, "Auditing and Protecting Your Work." Check the *Always Create Backup* setting to make Excel automatically create a backup of the file each time it is saved. See Chapter 7, "Productivity Basics," to learn more about this setting.

See Chapter 7 to learn about saving the workspace.

Closing a Workbook

Choose the File ➤ Close command to close the active workbook. If there are unsaved changes, you will be asked if you want to save.

TIP

To close all workbooks with one command, hold down the Shift key, then choose the File menu. The Close command will be changed to *Close All.*

Worksheets within Workbooks

Worksheets are the pages within a workbook. A workbook can contain one worksheet or hundreds of worksheets, memory allowing. Typically, worksheets within a workbook are related to one another. There may be one worksheet for each department, or one for each month, or a collection of sheets pertaining to a scientific experiment.

Activating Worksheets

Mouse Approach Click the worksheet tabs on the bottom of the workbook to activate the desired worksheet.

Keyboard Approach Press Ctrl+Page Down to activate the next worksheet, or Ctrl+Page Up to activate the previous worksheet.

The active worksheet is indicated by the highlighted tab.

Scrolling the Tabs

Only several worksheet tabs are visible at a given time. Use the tab scrolling buttons pictured in Table 2.1 to scroll the tabs. These four buttons control which tabs are displayed, but they do not change the active worksheet.

TABLE 2.1: Tab Scrolling Buttons

CLICK THIS BUTTON:	TO DISPLAY:
⏮	first tab in workbook
◀	previous tab (left)
▶	next tab (right)
⏭	last tab in workbook

You can change the number of visible tabs by moving the Tab Split Box (see below). Point to the tab split box, and slide it to the left or right.

Printing a Worksheet

To print a worksheet, choose the File ➤ Print command, then click OK. Chapter 6, "Printing," covers the many different settings and options related to printing.

Inserting a Worksheet

To insert a worksheet into the active workbook, choose the Insert ➤ Worksheet command. Or, right-click a tab, then choose the Insert command from the shortcut menu.

Deleting a Worksheet

To delete a worksheet from a workbook, activate the sheet, then choose the Edit ➤ Delete Sheet command. Excel will confirm this action by displaying a dialog box confirming the deletion. Or, right-click the tab, then choose the Delete command from the shortcut menu that appears.

Copying and Moving Worksheets

Worksheets can be copied or moved—within a workbook or to a different workbook.

Moving a Worksheet within the Same Workbook

Click the worksheet tab, then drag and drop it to a new location along the row of worksheet tabs.

Copying a Worksheet within the Same Workbook

Hold down the Ctrl key, and drag and drop the worksheet tab to a new location along the row of worksheet tabs. A copy of the worksheet is inserted.

Moving or Copying to a Different Workbook—The Easy Way

The simplest way to move or copy a sheet to a different workbook is to use the same procedure that you use within one workbook: drag and drop. Both workbooks must be open and visible. (The discussion on windows later in this chapter will explain how to make more than one workbook visible at the same time.) To move a sheet, drag and drop the tab to the row of tabs on the destination workbook. To copy, hold down Ctrl while you drag and drop.

Moving or Copying to a Different Workbook—The Hard(er) Way

If you do not want to rearrange workbooks to make them both visible, or if you want to move/copy to a *new* workbook, use this procedure: Choose the Edit ➤ Move or Edit ➤ Copy Sheet command, and the Move or Copy dialog box is displayed (Figure 2.3).

FIGURE 2.3

Move or Copy dialog box

The *To Book* drop-down list lets you specify the destination workbook. All open workbooks will display in this list, as will a (new book) choice. The *Before Sheet* list lets you specify where in the destination workbook the sheet will be placed. Check the *Create a Copy* setting to copy the sheet, or uncheck it to move the sheet.

Manipulating More Than One Worksheet at a Time

The procedures described above for copying, moving, and deleting a sheet can be performed on more than one sheet at the same time. This is accomplished by selecting more than one sheet before performing the desired operation. Selecting multiple tabs involves a procedure that is similar to selecting multiple items in a multi-select list box:

- To select and deselect the tabs individually, hold down the Ctrl key while clicking tabs.

- To select adjacent tabs, hold down the Shift key. If you click Sheet1, then hold down Shift while clicking Sheet4, the tabs for Sheet1 *through* Sheet4 will be selected.

The use of Ctrl to select multiple tabs, combined with the use of Ctrl to copy a sheet via drag and drop, can get a little bit confusing. Here is how to copy two sheets using drag and drop:

1. Click the tab of the first sheet to be copied.

2. Holding down the Ctrl key, click the tab of the second sheet to be copied.

3. Release the Ctrl key.

4. Holding down the Ctrl key, now drag and drop.

To cancel multiple tab selection:

- Click a tab that is not selected.

- Or right-click a tab, and choose Ungroup Sheets from the shortcut menu that appears.

TIP

Multiple worksheets can be edited and formatted simultaneously, by selecting more than one tab. This technique is explained in Chapter 7, "Productivity Basics."

Using Meaningful Worksheet Names

You are not required to use Excel's default worksheet names. Worksheet tabs become a very useful interface for navigating a workbook when sheets have names like *Sales Analysis* and *Forecast* instead of Sheet1 and Sheet2. Choose the Format ➤ Sheet ➤ Rename command to specify a meaningful name for the active sheet. Or, you can right-click a sheet tab,

then choose the Rename command from the shortcut menu that appears. A worksheet name is limited to 31 characters, including spaces.

Controlling the Default Number of Worksheets in New Workbooks

By default, there are 16 worksheets in a new workbook. This number conveniently accommodates one sheet per month, and one summary sheet per quarter, but you might not need to work with that number of sheets every time you open a new workbook. To change the number of worksheets shown by default in a new workbook, choose the Tools ➤ Options command, and select the General tab in the dialog box. This displays the General options available from the Options dialog box, as shown in Figure 2.4.

Change the *Sheets in New Workbook* setting according to preference. There is no limit to the number of sheets other than that imposed by available memory.

FIGURE 2.4

The General dialog box in the Tools ➤ Options dialog box

Windows in Excel

It comes as a surprise to many users to learn that "windows" and "workbooks" are not synonymous. One workbook can be displayed in more than one window. (If you are just learning about workbooks and worksheets, there is no compelling reason to tackle the windows topic right away—you may want to get comfortable with workbooks and revisit this section later.)

Displaying a Workbook in More Than One Window

Assume that the active workbook is Book1. Choose the Window ➤ New Window command to create a second window for Book1. There will then be two open windows: *Book1:1* and *Book1:2*.

Arranging Windows

There are several ways to quickly arrange multiple windows so that you can see them. To understand all of the ways that windows can be arranged, try this short exercise. Create three or more windows by choosing Window ➤ New Window a few times, then choose the Windows ➤ Arrange command. The following dialog box is displayed:

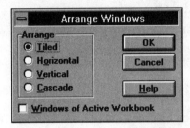

Now choose one of the Arrange options from the dialog box:

Tiled   Each window is made fully visible, and
                   Excel decides how to arrange them
                   based upon the number of open
                   windows.

Horizontal   Each window is made fully visible, and
                   arranged horizontally.

Vertical   Each window is made fully visible, and
                   arranged vertically.

Cascade   Windows are overlapped, with the title
                   of each window visible.

Arranging the Active Workbook Only

If you have more than one workbook open, and multiple windows have been created for each workbook, you can use the *Windows of Active Workbook* checkbox to limit the arranging of windows to the active workbook only:

- If checked, only the windows of the active workbook are arranged.

- If unchecked, all windows of all open workbooks are arranged.

Moving between Windows

There are various ways to move from one window to another in Excel.

- The bottom of the Window menu lists all open windows—choose the one you want to activate.

- If the windows are arranged so that more than one is visible, click on the window you want to activate.

- Press Ctrl+F6 to activate the next window, or Ctrl+Shift+F6 to activate the previous window.

Closing Windows

The File ➤ Close command is *not* necessarily the way to close a window—if the workbook is displayed in multiple windows, *all* of the windows will be closed. Instead, you must use the Close command on the Control menu for the specific window. The active window's Control menu is opened by clicking the control box on the left side of the window's title bar, as shown in Figure 2.5.

To close just one window, click the window's control box, then choose Close from the menu. Or just double-click the window control box. (The commands on the window Control menu are Microsoft Windows conventions, and not specific to Excel.)

Hiding Windows

You may want to temporarily hide a window to unclutter the workspace. Choose the Window ➤ Hide command to hide the active window, and choose the Window ➤ Unhide command to unhide a window.

A Tip to Avoid Windows/Workbooks Confusion

Remember, workbooks and windows are not necessarily synonymous—one workbook can be displayed in multiple windows. If a workbook is displayed in only one window, then the window and workbook are virtually synonymous—closing the window closes the workbook.

FIGURE 2.5

Click the active window's control box to display its Control menu.

Controlling the Display

There are many different settings that control how things are displayed, and these settings apply at different levels: workspace, workbook, worksheet, or window.

Controlling How the Workspace Displays

Workspace level settings are global to the entire Excel workspace, and are not specific to any workbook or worksheet.

Hiding the Formula Bar and Status Bar

There is one primary reason for hiding the formula and status bars: gaining additional screen real estate.

- The View ➤ Formula Bar command is used to hide or display the formula bar.

- The View ➤ Status Bar command is used to hide or display the status bar.

Excel "remembers" these settings from session to session. If you hide the formula bar and exit Excel, the formula bar will still be hidden the next time you run Excel.

Full Screen Display

The View ➤ Full Screen command maximizes Excel, and hides the title bar. A full screen display yields extra screen real estate. It is often used when doing an overhead presentation. Excel remembers this setting from session to session.

Controlling How the Workbook or Window Displays

Workbook settings are saved with the workbook. If you change any of these settings and then save the workbook, close the workbook, and later reopen it, the setting remains. These settings are accessed by choosing the Tools ➤ Options command, then choosing the View tab (see Figure 2.6).

Horizontal Scroll Bar/Vertical Scroll Bar Horizontal and/or vertical scrollbars can be displayed or hidden using the settings pictured in Figure 2.6. (In Excel 4, there was only one scrollbar setting, and it applied to the workspace, not to the workbooks or windows themselves.)

Sheet Tabs This option controls the display of the worksheet tabs at the bottom of the workbook. You may want to hide the tabs if you are distributing a workbook with multiple sheets but only one sheet is intended to be viewed. Use the Sheet Tabs checkbox pictured in Figure 2.6.

FIGURE 2.6

The Tools ➤ Options
➤ View dialog box

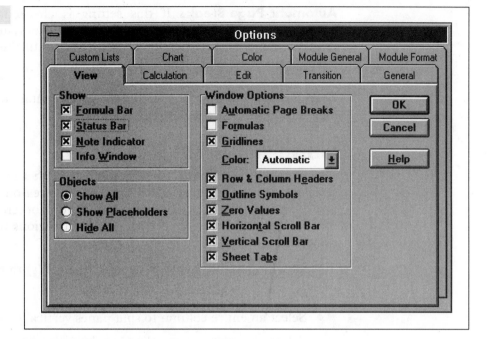

Controlling How the Worksheet Displays

Worksheet settings are applied only to the active worksheet, and are saved only for that worksheet. Worksheet settings, like the settings for controlling the display of workbooks and workbook windows, are accessed by choosing the Tools ➤ Options command, then choosing the View Dialog box tab (refer to Figure 2.6).

Row & Column Headings If this setting is checked, row and column headings are displayed; otherwise they are hidden.

Gridlines If this setting is checked, gridlines are displayed on the worksheet. If unchecked, gridline display is turned off for both the screen worksheet and the printed worksheet. Use the Gridlines setting in the dialog box shown in Figure 2.6.

Gridlines Color A different gridline color can be selected from the drop-down Color list in Figure 2.6.

Automatic Page Breaks If this setting is checked, automatic page breaks are displayed as broken lines along appropriate gridlines. If unchecked, page breaks will not be displayed until the page is printed. There is no effect on the hardcopy printout.

Zero Values If this setting is checked, cells containing zero values display zero; otherwise they display as blank.

To Split Window Panes

Windows can be split into *panes*, resulting in either two or four separate scrollable regions on the window. One common reason for splitting panes is to create row and/or column headings that do not scroll out of view. Another reason is to simply view two different regions of the sheet at the same time.

To split windows into panes, first select the cell(s) to represent the split point:

- Select an entire column to split panes vertically.
- Select an entire row to split panes horizontally.
- Select a single cell to split panes immediately above and to the left of the cell.

Then choose the Window ➤ Split command. Figure 2.7 shows a window with both vertical and horizontal splits. The four regions are *separately scrollable*.

To Freeze Panes

If the purpose of the split panes is to freeze row and/or column titles in place, choose the Window ➤ Freeze Panes command to lock the split in place. At that time,

- the split bar or bars turn into solid lines;
- the pane above a horizontal split can no longer be scrolled;
- and the pane to the left of a vertical split can no longer be scrolled.

The following simple exercise may help to clarify splitting and freezing panes.

FIGURE 2.7

Split windows

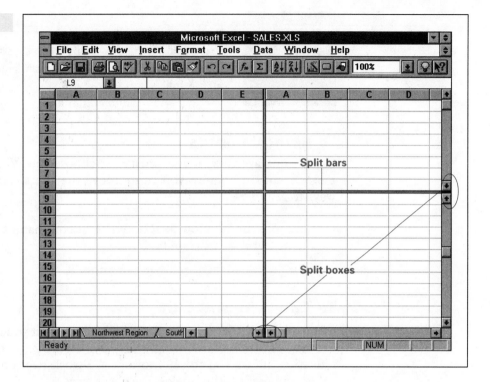

1. Enter the following onto a blank worksheet:

2. Select cell B2.

3. Choose the Window ➤ Split command. You should now have four panes, each of which is separately scrollable.

4. Choose the Window ➤ Freeze Panes command. Row 1 and column A are now frozen in place. When you scroll the worksheet, the headings stay in view.

TIP

Another way to split panes is by dragging the split boxes with the mouse. Splits created using this method do not have to lie on the cell border. (Figure 2.7 points out the split boxes.)

To Remove Splits

If the splits are frozen, you must first choose the Window ➤ Unfreeze Panes command before you can remove the splits. Then, there are two ways to remove them:

- Choose the Window ➤ Remove Split command to remove horizontal and vertical splits.
- Or double-click a split bar to remove it.

To Zoom In and Out

Choose View ➤ Zoom to display a dialog box to let you reduce or increase the magnification of the window display (Figure 2.8). Reducing the magnification allows you to see more of the worksheet on screen, while increasing magnification makes the sheet larger.

You can choose one of the several built-in magnification settings in this dialog box, or you can specify your own magnification setting using the *Custom* option. If you choose the *Fit Selection* option, the selected range is zoomed to fill the window.

NOTE

Splitting panes, freezing panes, and zooming do not affect the printed document.

FIGURE 2.8

The View ➤ Zoom
dialog box

Working inside
Worksheets

f a s t TRACK

To copy or move cells   67

- To move: select the cells to be moved, then use the mouse to drag the border of the selection to a new location.

- To copy: hold down Ctrl while dragging the border of the selection to a new location.

To insert cells   69

Select the cells, rows, or columns where you want to insert, and choose Insert ➤ Cells, Insert ➤ Rows, or Insert ➤ Columns.

To change column width   72

Click and drag the border on the right side of the column header.

To find a value   74

Choose Edit ➤ Find and type the characters to find in the *Find What* edit box, then click Find Next.

THIS chapter covers the basics of working inside a worksheet:

- *selecting cells*
- *types of data that can be contained in a cell*
- *entering and editing data into cells*
- *navigating the worksheet*
- *changing row height and column width*
- *copying and moving cells*
- *finding and replacing values*

About Cells

The basic element of an Excel worksheet is the cell. Cells possess these basic properties:

- They can contain text or numbers.
- They can contain formulas, which are used to perform calculations.
- They can be formatted using a wide variety of formatting options, such as font, borders, color, and alignment of data within the cell.
- Every worksheet contains 16,384 rows and 256 columns, whether you use them or not, for a total of 4,194,304 cells.

How Cells Are Identified

Cells are identified by their position in the worksheet grid, with letters used to designate the column, and numbers used to designate the row.

For example, cell B4 is located at the intersection of the second column and fourth row. A cell address, such as B4, is called a cell *reference*.

The Active Cell

One cell is always the *active cell*. The reference of the active cell is displayed in the *Name Box*, on the left part of the formula bar (see Figure 3.1). One easy way to activate a cell is by clicking it with the mouse. Then, whatever you type goes into the active cell.

NOTE There are times when there is *not* an active cell, like when a graphical object is selected. Macros you intend to be bulletproof need to take this factor into account.

FIGURE 3.1

The Worksheet grid

More Than One Cell Can Be Selected

A *range* of cells can be selected. The easiest way to select a range is to click a cell with the mouse, hold down the left mouse button, drag the mouse pointer across several cells, then release the mouse button. The selected cells are referred to as the *selection*. Even when a range of cells is selected, one cell is still the active cell.

In the selection shown here,

- Cell B2 is the active cell.

- Just as one cell has a reference, so does a range of cells. The selection here would be referred to as B2:D5—the colon is shorthand for the word *through*.

Types of Data

There are four distinct types of data that go into cells.

Text

Text can include any combination of letters, numbers, and special characters.

- A cell can contain up to 255 characters.

- If column width prevents a text string from fitting visually in a cell, the display extends over neighboring cells. However, if the neighboring cells are occupied, the display is truncated.

Numbers

There are some important things to understand about the way Excel treats numbers:

- There are many ways to format numbers. A number may be displayed using commas, scientific notation, or one of many built-in numeric formats. Do not confuse a number's *display format* with the *underlying value*. (Numeric formatting is covered in Chapter 5, "Formatting Cells.")

- Dates and times are numbers, but with special formatting.

- Excel tries very hard to guess the "meaning" of numeric input, and format it accordingly. If you try to enter **1-9** as a text string, Excel will interpret this as a date and display it as **9-Jan**.

- When an unformatted number does not fit in a cell, it is displayed in scientific notation.

- When a formatted number does not fit in a cell, number signs (####) are displayed.

Logical

The logical values TRUE and FALSE can be entered into cells.

Error

Formulas, covered in Chapter 4, "Using Formulas and Functions," can result in errors. An error value is a distinct type of data.

Entering, Editing, and Clearing Cells

Here are the common procedures for entering data into cells, editing data in a cell, and clearing the contents of cells.

Entering Data into a Cell

1. Select the cell by clicking it with the mouse.

2. Type numbers and/or text.

3. Press Enter (or select a different cell).

Entering Numbers

A numeric entry can include the numbers 0 through 9, and the special characters shown in Table 3.1.

TABLE 3.1: Characters Allowed for Numeric Entries

CHARACTER	FUNCTION
0 through 9	Any combination of numerals
+	Used in conjunction with E to indicate exponents
-	Indicates negative number
( )	Indicates negative number
, (comma)	Thousands marker
/	Fraction indicator
$	Currency indicator
%	Percentage indicator
. (period)	Decimal indicator
E	Exponent indicator
e	Exponent indicator

TIP

You can enter numbers with fixed decimal points by choosing Tools ➤ Options, then choosing the Edit tab. Check the *Fixed Decimal* checkbox, and select a number of decimal places. (Accountants often prefer to work with two fixed decimals.)

Entering Numbers as Text

An inventory product code may consist of only numeric characters, yet you do not want Excel to treat such an entry as a number. For example, when you enter **3-22**, Excel displays **22-Mar**. To force an entry to be text, use an apostrophe as the first character. The apostrophe will not display in the cell, nor will it print out. It will display when you edit the cell, however.

Entering Dates and Times

When you enter a number that Excel interprets as a date or time, it will be formatted as such. (You will usually appreciate this feature, but it will drive you crazy at times!)

TIP

By default, text is left-aligned within the cell, and numbers are right-aligned. This provides a quick visual cue as to whether Excel interpreted your entry as text or numeric.

Editing a Cell

There are two places where you can do your editing: on the formula bar or in the cell.

Formula Bar   Click the formula bar to begin editing.

In-Cell   In-cell editing is new to Excel 5, and will be much appreciated by those who have strained their eyes for years looking at the small font used in the formula bar. Double-click a cell to activate in-cell editing (see Figure 3.2).

Double-clicking to activate in-cell editing is a setting that can be turned on or off. Choose the Tools ➤ Options command, select the Edit tab, and set the *Edit Directly in Cell* checkbox. There are several advantages to turning off in-cell editing:

- Double-clicking a cell with a note displays the cell note dialog box (see Chapter 11 to learn about cell notes).

FIGURE 3.2

Double-clicking cell C6 here lets you perform in-cell editing.

	A	B	C	D	E	F	G	H
C6			=SUM(C3:C5)					
1								
2		Region	Sales					
3		East	$3,535					
4		Centrl	$45,646					
5		West	$56,756					
6		Total:	=SUM(C3:C5)					
7								
8								
9								

- Double-clicking a cell that refers to other cells takes you to the other cells.

The techniques for editing cells are similar, whether in-cell or in the formula bar:

If Edit Directly in Cell Is Turned On Double-click the cell. Or, select it and press F2. The insertion point is placed at the end of the cell contents.

Editing on the Formula Bar Select the cell, then click in the formula bar. (This works regardless of whether *Edit Directly in Cells* is on or off.) The insertion point is placed at the end of the cell contents.

Edit the cell contents using basic text editing techniques:

- Double-click a word to select it. Use the mouse to position the insertion point or to select text.

- Highlighted text is replaced by whatever you type.

- Press Home to go to the beginning, or End to go to the end.

- Use the left and right arrow keys to move left and right.

- While editing cell references in formulas, F2 toggles the meaning of the left and right arrow keys. The arrow keys can be used to edit the cell references by navigating the sheet, rather than navigating the formula.

Press Enter or click the enter box on the formula bar to finish editing.

Canceling Cell Entries/Edits

If you change your mind about an entry or edit while you are making it, you can undo it before moving on to the next entry:

- If you haven't yet pressed Enter while entering or editing, you can cancel your changes by pressing Esc or clicking the cancel button.

- If you've already pressed Enter, but haven't yet taken any other action, you can choose the Edit ➤ Undo command.

If, however, you've already initiated some action after making an entry or an edit, you'll need to edit the cell to get it back to what you want.

Clearing a Cell

Clearing a cell is like erasing a mistake. (Unlike deleting, which causes cells below and/or to the right to shift position.) Follow these steps to clear cells:

1. Select the cell(s) to be cleared.

2. The quickest way to clear the contents from the selected cell(s) is to press the Delete key. To see what types of cell elements you can clear separately, choose the Edit ➤ Clear command, then...

   - To clear just contents, choose *Contents* from the submenu.
   - To clear just formats, choose *Formats*.
   - To clear just cell notes, choose *Notes*.
   - To clear everything (contents, formats, and notes) from the cell, choose *All*.

TIP

If you want to replace a cell's contents with a different entry, there is no need to clear the cell first. Select the cell and begin typing the new entry; the old entry will be replaced.

Navigating Worksheets Using the Mouse

You can use some special mouse techniques for more efficient movement across the worksheet, as explained in the following paragraphs.

Jumping to the Beginning or the End of the Block

A quick way to jump to the end of a block of filled or blank cells is by double-clicking the *cell border* in the direction you want to move. For example, to move to the bottom of a column of data, double-click the bottom border of the cell. To move to the end of a row, double-click the right cell border.

How To Go Directly to Specific Cells

The fastest way to go directly to specific cells is to use the *Name box*:

- Click on the Name box and type a cell reference, then press Enter.
- If the cell is named, select the name from the Name box drop-down list (see Chapter 8 to learn about cell names).

Alternatively, use the *Go To* command:

1. Choose Edit ➤ Go To (or press F5).
2. Select a cell or range from the list of names, or type a cell reference into the *Reference* box.
3. Click OK.

Excel remembers the last four locations you selected using any of the methods described above and lists them at the top of the *GoTo* list in the dialog box (see Figure 3.3). Any named cells in the workbook will be listed below the last four locations.

FIGURE 3.3

The Edit ➤ GoTo
Dialog box

Navigating Worksheets Using the Keyboard

Table 3.2 explains the keystrokes for worksheet navigation. Make sure that Scroll Lock is off.

Moving within a Range of Cells

You can select a range of cells, and then use the keystrokes in Table 3.3 to navigate the selected range.

TABLE 3.2: Moving with Keystrokes

THIS KEYSTROKE	MOVES
Arrow keys	right, left, up and down (one cell at a time)
Ctrl+arrow keys	to edge of *current data region* (region the cell currently occupies)
Page Up, Page Down	up or down one window
Home	to beginning of row
Ctrl+Home	to cell A1
Ctrl+End	to lower right corner of worksheet
End, arrow key	by one block of data, within current row or column
End, Enter	to last cell in current row
End (with Scroll Lock on)	to lower right corner of window
Home (with Scroll Lock on)	to upper left corner of window

TABLE 3.3: Moving within a Selection

TO MOVE	PRESS
Down one cell	Enter
Up one cell	Shift+Enter
Right one cell	Tab
Left one cell	Shift+Tab

Selecting Cells Using the Mouse

There are several ways to select cells using the mouse, as explained in the following paragraphs.

Dragging a Range

1. Click on a cell, but don't release the mouse button.
2. Drag the mouse to select the range.
3. Once the desired range is selected, release the mouse.

N O T E

While selecting a range of cells, the Name box displays the dimensions of the selected range. If the selection is four rows by two columns, 4R X 2C will display. These dimensions only display *while selecting*—as soon as you release the mouse button, the dimensions are replaced with the cell reference.

Selecting a Large Range without Dragging

Selecting a very large range by dragging the mouse can be cumbersome. Here's another way to do it:

1. Click a cell in one corner of the range.
2. Hold down Shift and click the cell in the opposite corner of the range.

Other Ways to Select with the Mouse

Table 3.4 illustrates the variety of ways cells can be selected using the mouse.

Selecting Cells Using the Keyboard

Table 3.5 defines the keystrokes for making a wide variety of cell selections.

TABLE 3.4: Selecting Cells with the Mouse

TO SELECT	DO THIS
One Row	Click on row number at left side of worksheet
Multiple Rows	Click and drag up or down through row numbers
Noncontiguous Rows	Hold down Ctrl while selecting row numbers
Columns	Same as rows, but click column letters
Entire Worksheet	Click *Select All* button on upper left corner of worksheet (see Figure 1.1)
Multiple Ranges	Hold down Ctrl while selecting
Current Data Region	Select cell within data region, click *Select Current Region* tool

TABLE 3.5: Keystrokes for Selecting Cells

THIS KEYSTROKE	SELECTS
Ctrl+Spacebar	entire column
Shift+Spacebar	entire row
Ctrl+Shift+Spacebar	entire worksheet
End, Shift+Arrow keys	extends selection to end of data block
End, Shift+Home	extends selection to lower right corner of worksheet
End, Shift+Enter	extends selection to last cell in current row
Ctrl+Shift+* (asterisk)	current data region
F8, Arrow keys	same as holding down Shift while using arrow keys

Copying and Moving Cells

Cells can be copied and moved using drag and drop, or using menu commands.

Moving Cells Using Drag and Drop

1. Select the cells you want to move (range must be contiguous).

2. Point to an outside border of the selected range using the mouse. The mouse pointer will turn into an arrow.

WARNING

The lower right corner of the selected cells has a special marker called the *fill handle*. When you point at the fill handle, the mouse pointer becomes a black cross. When dragging and dropping, don't accidentally use the fill handle. (See Chapter 7, "Productivity Basics," for information about the fill handle and AutoFills.)

3. Click the mouse button, drag the cells to a new location, then release the mouse.

Copying Cells Using Drag and Drop

Copying via drag and drop is the same as moving, except the Ctrl key is held down during the procedure.

N O T E The drag and drop feature can be turned on or off by choosing the Tools ➤ Options command, selecting the Edit tab, and checking or clearing the *Allow Cell Drag and Drop* setting.

Using the Drag and Drop Shortcut Menu

If you hold down the right mouse button while dragging and dropping cells, the following *shortcut* menu will be displayed when the cells are dropped:

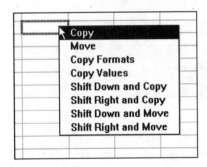

The commands on this shortcut menu are described in Table 3.6.

TABLE 3.6: Drag and Drop Shortcut Menu Commands

COMMAND	FUNCTION
Copy	copies cells
Move	moves cut cells
Copy Formats	copies formats only
Copy Values	copies values only
Shift Down and Copy	inserts copied cells, shifts existing cells down
Shift Right and Copy	inserts copied cells, shifts existing cells right
Shift Down and Move	inserts cut cells, shifts existing cells down
Shift Right and Move	inserts cut cells, shifts existing cells right

Copying and Moving Cells Using Menu Commands

Drag and drop is very efficient when cells are being copied or moved short distances. Menu commands (and toolbar shortcuts) may prove more effective when the target cells are a long distance from the source cells.

Moving Cells Using Menu Commands

1. Select the cell(s) to be moved.

 2. Choose the Edit ➤ Cut command.

3. Select the upper left cell of the region where the cells are to be pasted.

 4. Choose the Edit ➤ Paste command.

Copying Cells Using Menu Commands

1. Select the cell(s) to be copied.

 2. Choose the Edit ➤ Copy command.

3. Select the upper left cell of the region where the cells are to be pasted.

 4. Choose the Edit ➤ Paste command.

Inserting and Deleting Cells

The following procedures explain how to insert and delete cells, or entire rows and columns.

Inserting Cells

To insert cells,

1. Select the cell(s) where you want to perform the insertion. This can be one cell, a range of cells, entire rows, or entire columns.

2. From the Insert menu:

- Choose the Rows command to insert entire rows.
- Or choose the Columns command to insert entire columns.
- Or choose the Cells command to insert a range of cells. The Insert dialog box is displayed, asking how the insertion should occur.

The number of rows and columns in a worksheet is fixed—inserting does not actually create new cells, but rather shifts cells. An insertion will not cause data that is located at the end of the worksheet to "fall off the edge." For example, if there is data in cell IV2 (the second row of the *last* column) and you insert a column, Excel displays a warning and will not allow the insertion to occur.

NOTE Inserted cells will assume the formatting of the region into which they are inserted.

Inserting Cells That Have Been Cut or Copied from Another Location

Cells that have been moved or copied can be inserted into existing data using either menu commands or drag and drop.

Inserting Using Menu Commands

To insert cut or copied cells using menu commands:

1. Select the cells, then cut or copy them.
2. Select the cell where the insertion is to occur.

3. Choose the first command on the Insert menu. (The command will be either *Copied Cells* or *Cut Cells*, depending on which operation you performed in step 1.)

4. The Insert Paste Dialog box (pictured below) will display, letting you specify how to insert.

Inserting Using Drag and Drop

To insert cut or copied cells using drag and drop, use the same procedures as when cells are moved or copied with drag and drop (covered earlier in this chapter), but hold down the Shift key while dragging the cells. A grey insertion marker will display. The keystroke combinations get confusing when copying—here are the precise steps for a copy-insert:

1. Select the cells to be moved or copied.

2. Point to the edge of the range until the mouse pointer becomes an arrow. Click the mouse, and drag the cells to their new location.

3. Hold down Shift while dragging the cells. You'll see a grey insertion bar between rows and columns instead of a range outline. Then ...

- To insert cut cells, hold down Shift when dropping.
- To insert copied cells, hold down Ctrl+Shift when dropping.

Deleting Cells

When you delete one or more cells, the cells beneath or to the right shift position. (*Clearing* cells, on the other hand, does not cause other cells to shift position.)

1. Select the cell(s) that you want to delete. This can be one cell, a range of cells, entire rows, or entire columns.

2. Select the Edit ➤ Delete command:

- If an entire row or column was selected, the row or column is deleted immediately.
- Otherwise, the Delete dialog box (shown below) is displayed, giving you the opportunity to specify what to delete.

Controlling Row Height and Column Width

You can change row height and column width in several ways.

Setting Column Width Using Menu Commands

Select any cell(s) in the column you want to resize. Then choose the Format ➤ Column command. The following options are provided on the submenu:

Table 3.7 explains the commands available on the Format ➤ Column submenu.

TABLE 3.7: Format ➤ Column Commands

COMMAND	FUNCTION
Width	displays dialog prompting for column width
AutoFit Selection	sizes column(s) according to widest entry within selected range
Hide	hides selected column(s) from view
Unhide	unhides hidden columns
Standard Width	sets column to default column width (columns whose widths have previously been changed are unaffected)

TIP

Since a hidden column cannot be selected, how is it unhidden? If column B is hidden, select columns A through C, then choose the Unhide command. Nothing happens to columns A and C since they were not hidden to start with, but column B becomes unhidden. Alternatively, use the Name box to go to a cell in the hidden column (hidden cells can be selected even though the selection can't be seen), and choose the Unhide command.

Setting Column Width Using the Mouse

To use the mouse to change the column width:

1. Point to the line between column letters. The mouse pointer becomes a two-way arrow.

2. Click and drag to resize the column. (While dragging, the new width is displayed in the Name box.)

TIP

You can size several columns at once with the mouse. Select the columns you want to size (hold down Ctrl to select noncontiguous columns), and drag the border of any *one* of the selected columns.

Quick Best Fit

The mouse can be used to quickly perform the same function as the Format ➤ Column ➤ Autofit command. Double-click the border between column headings. The column will be sized according to the widest value within the entire column.

TIP

If you see ##### in a cell, it means the column is too narrow for the number to display. Use the double-click technique above to instantly size the column so that all values will fit.

Row Height

Row height works just like column width, except that rows will automatically increase in height to account for changing font size or wrapped text. Select a row or a cell in the row, and choose the appropriate Format ➤ Row commands to specify height or to hide/unhide rows. Row AutoFit is based on the largest font or wrapped text in the row.

Searching and Replacing

The Edit ➤ Find and Edit ➤ Replace commands are used to search the worksheet for user-specified values, and, optionally, to replace them with a different value. For example, suppose you have a worksheet which keeps track of payroll information, and employee Jane Smith changes her name to Jane Jones. Excel can search for every occurrence of *Jane Smith* and replace it with *Jane Jones*.

The Edit ➤ Find command displays the dialog box pictured in Figure 3.4.

FIGURE 3.4

The Find Dialog box

Finding a Value

To find a value:

1. Choose the Edit ➤ Find command.

2. Type the characters you want to find in the *FindWhat* box.

3. Use the *Look In* list box to specify where to search:

   • Select *Value* to search cell values.
   • Select *Formula* to search formulas.
   • Select *Note* to search cell notes.

4. Specify the row or column search sequence using the *Search* list.

5. Checking *Match Case* will limit the search to text strings that match the *FindWhat* entry in upper and lower case (for instance, if you search for **Bill**, the search will ignore **bill**).

6. Checking *Find Whole Words Only* will limit the search to exact matches. For example, if you are searching for **Rob**, the search will find **Robert** and **Robin**, but if you check *Find Whole Words Only*, only **Rob** will be found.

7. Click *Find Next* to find the next cell containing the search value.

Using the Replace Option

The Replace option works like Find, but allows the found value to be replaced with another value. Try the following exercise:

1. Enter the following on a blank worksheet:

2. Choose Edit ➤ Replace to display the Replace dialog box.

3. Type **Smith** in the *Find What* box.

4. Type **Jones** in *Replace With*.

5. Click *Replace All* to replace all instances of **Smith** with **Jones.**

Specifying the Search Range

You can search an entire worksheet, a range of cells, or multiple worksheets within a workbook. Before choosing the edit or replace command:

- Select only one cell to search the entire sheet.
- Or select a range of cells to search the range.
- Or select multiple sheets to search multiple sheets (see Chapter 2).

Using Wildcards

The question mark (?) and asterisk (*) can be used in your search text as wildcard characters.

- The asterisk represents one or more characters—a search for **A★Z** will find **ABZ** and **ABCZ**.
- A question mark represents one character—a search for **A?Z** will find **ABZ** and **ACZ**, but not **ABCZ**.

TIP If you want to search for a question mark or asterisk, precede these characters with a tilde (~). For example, to search for the string QUIT? enter QUIT~? as the search string.

PART TWO

Basic Skills

CHAPTER

4

Using Formulas and Functions

f a s t **TRACK**

● **To freeze a value**   89

    1. Select and copy cells to be frozen.

    2. Choose Edit ➤ Paste Special, select *Values*, and click OK.

● **To change a link**   100

    1. Choose the Edit ➤ Links command.

    2. Select the source file to be changed, then click the *Change Source* button.

    3. Select a new source file and click OK.

● **To use the FunctionWizard**   107

    Choose Insert ➤ Function, or click the FunctionWizard tool on the Standard toolbar.

THIS chapter covers some of the most important topics for new Excel users:

- *performing calculations with formulas*
- *understanding cell references*
- *linking workbooks*
- *introduction to functions*
- *controlling worksheet calculation*

Performing Calculations with Formulas

In Chapter 3 you learned about entering text and numbers into cells. In this chapter, you will learn how to do calculations using *formulas*. Formulas provide the real power when doing analysis and modeling in Excel. You can perform a wide variety of numeric calculations, including addition, subtraction, multiplication, and division. You can manipulate text, and do lookups into tables. By using formulas, the entry of a single number into a single cell can cause a ripple effect throughout a complex model.

Using the AutoSum Tool

 The SUM function is probably the most often used function, and the Auto-Sum tool makes it very easy to enter SUM functions. Try the following exercise to see how it's done in a very simple case:

BOOK1.XLS			
	A	B	C
1	12		
2	456		
3	98		
4	253		
5			
6			
7			

1. Enter the following:
2. Select cell A5.
3. Click the AutoSum tool.
4. Press Enter (or click the Enter box in the formula bar).

Excel guesses which cells you want to sum—the formula in cell A5 sums cells A1:A4.

Entering a Formula

To enter a formula into a cell, try the following as an example:

1. Select cell A1 on a blank worksheet.
2. Enter **=1+2** then press Enter. The resulting value, 3, displays in the cell.

Basic Properties of Formulas

Formulas in Excel share some basic properties:

- All formulas begin with an equal sign.
- After a formula is entered, the *resulting value* is displayed in the cell.
- When a cell containing a formula is selected, the underlying formula displays in the formula bar.

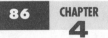

Editing Formulas

The procedure for editing formulas is the same as for editing numbers and text, which was covered in Chapter 3. You can use the formula bar, or you can edit directly in the cell. When you double-click a cell containing a formula, the formula is displayed in the cell.

T I P

Press Ctrl+ `(Ctrl plus the grave apostrophe, usually found to the left of the exclamation point) to switch back and forth from displaying formulas to displaying values on the worksheet.

Arithmetic Operators

Table 4.1 lists the arithmetic operators Excel supports in formulas:

TABLE 4.1: Arithmetic Operators Supported in Formulas

SYMBOL	FUNCTION
+	addition
-	subtraction
*	multiplication
/	division
^	exponentiation
%	percent when placed after a number

The following examples display some formulas utilizing arithmetic operators:

=1+1	Add 1 plus 1
=4/2	Divide 4 by 2
=2*2+10	Multiply 2 times 2, then add 10

Order of Calculation

It is very common for formulas to include more than one operator. Table 4.2 explains the order in which operators are evaluated:

TABLE 4.2: Order of Evaluating Operators

ORDER	OPERATOR	FUNCTION
1	%	percent
2	^	exponentiation
3	* and /	multiplication and division
4	+ and -	addition and subtraction
5	&	joining text

Following the order of precedence shown in the table, you can see that the multiplication operator is evaluated before the addition operator; therefore, the formula

=1+2*5

for example, evaluates to 11 (1 plus the result of 2 times 5), not 15 (the sum of 1 plus 2, which equals 3, times 5).

When there is more than one operator with the same priority level, the operators evaluate from left to right. For example, since multiplication and division are at the same priority level, the formula

=10/5*2

evaluates to 4 (10/5 times 2), not 1 (10 divided by 5*2).

Changing the Evaluation Order

Parentheses can be used to group expressions within a formula. An expression within parentheses evaluates *before* all arithmetic operators.

=1+2*3   evaluates to 7

=(1+2)*3   evaluates to 9

Joining Text

The ampersand character **&** joins text—a process referred to as *concatenation*. The formula

=″ABC″& ″DEF″

evaluates to ABCDEF.

NOTE Though earlier versions of Excel supported the & operator, calls to Microsoft's help line indicated that users didn't know where to find it in the manual. The Excel 5 CONCATENATE function adds nothing that the & operator doesn't already provide; it was added so that users could find it easier.

When Formulas Return Errors

When there is a problem with a formula, an error value is returned. One of the most common errors occurs when attempting to divide by zero. Enter the formula **=1/0** into a cell. The error **#DIV/0!** is returned. Table 4.3 explains the different errors that can result from an errant formula.

TABLE 4.3: Error Values

ERROR VALUE	CAUSE
#DIV/0!	divided by zero
#N/A!	different meanings depending on circumstance
#NAME!	reference to an invalid name
#NULL!	invalid intersection
#NUM!	incorrect use of a number
#REF!	invalid cell reference
#VALUE!	usually caused by incorrect argument(s)

How to Freeze Values

There are times when you will want to "freeze" a report by replacing formulas with values. Follow this procedure:

1. Select the cell(s) you want to freeze.

2. Choose the Edit ➤ Copy command.

3. Choose the Edit ➤ Paste Special command.

4. Select the *Values* option, then click OK.

Understanding Cell References

Each of the sample formulas presented so far in this chapter contains text and numeric *constants*. But a formula with only constants is not very useful. You can use *cell references* to incorporate *variables* into formulas, as demonstrated in the following examples.

=A1*2	multiplies the value in cell A1 times 2
=A1*B1	multiplies the value in cell A1 times the value in cell B1
="ABC"&A1	concatenates the characters ABC and the value in cell A1
=A1&B1	concatenates the value in cell A1 and the value in cell B1

Try this simple exercise on a blank worksheet:

1. Enter the number **2** in cell A1.

2. Enter the number **4** in cell A2.

3. Enter the formula **=A1+A2** in cell A3.

4. Change the value in A1, and watch the value in A3 change automatically.

You have just observed one of the basic features of a spreadsheet program—automatic recalculation of formulas as cell values change.

N O T E   A cell that refers to another cell is called a *dependent cell*. A cell that is referred to by another cell is called a *precedent* cell.

A1 and R1C1 Reference Styles

Excel supports two styles of cell references:

A1 Style This is the Excel default. Columns are labeled with letters A through IV, allowing for the maximum 256 columns. Rows are labeled by number, 1 through 16384.

R1C1 Style Rows and columns are both referred to by number. For example, R3C2 in this system is the same as B3 in the other system.

For better or for worse, A1-style references are the *de facto* standard for almost all spreadsheet products, including Excel. There is no compelling reason to work with both reference styles, and the inclusion of both styles in the Excel manuals only serves to further complicate an already complex subject. This book focuses exclusively on A1. Once you understand A1, it is easy to go back and understand R1C1 if so desired.

There are Three Ways to Reference, and You Need to Know All Three

You have just read about the two reference styles—A1 and R1C1. Regardless of which style you use, there are also three types of cell reference. A cell reference can be *relative*, *absolute*, or *mixed*. To explain, we will use a street address analogy:

Absolute Reference Refers to a specific cell or cells. The same as a home address, like 123 Elm Street.

Relative Reference Refers to cell(s) relative to a given position, such as "go one street down and two houses over."

Mixed Reference One of the coordinates is absolute, but the other is relative. "You're on the right street, but Ms. Jones lives three houses down."

N O T E

Excel supports three-dimensional cell references, which are used in conjunction with functions. 3-D references are covered later in this chapter.

Absolute References

A dollar sign in front of the cell coordinate denotes an *absolute* reference.

> **$A$1** is an absolute reference to cell A1.
>
> **$B$2** is an absolute reference to cell B2.

An absolute reference does not change when copied to another cell. The following exercise will demonstrate this:

1. Enter **=$A$1** into cell B1.

2. Copy and paste cell B1 to B2.

3. The formula in cell B2 is unchanged; it still reads **=$A$1**.

Relative References

The lack of a dollar sign in front of the cell coordinate denotes a *relative* reference. Use relative references to refer to cells *relative to the cell containing the formula*. The formula **=A1**, entered into cell B1, actually means "the contents of this cell are equal to the contents of the cell that is now one to the left" (A1 being one to the left of B1). Furthermore, since the formula uses a relative reference, the reference automatically adjusts when the cell is copied to another location.

1. Enter **=A1** into cell B1. This gives B1 the same content as A1, its neighbor directly to the left.

2. Copy and paste cell B1 to B2.

3. The formula in cell B2 automatically changes; Excel has adjusted it to read: **=A2**, giving B2 the same content once again as its neighbor directly to the left (in this case A2).

Try another example:

1. Enter numbers in cells B2, B3, C2, and C3.

2. Enter **=B2+B3** into cell B4.

3. Copy and paste B4 to C4; the formula in C4 reads **=C2+C3**.

NOTE

Unlike copy/paste, if you *cut* and paste a cell with relative references, the references will not change.

When to Use Absolute or Relative References

Here is an example that will illustrate the difference between absolute and relative references. Enter the constants in Figure 4.1 on a blank worksheet:

An Example of Doing It the Wrong Way

1. Enter the formula **=$B$5*$C$5** (absolute references) into cell D5.

2. Copy the formula in D5 to cells D6 and D7.

3. Since absolute references were used, cells D6 and D7 mistakenly extend (multiply) the figures on row 5—not what we intended.

FIGURE 4.1

Column D is intended to extend (multiply) the numbers in columns B and C.

	A	B	C	D	E
1					
2		Discount	10%		
3					
4		Qty	Price	Extension	
5		4	19.95		
6		7	12.55		
7		23	14.31		
8					
9					

BOOK1.XLS

An Example of Doing It the Right Way

1. Enter the formula **=B5*C5** (relative references) into cell D5.

2. Copy the formula in D5 to cells D6 and D7.

3. Since D5 contains relative references, Excel automatically adjusts the references when copied, and the extensions are now correct.

Now we will add an absolute reference to the equation. Assume that the discount in cell C2 (see Figure 4.1) applies to each row:

1. Enter the formula **=(B5*C5)-((B5*C5)*$C$2)** into cell D5. In English, this formula would translate to "The contents of this cell equal Extension minus Discount." Notice that cell $C$2 is being referred to absolutely.

2. Copy this formula into cells D6 and D7. Excel will adjust the relative references, but leave the absolute reference alone.

N O T E   The formula in step 1 above has extra parentheses that were added to enhance the readability of the formula. They do not affect the order of calculation.

Mixed References

You have now used absolute references (with a dollar sign in front of the coordinate), and relative references (with no dollar sign). A *mixed reference* has one absolute coordinate and one relative coordinate. **A$1** and **$A1** are both examples of mixed references. To illustrate, enter the following constants on a blank worksheet:

	A	B	C	D	E	F	G
		BOOK1.XLS					
1							
2		Freight	Red Widgets		Blue Widgets		
3		Per Unit	Units	Freight$	Units	Freight$	
4	North	11.95	5		9		
5	South	12.55	12		4		
6	East	13.52	6		2		
7	West	9.75	23		11		
8							
9							
10							

In this scenario, the freight calculation for red widgets and blue widgets are both based on the Freight Per Unit in column B. Formulas are required in columns D and F to calculate freight. The following paragraphs offer two ways to solve the problem.

An Example of Doing It the Less Efficient Way

1. Enter the formula **=B4*C4** in cell D4, and copy it to cells D5 through D7.

2. Enter the formula **=B4*E4** in cell F4, and copy it to cells F5 through F7. (If the formula in D4 is copied to column F, it would be *incorrect* due to the use of purely relative references.)

No problem, right? Not exactly. Using a mixed reference, the *same formula* can be used in columns D and F. This may seem like a trivial saving of time and energy, but this is a simple example. Anytime you can get away with using the same formula, a lot of time and hassle can be saved when the formula is originally entered, and when you go back later to change it.

An Example of Doing It the More Efficient Way

1. Enter the formula **=$B4*C4** in cell D4. **$B4** is a *mixed* reference—the first coordinate is absolute and the second coordinate is relative.

2. Copy D4 to cells F4 through F7.

Check out the formulas in columns D and F after you have copied them. Excel has adjusted the relative portion, but left the absolute portion alone.

TIP

The use of names can greatly simplify references. Names also add clarity: for example, a formula that reads =Sales–Cost makes a lot more sense than one that reads =$B$25–$B$47. See Chapter 8 to learn about naming.

Shortcut for Changing Reference Type

Instead of constantly typing and deleting dollar signs to switch reference type, the F4 key can be used to quickly change a reference.

1. Enter the formula **=A1** into cell B1.

2. In the formula bar (or in the cell), place the insertion point anywhere within the cell reference.

3. Press the F4 key repeatedly—the reference type will cycle through each of the ways the reference can be expressed.

Referring to Multiple Cells

In all of the examples so far, references have been made to *single cells*. A cell reference can also refer to a *range of cells*. In the cell reference **A1:A3**, the starting cell is **A1**, the colon means *through*, and **A3** is the ending cell. References to ranges of cells will take on greater significance when you start to work with formulas later in this chapter. In the meantime, here is a simple illustration:

1. Press F5 (the shortcut for Edit ➤ Go To)

2. Enter **A1:A3** as the reference, then click OK.

3. The range of cells A1 through A3 will be selected.

You Don't Have to Type Cell References

Fortunately, it is not necessary to actually type cell references when entering or editing formulas. References can be entered into formulas by pointing and clicking. Try this:

1. Enter numbers into cells A1 and A2 on a blank worksheet.

2. Select cell A3. Type an equal sign to start a formula.

3. Click on cell A1 with the mouse. Notice in the formula bar that the cell reference **A1** has been added to the formula.

4. Type a plus sign.

5. Click on cell A2 with the mouse to add it to the formula.

6. Press Enter to complete the formula, which adds cells A1 and A2.

Referring to Other Worksheets within the Same Workbook

In all of the examples so far, references have been made to cells located on the same worksheet. You can also refer to cells that are located on different worksheets. Let us return to the street address analogy: Instead of saying *123 Elm Street*, you must say *123 Elm Street, Chicago* because the address is located in another town. The same is true with references to other worksheets. Try this exercise in a new workbook:

1. On Sheet1, enter **10** into cell A1.

2. Activate Sheet2 by clicking its tab.

3. Enter an equal sign into cell B1 to begin a formula.

4. Activate Sheet1 by clicking its tab—notice that the formula is still being built.

5. Click cell A1 to add it to the formula.

6. Press Enter to complete the formula.

7. The formula in cell B1 (on Sheet2) will read =Sheet1!A1 and the number 10 will display in the cell.

Notice that the cell reference is preceded by the sheet name and an exclamation point. (The exclamation point separates the sheet name from the cell reference.) Don't be confused by references to other worksheets—they are essentially the same as references to the same sheet. All of the same rules apply.

If a worksheet name has a space in it, references to the sheet from other sheets must enclose the sheet name in single quotes, as in

='Sales Forecast'!B3

However, if a space is added to a sheet name *after* references have been made to the sheet, Excel automatically places single quotes in dependent cells for you.

Why Refer to Other Sheets?

Referring to cells on other worksheets is a very common practice. A workbook might contain departmental forecasts, with one worksheet for each of four departments. A fifth sheet might be used to summarize the departments, and this summary sheet might refer to cells on each of the four departmental sheets.

Referring to a Worksheet in Another Workbook: External References

This time, the address is not only located in another town, but in another state. And of course, the state must become part of the address. A reference to another workbook is called an *external reference*. Try this exercise:

1. Create two new workbooks, Book1 and Book2. Arrange them horizontally using the Window ➤ Arrange command.

2. On Sheet1 of Book1, enter **Hello** into cell A1.

3. On Sheet 1 of Book2, enter an equal sign into cell B1 to begin a formula.

4. Activate Book1 by clicking anywhere on the workbook.

5. Click cell A1 (on Sheet1, Book1) to add it to the formula.

6. Press Enter to complete the formula.

7. The formula in cell B1 (Sheet1, Book2) will read

    =[Book1]Sheet1!$A$1

and *Hello* will display in the cell.

The reference begins with the book name, enclosed in square brackets. (Notice that the reference defaults to absolute.)

What Happens to References As Cells Are Moved?

Various things can happen to cell references when cells are moved, depending on how and where they're moved.

Same Sheet   When a cell is moved to a different location on the same worksheet, cells that refer to that cell (*dependent cells*) are automatically updated to point to the new cell reference, regardless of the method you use to move the cell. This is true even if the dependent cell is located in a dependent workbook—but only if the dependent workbook is open when the cell is moved.

Different Sheet   When you cut and paste a cell to a different worksheet (in the same workbook or a different workbook), dependent cells are left with **#REF!** (a reference error).

Dependent Cell   When a dependent cell is moved, it will still point to the same cell(s) it originally pointed to, regardless of the method you use to move the cell. This holds true even if the dependent cell is moved to a different worksheet or workbook.

N O T E   If you are new to the subject of cell references, you may want to absorb what you have learned so far before reading about the next topic: links. Links are very important though—make sure to come back to this discussion.

Understanding File Links

When an external reference is entered, something special happens—a file *link* is automatically created. A file link always involves two workbooks:

- The workbook containing the external reference is dependent on the other workbook—it is called the *dependent workbook*.

- The workbook that is referred to by the external reference contains the source cell(s)—it is called the *source workbook*.

The dependent workbook is *linked* to the source workbook. The source workbook is not linked—it has no idea that one or more dependent workbooks may be linked to it.

Why Use Links?

Linked workbooks are used quite commonly—even in relatively simple models. Linked workbooks provide several key advantages compared to using multiple worksheets in one workbook:

- Workbooks can be edited concurrently by different users. The manager of the western region can be editing WEST.XLS while the manager of the eastern region is editing EAST.XLS.

- An entire model does not have to be opened at once, making opening, recalculating, and saving of workbooks faster. Also, a large model stored in one workbook may not "fit" in memory.

- Multi-level rollups can be achieved using multi-level linked workbooks.

Excel Keeps Track of the Full Path

Excel tracks the full path of the source book, and when the source book is closed, the full path appears in the external reference. For example, an external reference to a source workbook named SALES.XLS, located in a directory named FILES on the C drive, would look like this:

When source is open:

=[SALES.XLS]Sheet1!$A$1

When source is closed:

='C:\FILES\[SALES.XLS]Sheet1'!$A$1

There Can Be Lots of Links in Lots of Directions

Although a link always refers to a single workbook, a workbook can be linked many times, in many ways:

- One workbook can be linked to many different source workbooks.

- One source workbook can have many dependent workbooks.

- Workbook A can be linked to workbook B. Workbook B can be linked to workbook C. In other words, one workbook can be a dependent book *and* a source book.

- Two workbooks can be linked to each other, in which case each is dependent on the other.

Changing a Link

One way to change a link is by editing the formula containing the external reference. But what if a dependent workbook contains dozens of external references? Choose the Edit ➤ Links command to display the Links dialog box pictured in Figure 4.2.

Select the source file you want to change, then click the Change Source button to display the Change Links dialog box (Figure 4.3).

FIGURE 4.2

The Links dialog box lists all source workbooks for the active workbook.

FIGURE 4.3

The Change Links
dialog box

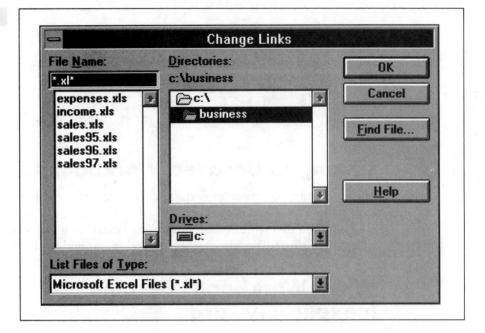

The Change Links dialog box looks and behaves very similarly to the File
➤ Open dialog box. You can navigate the file system to find the workbook
you want to link to. Once you have selected a new source file to link to,
all affected external references are automatically changed in one fell
swoop. Assume you have changed the source file EAST.XLS to
WEST.XLS. Every external reference in the dependent workbook is
automatically changed to WEST.XLS.

Opening a Dependent Workbook

Excel behaves differently depending on whether the source workbook is
opened or closed at the time the dependent book is opened.

- If the source workbook is already open, the dependent workbook recalculates automatically (unless you are in manual calculation mode).

- The source workbook does *not* have to be open for the dependent
  book to retrieve values from the source book. Excel will display the
  following dialog box. Click Yes to update the external references.

Linking to Unsaved Workbooks

Linking to a workbook that has *never* been saved is not a good idea; if you close the source workbook without saving it, the dependent workbook is linked to a workbook that does not exist. In general, it is good practice to save source workbooks before saving dependent books.

When Workbooks Become Inexplicably Large

Behind the scenes, dependent workbooks invisibly save values contained in source workbooks. There is one problematic manifestation of this feature: Sometimes a seemingly small workbook consumes an inexplicable amount of disk space. A workbook can be set to *not* save external values by choosing the Tools ➤ Options command, then selecting the Calculation tab. The *Save External Link Values* setting, shown in Figure 4.4, controls this behavior.

Using Functions

Picture a worksheet with numbers in cells A1 through A9, and these numbers need to be summed. You could enter the formula:

$$=A1+A2+A3+A4+A5+A7+A8+A9$$

FIGURE 4.4

The Tools ➤ Options
➤ Calculation dialog
box

This method is tiresome when summing nine cells, but becomes impossible if thousands of cells needed to be summed. The same result can be achieved using the SUM function:

=SUM(A1:A9)

The SUM function is one of several hundred built-in functions. These built-in functions provide the real power when it comes to the manipulation of text and numbers in Excel. A function can be used by itself, as with the SUM function above, or can be used as a piece of a complex formula. Formulas using functions must adhere to the following rules:

- All formulas must *begin* with an equal sign. (A function is *not* preceded by an equal sign unless the function is at the start of the formula.)

- Most functions need to be provided with one or more pieces of data to act upon, referred to as *arguments*. The arguments are enclosed in parentheses following the function name. If there are multiple arguments, they are separated by commas. The argument to the SUM function above is A1:A9.

Exercise

The following exercise will demonstrate the application of several critical skills:

- Entering functions with arguments.

- Using *nested functions*, where one function serves as an argument for another function.

- The use of the IF function, used to calculate a value conditionally.

N O T E   The functions used in this exercise do not have special significance—they are intended to illustrate the general syntax of functions within formulas.

1. Enter the following constants onto a blank worksheet.

2. Enter the following formula into cell C7 to calculate the average score:

=AVERAGE(C2:C5)

This averages the values in cells C2 through C5. The range C2:C5 is the argument for the AVERAGE function. (Remember, ranges don't have to be typed—they can be entered via point and click.)

3. Enter the following formula into cell B2 to calculate the student's last name:

   =LEFT(A2,SEARCH(",",A2)-1)

   This is an example of *nested* functions, which evaluate from the inside out. In order to calculate the last name, the LEFT function is used, which takes two arguments:

   - Text string found in cell A2.
   - Number of characters in the last name. We have to search for a comma, which is the separator between the last and first names, using the SEARCH function. The expression

   SEARCH(",",A2)-1

   translates to "get the position of the comma within the name, then subtract one. "This entire expression is the second argument to the LEFT function, and evaluates to 5.

   In simplified form, **=LEFT("Smith, Joe",5)** evaluates to Smith.

4. Copy the formula in cell B2 to cells B3 through B5.

5. The following formula, entered into cell D2, will display *No* if the student failed, or *Yes* if the student passed:

   =IF(C2<65,"No"," Yes")

This is an example of the all important IF function, which breaks down into five pieces:

IF	Function keyword
C2<65	Condition
"No"	Value if condition is true
,	ELSE clause (implied with a comma)
"Yes"	Value if condition is false

In English: "If score is less than 65 then *No*, otherwise *Yes*."

7. Copy the formula to cells D3 through D5. If the formulas were entered correctly, the worksheet will appear as follows:

	A	B	C	D	E
1	Full Name	Last Name	Score 1	Pass	
2	Smith, Joe	Smith	80	Yes	
3	Jones, Mary	Jones	92	Yes	
4	Dunn, Sam	Dunn	64	No	
5	Roberts, Jill	Roberts	76	Yes	
6					
7		Average:	78		
8					
9					

BOOK1.XLS

Checking Complex Conditions

In the above exercise, the IF function was used to apply conditional logic in a formula. The AND and OR functions allow more complex conditions to be tested.

AND Checks If More Than One Condition Is True

The general syntax of AND used with IF is as follows:

=IF(AND(Expression1, Expression2),Value if TRUE,Value if FALSE)

There can be up to 30 expressions as arguments to the AND function, and *all* must evaluate true for the AND function to evaluate true. On the following worksheet, it is OK to leave cells B1 and B3 blank. But, if a first name is entered in B1, a last name must be entered into B3.

	A	B	C	D	E
			BOOK1.XLS		
1	First Name	Smith			
2					
3	Last Name		Must enter last name		
4					
5					
6					
7					

The following formula, entered into cell C3, will remind the user to enter a last name if a first name has been entered:

=IF(AND(ISTEXT(B1),ISBLANK(B3)),"Must enter last name","")

In English: If there is text in B1 *and* B3 is blank, display a reminder or else display nothing. (The empty quotes represent null text.)

OR Checks If One Condition Is True

The AND function required that *all* expressions be true. The syntax of the OR function is identical, but with one fundamental difference: only *one* of the expressions must be true for the OR function to evaluate true.

Using the Function Wizard

Excel includes over three hundred built-in functions, and not even advanced users are familiar with each and every one. The Function Wizard is a great way to explore, learn, and build functions. Try the following exercise:

1. Enter **Smithers** in cell A1.

2. Select cell B1 and choose Insert ➤ Function (or click the Function Wizard tool). You'll see the following dialog box:

3. From the *Function Category* list, select **Text**.

4. From the *Function Name* list, select **LEFT**.

5. Click the Next button.

If you click Finish at this point, you can skip the rest of these steps. The argument placeholders are entered in the formula bar, where you can finish the formula without the Function Wizard.

6. Click on cell A1 to place its reference in the first argument. The value in the cell appears next to the argument.

7. Type 4 in the *num_chars* argument.

8. Click Finish. Cell B1 returns the value **Smit**.

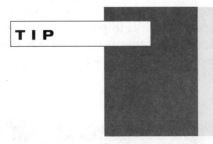

T I P

You can nest functions using the Function Wizard. To nest a function, click the Paste Function button (the *fx* button next to the argument window). A fresh Function Wizard dialog box will be displayed for the nested argument—when you complete the nested function, clicking Finish will return you to the previous level.

3-D Cell References

3-D cell references are used to reference cells in multiple, adjacent worksheets within a workbook. The following exercise demonstrates the use of a 3-D cell reference to sum cells spanning workbooks:

1. Create a new workbook.

2. Enter a number into cell A1 on Sheet1, Sheet2, Sheet3, and Sheet4.

3. Activate Sheet1. In cell B2, type **=SUM(**

4. Select Sheet1 through Sheet4 as a group (select Sheet1, hold down Shift and select Sheet4).

5. Select cell A1.

6. Type) and press Enter.

This formula sums cell A1 on sheets 1 through 4. You can also type the reference into the formula as follows:

=SUM(Sheet1:Sheet4!A1)

Controlling Worksheet Calculation

By default, Excel calculates worksheet formulas when changes to cell values so require. Automatic calculation is possibly the single most important feature of a spreadsheet program, and it is important to understand how to control it. To set calculation mode, choose the Tools ➤ Options command, then select the Calculation tab (Figure 4.5).

FIGURE 4.5

Calculation Settings

Calculation Modes

Calculation mode is a setting that is global to the workspace—it is not a workbook setting.

- *Automatic Calculation* is the default mode. Calculation automatically occurs if a cell value is changed and there are formulas referring to the changed cell. While calculation is taking place, a message is displayed on the status bar indicating what percentage of the calculation is complete.

TIP You can continue to work while Excel is calculating, though the calculation process pauses until you stop working.

- *Manual Calculation* is used to speed up response time. When working with a large model, it is often desirable to suppress calculation until after data entry is complete. The word **Calculate** will display on the status bar as a reminder that recalculation is required. Press F9 to perform a one-time calculation, yet remain in manual calculation mode. Click the Calc Sheet button pictured in Figure 4.5 to calculate just the active workbook rather than the entire workspace.
- *Automatic Except Tables* is a special mode that recalculates everything except data tables.

Precision as Displayed

The value that appears in a cell is not necessarily the same as the actual value stored in the cell. Excel stores numbers with 15-digit accuracy, yet a cell may be formatted to display dollars and cents. (The formula bar always displays the actual underlying value.) Variation between formatted numbers and underlying values can cause results to appear incorrect, which vexes accountants to no end. Check the *Precision as Displayed* setting, pictured in Figure 4.5, to recalculate based on the formatted values.

CAUTION This is a workbook setting that is saved with the workbook, unlike the automatic and manual calculation settings.

Putting Formulas and Functions to Work

This section will demonstrate how to use formulas and functions to create two simple but useful worksheets: a loan calculator and a loan amortization table.

Creating a Loan Calculator

Suppose you are taking out a car loan, and want to analyze the various loan options that are available. This exercise will show you how to create a simple, reusable loan calculator to determine what the monthly payments will be based on the loan amount, interest rate, and term.

Enter the following information onto a blank worksheet:

CELL	ENTRY
B2	Loan Calculator
B5	Interest rate
C5	Term (months)
D5	Loan amount
G5	Monthly Payment
G6	=PMT(B6/12,C6,-D6)
B6	10.0% (be sure to type the % sign)
C6	24
D6	2000

You can play "what if?" by changing the interest rate, the number of monthly payments, and the loan amount.

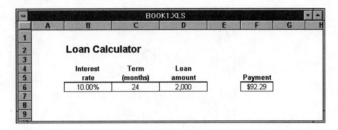

Creating a Loan Amortization Schedule

The loan calculator tells you what the monthly payment is. Suppose that you want to know how much interest is being paid in a given year. This exercise will add a loan amortization schedule to the loan calculator.

The basic calculations used in the table are:

- beginning balance (except for initial) = ending balance from previous period
- interest (compounded monthly) = annual interest rate divided by 12, multiplied by the beginning balance for the period
- principal = payment less interest
- ending balance = beginning balance less principal

1. On the same worksheet as the loan calculator, make the following entries:

B10	Amortization Schedule
B17	Period
C17	Beginning Balance
D17	Payment
E17	Interest
F17	Principal
G17	Ending Balance

CELL	ENTRY
B18	May-96
C18	=$D$6
D18	=$G$6
E18	=$B$6*C18/12
F18	=D18-E18
G18	=C18-F18
B19	Jun-96
C19	=G18
D19	=$G$6(copy from D18)
E19	=$B$6*C19/12 (copy from E18)
F19	=D19-E19 (copy from F18)
G19	=C19-F19 (copy from G18)
C14	Totals
D13	Payments
E13	Interest
F13	Principal
D14	=SUM(D18:D378)
E14	=SUM(E18:E378)
F14	=SUM(F18:F378)

NOTE The SUM formulas in cells D14:F14 allow for up to 360 payments (monthly payments on a 30-year mortgage), so this template can be used to test much larger loans without recreating the SUM formulas. The formulas are placed above the table so that you can put unlimited rows into the schedule without overwriting the totals.

2. Select cells B19:G41. Choose the Edit ➤ Fill ➤ Series command, select the AutoFill option, then click OK. (See Chapter 7 to learn more about AutoFill.)

3. Select cells C18:G41, then choose the Format ➤ Cells command and select the Number tab. Select Category **Number** and Format Codes **#,##0.00**. (See the next chapter to learn more about cell formatting.)

NOTE Excel performs these calculations with 15-digit precision, and will display the full precision unless you format the cells otherwise. Changing the format doesn't change the actual underlying cell value.

CHAPTER

5

Formatting Cells

fast **TRACK**

To format a number   **132**

Choose Format ➤ Cells, then select the Number tab.

To apply an AutoFormat   **141**

Select a cell within the table to be formatted, then choose Format ➤ AutoFormat and select a table format.

To apply a style   **143**

Choose Format ➤ Style and select a *Style Name* from the list box.

SOME people are of the opinion that the substance of a document is all that counts. Even if you are in this camp, much of the world is not. As a user of a graphically rich spreadsheet program, you probably appreciate how important the appearance of a report can be. Fairly simple formatting practices can yield the following benefits:

- *Important information can be highlighted with formatting.*
- *Simple formatting procedures can greatly enhance overall readability of reports.*
- *Styles can be used to easily create a consistent look, and consistency enhances professionalism.*

Basic Formatting Procedures

This chapter will cover many formatting options, all of which follow the same basic procedure:

1. Select the cell(s) you want to format.
2. Choose the desired formatting command.

Fonts

In Excel, the font format property encompasses several aspects of the character:

- typeface, such as *Times New Roman*, *Arial*, and *Courier*

- size measured in points
- bold and/or italic
- color
- underline
- special effects—strikethrough, superscript, and subscript

Three important new font formatting features have been added in Excel 5:

- Accountants will appreciate the support of underlining that adheres to rigid accounting standards.
- The scientific community will appreciate the addition of superscript and subscript as global font options.
- Everyone will appreciate that fonts can be applied to individual characters within a cell.

Applying Fonts

Choose the Format ➤ Cells command, then select the Font tab to display the dialog box pictured in Figure 5.1. Select the font properties you want to apply and click OK.

Font

- Available fonts are not specific to Excel—the list includes all fonts available under Microsoft Windows.
- TrueType fonts are indicated by a TT symbol next to the typeface—TrueType is a scalable font technology built into Microsoft Windows.
- Fonts available for the currently selected printer are indicated by a printer symbol next to the typeface.

Size

Font size is measured in points. There are 72 points per inch (measured from the top of the **b** upstroke to the bottom of the **p** downstroke), so a 12-point font is $\frac{1}{6}$th of an inch from top to bottom when printed.

FIGURE 5.1

The Format ➤ Cells, Font dialog box

Underline

- *Single* and *Double* underlines apply to all characters.

- *Single Accounting* and *Double Accounting* underline the entire cell if text, or characters only if number.

Normal Font

Checking *Normal Font* resets font selections to default settings.

Changing the Default Workbook Font

To change the default workbook font, choose the Tools ➤ Options command, then select the General tab. The *Standard Font* and *Size* settings determine the default font. This setting is applied every time you create a new workbook. (Excel must be restarted before changes in this setting take effect.)

Tools for Setting Fonts

Table 5.1 describes the various font tools available in Excel. Note that the tools marked with ★ do not appear on a built-in toolbar—see Chapter 26 to learn how to display them by customizing toolbars.

TABLE 5.1: Font Formatting Tools

TOOL	FUNCTION
Arial	Font (typeface)
10	Size (in points)
B	Bold
I	Italic
U	Single Underline
D	Double Underline ★
K	Strikethrough ★
A	Increase Font Size ★
A	Decrease Font Size ★
T	Font Color Palette (tearaway)
A	Cycle Font Color ★

Borders

Cell borders add clarity and organization to a worksheet, and when used judiciously are one of the most useful formatting options. To set borders, choose the Format ➤ Cells command, then select the Border tab to display the dialog box shown in Figure 5.2.

FIGURE 5.2

The Format ➤ Cells, Border dialog box

Understanding the Border Options

The following list describes the options available in the Format Cells, Border dialog box:

- *Style* controls the line style of selected borders, including varied line weight, solid or broken, and single or double.

- *Color* controls the color of selected borders.

- *Border* controls which borders are applied to selected cells, and displays the *Style* and *Color* selected for each border.

NOTE If a *Border* option is shaded grey, it means that that specific option is applied to only some of the selected cells (or that different styles are applied to the selected cells). For example, select cell B2 and apply a left border. Now select cells B2:B3 and display the Border dialog box. *Border, left* is shaded grey because only part of the selection is left-bordered.

To remove a border, display the Border dialog box and click the *Border* you want to remove.

NOTE Sometimes when you remove a border, the border doesn't disappear from the cell. This happens because there are two borders applied to the gridline, and you must remove both. For example, select cells B2:C2 and apply left and right borders. Now try to remove the border between the two cells by removing the right border from cell B2. The border still displayed on the worksheet is the left border of cell C2. Remove the left border from cell C2, and the border between the two cells on the worksheet disappears.

Gridlines Are Not the Same as Borders

Cell gridlines are not the same as cell borders. Gridlines are global to the worksheet, and they diminish the impact of borders. To remove gridlines:

1. Choose the Tools ➤ Options command, then select the View tab.

2. Uncheck the *Gridlines* option.

TIP

Light grey borders, or thin borders, can provide a less visually obtrusive border, and a more professional look. The appearance of these effects will vary depending on monitor or printer resolution.

Tools for Applying Borders

The Border tool displays a palette of various border styles (see Chapter 1 to learn about tear-off palettes). Table 5.2 describes each tool on the Border tool palette.

TABLE 5.2: Border Formatting Tools on the Border Tool Drop-down Palette

TOOL	FUNCTION
	No border (removes existing borders)
	Bottom
	Left
	Right
	Bottom double
	Bottom heavy
	Top and bottom
	Top and double bottom
	Top and heavy bottom

TABLE 5.2: Border Formatting Tools on the Border Tool Drop-down Palette (continued)

TOOL	FUNCTION
	Outline (each cell in selection)
	Outline (around selection)
	Heavy outline (around selection)

Patterns

Patterns and colors can improve the appearance of a worksheet or emphasize specific information. To apply colors and patterns to selected cells, choose Format ➤ Cells, then select the Patterns tab.

- Select a color.
- Select a pattern and a pattern color from the *Pattern* drop-down.

Bright colors can be muted by mixing with a white pattern, or by applying the bright color as a pattern over a white background.

Make large tables easy to read across by shading every other row in a light color or grey:

	A	B	C	D	E	F	G
EXPENSES.XLS							
1	7180	5921	826	9781	8295	145	6480
2	1972	8060	4033	7807	6401	7591	3902
3	6170	1233	7893	4038	8415	3690	1710
4	5308	9073	7691	5232	7970	1592	7173
5	977	7395	1392	8186	647	535	1889
6	3204	824	5934	1473	1810	239	5114
7	1154	4232	7140	8979	8746	4792	8837
8	7242	4718	717	802	9785	7469	4818
9	8595	2072	1535	3314	7203	161	9272
10	968	4829	1564	8806	4164	3737	365
11	2368	6005	5305	7459	7588	6353	3723

Tools for Applying Patterns

 The Color tool is found on the Formatting toolbar. When clicked it displays a tear-off palette of colors. To tear the palette away from the toolbar, click on the palette and drag it onto the worksheet (where it will act like a floating toolbar).

 The Pattern tool is found on the Drawing toolbar, and also has a drop-down, tear-off palette.

Alignment

Alignment refers to the positioning of characters within the cell. By default, text is left-aligned and numbers are right-aligned. To set alignment, choose the Format ➤ Cells command, then select the Alignment tab to display the dialog box in Figure 5.3.

FIGURE 5.3

The Format ➤ Cells, Alignment dialog box

Format Cells

| Number | **Alignment** | Font | Border | Patterns | Protection |

Horizontal
- ● General
- ○ Left
- ○ Center
- ○ Right
- ○ Fill
- ○ Justify
- ○ Center across selection

Vertical
- ○ Top
- ○ Center
- ● Bottom
- ○ Justify

☐ Wrap Text

Orientation

Text

OK

Cancel

Help

Horizontal Alignment

The following describes the options for horizontally aligning the text:

General aligns text to the left, numbers to the right.

Left aligns cell contents to the left.

Center centers characters within the cell.

Right aligns cell contents to the right.

Fill fills selected cells evenly with a single character.

Justify aligns wrapped text right and left (text is automatically wrapped). Results are visible only with multiple lines.

Center Across Selection centers text across multiple columns.

Center Across Selection

The *Center Across Selection* option is very useful for titles, as it centers the text across the selected cells regardless of varying column widths. For example, suppose you want to center the title **1996 Quarterly Revenue** over columns A through D (in row 2).

1. Enter text in cell A2.

2. Select cells A2:D2.

3. Choose *Center Across Selection* from the Alignment dialog box.

Wrap Text

The *Wrap Text* option breaks a long line of text into multiple lines to fit within the cell. Excel breaks the lines to fit column width, but you can insert specific line breaks with Alt+Enter. Rows automatically heighten to fit multiple lines of text.

Vertical Alignment

The vertical alignment settings control alignment between the top and bottom of the cell.

Top positions contents at the top of the cell.

Center centers contents vertically within the cell.

Bottom positions contents on the bottom of the cell.

Justify justifies lines vertically, from top to bottom of the cell, and automatically wraps text.

To demonstrate the effect of vertical alignment, try this:

1. Enter some text in cell B2.

2. Increase the height of row 2.

3. Change the vertical alignment in cell B2 to *Top*.

Notice that the vertical alignment in a cell is not apparent unless the row height is increased.

Orientation

The Orientation settings control how the text is oriented within the cell. The four settings on the dialog box (see Figure 5.3) display what the text will look like.

Row height automatically adjusts when the cell is oriented vertically or sideways. For instance, if you format a cell for vertical orientation, the row height will increase to fit the entire entry into the cell.

Alignment Tools

Table 5.3 lists and describes Excel's alignment tools. Note that the tools marked with ★ do not appear on a built-in toolbar—see Chapter 26 to learn how to display them by customizing toolbars.

TABLE 5.3: Alignment Tools

TOOL	FUNCTION
	Left-align
	Center-align
	Right-align
	Justify ★
	Center across Selection
	Vertical orientation ★
	Sideways (read bottom-to-top) ★
	Sideways (read top-to-bottom) ★

Numbers

Number formats control how numbers, including date and time, are displayed.

Using Number Formats

1. Choose Format ➤ Cells, then select the Number tab (see Figure 5.4).

2. Select a *Category* of formats (to narrow the search for a formatting code).

3. Select a *Format Code*. (*Sample* displays the selected format applied to the data in the active cell.)

4. Click OK.

FIGURE 5.4

The Format ➤ Cells, Number dialog box

Format Symbols

Excel's number format symbols are listed in Table 5.4.

TABLE 5.4: Number Format Symbols

SYMBOL	FUNCTION	REMARKS
0	digit placeholder	Determines number of decimal places displayed; rounds to number of 0's right of decimal point, displays leading and trailing zeros
#	digit placeholder	Same as 0; doesn't display leading or trailing zeros
?	digit placeholder	Same as 0; insignificant 0's removed, spaces inserted to align numbers correctly
. (period)	decimal point	Marks location of decimal point
%	percent	Displays % sign, and treats number as percent
, (comma)	thousands separator	Marks thousands position
_ (underscore)	alignment feature	Skips width of character following underscore; aligns positives with negatives enclosed in ( ) so that numbers and commas remain aligned
E- E+ e- e+	exponent indicator	Displays number in scientific format
: $ _ + ( ) - /	characters	These characters displayed
/	fraction separator	Indicates fraction
\	text indicator	Character following is text
" "	text indicator	Entry within quotes is text
★	fill indicator	Fills remaining cell width with character following asterisk

TABLE 5.4: Number Format Symbols (continued)

SYMBOL	FUNCTION	REMARKS
@	format code	Indicates where user-input text will appear
[*color*]	color indicator	Displays characters in indicated color (black, blue, white, green, cyan, magenta, red, yellow)
[*color n*]	color indicator	Displays characters in corresponding color from color palette (*n* is number from 0–56)
[*condition value*]	conditional statement	Sets criteria for each section of number format; uses conditions **<,>,=,<=,>=,<>**, and numeric values

Date and Time Formatting Symbols

When a date or time is entered, it is recognized and displayed in a date or time format. Table 5.5 shows the variety of formats available for dates and times.

Inexplicably, there is no built-in format to display a date in the format **January 7, 1998**. To display a date in this format, either enter it as text (by preceding the entry with an apostrophe), or create the custom format **mmmm d, yyyy**. Keep in mind that the date cannot be used in calculations if entered as text.

TIP

When you enter a fraction, such as 1/2, Excel interprets your entry as a date, and displays *2-Jan*. To "force the fraction," enter it as a mixed fraction: *0 1/2*.

TABLE 5.5: Date and Time Format Symbols

SYMBOL	DISPLAY	REMARKS
YYYY	1997	Year—four-digits
YY	97	Year—two-digits
MMMM	January	Month—full name
MMM	Jan	Month, abbreviated to three characters
MM	01	Month—number, leading zeros
M	1	Month—number, no leading zeros
DD	07	Day—number, leading zeros
D	7	Day—number, no leading zeros
h	1	Hour
mm	01	Minute (displays leading zeros)
ss	01	Second (displays leading zeros)

NOTE M or mm immediately following h or hh signifies minutes, not months.

Samples

Table 5.6 shows some of Excel's many number formatting options at work.

TIP When you enter a formula that refers to other cells, the cell inherits the formatting of the first referenced cell in the formula (unless a specific format has already been applied to the cell containing the formula).

TABLE 5.6: Sample Built-in Formats

VALUE	FORMAT	DISPLAY
1234.335	0	1234
1234.335	#,##0	1,234
1234.335	#,##0.00	1,234.34
1234	0.00	1234.00
1234.335	# ?/?	1234 1/3
.1234	0%	12%
1234.335	0.00E+00	1.23E+03
June 11, 1998	mm/dd/yy	06/11/98
June 11, 1998	d/mmm/yy	11-Jun-98
June 11, 1998	mmm/yy	Jun-98
8:07 PM	h:mm AM/PM	8:07 PM
8:07 PM	h:mm	20:07
8:07:32	h:mm:ss	8:07:32

Custom Number Formats

You are not limited to the built-in number formats. Using the format symbols in Table 5.4 and Table 5.5, you can construct your own custom number formats.

Creating a Custom Number Format

Suppose that you want to display numbers in thousands, without changing the values:

1. Select cell A1 and enter **1234567**.

2. Choose Format ➤ Cells, then select the Number tab.

3. Type **#,###,** in the *Code* box (be sure to type both commas).

4. Click OK. The number will display as **1,235**.

Applying Custom Number Formats

Once a custom number format is defined, it is stored in the workbook and can be applied just like built-in formats. Custom formats will display in the *Number* dialog box (see Figure 5.4) at the end of the appropriate category, the end of the *All* category, and in the *Custom* category.

Deleting Custom Number Formats

Custom number formats are stored in the workbook in which they were defined. To delete them, activate the workbook, then follow these steps:

1. Display the Number dialog box.

2. Select the *Custom* category.

3. Select the custom format you want to delete, then click the Delete button.

Number Formats Based on Cell Value

Numbers can be formatted to display differently, based on cell value. For example, a cell can be formatted to display negative numbers red and positive numbers blue. Several of the built-in formats use this type of conditional formatting. Examples 1 and 2 are built-in formats, and are included as a first step in understanding the tedious, complex syntax involved.

TIP There is one element common to all conditional formats: the different segments are separated by a semicolon.

The easiest way to create a custom conditional format is to modify one of the built-in formats. Select the built-in format, then edit the format in the *Code* edit box (see Figure 5.4).

FORMATTING CELLS

EXAMPLE 1: **#,##0_);(#,##0)**

#,##0_)   Format for positive number—right parenthesis does not display; underscore causes format to skip width of right parenthesis, so positive numbers align properly with negative numbers displaying parentheses; value displayed as whole number with commas marking thousands

(#,##0)   Format for negative number—parentheses placed around number; value displayed as whole number with commas marking thousands

EXAMPLE 2: **#,##0_);[Red](#,##0)**

#,##0_)   Format for positive number, same as Example 1

[Red](#,##0)   Negative number displayed in red, in parentheses

Examples 1 and 2 use *implicit* thresholds; the remaining examples include expressions that *explicitly* set the conditional value thresholds.

EXAMPLE 3: **[Red][<10]#,##0;[Green][>20]#,##0;[Yellow]#,##0**

[Red][<10]#,##0   Numbers less than 10 displayed red

[Green][>20]#,##0   Numbers greater than 20 displayed green

[Yellow]#,##0   All other numbers (from 10 to 20) displayed yellow

EXAMPLE 4: **[Red][<=10]#,##0;[Green][>=20]#,##0;[Yellow#,##0**

[Red][<=10]#,##0   Numbers less than or equal to 10 displayed red

[Green][>=20]#,##0   Numbers greater than or equal to 20 displayed green

[Yellow]#,##0   All other numbers (between 10 and 20) displayed yellow

Examples 5 through 7 use text constants in place of number formats:

EXAMPLE 5: **[<10]"Few";[>100]"Many";"Some"**

[<10]"Few"   Numbers less than 10 displayed as *Few*

[>100]"Many"   Numbers greater than 100 displayed as *Many*

Some   All other numbers (from 10 to 100) displayed as *Some*

EXAMPLE 6: **[<-100][GREEN]"Too small";[>100][RED]"Too large";###0**

[<-100][GREEN]"Too small"   Numbers less than −100 displayed as *Too small*, in green

[>100][RED]"Too large"   Numbers greater than 100 displayed as *Too large*, in red

###0   All other numbers (from −100 to 100) displayed as whole numbers, in default color; no comma marking thousands

EXAMPLE 7: **"Quantity: "#,##0**

"Quantity: "   Numbers display following this text string (e.g., *Quantity: 2,345*)

#,##0   Number format

A number format may contain up to four segments, separated by semi-colons. Up to three value ranges may be formatted (as you have seen in the preceding examples). If the value ranges are not explicitly specified (for instance, *[<100]*) then Excel assumes a syntax of

Positive values;negative values;zero values;text values

Example 8 uses a fourth segment to specify the format for a text value:

EXAMPLE 8: **#,##0;(#,##0);0;"Enter a number!"**

#,##0   Positive numbers displayed whole, with comma; no space-holder to align with parentheses around negative numbers

(#,##0)   Negative numbers displayed whole, with comma, in parentheses

0   zero values displayed as **0**

"Enter a number!"   Text values displayed as **Enter a number!**

CAUTION

As you have seen,, custom formats can be used to display information that is very different than the underlying cell value. This can be very confusing down the road when 2 + 2 does not equal 4. Look to the formula bar to see actual underlying cell values.

Some Useful Custom Formats

Here are some custom formats which may come in handy, and will further illuminate format code syntax:

;;   Hides all numbers (but not text)

;;;   Hides all values (including text)

0;0;   Displays both positive and negative values as whole positive numbers; zero values as blank cells; text as entered

Format Painter

 A new feature in Excel 5 is the *Format Painter* tool, available on the Standard toolbar. Format Painter copies and pastes formats by "painting" them onto cells. To use Format Painter:

1. Select a cell containing formatting you want to copy.

2. Click the *Format Painter* tool.

3. Click and drag through cells where you want to apply the formatting.

You can paint formatting repeatedly without clicking the tool each time if you double-click the *Format Painter* tool. The *Format Painter* cursor remains active until you click the *Format Painter* tool again.

AutoFormats

An *AutoFormat* is a built-in table format which can be quickly applied to a range of cells. AutoFormats include formatting for numbers, alignment, font, border, pattern, color, row height, and column width.

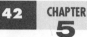

Applying an Autoformat

Follow these steps to apply an AutoFormat to a range of cells:

1. Select a range of data (either an entire contiguous range or a single cell within a range of data).

2. Choose Format ➤ AutoFormat.

3. Select an AutoFormat from the *Table Format* list.

4. Click OK.

Selectively Applying an AutoFormat

An AutoFormat includes six attributes, but when you apply an AutoFormat you can elect to include only selected attributes, so that when the AutoFormat is applied it won't erase previously applied formatting. For example, suppose you want to apply an AutoFormat without changing the current row and column sizing on the worksheet:

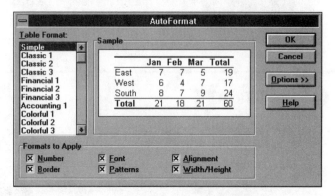

1. Select a range of data and choose Format ➤ AutoFormat.

2. Select an AutoFormat from the *Table Formats* list, then click the Options button.

3. Under *Formats to Apply*, uncheck the *Width/Height* option.

4. Click OK. The AutoFormat will be applied without any column width or row height attributes.

TIP

Format Painter will paint an AutoFormat from one table to another (but without row/column sizing). Select the entire AutoFormatted range, click Format Painter, then select (paint) the entire range to be formatted.

Styles

Picture a worksheet that has dozens of subheadings throughout the sheet, each one formatted Times New Roman, 12, Bold, with a bottom border. You can define a *style*, which is a named combination of formats, then rapidly apply the style to cells. If you change the style, all cells using the style change automatically.

Styles are vitally important when it comes to simplifying sheet formatting. The small amount of time it will take you to learn about styles will save you a lot of time and hassle in the long run. Some of the benefits of styles are…

- time savings when developing sheets
- time savings when changing formats later
- establishment of formatting standards

For example, when standardizing the look of reports, you might want to define styles for section titles, total rows, subtotal rows, and column headings.

Creating Styles by Example

When you create a style by example, you first format a cell, then define a style using the cell's formatting. (This is the fastest way to create a new style.)

1. Format a cell using desired formatting commands, and leave that cell selected.

2. Choose the Format ➤ Style command. The Style dialog box is displayed (see Figure 5.5).

3. Type a name for the new style into the *Style Name* box.

FIGURE 5.5

The Format ➤ Style
dialog box

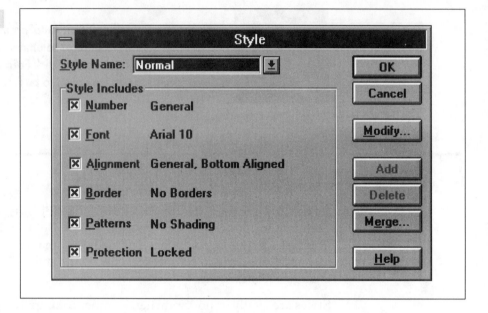

4. Click OK.

The new style will contain all the formatting characteristics of the selected cell.

TIP You can create a new style by typing the name directly into the style tool rather than using the Style dialog box. To use the Style tool, add it to a toolbar (see Chapter 26 to learn how).

Creating Styles Explicitly

Previously, you learned how to create styles by example. The following procedure lets you define a style explicitly, using the options in the Style dialog box.

1. Choose the Format ➤ Style command.

2. Type a name for the new style in the *Style Name* box.

3. Click *Modify*. The Format Cells dialog box is displayed.

4. Select the formatting options you want from the dialog box tabs, then click OK.

5. The Style dialog box is displayed again:

   - To apply the new style, click OK.
   - To define the style without applying it, click Add, then click Close.

The Style dialog box displays a list of the six attributes a style can include (see *Style Includes* in Figure 5.5), and the settings for each attribute in the selected style. You can uncheck any attributes that you don't want to include. For example, you can create a style that doesn't include border or patterns attributes, so that the style, when applied, won't alter existing borders or patterns.

N O T E Row height and column width are not part of the style definition.

Changing a Style Definition

The steps involved in changing the style are very similar to creating a style:

1. Choose Format ➤ Style.

2. Select or type the name of the style you want to change.

   - If you *select* the name, the existing style formats serve as the starting point for changes.
   - If you *type* the name, the formatting of the active cell serves as the starting point for changes.

3. Click *Modify*, and change the formats using the Format Cells dialog box tabs.

4. Click OK. The Style dialog box is displayed again.

5. Click OK to apply the new style, or click *Add* to keep the Style dialog box open (to create or redefine more styles).

TIP

You can also change a style using the Style tool. Select a cell containing the style and change the formatting. Use the Style tool to reselect or retype the same style name. Excel will ask if you want to redefine the style name based on selected cells—click Yes.

Applying a Style

You have learned how to create styles. Here is the procedure for *applying* a style to one or more cells:

1. Select the cell(s) that you want to apply the style to.

2. Apply the style in one of two ways:

   • Choose Format ➤ Style, then select a style from the *Style Name* list, then click OK.

   • Select a style from the Style tool (see Chapter 26 to learn how to add the Style tool to a toolbar).

Deleting a Style

Styles are stored inside the workbook in which they were created. To delete a style:

1. Activate the workbook containing the style.

2. Choose Format ➤ Style.

3. Select the style to delete from the *Style Name* list.

4. Click Delete, then click OK.

NOTE

You can't delete the Normal style, but you can change its properties.

Merging Styles

Styles are stored in workbooks, and are only available in the workbook where the style was created. Assume that you have created some styles in a workbook, and want to merge them into a different workbook without having to redefine them:

1. Open the *source* workbook containing the style(s) to be copied from, and the *target* workbook the style(s) are to be merged into.

2. Activate the target workbook.

3. Choose the Format ➤ Style command.

4. Click *Merge*.

5. Select the source workbook from the *Merge Styles From* list.

6. Click OK to copy the styles into the target workbook—all styles in the source workbook will be merged.

7. Click OK to close the Style dialog box.

TIP

Use styles in conjunction with templates to create standardized worksheet formats. See Chapter 10 to learn about templates.

Copying Formats and Styles to a Different Workbook

When you copy a cell from one workbook to another, the formatting moves with the cell. This is most beneficial with custom number formats and styles, since it can be time consuming to recreate the definitions.

To copy a custom number format or style to another workbook, select a cell containing the format or style and copy it to the new workbook. Custom number formats and styles will be added to the lists in the new workbook.

Design Tips

Here are some simple tips for designing aesthetically pleasing and easy-to-use worksheets:

- **Keep it simple!** Too many fonts and colors can be overwhelming. Limit a given worksheet to one or two typefaces, with variations in size and style (bold, italic).

- **Use scalable fonts,** such as TrueType, to keep your figures sharp and clear on the screen.

- **Use color meaningfully,** to highlight information or focus the reader's attention. Use muted colors, like grey, for backgrounds.

- **Turn off gridlines,** and use borders for clarity.

- **Incorporate plenty of white space**—a lot of condensed data can be difficult to digest.

- **Incorporate graphic features** (charts, logos, etc.) to make the worksheet more visually appealing. See Chapter 12 to learn more about graphic objects.

A Formatting Exercise

As an exercise, let's create the example worksheet shown in Figure 5.6 and then take the steps to format it differently. (Don't worry about having to enter all the numbers as shown here; in these steps you'll learn how to use a function that will fill in the number cells with random data.)

FIGURE 5.6

A typical hard-to-read worksheet

	Northwest Athletic Wear Quarterly Sales – By Product				
Shoes	Qtr 1	Qtr 2	Qtr 3	Qtr 4	
	-----------	-----------	-----------	-----------	
Running	616	963	539	119	
Tennis	21	539	647	140	
Basketball	807	663	487	958	
	========	========	========	========	
subtotal	1444	2165	1673	1217	
Shirts	Qtr 1	Qtr 2	Qtr 3	Qtr 4	
	-----------	-----------	-----------	-----------	
Tee	106	321	853	728	
Polo	608	515	205	570	
Sweat	447	228	507	449	
	========	========	========	========	
subtotal	1161	1064	1565	1747	
	========	========	========	========	
Total	2605	3229	3238	2964	

1. Open a new worksheet and enter the following:

CELL	ENTRY
B2	Northwest Athletic Wear
B3	Quarterly Sales—By Product
B6	Shoes
C7	Qtr 1
D7	Qtr 2
E7	Qtr 3
F7	Qtr 4
B8	Running
B9	Tennis
B10	Basketball
B11	Subtotal
C11	=SUBTOTAL(9,C8:C10)
D11:F11	(copy formula from C11)

2. Apply the following formatting:

CELL	FORMATTING
B2	bold, italic, 16 points
B3	bold, italic, 12 points
B2:B3	center across worksheet (select B2:F3; choose Format ➤ Cells, Alignment tab, *Center Across Selection* setting)
B6	bold, italic, 11 points
B8:B10	right-align
B11:F11	bold
C7:F7	bold, center-align
C8:F10	thin, grey borders to left, right, top, and bottom
C11:F11	grey double borders to top; built-in number format #,##0
C8:F10	custom number format **[Red][<300]#,##0; [Blue][>600]#,##0;#,##0**

3. Turn the gridlines off.

4. Create a style for the title cells:

   • Select cell B6.

   • Choose Format ➤ Style, type **Title** in the *Style Name* edit box, then click OK.

N O T E

If you change the properties of a style, all the cells using that style will change. This may seem a minor efficiency with only a few titles, but picture a worksheet with hundreds of titles. If the titles have been formatted using a style, a single change to the style will automatically change the formatting of all of the titles.

5. Create a second section by copying the first:

   • Select cells B6:F11.

   • Copy and paste to cell B13.

6. Change these values in the second section:

   • Enter **Shirts** in cell B13.

   • Enter **Tee, Polo,** and **Sweat** in cells B15:B17.

7. Enter the following function to enter random data:

   • Select cells C8:F10 and C15:F17 (hold down Ctrl to select both ranges).

   • Type **=INT(RAND()*1000)** and press Ctrl+Enter.

8. Freeze the random values:

   • Select C8:F10, Edit ➤ Copy, choose Edit ➤ Paste Special, select *Values,* and click OK.

   • Repeat this freeze procedure for cells C15:F17.

9. Create a Grand Total row:

   - Enter **Total** (right-aligned and bold) in cell B19.
   - Enter the formula **=SUBTOTAL(9,C8:C10,C15:C17)** in cell C19, then copy the formula to cells D19:F19 (see Chapter 9 to learn more about the SUBTOTAL function).

10. Apply a grey double border to the tops of the Grand Total cells.

11. Give the totals some visual separation from the data:

    - Select rows 11, 18, and 19.
    - Choose Format ➤ Row ➤ Height, and enter a row height of **19**.

When completed, the exercise worksheet should look like Figure 5.7.

FIGURE 5.7

The worksheet from Figure 5.6, newly formatted

Northwest Athletic Wear
Quarterly Sales - By Product

Shoes

	Qtr 1	Qtr 2	Qtr 3	Qtr 4
Running	616	963	539	119
Tennis	21	539	647	140
Basketball	807	663	487	958
subtotal	**1444**	**2165**	**1673**	**1217**

Shirts

	Qtr 1	Qtr 2	Qtr 3	Qtr 4
Tee	106	321	853	728
Polo	608	515	205	570
Sweat	447	228	507	449
subtotal	**1161**	**1064**	**1565**	**1747**
Total	**2605**	**3229**	**3238**	**2964**

CHAPTER

6

Printing

fast TRACK

IN spite of trends towards the paperless office, hardcopy reports will likely be a fixture for the foreseeable future. Preparing and printing reports is one of the most common activities performed with Excel, according to Microsoft surveys. This chapter will cover:

- *how to select a printer*
- *setting up headers, footers, margins, and pagination*
- *special printing considerations*

Selecting a Printer

Your computer may be connected to more than one printer. If so, the following procedure allows you to select which printer to use.

1. Choose File ➤ Print, then click the Printer button.
2. Select a printer from the list in the Printer Setup dialog box.
3. Click OK to close the printer setup dialog box.
4. Click OK to print (when Cancel is clicked, the print job is canceled, but the chosen printer remains in effect).

Setting Up Worksheets for Printing

The File ➤ Page Setup command displays a tabbed dialog box which provides access to most print-related settings. The four tabs are: Page, Margins, Header/Footer, and Sheet.

Page Setup

The Page tab, pictured in Figure 6.1, controls the basic layout of the printed pages.

Table 6.1 describes the settings found on the Page tab.

Margins

The Margins tab, pictured in Figure 6.2, is where margins, headers, and footers are positioned on the page.

FIGURE 6.1

File ➤ Page
Setup—Page tab

PRINTING

TABLE 6.1: Page Options

OPTION	REMARKS
Orientation	Select portrait (tall) or landscape (wide).
Scaling—Adjust To	Increases (magnifies) or decreases (shrinks) scale of worksheet to fit printed page
Scaling—Fit To	Adjusts scale to fit specified number of pages
Paper Size	Select paper size from drop-down list.
Print Quality	Select resolution (dpi) from list.
First Page Number	Begins numbering at specified page number
Options button	Displays dialog box for settings on selected printer

FIGURE 6.2

File ➤ Page
Setup—Margins tab

The settings on the Margin tab are described in Table 6.2. The *Preview* indicates which margin is being set. (Select a margin, and the corresponding line on the *Preview* will be highlighted.)

TABLE 6.2: Margins Options

OPTIONS	REMARKS
Top, Bottom, Left, Right	Sets margins (inches from edge)
From Edge	Sets header/footer placement (inches from edge)—Should be less than top/bottom margins
Center on Page	Check to center vertically/horizontally within margins.

Creating Page Headers and Footers

The Header/Footer tab, pictured in Figure 6.3, is where page headers and page footers are entered and formatted.

FIGURE 6.3

File ➤ Page Setup—Header/Footer tab

PRINTING

Headers and Footers work exactly alike—you can choose a built-in header/footer, or define a custom one.

Using Built-in Headers/Footers

Select from a variety of built-in headers and footers using the two drop-down lists on the Header/Footer tab. The lists include several commonly-used header/footer formats.

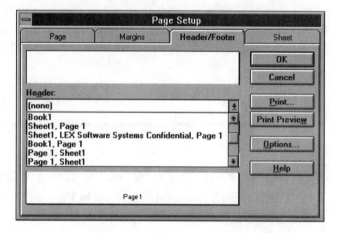

Creating Custom Headers/Footers

Click the Custom Header or Custom Footer buttons to customize headers/footers.

Click on the section (left, center, or right) where you want to place a header/footer. The left section is left-justified, the center section is centered on the page, and the right section is right-justified. Type text into any of these three sections. (Press Alt+Enter for a new line.) The buttons in the center of the dialog box, defined in Table 6.3, are used to format the text, and to insert special values into the header/footer.

TABLE 6.3: Custom Header/Footer Buttons

CLICK ON:	TO INSERT:
A	font format (Select text, click button, select formatting options.)
#	page number
(page)	number of pages
(date)	current date
(time)	current time
(workbook)	workbook name
(worksheet)	worksheet name

Sheet Options

The Sheet tab, pictured in Figure 6.4, allows you to specify a print area, print titles, and several other print options.

Table 6.4 describes the options found on the Sheet tab.

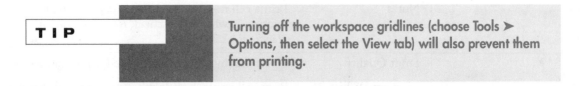

TIP Turning off the workspace gridlines (choose Tools ➤ Options, then select the View tab) will also prevent them from printing.

Setting a Print Area

To set a Print Area, click in the *Print Area* edit box, then select a range of cells using the mouse (or type in a cell range reference).

FIGURE 6.4

File ➤ Page Setup,
Sheet Tab

TABLE 6.4: Sheet Options

OPTIONS	REMARKS
Print Area	Select area of worksheet to print (select or type reference).
Print Titles	Select or type rows/columns to print on every page.
Gridlines	Turns gridlines on/off (only affects printed pages)
Notes	Prints cell notes on additional pages. (To print references with notes, check *Row and Column Headings*.)
Draft Quality	Fewer graphics, no gridlines—reduces printing time
Black and White	Prints all in black and white (no shades of grey for colors)
Row and Column Headings	Includes row and column headings on printed page
Page Order	Select page order for multi-page worksheet.

You can set a Print Area quickly by selecting the range to print and clicking the Set Print Area tool. This tool is not available on a built-in toolbar—see Chapter 26 to learn how to add it to a customized toolbar.

A worksheet can have only one Print Area at a time, but there's no need to delete the old Print Area to set a new one.

TIP

You don't have to define a print area in order to print a certain range of cells. Select the cells to print, choose File ➤ Print, and choose *Selection* from the *Print What* options.

Setting Print Titles

When printing a multiple-page document, you may want certain rows or columns to appear on each page.

For example, suppose you have a worksheet of scientific air-quality data, with a year's worth of daily readings from 150 sites. The worksheet is 365 rows (dates) long by 150 columns (sites) wide, and requires several pages to print. Each data point must be identified by date (down the left column) and by site (along the top row). A page containing, for example, data for Sites 95–106 in June must have appropriate dates and sites along the left and top of the page (as in Figure 6.5).

The page shown in Figure 6.5 is just one page out of 144 pages (the worksheet is 12 pages tall by 12 pages wide). Setting the Date column (Column A) and the Site row (Row 1) as Print Titles makes it possible to print any range of cells in the worksheet without having to paste in the identifying dates and sites (the appropriate date and site titles are printed automatically with whatever portion of the worksheet is printed).

NOTE

Print titles are not the same as page headers, though they can be used for similar purposes. A page can be set up for both print titles and page headers.

PRINTING

FIGURE 6.5

A portion of a spreadsheet with data for 150 sites recorded every day for a year

Site#	95	96	97	98	99	100	101	102
6/1/97	604	248	429	502	634	881	175	933
6/2/97	127	579	156	36	954	912	596	797
6/3/97	555	235	970	936	558	740	85	230
6/4/97	394	995	916	458	873	924	358	309
6/5/97	457	272	140	522	781	104	558	275
6/6/97	624	523	638	995	4	475	409	832
6/7/97	748	473	565	453	64	311	18	731
6/8/97	48	275	343	356	672	2	899	613
6/9/97	277	453	408	257	632	818	784	919
6/10/97	480	120	159	803	223	337	489	809
6/11/97	851	475	564	47	190	858	470	358
6/12/97	525	861	890	163	189	154	628	217
6/13/97	998	934	23	114	388	916	693	274
6/14/97	308	842	172	371	619	176	769	892
6/15/97	772	865	605	273	640	618	700	733
6/16/97	69	998	197	269	134	574	235	951
6/17/97	680	974	829	26	557	988	155	817
6/18/97	10	955	353	446	222	97	33	837
6/19/97	267	135	68	779	853	472	178	989
6/20/97	949	331	981	10	278	729	584	292

To set Print Titles:

1. Choose the File ➤ Page Setup command, then select the Sheet tab.

2. Click in the *Rows to Repeat at Top* edit box.

3. On the worksheet, select the rows to be repeated. (Or type the cell reference.)

4. Click in the *Columns to Repeat at Left* edit box.

5. On the worksheet, select the columns to be repeated. (Or type the cell reference.)

6. Click OK.

CAUTION

If you set Print Titles *and* a Print Area, do not include the title rows and/or columns in the Print Area. Otherwise, the titles will print twice.

Deleting a Print Area or Print Titles

If a print area has been defined, and you want to print the entire worksheet, you must first delete the Print Area.

To delete the Print Area, choose the File ➤ Page Setup command, then select the Sheet tab and clear the *Print Area* edit box. To delete print titles, clear *Rows to Repeat* and/or *Columns to Repeat*.

When you set the print area or print titles, range names are automatically defined on the worksheet. Setting the print area causes the name **Print_Area** to be defined. Setting print titles causes the name **Print_Titles** to be defined. If you want to see either of these ranges, select them from the Name box. Because they are named ranges, they can be deleted using the Insert ➤ Name ➤ Define command. (See Chapter 8 to learn more about names.)

Preview before Printing

 Choose the File ➤ Print Preview command to see what the printed pages will look like before actually printing. There are also several settings that can be controlled while in print preview mode. Figure 6.6 displays the Print Preview workspace.

Zooming In and Out

 When in print preview, the mouse pointer becomes a magnifying glass. Click on the part of the worksheet that you wish to zoom in on. The sheet will be magnified, and the pointer becomes an arrow. Click on the worksheet again to zoom back out. (Alternately, use the Zoom button on the top of the window.)

Print Preview buttons

The following list explains the buttons that are displayed along the top of the workspace in print preview mode (see Figure 6.6):

Next   Displays the next page (this button is dimmed when there is no next page)

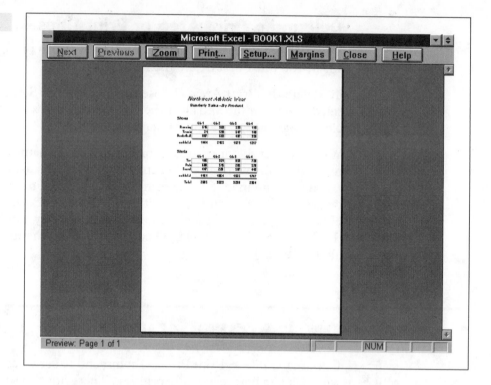

Previous   Displays the previous page (dimmed when there is no previous page)

Zoom   Toggles between magnified and full page display

Print   Displays the Print dialog box

Setup   displays the Page Setup dialog box

Margins   Toggles on/off lines depicting page margins, header/footer margins, and column width (drag the lines to reposition)

Close   Closes the Preview window and returns to the worksheet.

The Margins button, which toggles the display of margin and column lines, is a particularly useful feature. When margin and column lines are in view, they can be dragged with the mouse to a new position. To reposition a line, place the mouse pointer on a margin line, a column gridline, or a handle at the edge of the page, and drag the line with the two-headed arrow (Figure 6.7).

The inner horizontal margins are text margins; the outer horizontal margins are header/footer margins. The extra handles along the top of the page correspond to column lines.

Pagination

When you print, Excel automatically creates page breaks where needed. If automatic page breaks cause a page break to occur in an undesirable place on the worksheet, you can insert manual page breaks.

Automatic Page Breaks

By default, automatic page breaks are not indicated on the worksheet until the sheet is printed (or print previewed) for the first time. To display page breaks, choose Tools ➤ Options, then select the View tab, and check the *Automatic Page Breaks* option. Automatic page breaks are indicated by broken lines which run along the gridlines.

Manual Page Breaks

Suppose there is a multi-page worksheet with a table of numbers, and an automatic page break is occuring in the middle of the table (causing the table to print on pages two and three). But the table is only several rows tall, and by placing a manual page break just before the table begins, the table will fit on a single page. The following paragraphs explain how to accomplish this.

Inserting a Manual Page Break

Table 6.5 explains the three ways to insert page breaks.

TABLE 6.5: Inserting Page Breaks

TO INSERT:	DO THIS:
Vertical-only page break	Select column right of break, choose Insert ➤ Page Break.
Horizontal-only page break	Select row below break, choose Insert ➤ Page Break.
Vertical and horizontal page break	Select single cell, choose Insert ➤ Page Break. (Breaks insert along top and left side of cell)

Manual page breaks are indicated by heavier broken lines than automatic page breaks, as shown below. Automatic page breaks automatically adjust when manual page breaks are inserted.

Removing a Manual Page Break

Select a cell to the right of a vertical break or immediately below a horizontal break, and choose Insert ➤ Remove Page Break. (If the Insert menu doesn't list the Remove Page Break command, there is no manual page break at the selected cell.)

Printing Worksheets

 The File ➤ Print command displays a dialog box which offers options for printing selected cells, specific sheets or pages, or an entire workbook.

NOTE The Print tool will begin printing immediately without displaying a dialog box.

Printing Sections of a Worksheet

Often you won't want to print an entire worksheet. For example, you might have a year's worth of data accumulating in a given worksheet, and want to print just one month's worth, or perhaps you want to print it all but in small chunks.

1. Select the range of cells to print.

2. Choose File ➤ Print, and under *Print What* choose *Selection*.

Excel ignores any Print Area that has been set, and prints the selected range.

Printing More Than One Worksheet at a Time

To print several worksheets with one command, select all the sheets you want to print and choose File ➤ Print Selected Sheet(s) (the worksheets must be within the same workbook). See Chapter 3 to learn how to select multiple sheets.

Printing a Few Pages

Follow these steps to print selected pages from a multi-page printout. This example will print only page two:

1. Choose File ➤ Print.

2. Under *Page Range*, select *Page*.

3. Type **2** in both the *From*: and the *To*: boxes.

Printing Formulas

Naturally, when you print a worksheet, formulas do not print—just the resulting values. Here is how to print formulas instead of values:

1. Display the formulas by choosing Tools ➤ Options, then selecting the View tab, and checking the *Formulas* checkbox (or press Ctrl+è).

2. Print the worksheet.

TIP

Make the formula printout more useful by printing row and column headings. Choose File ➤ Page Setup, then select the Sheet tab and check the *Row and Column Headings* option.

	A	B	C	D	E
1	Full Name	Last Name	Score 1	Pass	
2	Smith, Joe	=LEFT(A2,SEARCH(",",A2)-1)	80	=IF(C2<65,"No","Yes")	
3	Jones, Mary	=LEFT(A3,SEARCH(",",A3)-1)	92	=IF(C3<65,"No","Yes")	
4	Dunn, Sam	=LEFT(A4,SEARCH(",",A4)-1)	64	=IF(C4<65,"No","Yes")	
5	Roberts, Jill	=LEFT(A5,SEARCH(",",A5)-1)	76	=IF(C5<65,"No","Yes")	
6					
7		Average:	=AVERAGE(C2:C5)		
8					
9					
10					
11					

Info Windows

An Info Window displays underlying information about a cell (see Chapter 11 to learn about Info Windows).

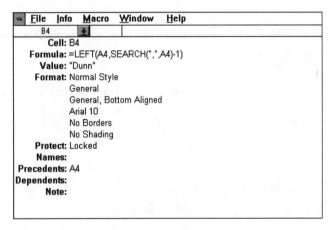

To print the Info Window for a cell:

1. Select the cell you want information for.

2. Display the Info Window by choosing Tools ➤ Options, then selecting the View tab, and checking the *Info Window* checkbox.

3. Choose the Info menu, then select cell information to be displayed.

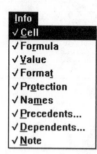

4. Choose File ➤ Print.

Using Colors

Colors are invaluable for adding emphasis to certain points and increasing overall visual appeal and readability. There are a wide variety of colors for fonts, borders, backgrounds, and background patterns, limited only by what your printer is capable of printing.

Translating Colorful Worksheets into Black and White Reports

To print a color worksheet in black and white (no shades of grey), choose File ➤ Page Setup and check the *Black and White* checkbox.

CHAPTER

7

Productivity Basics

fast TRACK

To enter the current date and time   **189**

  • Enter the current date with the keystrokes **Ctrl+;** (semicolon)

  • Enter the current time with the keystrokes **Ctrl+:** (colon)

To save the workspace   **189**

Choose File ➤ Save Workspace.

To use AutoFill   **195**

Drag the lower right corner of the cell selection up, down, left, or right to fill values or extend series.

THIS chapter covers a number of skills, techniques, and shortcuts to enhance your overall productivity. The tips are organized in the following categories:

- *getting help*
- *editing and navigating worksheets*
- *working with workbooks, worksheets, and windows*
- *productivity with Microsoft Windows*
- *using shortcut menus*
- *working with AutoFill*
- *using reversible tools*

Getting Help

The following paragraphs will help you to get help from Excel.

Getting Tips from the TipWizard

 The TipWizard is a tool that, when activated, can provide valuable productivity tips while you work. It "watches" you work, and displays a tip when there is a more efficient way to perform a given task. Click the TipWizard tool to activate this feature.

 The tips are brief in nature. But the Tip Help tool (on the right end of the Tip Wizard) will provide a fuller explanation by accessing Excel's online help.

Tip of the Day: To add a sheet to a workbook, choose Worksheet, Chart, or Macro from the Insert menu.

You don't have to notice the tip immediately. You can resume working, then later use the up and down arrows on the TipWizard to scroll through the tips at your leisure. When the TipWizard is displayed, the TipWizard button will hide it.

Keeping the Help Window in View

After accessing online help, it is often desirable to switch back and forth between viewing your worksheet and the online help window. But if Excel is maximized, the help window is obscured when you switch back to Excel. To keep the help window in view as you work, choose the Help ➤ Always On Top command while help is displayed. You can reduce the size of the help window, and the help text will automatically wrap accordingly.

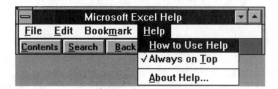

Placing a Bookmark in Help

Sometimes it takes a fair amount of searching to find the online Help topic you need. If it is a topic that you access often, such as the worksheet function reference, a bookmark can be used to speed up the search.

To place a bookmark into online help, find the topic that you want to mark, then choose the Bookmark ➤ Define command from the Help menu bar. Type your own name for the bookmark if desired, then click OK.

To use the bookmark, choose the Help ➤ Contents command. Select your bookmark from the Bookmark menu.

To delete a bookmark, choose Bookmark ➤ Define, select the bookmark to be deleted, and click Delete.

Editing Cells and Navigating Worksheets

The following paragraphs include a number of skills that will help you to effectively enter and edit formulas, fix mistakes, and navigate worksheets.

How to Undo Mistakes

 Most things you do in Excel can be undone if you use the Edit ➤ Undo command from the menu *immediately* following the action you want to reverse. You can undo typing, editing, inserting, deleting, and many other tasks where errors often occur.

However, some things cannot be undone:

- Some actions, due to their inherent nature, cannot be undone. For example, you cannot undo a File ➤ Save command or File ➤ Close command.

- Some actions cannot be undone due to memory restrictions. For example, if you change the formatting for a huge range of cells, you may have insufficient memory for Excel to "remember" the status of the sheet prior to the change. In these cases, Excel will issue the following warning:

If a serious mistake is not noticed until it is too late to be undone, you can close the file without saving it, and then reopen it.

Repeat the Last Command Using Edit ➤ Repeat

 The Edit ➤ Repeat command is used to quickly repeat the last command that you issued.

For example, you might format a cell, which takes several keystrokes. Then repeat the procedure on other cells using Edit ➤ Repeat.

The Quickest Way to Clear Cell Contents

The common task of clearing the contents of one or more cells requires only one keystroke:

1. Select the cells to be cleared (selection may be noncontiguous).

2. Press the Delete key.

Paste Copied Cells with Enter

Copied cells can be pasted by pressing Enter rather than using a Paste command:

1. Copy cell(s).

2. Select the cell where you want to paste.

3. Press Enter.

You can also use the Enter key to fill a range. Copy a cell, select the range to fill, and press Enter.

Evaluating Expressions within a Formula

Often a formula refers to cells that are out of view. When entering, editing, or debugging such a formula, a lot of time can be spent scrolling the sheet to check the value of the cell(s) being referred to.

Instead, you can highlight the cell reference within the formula bar (or in-cell), and press F9. The cell reference is replaced with the cell value. This technique is not limited to cell references; you can highlight any expression, such as **(A1*B1)/C1**, and when F9 is pressed, the entire expression is replaced with the calculated value.

After evaluating an expression, remember to cancel the changes (press Esc). Otherwise, if you press Enter, the expression is replaced with the calculated value.

Quickly Selecting a Word within a Formula

Most standard text-editing techniques can be used when editing formulas. One of the most useful techniques is double-clicking words to select them, rather than painstakingly selecting the word with the mouse. This works whether editing is taking place in the formula bar or in the cell.

Enter the Same Formula into Multiple Cells

The following procedure allows you to enter the same formula (or constant) into multiple cells:

1. Select the cells (selections can be noncontiguous).

2. Type the entry.

3. Press Ctrl+Enter instead of Enter.

Quickly Create a Table of Numbers

When prototyping a worksheet model, sometimes actual data is not available, and test data is used instead. Here is a technique to quickly place a range of numbers onto a worksheet:

1. Select a range of cells.

2. Enter the formula **=RAND( )** then press Ctrl+Enter. This places the random number function into the range of cells.

To keep the RAND( ) functions from recalculating:

3. Select the range of cells.

4. Choose Edit ➤ Copy.

5. Choose Edit ➤ Paste Special, select *Values*, and click OK.

The numbers generated by the **RAND** function are fractions. Here are two variations to generate numbers bearing more similarity to the data you are emulating:

=RAND( )*1000	Creates random numbers between 1 and 1000
=INT(RAND( )*1000)	Creates whole random numbers between 1 and 1000

Entering Numbers with Automatic Decimal Places

Accountants typically prefer to enter numbers with two automatic decimal places. Excel can be configured for this type of data entry:

1. Choose Tools ➤ Options as shown in Figure 7.1, then select the Edit tab. Check the *Fixed Decimal* box.

2. Enter the desired number of decimal places.

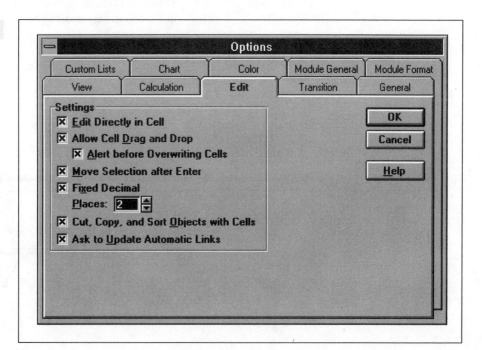

Automatically Move Down after Pressing Enter

By default, the active cell selection moves down one cell after pressing Enter. This behavior is controlled by choosing the Tools ➤ Options command, then selecting the Edit tab to access the *Move Selection after Enter* setting.

Move from Corner to Corner in a Selection

The keystroke combination Ctrl+ . (period) changes the active cell from corner to corner, clockwise, within a selected cell range.

Using Spell Check

To check spelling, choose the Tools ➤ Spelling command. Table 7.1 explains the various items which can be selected for spell-checking.

TABLE 7.1: Spell-Checking Selections

SELECT:	TO CHECK:
a single cell	entire worksheet, including headers, footers, cells, cell notes, text boxes, buttons
multiple cells	selected cells
one or more objects	selected objects (text boxes and buttons only)
multiple sheets	contents of selected sheets
formula bar	entire formula bar
words within a cell or formula bar	selected words

NOTE Spell-checking checks hidden cells and cells in collapsed outlines; formulas and Visual Basic modules are not checked.

When Excel finds a word not in its dictionary, the Spelling dialog box is displayed. Table 7.2 explains the options on the Spelling dialog box.

TABLE 7.2: Spelling Options

DIALOG OPTION	FUNCTION
Change To	Replacement for unrecognized word (select or type)
Suggestions	Select replacement from list of suggestions.
Add Words To	Lists available custom dictionaries
Ignore	Leaves unrecognized word unchanged
Ignore All	Leaves unrecognized word unchanged throughout spell-check selection
Change	Replaces unrecognized word with *Change To* word
Change All	Replaces unrecognized word with *Change To* word throughout spell-check selection
Add	Adds unrecognized word to dictionary in *Add Words To*
Always Suggest	If checked, *Suggestions* list is always displayed
Suggest	Displays *Suggestions* list when *Always Suggest* box is unchecked
Ignore UPPER-CASE	Ignores words containing only capital letters
Undo Last	Undoes last change

PRODUCTIVITY BASICS

If you only want to spell-check a certain range of cells, select the range before choosing the spell-check command.

Creating and Using Custom Dictionaries

If you use lots of technical words or acronyms, you may be spell-checking those same words repeatedly. Custom dictionaries save you the time spent clicking the Ignore button over and over again.

To create a custom dictionary, spell-check the worksheet. When Excel finds an unrecognized word, follow these steps:

1. Type a name for the custom dictionary in the *Add Words To* edit box.

2. Click the Add button. The following message will be displayed:

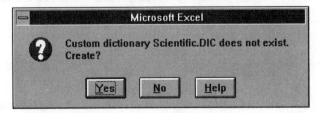

Microsoft Excel

Custom dictionary Scientific.DIC does not exist. Create?

Yes   No   Help

3. Click Yes to create the new dictionary.

To add a word to an existing custom dictionary, select the dictionary from the *Add Words To* list, then click Add.

Entering a Number as Text

Sometimes a number should be entered as text (for example, the zip code 07384, which will lose its leading zero if entered as a number). To enter a number as text, type an apostrophe first: **'07384**.

Format Numbers to Retain Leading Zeros

Sometimes numbers need to be entered as numbers which retain their leading zeros (for example, inventory part number 00284). The solution is the custom number format **00000**, which retains leading zeros in a 5-digit number.

Entering the Current Date and Current Time

The following keystrokes will place the current date or time into a cell, or into the middle of a formula:

Ctrl+;   (Ctrl+semicolon) Enters the current date

Ctrl+:   (Ctrl+colon) Enters the current time

Workbooks, Worksheets and Windows

The following paragraphs will help you work more effectively with workbooks, worksheets, and windows.

Open Several Workbooks at Once

Select multiple workbooks in the File ➤ Open dialog box by holding down Ctrl or Shift keys while selecting file names, then click OK to open all selected files at once.

Editing Multiple Worksheets Simultaneously

Workbooks often contain many similar worksheets. A lot of time can be saved by editing and formatting similar sheets simultaneously.

Select the group of worksheets that you want to edit. One way to select multiple sheets is to hold down the Ctrl key while clicking the worksheet tabs (see Chapter 2 for other ways to select groups of worksheets). All input, editing, and formatting are applied to each sheet in the group.

Saving the Workspace

Perhaps there are several workbooks you use regularly, and the process of opening each of them and arranging them on the screen is time-consuming. When you choose the File ➤ Save Workspace command, Excel "remembers" the names of all open workbooks, and how the windows are arranged. This information is saved in a workspace file with a .XLW extension. Later, when you open the workspace file using the File ➤ Open command, the individual workbooks are opened and arranged automatically.

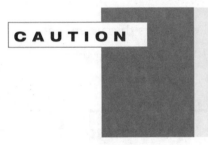

CAUTION

Workbooks are not physically stored inside the workspace file—only the workbook names and how the windows are arranged. Thus, saving a workspace file does not obviate the need to save the workbooks (you will be queried about saving each workbook before it is closed).

Removing Add-Ins That Are Not Used

Add-Ins are workbooks that add commands and functionality to Excel. An example is the Analysis Toolpak, which provides a number of engineering and financial functions.

When you install Excel, you are given the opportunity to install the many add-ins that are included with Excel. What the install program fails to point out is that the add-ins will not only be installed on your hard disk, but in some cases are automatically loaded into memory every time you start Excel. This uses up memory and system resources, and increases the amount of time it takes to start Excel.

To remove unused (or seldom used) add-ins from memory, choose the Tools ➤ Add-Ins command to display the Add-Ins dialog box (Figure 7.2).

Clear the checkboxes next to the add-ins you want to remove, and click OK. The add-ins are not actually removed from your disk; rather, Excel's configuration is changed so that they will not load into memory automatically the next time you start Excel. You can still open the add-in on demand. (See Chapter 24 to learn more about these useful workbooks.)

Viewing Two Worksheets within the Same Workbook at Once

Suppose you have a workbook with lots of details on one sheet and with summaries on another sheet. You want to be able to see the summaries and various details at the same time—the solution is to open two windows into the workbook, as shown in Figure 7.3.

FIGURE 7.2

The Tools ➤ Add-Ins
dialog box

FIGURE 7.3

Two windows into the
same workbook

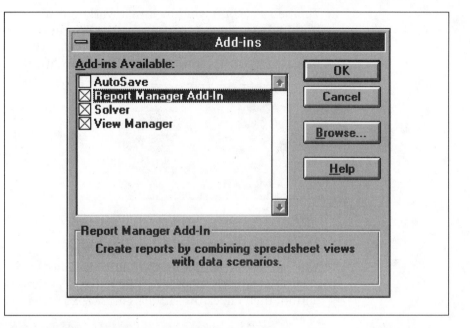

PRODUCTIVITY BASICS

To open a second window into a workbook, choose the Window ➤ New Window command. Then choose the Window ➤ Arrange command, and select an arrangement (check the *Windows of Active Workbook* setting to arrange only the windows into the active workbook).

Using Automatic File Backups

You can choose a setting that automatically creates a copy of your file prior to saving it. Choose the File ➤ Save As command, click the Options button, then check the *Always Create Backup* setting.

This setting provides an extra safety net. For example, say you make mistakes editing a file named SALES.XLS, the mistakes cannot be undone using Edit ➤ Undo, and the file is set to create backups. You can revert to an older copy of the file using one of these two methods:

• If the mistake was made *after* the file was last saved, choose File ➤ Open SALES.XLS. You will be prompted:

Click Yes. All changes made since the file was last saved will
be lost.

- If the mistake occured *before* the file was last saved, close the file
  without saving. File ➤ Open SALES.BAK. By default the Open
  dialog box displays only files with a .XL* extension, so you will
  have to type in the file name. (Since it is unwise to resume work
  on a file with a .BAK extension, save the file under a different
  name immediately.)

CAUTION

Automatic backups are saved with a .BAK extension. If
you have files named FINANCE.XLS and FINANCE.XLT
in the same directory, and both files are set to create
backups, both backups will be saved as FINANCE.BAK.

Working Productively with Microsoft Windows

The following tips are not specific to Excel. They are applicable throughout Microsoft Windows.

Switching to Another Application during a Lengthy Procedure

When Excel is maximized, and a time-consuming procedure is in process,
the mouse cannot be used to switch applications. Press Alt+Tab as an alternative method for switching applications.

Adding an Icon to Program Manager to Open a Specific Workbook

Typically, after starting Excel, you use the File ➤ Open dialog box to open
the file that you want to work with. This can be time-consuming, especially if the file is buried in an obscure subdirectory. Instead, you can place
icons on Program Manager to start Excel and open the workbooks that

you access most frequently. Follow these steps:

1. Start File Manager.

2. Resize File Manager and Program Manager so that they are both in view, as shown in Figure 7.4.

3. Use File Manager to locate the Excel workbook.

4. Click on the workbook, then drag it to Program Manager—drop it in the desired group.

5. An Excel icon will be added to the group—you can change its description using Program Manager's File ➤ Properties command.

Remember, this procedure is not specific to Excel; it can be used for files created by (most) other Windows programs.

FIGURE 7.4

To place an icon for an Excel workbook on Program Manager, arrange Program Manager and File Manager so that you can work with both of them.

Shortcut Menus

The right mouse button is used to display context-sensitive shortcut menus. Here are the items in the workspace you can right-click to display a shortcut menu:

- menu bar
- toolbars
- column/row headers
- cells
- sheet tabs
- objects
- charts—each element has a specific shortcut menu
- tools—when the Toolbars or Customize dialog box is displayed

AutoFill

The AutoFill feature, explained in the paragraphs below, is an important feature that can save you countless hours of data entry.

Using the Fill Handle

The *Fill Handle* provides a shortcut for automatically filling a range of cells with a series of values. The fill handle is the small black square located on the lower right corner of the selected cell(s).

NOTE If the fill handle does not display on a worksheet, choose the Tools ➤ Options command, then select the Edit tab, and make sure the *Drag and Drop* setting is checked.

Filling Months

Follow these steps to fill month names in a range of cells:

1. Enter **Jan** into cell A1.

2. Point to the fill handle with the mouse—the mouse pointer will become a black cross.

3. Click and drag thru cell L1, then release the mouse button. **Jan** through **Dec** will be filled into cells A1 through L1.

More Simple AutoFills

This exercise will demonstrate some of the other types of data that can be filled:

1. Enter the following values:

	A	B	C	D
1	January			
2	Jan			
3	1/1/93			
4	Monday			
5	Mon			
6	Q1			
7	1			
8	9:00 AM			
9				
10				

Book1

2. Select cells A1 through A8.

3. Select the fill handle, and drag thru cell L8.

Establishing an AutoFill Trend

In the previous exercise, each AutoFill was based on a single starting value. If two or more values are selected as the starting range for an AutoFill, Excel tries to determine a trend and AutoFills accordingly.

1. Enter the following values:

	A	B	C	D
1	2	4		
2	Jan	Apr		
3	Mon	Wed		
4	1995	2000		
5	1:00	1:15		
6				
7				
8				

2. Select cells A1 through B5.

3. Select the fill handle, and drag thru cell H5. The result will be:

	A	B	C	D	E	F	G	H	I
1	2	4	6	8	10	12	14	16	
2	Jan	Apr	Jul	Oct	Jan	Apr	Jul	Oct	
3	Mon	Wed	Fri	Sun	Tue	Thu	Sat	Mon	
4	1995	2000	2005	2010	2015	2020	2025	2030	
5	1:00	1:15	1:30	1:45	2:00	2:15	2:30	2:45	
6									
7									

AutoFill Based on Adjacent Cells

You can AutoFill a range of cells adjacent to a range of data by double-clicking the Fill Handle. This AutoFills the row or column where values are found in the adjacent row or column:

1. Type numbers into cells B1 through B4.

2. Enter **Q1** into cell A1.

3. Double-click the fill handle on cell A1. Cells A1 through A4 will be filled with **Q1** through **Q4**.

See Chapter 26 to learn how to create custom AutoFill lists.

Reversible Tools

Many tools are reversible, meaning that one tool can perform two functions. A reversible tool:

- performs an action when the tool is clicked
- performs an alternate action when the Shift key is held down and the tool is clicked

For example, the Zoom In tool normally zooms in. But with Shift pressed, it changes to *Zoom Out*. (The tool face and status bar description change to reflect the alternate function). The Zoom Out tool does just the opposite. By using only one of a pair of reversible tools, you can create space for more tools on a favorite toolbar. Table 7.3 displays pairs of reversible tools.

TABLE 7.3: Reversible Tool Pairs

TOOL FACE	ACTION	SHIFTED TOOL FACE	SHIFTED ACTION
	Zoom in		Zoom Out
	Print		Print Preview
	Paste Formats		Paste Values
	Clear Contents		Clear Formats
	Increase Font Size		Decrease Font Size
	Sort Ascending		Sort Descending
	Increase Decimal		Decrease Decimal
	Insert Cells		Delete Cells

TABLE 7.3: Reversible Tool Pairs (continued)

TOOL FACE	ACTION	SHIFTED TOOL FACE	SHIFTED ACTION
	Insert Row		Delete Row
	Insert Column		Delete Column
	Group Objects		Ungroup Objects
	Bring to Front		Send To Back
	Draw Unfilled Rectangle		Draw Filled Rectangle
	Draw Unfilled Ellipse		Draw Filled Ellipse
	Draw Unfilled Arc		Draw Filled Arc
	Draw Unfilled Polygon		Draw Filled Polygon
	Draw Unfilled Freeform		Draw Filled Freeform
	Run Macro		Step Macro
	Group Selected Rows or Columns		Ungroup Selected Rows or Columns
	Trace Precedents		Remove Precedent Arrows
	Trace Dependents		Remove Dependent Arrows

PART THREE

Tapping Excel's Power

CHAPTER

8

The Power of Names

fast TRACK

To select a named cell or range   **216**

- Select the name from the Name-box list.

- Or choose Edit ➤ Go To or press the F5 key, then select a name from the *Go To* list and click OK.

To name a constant value   **218**

Choose Insert ➤ Name ➤ Define. Enter the name in the *Names in Workbook* edit box. Type a constant value in *Refers To*, and click OK.

To name a formula   **225**

Choose Insert ➤ Name ➤ Define. Enter the name in the *Names in Workbook* edit box. Type a formula in *Refers To*, and click OK.

USING names is an important practice overlooked by many Excel users. If you are creating models of moderate complexity, or even simple models with linked workbooks, it is important that you learn basic naming techniques. This chapter covers the following topics:

- *why use names*
- *naming cells*
- *naming constants*
- *naming formulas*
- *using names in formulas*
- *advanced naming techniques*

Why Use Names?

There are several important benefits to names, outlined in the following paragraphs.

Clarity and Documentation

Names add clarity to worksheets:

- Names make formulas easier to understand and maintain. The formula **=Sales-Cost** makes a lot more sense than **=C3-B3**, especially six months later when you need to revise the worksheet.

- Organization-wide naming conventions let users of shared workbooks better understand formulas.

Integrity of External References

Referring to cells by name rather than by cell address can help ensure the integrity of cell references. Consider the following scenario:

1. Two workbooks, DETAIL.XLS and SUMMARY.XLS, are open. SUMMARY.XLS has an external reference pointing to cell A3 on DETAIL.XLS.

2. The dependent workbook, SUMMARY.XLS, is closed.

3. A new row is inserted at the top of DETAIL.XLS. The value in cell A3 is now in cell A4.

4. When SUMMARY.XLS is reopened, the external reference incorrectly points to cell A3 instead of A4.

When a cell moves, its name moves with it. Had the external reference on SUMMARY.XLS been referring to cell DETAIL.XLS!A3 by name, there would be no adverse side effect caused by the insertion.

Names Provide Added Power

Names are more than cosmetic! The advanced naming techniques covered in this chapter provide important *functional* benefits:

- Named formulas serve to centralize logic, and can be used as powerful building blocks in complex formulas.

- Names can be used to create ranges that dynamically expand and contract.

General Productivity

Names can help to make you more productive by speeding up worksheet navigation, and by simplifying the entering of formulas:

- Worksheet navigation is enhanced with names. The *Name box* drop-down can be used to rapidly go to a named range.

- Names reduce errors caused by mistyped entries. A formula will accept any valid cell reference, even the wrong cell reference. But an error displays when a name is misspelled.

- Writing formulas is simplified by inserting names into the formula.

Valid and Invalid Names

Here are the rules for defining names:

- A name can only contain the following characters: A–Z (upper or lower case allowed), 0–9, period, and underscore.
- The first character must be a letter or underscore.
- Names cannot be longer than 255 characters.
- A name cannot be the same as a cell reference, such as **B3** or **Y1998**.

Here are some examples of valid and invalid names:

VALID NAMES	INVALID NAMES
Last.Year.Sales	95.Sales (starts with a number)
Profit_1995	Gross Profit (contains a space)
UnitPrice	A1 (same as a cell reference)
Labor	R2C2 (same as a cell reference)

Naming Cells

The most common use of names is the naming of cells and ranges of cells. There are several ways to name cells:

Using the Name Box

The name box, found on the left part of the formula bar, is the quickest way to name cells:

1. Select the cell(s) you want to name.

2. Click in the Name box (not the drop-down):

3. Type the name, then press Enter.

Using the Define Name Dialog Box

The Define Name dialog box lets you name cells, and will also be used later in this chapter to name constants and formulas:

1. Select the cell(s) you want to name.

2. Choose the Insert ➤ Name ➤ Define command, or press Ctrl+F3, to display the Define Name dialog box pictured in Figure 8.1.

3. Type a valid name in the *Name* edit box.

4. The *Refers To* entry defaults to the current selection. (If not correct, enter a new cell reference—this is a range edit which can be filled in by pointing and clicking on the worksheet.)

5. Click OK to finish, or click Add to accept the name without closing the Define Name dialog box.

FIGURE 8.1

The Define Name
dialog box

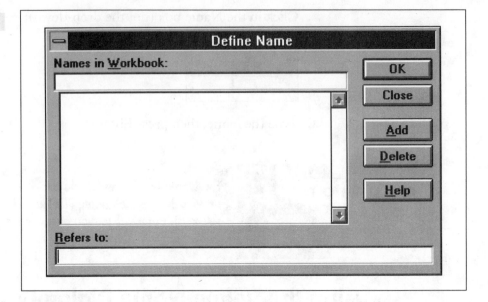

CAUTION

The Define Name dialog box will let you overwrite previously used names without warning, though existing
names are displayed in the *Names in Workbook* list,
and can be scanned to see if the name is in use.

Using the Create Name Dialog Box

The Create Name dialog box provides two key advantages over the Define
Name dialog box:

- You are warned if you attempt to overwrite an existing name.
- Many cells can be named with one command.

Choose the Insert ➤ Name ➤ Create command, or press Ctrl+Shift+F3,
to display the Create Name dialog box pictured in Figure 8.2.

The Create Name dialog box lets you name cells based upon the contents of
adjacent cells. The exercise on the following page illustrates the procedure.

FIGURE 8.2

The Create Name
dialog box

1. On a blank worksheet, enter the values pictured below.

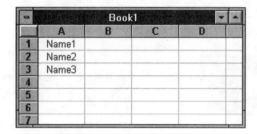

2. Select cells A1 through B3, then choose the Insert ➤ Name ➤ Create command.

3. Only the *Left Column* setting should be checked.

4. Click OK. Cells B1, B2, and B3 have *each* been named according to the text in cells A1 through A3.

If a name is already used, the following warning is displayed:

Naming Noncontiguous Cells

A named range does not have to be contiguous. You can name non-contiguous ranges using the Define Name dialog box or the Name box (the Create Name dialog box cannot be used). If you are attempting to name a range consisting of many noncontiguous sections, the *Refers To* can become quite long. Be careful, because *Refers To* is limited to 255 characters.

Deleting Names

Follow these steps to delete a name, regardless of the type of name (cell, constant, formula):

1. Choose the Insert ➤ Name ➤ Define command to display the Define Name dialog box pictured in Figure 8.1.

2. Select the name you want to delete in the *Names in Workbook* list.

3. Click the Delete button.

CAUTION   Any cell referring to a deleted name will display the #NAME? error, since the name will no longer be valid.

Referring to Named Cells in Formulas

Very simply, a named cell, or range of cells, is an *absolute cell address.* The following formulas assume that cell **$A$1** is named **Profit** and cells **$B$1:$B$3** are named **Detail**.

=Profit	equal to cell A1
=Profit*2	multiply A1 by 2
=SUM(Detail)	sum cells B1:B3
=AVERAGE(Detail)	average cells B1:B3
=Profit+SUM(Detail)	add A1 to the sum of B1:B3

Referring to cells by name is very simple. The cell name is used in place of the cell address in your formulas.

Inserting Names into Formulas

While entering or editing a formula, names can be pasted into the formula rather than typing them. This is a helpful procedure if you forget the name, don't want to misspell the name, or are too lazy to type the name.

...If the Name Is on the Same Workbook

1. Name cell A1 **GrossProfit** and enter **100** into it.

2. Select cell B1. Type an equal sign to begin the formula.

3. Use the Name box drop-down list, and select the name **GrossProfit**. The name will be added to the formula.

4. Type ***2** (to multiply by 2) then press Enter. Cell B1 will equal 200.

TIP

The Name box only lists named cells and named ranges. To paste in a name that refers to a formula or constant, use the Insert ➤ Name ➤ Paste command.

...If the Name Is from a Different Workbook

Assume that SUMMARY.XLS and DETAIL.XLS are open, and DETAIL.XLS has a cell named **Cost**.

1. Activate SUMMARY.XLS, select cell A1, and enter an equal sign to begin the formula.

2. Activate DETAIL.XLS. (Use the Window menu, or click on DETAIL.XLS if visible.)

3. Use the Name box drop-down list, and select the name **Cost**. The name will be added to the formula.

4. Press Enter to complete the formula. SUMMARY.XLS is automatically reactivated.

Referencing a Row-and-Column Intersection

There is a special way to reference a cell that lies at the intersection point of a given row and column. The *space character* implies an intersection. For example, the formula **=C:C 2:2** is a roundabout way of referring to cell C2, and breaks down as follows:

C:C	Reference to column C
Space	Intersection operator
2:2	Reference to row 2

While an intersection reference does not require the use of names, the power of this construct is realized when used in conjunction with names:

1. Enter the following values onto a new worksheet:

	A	B	C	D	E	
1						
2			East	West		
3		Gadgets	3897	4123		
4		Gizmos	9000	2721		
5		Widgets	8521	9699		
6						
7						
8						

Book2

2. Select cells B2:D5. Choose the Insert ➤ Name ➤ Create command.

3. The Create Name dialog box is displayed (see Figure 8.2). Check the *Top Row* and *Left Column* settings, then click OK. Five names have been created:

NAME	REFERS TO
Gadgets	C3:D3
Gizmos	C4:D4
Widgets	C5:D5
East	C3:C5
West	D3:D5

4. The following formulas can be used to refer to the intersection point of these names:

FORMULA	REFERS TO
=East Gadgets	C3
=West Widgets	D5
=Gizmos East	C4

Implied Intersection

Using the worksheet from the above exercise, enter the formula **=East+West** into cells E3, E4, and E5. Even though **East** and **West** are ranges, the formulas calculate correctly based on the values on the same row. This is due to an *implied intersection*. Now enter the formula **=East+West** into cell E6. The **#VALUE!** error will display because the names East and West do not extend to row 6.

Names Are Not Case-Sensitive, but They Are Case-Retentive

Names are *not* case-sensitive. If you define the name **SALES**, then define the name **Sales**, the second name will replace the first name. On the other hand, names *are* case-retentive. When a name is used in a formula, it will automatically revert to the same case used when the name was defined. If a name is defined as **GrossProfit**, and you enter the formula **=grossprofit**, the formula will automatically change to **=GrossProfit** when Enter is pressed.

TIP

There is a benefit to always using mixed case in names. Formulas are typically entered in all upper or all lower case. Since names revert to their original case, you get immediate visual feedback if a name was misspelled—it will not revert to mixed case.

Quickly Selecting Named Cells

Names can be used to help navigate a workbook. Select a name using the Name box dropdown list. The named cell(s) will be selected. The Edit ➤ Go To command, or F5 key, provides the same functionality.

Applying Names After the Fact

In the short run, it is easier to construct formulas by clicking cells. Using names requires that the names be defined, and then used. Here is how to work quick and dirty with cell references, and then quickly clean up later:

1. On a blank worksheet, enter the formula =A1 into cells A2, A3, and A4.

2. Name cell A1 **TestApply**.

3. Choose the Insert ➤ Name ➤ Apply command; the Apply Name dialog box (Figure 8.3) is displayed.

4. Make sure **TestApply** is selected in the *Apply Names* list. Click OK.

5. Look at the formulas in cells A2, A3, and A4—they now refer to cell A1 by name.

FIGURE 8.3

The Apply Name dialog box

Apply Names

Apply **N**ames:
TestApply

[OK]
[Cancel]
[**O**ptions >>]
[**H**elp]

[X] **I**gnore Relative/Absolute
[X] **U**se Row and Column Names

Ignore Relative/Absolute

The Ignore Relative/Absolute checkbox toggles between two useful settings:

- If checked (default setting), replaces reference with name regardless of whether reference is relative, absolute, or mixed.

- If unchecked, will only replace absolute references with absolute names, relative references with relative names, and mixed references with mixed names.

Use Row and Column Names

Use Row and Column Names uses intersection names (covered above) if an actual cell name does not exist. For example, if an unnamed cell sits at the intersection of a column named *January* and a row named *Profits*, this setting allows Excel to apply the name *January Profits*.

Advanced Options

Click the Options button (see Figure 8.3) to expand the dialog box to include the options pictured in Figure 8.4:

Omit Column Name If Same Column

In the worksheet pictured below, the columns and rows are named ranges. **Profit** is equal to **Revenue** less **Expenses**. Suppose you set up the profit formulas quickly, using point-and-click cell references (e.g., the formula in C5 is **=C3-C4**), and you want to replace the cell references with cell names:

	A	B	C	D	E	F	G	H
1								
2			Fiscal.96	Fiscal.97		*Named Ranges*		
3		Revenue	10000	13000		Fiscal.96	C3:C5	
4		Expenses	8000	7000		Fiscal.97	D3:D5	
5		Profit	2000	6000		Revenue	C3:D3	
6						Expenses	C4:D4	
7						Profit	C5:D5	
8								

BOOK1.XLS

The *Omit Column Name if Same Column* setting is checked by default. If you apply names without changing this setting, the formula in cell C5 will be **=Revenue-Expenses**. If you clear the setting and apply names, the formula in cell C5 will be **=Fiscal.96 Revenue–Fiscal.96 Expenses**.

FIGURE 8.4

Advanced Apply
Name options

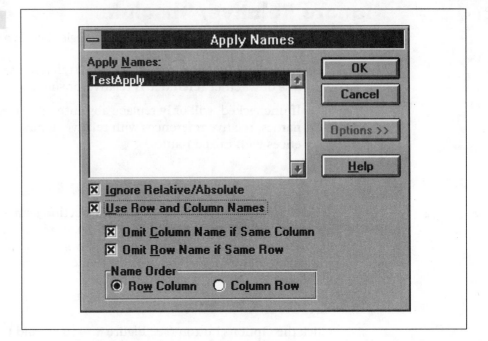

Omit Row Name If Same Row

This is the same as the previous setting, but works on formulas which reside in the same rows as the cells referenced in the formulas.

Name Order

Name Order determines the name order for an intersection name: row-column or column-row.

Named Constants

So far, the names used in this chapter have all been named cells. You can also name *constants*. Probably the most common reason for naming a constant is to discourage users from inadvertently changing values. Consider the following:

1. A commission rate of 12% is to be used throughout a sheet.

2. Knowing that the commission rate may change, you don't want to embed the 12% constant in formulas throughout the sheet.

3. If the 12% is stored in a cell, the user is invited to change it. A named constant provides the flexibility of a named cell, with some added security.

Use the Insert ➤ Name ➤ Define command, which displays the Define Name dialog box pictured in Figure 8.1.

1. Enter the name as usual.

2. In *Refers To*, type in a constant value. The constant can be a number, text, logical (TRUE/FALSE), or even an array.

3. Click OK to add the name and close the dialog box. Click Add to add the name and keep the dialog box.

T I P

When you define a named constant, Excel automatically places an equal sign (and quotation marks surrounding text constants), in *Refers To*. Remember, you do not have to type the equal sign or quotation marks—let Excel do it for you.

Fixing #NAME? Errors

The **#NAME?** error displays when a formula refers to a non-existent name. If this happens, check that:

- Name(s) in the formula are typed correctly.
- Function name(s) in the formula are typed correctly.
- The name is not enclosed in quotes.

N O T E   The remainder of this chapter deals with advanced naming techniques. You may want to revisit this section after becoming comfortable with the topics covered earlier in the chapter. You will also need to understand external references (covered in Chapter 4).

Names That Refer to Cells on Other Worksheets

A name can refer to cells on external workbooks. This technique is critically important when developing templates, and in worksheet development in general. Suppose that the names below are defined in Book1:

NAME	REFERS TO	COMMENTS
Sales	=[XYZ.XLS]Sheet1!A1:A3	Refer by cell address
Profit_1	=[DEPT1.XLS]Sheet1!Profit	Refer by cell name
YTD.Table	=SUM([SALES.XLS]Sheet1!A1:A3)	Refer to range

Formulas in Book1 can now use the names **Sales**, **Profit_1**, and **YTD.Table** as if the ranges were actually in Book1, without concern for the book name prefix. The following formulas are valid:

=SUM(Sales)

=ROWS(YTD.Table)

=INDEX(YTD.Table,1,1)

=Profit_1*2

To create a name that refers to an external reference:

1. Choose the Insert ➤ Name ➤ Define command.

2. Type in the name.

3. In *Refers To*, type **=[BOOK1.XLS]Sheet1!Cell** (In this exercise, **BOOK1.XLS** is the name of the external workbook, and **Cell** is the cell reference, or cell name).

Saving External Link Values

Any time you create names referring to other worksheets, you should be aware of the *Save External Link Values* setting, which determines whether the external data is saved inside the worksheet (though not visible). Consider the following:

1. The name **YTD.Sales**, created in Book1, refers to the external range **SALES95.XLS!Database**, which is 5000 rows by 20 columns.

2. The Tools ➤ Options ➤ Calculation *Save External Link Values* setting is checked by default. This causes the values from **SALES95.XLS!Database** to be stored, invisibly, in Book1.

3. When Book1 is saved, a huge workbook has been created because the external link values were saved.

Uncheck this setting if the external values do not need to be saved with the sheet, as will often be the case.

Centralize Logic Using Named Formulas

You are now accustomed to naming cells, and naming constants. If you observe the syntax of defined names using the Define Name dialog box (see Figure 8.1), you will notice that the *Refers To* for *all* names begins with an equal sign. *All names are essentially named formulas—some more complex than others.* Almost any formula that can be entered into a cell can also be defined as a *named formula*. One important way that named formulas are used is to centralize logic. Consider this problem:

1. A complex formula is used to calculate the rate of return for an investment.

2. This same formula is used in hundreds of cells on a sheet. The cells are not contiguous.

3. The formula needs to be changed. You can do a find/replace, but there are other similar formulas that you must be careful not to overwrite.

This problem can be solved by defining a single named formula, and then referring to this formula by name. Because the *Refers To* edit box in the Define Name dialog box is awkward to work with, it is easier to name formulas by first entering the formula into a cell, and then copying it into the Define Name dialog box. Follow this simple exercise:

1. Enter the following constants onto a blank worksheet:

	A	B	C	D	E	F
1						
2		Item	Qty	Price	Extension	
3		Widgets	7	22.95		
4		Gadgets	15	19.55		
5		Gizmos	11	8.98		
6						
7						
8						

BOOK1.XLS

2. Enter the formula **=C3*D3** into cell E3.

3. Select the formula (on the formula bar, or using in-cell formula editing), then choose the Edit ➤ Copy command.

4. Press Esc.

5. Choose the Insert ➤ Name ➤ Define command to display the Define Name dialog box.

6. Enter the name **Extension**.

7. Clear the entry in the *Refers To* edit box.

8. Choose the Edit ➤ Paste command to paste in the formula.

9. Click OK.

The named formula **Extension** has been defined, but has not yet been used:

10. Select cells E3:E5.

11. Type **=Extension**, then press Ctrl+Enter to place the formula in all three cells.

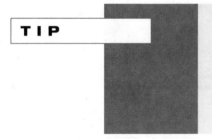

TIP

Select cell E3, display the Define Name dialog box, and select the name Extension. It will refer to =Sheet1!C3*Sheet1!D3. Close the dialog box, select E4, and look at the definition of Extension again. It will refer to =Sheet1!C4*Sheet1!D4. The definition depends on the active cell because it contains relative references.

Named 3-D References

Three-dimensional references can be named. (See Chapter 4 for an explanation of 3-D references.) Consider the scenario pictured in Figure 8.5: A workbook has five worksheets, one for each of four regions (East, West, North and South) and a summary sheet. Cell C5 on each of the regional sheets contains annual sales for the region.

NOTE

Figure 8.5 shows two worksheets from the same workbook in separate windows. This is accomplished with the Window ➤ New Window command.

FIGURE 8.5

Summary and
Regional sheets

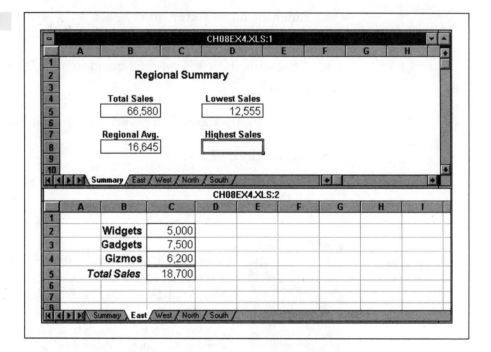

Cells B5, B8, D5, and D8 can each contain a formula referring to the 3-D range **=East:South!$C$5**. But if a new region sheet is added, and it is not placed between East and West, all formulas require modifications. Instead, define the name **TotalSales** to refer to:

=East:South!$C$5

Then enter the following formulas onto Summary:

CELL	FORMULA
B5	**=SUM(TotalSales)**
B8	**=AVERAGE(TotalSales)**
D5	**=MIN(TotalSales)**
D8	**=MAX(TotalSales)**

These formulas never require modification. When a new region sheet is added, only the name **TotalSales** requires modification.

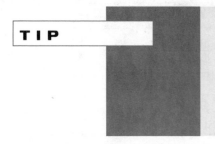

TIP

As you read about the different types of names explained in this chapter, remember that *all names* are essentially named formulas, even named ranges. Almost any formula that can be entered into a cell can also be named, including 3-D formulas, and formulas referring to external workbooks.

Using Named Formulas to Create Dynamic Named Ranges

Dynamic named ranges are ranges that automatically change based upon certain conditions. There is no formal *dynamic named range* construct; they are simply named formulas that refer to a range of cells. Consider the following problem:

1. A range of cells is named **Portfolio_Details**.

2. Various complex formulas and charts refer to the named range **Portfolio_Details** for the purpose of analyzing the portfolio.

3. The need to analyze two portfolios emerges. Using traditional methods, a second set of complex formulas and charts can be created which refer to the second portfolio range. Since the model requires modification to accommodate a second portfolio, a design that will easily accommodate a third and fourth portfolio is highly desirable.

The problem can be solved using a dynamic named range—with no change to the complex formulas that refer to *Portfolio_Details*. User input will determine which portfolio is being analyzed. Follow this exercise:

1. Enter the following onto a blank worksheet:

2. Name cells B2:C6 **Portfolio1**.

3. Name cell E2:F6 **Portfolio2**.

4. Name cell D8 **Choice**. (User input into this cell determines which portfolio is analyzed.)

5. Choose the Insert ➤ Name ➤ Define command.

6. Enter **Portfolio_Details** as the name.

7. Enter the following formula in *Refers To*:

   =IF(Choice=1,Portfolio1,Portfolio2)

8. Click OK.

Now test the dynamic name:

9. Enter **1** into cell **Choice**.

10. Choose the Edit ➤ Go To command. In the *Reference* edit box, type the name **Portfolio_Details** and click OK. The range **Portfolio1** will be selected.

11. Enter **2** into cell **Choice**, then repeat step 10.

Suppose that, in the future, a third portfolio is added. All you need to do is add the portolio data, name it **Portfolio3**, then change the definition of **Portfolio_Details** to refer to:

   =IF(Choice=1,Portfolio1,IF(Choice=2,Portfolio2,Portfolio3))

N O T E   Excel will not display dynamic named ranges in the Go To dialog box or in the Name box drop-down.

Named Array Constants

Array constants are very useful, though awkward to construct. An array constant is similar to a range of cells, but it does not reside in rows and columns and thus is not easily visible. One use of array constants is to store tables of data out of view from the user of the worksheet. As with other named constants, array constants are defined using the Insert ➤ Name ➤ Define command, which displays the Define Name dialog box pictured in Figure 8.1.

An array constant stores multiple values which, like cells, are oriented in rows and columns. But since the array does not reside in the worksheet grid, the rows and columns are indicated by the use of two separators, as shown in Table 8.1:

TABLE 8.1: Array Separators

SEPARATOR	MEANING
Comma	Denotes new column
Semicolon	Denotes new row

In the following examples, the boldfaced entry indicates what would be typed into the *Refers To* edit box of the Define Name dialog box to create the array that follows:

={2;4;6;8}   4 rows, 1 column of numbers

={"East",12,100;"West",15,135}   2 rows, 3 columns of text and numbers

={"A",TRUE,99.99}   1 row, 3 columns—text, logical, and number

Accessing the data in an array constant is similar to accessing data stored in cells. The INDEX function can be used to refer to an individual data element. The ROWS functions will return the number of rows in the array, and the COLUMNS function will return the number of columns.

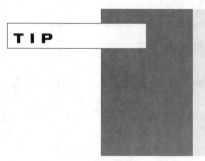

T I P

Application developers often store information in array constants, but the process of building the arrays is controlled programmatically. This allows the use of the construct, without the tedium of defining the names. Also, since names that are defined programmatically can be hidden, another layer of security can be achieved.

Names Can Be Workbook or Worksheet Level

Names can be *global* to the workbook, or can be *local* to a specific worksheet. This is a distinction that is very important to understand in order to use names effectively.

Global Names

By default, all names are global to the workbook. This means that when cell B2, on Sheet1 in Book1, is named **Total**...

- The name Total can be referred to from any worksheet (in the same workbook) without having to specify the sheet name prefix—Sheet2 can contain the formula **=Total**.

- If the name Total is defined again, anywhere in the workbook, the new definition will replace the old definition.

- Regardless of which sheet is active, the name will appear in the Name Box drop-down.

- If a sheet from a different workbook with the global name Total is moved or copied to Book1, the original name on Sheet1 takes precedence—the name defined on the just-copied sheet is changed to a local name.

Local Names

A local name is defined by including the sheet name as part of the name using the Define Name dialog box (see Figure 8.1), or the Name box. To create a local name **Total** on Sheet1:

1. Activate Sheet1.

2. Select cell(s) you want to name.

3. Enter name **Sheet1!Total** in the Name box—the sheet name is included as part of the name.

The implications of the local name **Total**, defined on Sheet1, are as follows:

- Total can be referred to from any worksheet, but the sheet name prefix must be included (e.g., Sheet2 can contain the formula **=Sheet1!Total**).

- The formula **=Total** entered onto Sheet2 will return a #NAME? error.

- Total can be defined on other worksheets, and Sheet1!Total will *not* be overwritten (even if the new definition for Total is global).

- If Total is redefined on Sheet1 with the sheet name prefix omitted (as if it were a global name), it will still be a local name.

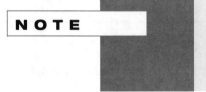

NOTE

The explanations of global and local names above use named cells to illustrate the concept. The same rules apply for all other worksheet names, including named formulas and named constants.

Naming Conventions

Once you start to use names, you are apt to use them a lot. A complex model might contain hundreds of names, and the list of names in the Define Name dialog box can become unwieldy. Special prefixes and/or suffixes can be used to help document and manage the names. The naming conventions in the following examples are not intended to be used verbatim, but rather to provide ideas on how to create meaningful conventions that work for you.

Convention Based on Type of Name

The naming conventions listed in Table 8.2 are based on the type of name created:

TABLE 8.2: Convention Based on Type of Name

PREFIX	MEANING
NF	Named formula
AC	Array constant
ER	External reference
DC	Database criteria
DB	Database table
DE	Database extract range
CR	Calculated (dynamic) range

Conventions Specific to a Model

Naming conventions can also be specific to a worksheet model, as in the following examples:

- Several ranges on one sheet that are printed as separate reports— Use prefix of **Report**, as in Report_Summary and Report_Detail.

- Worksheet contains data for multiple regions—Use prefix of **Region**, as in Region_East and Region_West.

- Worksheet used to track investments—Use prefix identifying type of investment, as in Stock.IBM, Stock.ATT, Bonds.Muni, Bonds.TB.

How to See All Names at Once

A complex workbook might contain hundreds of names. The Define Name dialog box only lets you view the definition for one name at a time. The Insert ➤ Name Paste command displays the following dialog box:

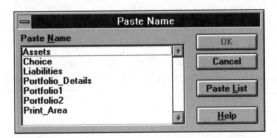

Click the Paste List button to paste all of the definitions onto the active worksheet, starting at the active cell.

CAUTION

Since the names are pasted starting at the active cell, you must be careful not to overwrite data on the worksheet. One way to avoid this pitfall is to add a new worksheet to the workbook, then paste the names onto the new worksheet.

CHAPTER

9

Essential Worksheet Functions

fast TRACK

THERE are hundreds of built-in Excel functions, and it is a given that most users will learn the ones needed for basic worksheet arithmetic, such as SUM. But as you start to create more powerful models, the inherently dry nature of Excel's function reference manual falls short—it fails to point out which functions are *essential* for serious worksheet modeling and data analysis.

What makes a particular function essential? Even the most obscure functions are momentarily essential when required to solve a specific problem. But the functions covered in this chapter are important generic tools. A case in point is the OFFSET function—the thought of doing even simple modeling and analysis without OFFSET is literally inconceivable, yet few Excel users are even *aware* of it.

This chapter covers the following worksheet functions:

Totals and Subtotals	*SUMIF, SUBTOTAL*
Lookup and Reference	*VLOOKUP, MATCH, INDEX, OFFSET, INDIRECT, ROW, ROWS, COLUMN, COLUMNS*
Counting	*COUNT, COUNTA, COUNTBLANK, COUNTIF*
Text	*LEN, LEFT, RIGHT, MID, SEARCH, FIND*
Date & Time	*TODAY, NOW, DATE, DAY, HOUR, MINUTE, MONTH, WEEKDAY, YEAR*

Totals and Subtotals

The SUBTOTAL and SUMIF functions are very important new additions in Excel 5, and serve to streamline two very common calculations: *conditional totals* and *nested subtotals*.

SUMIF

In previous versions of Excel, there were two ways to conditionally calculate a sum of certain of the cells within a range (based on specified criteria):

- Array formulas—powerful but inordinately complex
- Criteria ranges combined with the DSUM function—again, powerful but tedious to construct

Array formulas and criteria ranges still provide important functionality, but SUMIF provides simple solutions for common conditional summing problems.

Syntax

The following options are used with SUMIF:

```
SUMIF(CheckRange,Criteria,SumRange)
```

CheckRange range of cells being compared against the *Criteria*

Criteria an expression specifying which cells in *CheckRange* meet the evaluation criteria

SumRange range of cells being summed—only cells that correspond to qualifying *CheckRange* cells are summed

Examples

```
┌─────────────────────────────────────────────────────────────┐
│ ─                        BOOK1.XLS                    ▼  ▲  │
├─────────────────────────────────────────────────────────────┤
│        A       B         C         D         E      F    G  │
│  1                                                          │
│  2          Region    Category   Units   Dollars            │
│  3          East      Coffee       22      154              │
│  4          East      Juice        15       75              │
│  5          East      Soda         18       90              │
│  6          East      Tea          34      170              │
│  7          West      Coffee       13       91              │
│  8          West      Juice        30      144              │
│  9          West      Soda         41      205              │
│ 10          West      Tea          23      115              │
│ 11                                                          │
│ 12          Filter1              Filter2                     │
│ 13          West                 <20                         │
│ 14                                                          │
│ 15                                                          │
│ 16                   Named Ranges                            │
│ 17                   Region    B3:B10                        │
│ 18                   Category  C3:C10                        │
│ 19                   Units     D3:D10                        │
│ 20                   Dollars   E3:E10                        │
│ 21                   Filter1   B13                           │
│ 22                   Filter2   D13                           │
│ 23                                                          │
└─────────────────────────────────────────────────────────────┘
```

EXAMPLE 1:

    =SUMIF(C3:C10,"Soda",E3:E10)

returns *295*—total dollars for category Soda

EXAMPLE 2:

    =SUMIF(Category,"<>Tea",Dollars)

returns *759*—total dollars for all categories except Tea

EXAMPLE 3:

    =SUMIF(Region,Filter1,Units)

returns *107*—total units for region West

EXAMPLE 4:

    =SUMIF(Units,Filter2,Dollars)

returns *256*—total dollars for every row where units are less than 20

Notes

- Use the COUNTIF function, covered in this chapter, to count values conditionally.
- Use the SUBTOTAL function to place nested subtotals in a row or column.

SUBTOTAL

The SUBTOTAL function is new to Excel 5, and long overdue.

- Subtotals can be easily calculated using several calculation methods.
- Multiple levels of subtotals can be nested in a column, and a grand subtotal will ignore nested subtotals.
- Rows that are hidden as a result of a data filter (see Chapter 15) are not included in the calculation.

Syntax

The following options are used with SUBTOTAL:

SUBTOTAL(Type,Ref)

Type   a number from 1 to 11 that specifies type of calculation, as listed below:

1	AVERAGE	(arithmetic mean of values)
2	COUNT	(count numeric values)
3	COUNTA	(count non-blanks)
4	MAX	(maximum value)
5	MIN	(minimum value)
6	PRODUCT	(multiply)
7	STDEV	(standard deviation based on a sample)
8	STDEVP	(standard deviation based on entire population)

ESSENTIAL WORKSHEET FUNCTIONS

9	SUM	(add values)
10	VAR	(variance based on a sample)
11	VARP	(variance based on entire population)

Ref the range being subtotaled

Examples

EXAMPLE 1:

The following exercise demonstrates the versatility of the SUBTOTAL function:

1. Enter the following on a blank worksheet:

	A	B	C	D	E	F
1						
2		Region	Category	Units	Dollars	
3		East	Coffee	22	154	
4		East	Juice	15	75	
5		East	Soda	18	90	
6		East	Tea	34	170	
7		West	Coffee	13	91	
8		West	Juice	30	144	
9		West	Soda	41	205	
10		West	Tea	23	115	
11						
12						
13						
14						

BOOK1.XLS

2. Insert one row below the "East" rows, and insert two rows below the "West" rows (to make room for subtotals and grand totals).

3. Enter the following formulas to calculate subtotals and a grand total:

CELL	FORMULA
E7	=SUBTOTAL(9,E3:E6)
E12	=SUBTOTAL(9,E8:E11)
E13	=SUBTOTAL(9,E3:E12)

EXAMPLE 2:

The second part of this exercise makes the formulas dynamic, and demonstrates the versatility of SUBTOTAL:

1. Name cell F16 **CalcType**.

2. In each of the three SUBTOTAL formulas, replace the *Type* argument **9** with a reference to cell **CalcType**, for example:

    =SUBTOTAL(CalcType,E3:E6)

3. Enter numbers from 1 to 11 in cell **CalcType** and watch the SUBTOTAL calculations change.

TIP   The Data ➤ Subtotals command can quickly insert embedded subtotals, without the need to manually insert rows, and will create an outline in the process. See Chapter 16 to learn more about this command.

Lookup and Reference Functions

A worksheet is one great big table, which typically contains one or more tables of data. Accordingly, the ability to access data stored in tables is an essential skill, regardless of the type of analysis and modeling you are performing. Functions such as INDEX, OFFSET, and VLOOKUP are some of the most important worksheet functions for serious users.

VLOOKUP

The VLOOKUP function is used to search the leftmost column of a range (or array) for a specific value, then return a corresponding value from a different column in the table.

- Used for traditional table lookups requiring exact matches— Retrieving a customer address by using a customer code, or retrieving sales figures using a product number

- Search for the closest value less than or equal to a search value, then retrieve value from corresponding column—Used, for example, for lookups into tax tables

- The search is *not* case-sensitive

Syntax

The following options are used with VLOOKUP:

```
VLOOKUP(LookupValue,LookupRef,ColumnNo,Nearest)
```

LookupValue value being searched for in the first column of *LookupRef*

LookupRef rectangular range or array

ColumnNo column number within the range containing the lookup value; must be a number greater than or equal to 1, and less than or equal to the number of columns in the table

Nearest specifies if the search value must be an exact match to a value in the 1st column of *LookupRef*

- If Nearest is TRUE, the first column of *LookupRef* is searched for the closest value less than or equal to *LookupValue* in first column of *LookupRef*—The values in the first column of *LookupRef* must be sorted in ascending order, otherwise VLOOKUP will not work properly.

- If Nearest is FALSE, the first column of *LookupRef* is searched for an exact match to *LookupValue*—Values in first column of *LookupRef* do not have to be sorted.

Examples: Exact Lookups

	A	B	C	D	E
		BOOK1.XLS			
1					
2		Storage_Data			
3		Tank ID	Capacity	Contains	
4		N1	145	Oxygen	
5		A1	190	Nitrogen	
6		A2	380	Helium	
7		T6	242	Empty	
8					
9					
10		Tank	A2		
11					
12					
13					
14		*Named Ranges:*			
15		Storage_Data	B4:D7		
16		Tank	C10		
17					
18					

EXAMPLE 1:

```
=VLOOKUP("T6",B4:D7,2,FALSE)
```

returns *242*—T6 is located in the 4th row, and 242 found in 2nd column of range.

EXAMPLE 2:

```
=VLOOKUP(Tank,Storage_Data,3,FALSE)
```

returns *Helium*.

EXAMPLE 3:

```
=VLOOKUP(Tank,Storage_Data,2,TRUE)
```

mistakenly returns *#N/A* due to improper use of TRUE as the *Nearest* argument.

Examples: Lookup Based on Closest Value

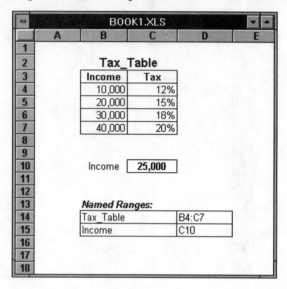

EXAMPLE 1:

    =VLOOKUP(15000,B4:C7,2,TRUE)

returns .*12* (12%)—10,000 is the closest value less than or equal to 15,000.

EXAMPLE 2:

    =VLOOKUP(Income,Tax_Table,2,TRUE)

returns .*15* (15%)—20,000 is the closest value less than or equal to 25,000.

EXAMPLE 3:

    =VLOOKUP(5000,Tax_Table,2,TRUE)

returns .*#N/A*—there is no value equal to or less than 5000 in the first column of *Tax_Table*.

There are two functions closely related to VLOOKUP: HLOOKUP and LOOKUP. The HLOOKUP function is identical to VLOOKUP, except it searches a row for a given value, and returns a value from a corresponding row—once you understand VLOOKUP you will understand HLOOKUP. The LOOKUP function is not covered in this chapter because the sort requirements severely limit its usefulness.

MATCH

Use MATCH when there is a known value, and you need to determine the *position* of this value within a list.

- Use for input verification, when an input value must exist within a list in order to be valid.

- Use to determine the exact position of a value within a list where the list may or may not be sorted.

- Use to determine where within a sorted list a given value falls (without the requirement for an exact match).

Syntax

The following options are used with MATCH:

```
MATCH(LookupValue,LookupRef,Type)
```

LookupValue   value being searched for

LookupRef   range, or array constant, being searched; the range or array must be one-dimensional (a single row or column)

Type   type of match being performed, as listed below:

0   search for an exact match—if match not found, returns **#N/A**

1   search for the largest value that is less than or equal to the *LookupValue*; *LookupRef* must be sorted in ascending order; if all values in Ref are greater than *LookupValue*, returns **#NA**

-1 search for the smallest value that is greater than or equal to *LookupValue*; *LookupRef* must be sorted in descending order; if all values in Ref are less than *LookupValue*, returns **#NA**

Examples: Exact Matches

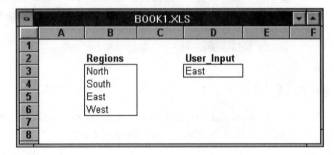

EXAMPLE 1:

    =MATCH("South",B3:B6,0)

returns 2, because *South* is the 2nd value within the range B3:B6.

EXAMPLE 2:

    =MATCH(User_Input,Regions,0)

returns 3, because cell **User_Input** is the 3rd value within the named range **Regions**.

EXAMPLE 3:

    =MATCH("Central",Regions,0)

returns #N/A, because *Central* is not found in the named range **Regions**.

EXAMPLE 4:

    =IF(ISNA(MATCH(User_Input,Regions,0)),"Invalid region!","")

returns text string intended as an error message if the entry in cell **User_Input** is not found in the range **Regions**, otherwise returns null text.

Examples: Match Closest Value

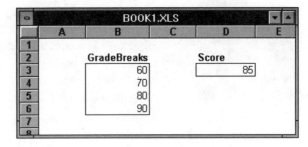

EXAMPLE 1:

```
=MATCH(92,B3:B6,1)
```

returns 4, because the 4th value in the range is the largest value less than or equal to 92.

EXAMPLE 2:

```
=MATCH(Score,GradeBreaks,1)
```

returns 3, because the 3rd value in the range is the largest value less than or equal to 85.

EXAMPLE 3:

```
=MATCH(74,GradeBreaks,-1)
```

returns #N/A. Since **GradeBreaks** is sorted in *ascending* order, this is an improper use of match type -1.

INDEX

Use the INDEX function to refer to a cell within a range of cells (or to an element within an array) when the position of the cell is known.

- Use to refer to a cell within a range when the row and/or column is variable.
- Use in conjunction with MATCH to perform lookups.
- Use to refer into one-dimensional or two-dimensional ranges.

NOTE

The Excel function reference manual provides a thoroughly confusing treatment of this essential function. The distinction between the two forms, array and reference, is confusing and inaccurate. Even in its simpler variations, INDEX is very powerful, fairly easy to use, and is a must-know function.

Syntax

The following options are used with INDEX:

```
INDEX(LookupRange,Coordinate1,Coordinate2,AreaNum)
```

LookupRange   range or array being referred to

Coordinate1   if *LookupRange* is one-dimensional, specifies row or column number within range; if *LookupRange* is two-dimensional, specifies row number

Coordinate2   column number within *LookupRange*; use this argument only when LookupRange is two-dimensional

AreaNum   LookupRange can include multiple noncontiguous areas, in which case AreaNum specifies which area number

Examples: One-Dimensional Range

EXAMPLE 1:

```
=INDEX(B3:B6,1)
```

returns *North,* the 1st element of range B3:B6.

EXAMPLE 2:

```
=INDEX(Products,RowNum)
```

returns *Gizmos,* the 2nd element of **Products**.

EXAMPLE 3:

```
=INDEX(Regions,5)
```

returns *#REF!*—there are only 4 cells in **Regions**.

Examples: Two-Dimensional Range

EXAMPLE 1:

```
=INDEX(Stats,1,3)
```

returns *3*—the intersection of 1st row and 3rd column of range **Stats**.

EXAMPLE 2:

```
=INDEX(Stats,RowNum,ColNum)
```

returns *6*—the intersection of 2nd row and 4th column of range **Stats**.

Referring to an Entire Row or Column

If zero is specified for either coordinate, the entire row or column is referred to.

EXAMPLE 1:

```
=SUM(INDEX(Stats,0,1))
```

returns *20*—the sum of the 1st column of **Stats**.

EXAMPLE 2:

```
=AVERAGE(INDEX(Stats,RowNum,0))
```

returns *4*—the average of the 2nd row of **Stats**.

Examples: Range Consisting of Multiple Areas

On the following worksheet, the noncontiguous range C4:F7,C12:F15 is named **Calls**.

	A	B	C	D	E	F	G
1							
2			Service Calls - 1994				
3			Q1	Q2	Q3	Q4	
4		North	159	287	523	705	
5		South	378	777	20	219	
6		East	639	779	334	622	
7		West	928	559	977	68	
8							
9							
10			Service Calls - 1995				
11			Q1	Q2	Q3	Q4	
12		North	665	784	229	705	
13		South	192	707	947	910	
14		East	434	951	75	889	
15		West	91	178	184	99	
16							
17							
18							

BOOK1.XLS

EXAMPLE 1:

    =INDEX(Calls,4,3,1)

returns *977*—the intersection of 4th row and 3rd column within the 1st area of range **Stats**.

EXAMPLE 2:

    =INDEX(Calls,4,3,2)

returns *184*—the intersection of 4th row and 3rd column within the 2nd area of range **Stats**.

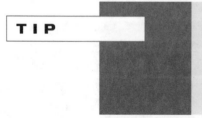

TIP

When used together, MATCH and INDEX can be used to do lookups similar to lookups performed by the VLOOKUP and HLOOKUP functions. MATCH and INDEX require more effort (two functions instead of one) but with somewhat more flexibility.

Reference Functions

The functions in this category are closely related to those in the *Lookup* category.

OFFSET

OFFSET is arguably the single most powerful general-purpose worksheet function. It allows you to refer to one or more cells that are *offset* from a given starting point.

Main points:

- Similar uses as the INDEX function
- Unlike INDEX, not limited to cells within a range
- Range referred to can be any height or width

Syntax

The following options are used with OFFSET:

```
OFFSET(AnchorRange,RowOffset,ColOffset,Height,Width)
```

AnchorRange   position on the worksheet being offset from

RowOffset   vertical offset, measured in rows, from upper left corner of *AnchorRange*:

- Positive number moves down
- Zero performs no vertical offset
- Negative number moves up

ColOffset   horizontal offset, measured in columns, from upper left corner of *AnchorRange*:

- Positive number moves right
- Zero performs no horizontal offset
- Negative number moves left

Height   number of rows in the offset range; if omitted defaults to same number of rows in *AnchorRange*

Width   number of columns in the offset range; if omitted defaults to same number of columns in *AnchorRange*

Examples: Referring to One Cell

EXAMPLE 1:

```
=OFFSET(B2,1,3)
```

returns *24*—one row down and three columns over from cell B2 (height and width default to 1—the same height and width of B2)**.**

EXAMPLE 2:

```
=OFFSET(Employees,4,NoCols,1,1)
```

returns *98*—four rows down and four columns over from upper left corner of range **Employees**.

EXAMPLE 3:

```
=OFFSET(Corner,-1,0)
```

returns *Draft*—one row up, same column as cell **Corner**.

EXAMPLE 4:

```
=OFFSET(Corner,NoRows,-3)
```

returns *#REF!*—there is no column three to the left of cell **Corner**.

Examples: Referring to Range of Cells

EXAMPLE 1:

```
=AVERAGE(OFFSET(Employees,3,0,1,))
```

returns *33.33*—the average number of technical employees 1990 thru 1995; refers to range offset from **Employees** three rows down and zero columns right, with dimensions one row high and six columns wide (defaults to six wide because last argument is omitted and **Employees** is six columns wide).

EXAMPLE 2:

```
=SUM(OFFSET(Employees,0,2,,1))
```

returns *73*—the total number of employees in 1992; refers to range offset from **Employees** by zero rows and two columns right, with dimensions four rows high and one column wide (defaults to four high because fourth argument is omitted and **Employees** is four rows high).

EXAMPLE 3:

```
=OFFSET(Employees,3,1)
```

returns *#VALUE!*—one cell cannot equal a range of cells; since last two arguments omitted, offset range is four rows high and six wide.

TIP

The OFFSET function actually returns a cell reference, but that reference is automatically converted to a value when the formula syntax so dictates. This is apparent when OFFSET is used as an argument to a function that expects a reference, such as the AVERAGE and SUM functions above. For a visual demonstration: choose Edit ➤ Go To, then enter OFFSET(A1,1,2,3,4) as the reference—cells C2:F4 will be selected. You can perform a similar test with the INDEX function: go to the reference INDEX(A1:A9,3); cell A3 will be selected.

INDIRECT

The INDIRECT function allows a text string to be treated as a cell reference. You are better off if a problem can be solved *without* using INDIRECT because it is slower than "normal" functions. But in special cases, INDIRECT provides unique, powerful functionality.

Main points:

- Used in template development when trying to achieve extraordinary modularity
- Used under the rare circumstances when a cell reference is only known in textual form

Syntax

The following options are used with INDIRECT:

```
INDIRECT(Text)
```

Text   text that is equal to a cell reference

Examples

	A	B	C	D
1				
2		ABC		
3				
4		B2		
5				
6		Sheet2!A1		
7				
8				
9				
10				

BOOK1.XLS

EXAMPLE 1:

```
=INDIRECT("B2")
```

returns *ABC*—the contents of cell B2.

EXAMPLE 2:

```
=INDIRECT(B4)
```

returns *ABC*—since cell B4 contains "B2", this returns the contents of cell B2.

EXAMPLE 3:

```
=INDIRECT("ABC")
```

returns *#REF!*—there is no cell reference ABC.

EXAMPLE 4:

```
=INDIRECT(B6)
```

returns the value in cell **Sheet2!A1**—INDIRECT can refer to cells on other worksheets on the same workbook, or other workbooks.

T I P

In many cases, users solve problems with INDIRECT that could, and should, be solved with OFFSET and INDEX.

ROW and COLUMN

The ROW function returns the row number of a given reference. The COLUMN function returns a column number. Though seemingly obscure, these functions can play a key role in your modeling strategies.

Syntax

The following options are used with ROW and COLUMN:

```
ROW(Reference)
COLUMN(Reference)
```

Reference   cell reference or name

Examples
EXAMPLE 1:

```
=ROW(B3)
```

returns *3*—the row number of cell B3.

EXAMPLE 2:

```
=COLUMN(B3)
```

returns *2*—the column number of cell B3.

EXAMPLE 3:

```
=ROW(MyTable)
```

returns the starting row number of named range *MyTable*.

EXAMPLE 4:

```
=ROW()
```

when *Reference* omitted, row number of cell containing the formula is returned.

EXAMPLE 5:

```
=COLUMN()
```

when *Reference* omitted, column number of cell containing the formula is returned.

ROWS and COLUMNS

The ROWS function returns the number of rows in a given reference. The COLUMNS function returns the number of columns.

Syntax

The following options are used with ROWS and COLUMNS:

```
ROWS(Reference)
COLUMNS(Reference)
```

Reference   cell reference or name

Examples

EXAMPLE 1:

```
=ROWS(B3:B4)
```

returns *2*—B3:B4 consists of 2 rows.

EXAMPLE 2:

```
=COLUMNS(B3)
```

returns *1*—B3 consists of 1 column.

EXAMPLE 3:

```
=ROWS(MyTable)
```

returns the number of rows in named range *MyTable.*

Exercise

Whenever a range of cells is named, an age-old quandary is whether to include a header row as part of the named range. Some functions are easier to use one way and some the other. Both ranges can be named, but if a row is inserted immediately under the header row and the named range does not include the header row, the data area will not expand. The following exercise uses the OFFSET and ROWS functions, used in a named formula, to automatically keep a named data range in sync with the data-plus-header range.

1. Enter the following onto a blank sheet:

2. Name the range B2:C6 *Database.*

3. Use the Insert ➤ Name ➤ Define command to define the name *Data* to refer to:

```
=OFFSET(Database,1,0,ROWS(Database)-1)
```

4. Test the name using the Edit ➤ Go To command, and type *Data* as the reference (it will not display in the list box). Cells B3:C6 should be selected.

5. Insert a row under the headings (at row 3). Go to Data again, and cells B3:C7 will be selected.

Counting Functions

The various counting functions provide important generic functionality, and should be an integral part of your worksheet development strategy.

COUNT (and COUNTA, COUNTBLANK)

The COUNT function counts the numeric values found in a range of cells (or array).

Main points:

- Used to determine number of entries in a column or row
- Used as an argument to functions such as INDEX and OFFSET

Syntax

The following options are used with COUNT:

```
COUNT(Arg1, Arg2, etc.)
```

Arg1   there can be up to 30 arguments, each of which can be a constant or a range of cells

Examples

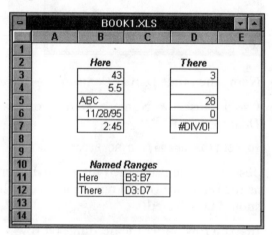

EXAMPLE 1:

    =COUNT(B3:B7)

returns *4*—every value is numeric except for ABC.

EXAMPLE 2:

    =COUNT(There)

returns *3*—every cell is numeric except for blank cell and cell with error.

EXAMPLE 3:

    =COUNT(Here,There)

returns *7*—counts numeric values in both ranges.

Notes

- The COUNTA function is identical to COUNT, except it counts nonblanks (any cell with text, number, or error value).

- The COUNTBLANK function is identical to COUNT, except it counts blank cells. Cells that are empty and cells containing null text are both considered blank.

Exercise

The following exercise uses the OFFSET and COUNTA functions in a named formula to create a dynamic named range that automatically expands based on the number of rows of data.

1. Enter the following values onto a blank sheet:

	A	B	C
1		North	
2		South	
3		East	
4		West	
5			
6			
7			
8			

BOOK1.XLS

2. Use the Insert ➤ Name ➤ Define command to define the name
   Regions as:

   ```
   =OFFSET($B$1,0,0,COUNTA(OFFSET($B$1,0,0,9999,1)),1)
   ```

In English, *Regions* is defined to start at $B$1, and the number of rows is
based on the number of values found in the first 9,999 cells of column B.
(Blank cells inside the range defeat this technique.)

3. Edit ➤ Go To *Regions* (the name will not appear in the list box)—
   if defined correctly cells B1:B4 will be selected.

4. Enter a value in cell B5.

5. Edit ➤ Go To *Regions* again—cells B1:B5 will be selected—the
   range has automatically expanded.

COUNTIF

In previous versions of Excel, there were two ways to count conditionally:

- array formulas—powerful but inordinately complex
- criteria ranges combined with the DCOUNT function—again,
  powerful but tedious to construct

Array formulas and criteria ranges are still applicable for counts requiring
multiple criteria. But COUNTIF is a far simpler solution for counts
based on a single criterion.

- Use COUNT to count numeric values (covered in this chapter).
- Use COUNTA to count non-blank cells (covered in this chapter).
- Use COUNTBLANK to count blank cells (covered in this chapter).

Syntax

The following options are used with COUNTIF.

```
COUNTIF(Range,Criteria)
```

Range   range of cells being counted

Criteria   an expression specifying which cells in *Range* are to be
counted

Examples

```
┌─────────────────────────────────────────┐
│ ▭           BOOK1.XLS            ▼ ▲      │
├─────┬──────┬──────┬──────┬──────┬────────┤
│     │  A   │  B   │  C   │  D   │   E    │
├─────┼──────┴──────┴──────┴──────┴────────┤
│  1  │                                    │
│  2  │            Stuff                   │
│  3  │         12│Smith    │      0       │
│  4  │         20│XYZ      │    107       │
│  5  │         14│         │SMITH         │
│  6  │         37│7/4/96   │    235       │
│  7  │                                    │
│  8  │      Filter  <>Smith               │
│  9  │                                    │
│ 10  │                                    │
│ 11  │        Named Ranges                │
│ 12  │      Stuff  │B3:D6                  │
│ 13  │      Filter │C8                     │
│ 14  │                                    │
│ 15  │                                    │
└─────┴────────────────────────────────────┘
```

EXAMPLE 1:

    =COUNTIF(B3:B6,">30")

returns *1*—the number of cells greater than 30.

EXAMPLE 2:

    =COUNTIF(Stuff,"Smith")

returns *2*—the number of cells equal to *Smith*—notice that COUNTIF is *not* case-sensitive.

EXAMPLE 3:

    =COUNTIF(Stuff,Filter)

returns *10*—the number of cells not equal to *Smith*.

EXAMPLE 4:

    =COUNTIF(Stuff,"<=20")

returns *4*—the number of cells less than or equal to 20 (notice that the blank cell was not counted).

Text Functions

Excel has many powerful text-manipulation functions, most of which are very simple to learn and apply.

LEN

Determines the length of a text string.

Syntax

The following options are used with LEN.

```
LEN(Text)
```

Text   text string

Examples

EXAMPLE 1:

```
=LEN("ABCDE")
```

returns 5—there are 5 characters in the text string.

EXAMPLE 2:

```
=LEN(B2)
```

returns length of text string in cell B2.

EXAMPLE 3:

```
=IF(LEN(B2)>7,"Entry in B2 too long!","")
```

displays error message if text in cell B2 is longer than 7 characters, or null text (" ") if less than or equal to 7 characters.

LEFT (and RIGHT)

Returns the leftmost characters of a text string.

Syntax

The following options are used with LEFT and RIGHT.

```
LEFT(Text,Chars)
RIGHT(Text,Chars)
```

Text   text string

Chars   number of characters—defaults to 1 if omitted

Examples

EXAMPLE 1:

```
=LEFT("ABCDE",3)
```

returns *ABC*—the left 3 characters of text string ABCDE.

EXAMPLE 2:

```
=LEFT("ABCDE")
```

returns *A*—when *Chars* argument omitted it defaults to 1.

EXAMPLE 3:

```
=LEFT("ABC",5)
```

returns *ABC*—if *Chars* is larger than length of *Text*, entire text string is returned.

EXAMPLE 4:

```
=LEFT(A1,2)
```

returns the 2 left characters of text string contained in cell A1.

The RIGHT function works identically to LEFT, except it returns the rightmost characters of a text string.

MID

Returns characters from the middle of a text string

Syntax

The following options are used with MID.

```
MID(Text,Start,Chars)
```

Text   text string

Start   starting character

Chars   number of characters

Examples

EXAMPLE 1:

```
=MID("ABCDE",2,3)
```

returns *BCD*—three characters beginning with the 2nd character.

EXAMPLE 2:

```
=MID("ABCDE",1,2)
```

returns *AB*—two characters starting at the 1st character.

EXAMPLE 3:

```
=MID("ABCDE",4,99)
```

returns *DE*—if *Chars* extends beyond length of *Text*, entire text string beginning with *Start* is returned.

EXAMPLE 4:

```
=MID(A1,10,5)
```

returns 5 characters beginning at the 10th character of text string contained in cell A1.

SEARCH (and FIND)

Returns the position of one text string within another text string.

Main points:

- SEARCH is not case-sensitive
- Allows wildcard characters to be included in search text

Syntax

The following options are used with SEARCH.

```
SEARCH(SearchText,InText,Start)
```

Search Text   text string being searched for—supports wildcards:

    *   matches any sequence of characters

    ?   matches a single character

InText   text string being searched for an occurrence of *SearchText*

Start   character number within *SearchText* to begin searching at; if omitted defaults to 1

Examples

The following examples assume that cell A1 contains the text string *Smith, Janet.*

EXAMPLE 1:

```
=SEARCH("C","ABCDE")
```

returns *3*—C is the 3rd character of ABCDE.

EXAMPLE 2:

```
=SEARCH("Jan",A1)
```

returns *8*—Jan begins at the 8th character in cell A1.

EXAMPLE 3:

```
=SEARCH("T",A1,8)
```

returns *12*—the 12th character is the first occurrence of T after the 8th character.

EXAMPLE 4:

```
=SEARCH("XYZ",A1)
```

returns *#VALUE!*—XYZ not found in cell A1.

EXAMPLE 5:

```
=SEARCH("J?N",A1)
```

returns *8*—question mark used as single-character wildcard.

EXAMPLE 6:

```
=SEARCH("J*T",A1)
```

returns *8*—asterisk used as multi-character wildcard.

EXAMPLE 7:

```
=LEFT(A1,SEARCH(",",A1)-1)
```

returns *Smith*—searches for comma and subtracts 1 in order to determine the last name.

Notes

The FIND function is identical to SEARCH except:

- FIND is case-sensitive
- FIND does not allow wildcards

Date and Time Functions

Working with dates and times is a common worksheet task, and Excel includes a rich set of date and time functions. First, it is important to understand how Excel works with date and time values:

- Date and time values are numbers, regardless of how the cells are formatted.

- Dates and times are stored as serial numbers—by default, Excel uses a 1900 date system in which serial numbers range from 1 to 65,380 corresponding to dates Jan 1, 1900 through Dec 31, 2078.

- In the serial number, digits to the right of the decimal point represent time of day (as a fraction of 24 hrs); 12:00 PM is the equivalent of .5.

- The 1900 date system was employed for Lotus compatibility; a 1904 date system can be chosen (for Macintosh compatibility) using the Tools ➤ Options ➤ Calculation dialog box.

TODAY

Returns the serial number of the current date. The TODAY function takes no arguments. It recalculates every time the worksheet recalculates.

Examples

EXAMPLE 1:

```
=TODAY()
```

returns 35703 on 9/30/97.

EXAMPLE 2:

```
=IF(DAY(TODAY())=15,"Check inventory today!","")
```

displays message on the 15th day of the month.

NOTE

If you enter the formula =TODAY() into an unformatted cell, Excel will automatically format the cell using M/D/YY format. Do not confuse the formatted cell with the underlying value. This holds true for many of the date/time functions.

NOW

Returns the serial number of the current date and time (unlike TODAY, which returns only the date). The NOW function takes no arguments. It recalculates every time the worksheet recalculates.

Example

EXAMPLE 1:

```
=NOW()
```

returns 35703.57639 on 9/30/97 at 1:50 pm (35703 is the serial number for the date, and .57639 is for the time).

TIP To freeze the date and time, use the Edit ➤ Copy and Edit ➤ Paste Special commands, then paste values.

DATE

Returns serial number of a date.

Syntax

The following options are used with DATE.

    DATE(Year,Month,Day)

Year   number from 1900 to 2078 (1904–2078 if 1904 date system is selected)

Month   number representing month of the year (can be greater than 12—see examples)

Day   number representing day of the month (can be greater than number of days in month specified—see examples)

Examples

EXAMPLE 1:

    =DATE(97,9,15)

returns 35688, the serial number for 9/15/97.

EXAMPLE 2:

    =DATE(97,14,15)

returns 35841, the serial number for 2/15/98 (month 14 of 1997 translates to month 2 of 1998).

EXAMPLE 3:

    =DATE(97,9,35)

returns 35708, the serial number for 10/5/97 (day 35 of September translates to day 5 of October).

EXAMPLE 4:

```
=DATE(A1,A2,A3)
```

returns the serial number for the date defined by the year in A1, the month in A2, and the day in A3.

DAY

Calculates day of month (1–31) given date as serial number or text.

Syntax

The following options are used with DAY.

```
DAY(SerialNumber)
```

SerialNumber   date as serial number or text

Examples

EXAMPLE 1:

```
=DAY(35688)
```

returns 15—the day in 9/15/97.

EXAMPLE 2:

```
=DAY("9/15/97")
```

returns 15.

EXAMPLE 3:

```
=DAY("15-Sep-97")
```

returns 15.

EXAMPLE 4:

```
=DAY(A2)
```

returns day of the date in cell A2.

EXAMPLE 5:

```
=IF(OR(DAY(F2)=1,DAY(F2)=15),"Payday!","")
```

displays message if date in F2 is 1st or 15th of month.

HOUR

Converts serial number to an hour.

Syntax

The following options are used with HOUR.

```
HOUR(SerialNumber)
```

SerialNumber   time as serial number or text

Examples

EXAMPLE 1:

```
=HOUR(0.75)
```

returns 18—0.75 times 24 hrs equals 18 hours.

EXAMPLE 2:

```
=HOUR("1:50 pm")
```

returns 13—the hour, using 24-hour clock, of the given time.

EXAMPLE 3:

```
=HOUR(35688.75)
```

returns 18—the hour, using 24-hour clock, of 9/15/97, 6:00pm.

EXAMPLE 4:

```
=HOUR(NOW())
```

returns hour of the current time.

EXAMPLE 5:

```
=IF(HOUR(C9)>8,"Enter reason for late arrival","")
```

displays message if time in C9 is later than 8:00 am.

MINUTE

Converts serial numbers into minutes, displayed as an integer from 1 to 59.

Syntax

The following options are used with MINUTE.

```
MINUTE(SerialNumber)
```

SerialNumber   time as serial number or text

Examples

EXAMPLE 1:

```
=MINUTE(0.3)
```

returns 12—0.3 times 24 hrs equals 7.2 hours, which equals 7 hrs, 12 minutes.

EXAMPLE 2:

```
=MINUTE(35688.3)
```

returns 12—the minutes of 9/15/97, 7:12am.

EXAMPLE 3:

```
=MINUTE("1:50:36 pm")
```

returns 50—the minutes of the given time.

EXAMPLE 4:

```
=MINUTE(B3)
```

returns minutes of the time in cell B3.

MONTH

Converts a serial number to a month.

Syntax

The following options are used with MONTH.

```
MONTH(SerialNumber)
```

SerialNumber   date as serial number or text

Examples

EXAMPLE 1:

```
=MONTH("15-Sep")
```

returns 9—the month number of the given date.

EXAMPLE 2:

```
=MONTH(35688)
```

returns 9—the month number of the given date.

EXAMPLE 3:

```
=MONTH(B5)
```

returns month number of date in cell B5.

EXAMPLE 4:

```
=IF(MONTH(B5)=4,"Tax Time!","")
```

displays message if date in B5 is in April.

WEEKDAY

Converts serial number to day of the week.

Syntax

The following options are used with WEEKDAY.

```
WEEKDAY(SerialNumber,ReturnType)
```

SerialNumber   date as serial number or text

ReturnType   number which determines type of return value:

1	returns 1 through 7 representing Sunday through Saturday
2	returns 1 through 7 representing Monday through Sunday
3	returns 0 through 6 representing Monday through Sunday

NOTE If you omit the ReturnType argument, the result is the same as if you entered 1—i.e., it returns 1 through 7 representing Sunday through Saturday.

Examples

EXAMPLE 1:

```
=WEEKDAY("9/15/97")
```

returns 2—date is a Monday, ReturnType omitted.

EXAMPLE 2:

```
=WEEKDAY(35688)
```

returns 2—date is a Monday, ReturnType omitted.

EXAMPLE 3:

```
=WEEKDAY(35688,2)
```

returns 1—date is a Monday, ReturnType is 2.

EXAMPLE 4:

```
=IF(WEEKDAY(A1,2)>5,"Entry must be weekday!","")
```

displays error message if entry in A1 is not a weekday.

YEAR

Converts serial number to a year.

Syntax

The following options are used with YEAR.

```
YEAR(SerialNumber)
```

SerialNumber   date as serial number or text

Examples

EXAMPLE 1:

```
=YEAR("9/15/97")
```

returns 1997.

EXAMPLE 2:

```
=YEAR(35688)
```

returns 1997.

EXAMPLE 3:

```
=IF(YEAR(A1)<>YEAR(NOW()),"Entry must be in current year.","")
```

displays error message if date in A1 is not in the current year.

CHAPTER

10

Using Templates

f *a* *s* *t* TRACK

● **If a template named CHART.XLT is saved in the XLSTART directory** 283

All newly created charts will be based on CHART.XLT.

● **To modify a template** 285

Hold down the Shift key while opening the file. This opens the original template rather than a copy.

● **To validate data entry** 290

Use IS functions (ISTEXT, ISNUMBER, etc.).

A **CARPENTER** uses templates to simplify tasks, save time, and avoid making mistakes. You can use workbook templates to realize similar efficiencies in several distinct areas:

- *Control the appearance of new workbooks, worksheets, and charts.*

- *Create business forms, such as purchase orders, time sheets, and expense reports.*

- *Standardize the look of your reports.*

- *Use templates as modular building blocks in the development of complex models—for instance, a template can be used to "slice and dice" data from a variety of sources without having to reinvent the wheel every time.*

What Is a Template?

This chapter will deal with templates using two distinct definitions of the word:

"Official" Excel Definition There is a file-save option that allows you to save a workbook as a *Template*. Very simply, this kind of template has one special characteristic: When opened, a copy of the template is placed in memory instead of the original copy. The first part of this chapter is dedicated to explaining the simple task of creating and using such templates.

Broader Definition Generally speaking, the word *template* implies a reusable form or model. Reusability is not limited to *official* Excel templates. Any workbook can perform a template-like function (though without the special characteristic of official templates described above).

Gradually, this chapter will expand the topic of templates, and explain how to create powerful reusable worksheets that can be used as building blocks in worksheet development.

Creating Templates

Any workbook can easily be made into a template:

1. Create a new workbook, or open an old one.

2. Enter constants, formulas, and formatting (anything goes—a template can include charts, macros, and dialog boxes).

3. Choose the File ➤ Save As command.

4. Use the *Save File as Type* drop-down list to select *Template*.

N O T E   Excel will change the file suffix from .XLS to .XLT. As with any workbook, you can override the suffix. However, the .XLT suffix serves as a visual reminder that the workbook is a template.

Opening a Template

Open a template just as you would a normal workbook. A copy of the template is opened rather than the original, which prevents users from accidently changing the original template. Assume that you have just opened a template named REPORT.XLT:

- The workbook in memory will be an unsaved file, similar to new workbooks created with the File ➤ New command (though it will contain all of the data, formulas, and formatting from the template REPORT.XLT).

- The unsaved workbook will be named REPORT1.

- If you open the template again (during the same Excel session) the workbook in memory will be named REPORT2. (There can be multiple copies of the same template opened at the same time.)

- Saving REPORT1 is no different than saving any new workbook—by default, it is saved as a workbook with a .XLS suffix.

C A U T I O N

Never link other workbooks to a template. The link breaks when copies of the template are opened (since the name of the template is different when opened). However, templates can be linked to other workbooks.

Making Templates Readily Available

Templates that are placed in the XLSTART directory or the *alternate startup* directory automatically appear as options whenever you choose the File ➤ New command. For instance, if you have two templates named REPORT.XLT and INVOICE.XLT saved in the XLSTART directory, the New dialog box would display as follows:

Selecting *Report* or *Invoice* from the list is simply a shortcut for opening the templates using the File ➤ Open command.

Creating AutoTemplates

You can control the characteristics of *all* new workbooks and worksheets with special templates called *AutoTemplates*. Very simply, an AutoTemplate is a template placed into the XLSTART or *alternate startup* directories, and which has been named using one of the special names listed in Table 10.1:

TABLE 10.1: Template Names

NAME	CONTROLS
BOOK.XLT	all new workbooks
SHEET.XLT	newly inserted worksheets
CHART.XLT	new chart sheets
MODULE.XLT	newly inserted VBA modules
DIALOG BOX.XLT	newly inserted dialog-box sheets
MACRO.XLT	newly inserted .XLM-macro sheets

If there is a template named BOOK.XLT in XLSTART (or the alternate startup directory), the File ➤ New command will cause BOOK.XLT to be opened. If there is a template named SHEET.XLT in XLSTART, the Insert ➤ Worksheet command will cause SHEET.XLT to be inserted.

NOTE All of the AutoTemplates other than BOOK.XLT control individual sheets; these templates should contain only one sheet.

The following AutoTemplate possibilities are not necessarily recommendations—they are just ideas to show what is possible with AutoTemplates.

New Workbooks (BOOK.XLT)

- customize the names of worksheet tabs, or hide tabs entirely
- uncheck the *Save External Link Values* setting
- change the standard colors
- change page setup settings
- add company logo

New Worksheets (SHEET.XLT)

- hide gridlines
- sheet formatting (fonts, borders, styles, etc.)

New Charts (CHART.XLT)

- define chart type
- chart formatting (colors, fonts, etc.)

TIP Programmers can use MODULE.XLT and/or MACRO.XLT to include basic code framework used in all modules and/or macro sheets.

Modifying a Template

When a template is opened, a copy of the template is opened into memory. However, you may want to edit the original template. To edit the original template, follow these steps:

1. Choose the File ➤ Open command.

2. Select the template in the file list (do not open it yet).

3. Hold down Shift and click OK—the original template will be opened.

4. Modify and save.

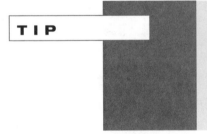

TIP

A common mistake is to open a copy of a template when you intended to open the original template, then not notice the mistake until after changes have been made. To avoid losing changes, save the copy on top of the original—you must *explicitly* save it as a template in this circumstance.

Invoice Template

The following exercise draws upon several important skills in the creation of an invoice template for a fictitious consulting firm:

- lookups into a database using the VLOOKUP function
- using the NOW function to suggest a unique invoice number
- input verification using IS functions

N O T E   The exercise instructs you to save the file as the final step—you may actually want to save your work from time to time as you progress.

1. Create a new workbook consisting of three worksheets (see Chapter 2).

2. Name the sheets **Invoice, Clients,** and **Consultants**.

3. Enter the following information onto the *Clients* sheet:

	A	B	C	D	E
1	Code	Name	Address1	Address2	Address3
2	ARGUS	Argus Industries	123 Industrial Way		Seattle, WA 98023
3	BC	B&C Paper Products	456 Cedar Lane	Suite 1105	Seattle, WA 98105
4	SALTY	Salty Dog Chandlery	12 Marine Drive		Everett, WA 92654
5	TALLY	Tally-Ho Clothing, Inc.	11205 First Ave	Suite 121	Seattle, WA 98102
6	GREEN	Greentrees Nursery	521 Rose Lane		Cle Elum, WA 95642
7					
8					
9					

BOOK1.XLS

4. Name the range A2:E6 **ClientData** (see Chapter 8 to learn about naming).

5. Enter the following information onto the *Consultants* sheet:

	A	B	C	D
1	Code	Name	Level	
2	BG	Ben Gomez	SR	
3	ES	Ellen Smith	JR	
4	JN	John Norris	JR	
5	MW	Mary West	SR	
6				
7				
8				
9	Rate_Jr			
10	65			
11				
12	Rate_Sr			
13	95			
14				

BOOK1.XLS

6. Name the range A2:C5 **ConsultantData**.

7. Name cell A10 **Rate_Jr** and name cell A13 **Rate_Sr**. (These cells define the billing rate for junior and senior consultants.)

8. Activate the *Invoice* sheet. Remove gridlines using Tools ➤ Options ➤ View.

9. Enter the constants, set approximate column widths, and apply cell borders as pictured below:

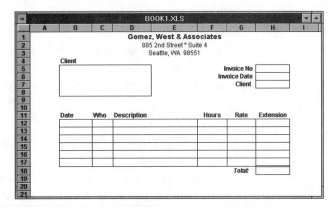

10. Apply the following built-in number formats to the *Invoice* sheet:

CELL(S)	FORMAT
B12:B17	Date—m/d/yy
F12:F17	Number—0.00
G12:G17	Number—0
H6	Date—m/d/yy
H12:H18	Number—#,##0.00

11. Enter the following formulas on the *Invoice* Sheet:

a Enter the following formula into cell B5—it looks up the client name based on client number entered in cell ClientCode:

```
=IF(ISTEXT(ClientCode),VLOOKUP(ClientCode,ClientData,2,
FALSE),"")
```

b Enter the following formula into cell B6—it looks up address line 1:

```
=IF(ISTEXT(ClientCode),VLOOKUP(ClientCode,ClientData,3,
FALSE),"")
```

c Enter the following formula into cell B7—it looks up address line 2:

```
=IF(ISTEXT(ClientCode),VLOOKUP(ClientCode,ClientData,4,
FALSE),"")
```

d Enter the following formula into cell B8—it looks up address line 3:

```
=IF(ISTEXT(ClientCode),VLOOKUP(ClientCode,ClientData,5,
FALSE),"")
```

e Enter the following formula into cell H4—it suggests a unique invoice number based on current date if an invoice number has not been entered and workbook is unsaved:

```
=IF(AND(ISBLANK(H5),CELL("filename")=""),"Suggested
invoice:"&RIGHT(YEAR(NOW()),1)&TEXT(MONTH(NOW()),
"00")&RIGHT(TEXT(NOW()*100 00,"#####"),3),"")
```

f Enter the following formula into cell I6—it displays a prompt if there is not a valid date in H6, or if the date in H6 is more than 30 days ago, or if the date in H6 is later than the current date:

```
=IF(OR(ISERROR(YEAR(H6)),H6<TODAY()-30,H6>TODAY()),"Enter
valid date","")
```

g Enter the following formula into cell I7—it displays an error message if the value in B5 is #N/A:

```
=IF(ISNA(B5),"Invalid Client!","")
```

h Enter the following formula into cell G12 (and copy it to G13:G17)—it looks up the consultant rate:

```
=IF(ISTEXT(C12),IF(VLOOKUP(C12,ConsultantData,3,FALSE)="SR",
Rate_Sr,Rate_Jr),0)
```

i Enter this formula into cell H12 (copy to H13:H17)—it calculates the extension:

```
=F12*G12
```

j Enter the following formula into cell I12 (and copy it to G13:G17)—it displays an error message if the value in G12 is #N/A:

```
=IF(ISNA(G12),"Invalid Consultant Code!","")
```

   k Enter this formula into cell H18—it totals the extensions:

`=SUM(H12:H17)`

12. Choose the Tools ➤ Options ➤ View command and uncheck the *Zero Values* setting (to suppress the display of zero values).

13. Choose the File ➤ Save command—enter file name *Invoice*. Use the *File Save as Type* drop-down to specify Template.

14. Close the template, then reopen it and test it.

Bulletproofing the Template

Depending on how a template is used, varying levels of security measures may be required. Here are some additional features that could be added to the Invoice template to make it more bulletproof:

- Add an on-sheet list box control for entering client code (see Chapter 19).

- Unlock cells where data entry is allowed, then protect the sheet (see Chapter 11).

- Add validation to warn if entry in date or hours columns is invalid.

- The list of clients and consultants is part of the template, and thus is saved with each copy of the template. (Often, it is desirable to store such data in separate workbooks, or in an external database—see Chapter 18.)

Using IS Functions for Data Validation

Input verification is a common requirement for templates. You can place formulas on a template (or any worksheet) to display error messages when data entry is invalid. There is a family of functions, all beginning with IS, that check the type of data that is in a certain cell. Table 10.2 lists all of the IS functions.

TABLE 10.2: IS Functions

FUNCTION	RETURNS
ISBLANK	TRUE if value is blank
ISERR	TRUE if value is any error value except #N/A
ISERROR	TRUE if value is any error value
ISLOGICAL	TRUE if value is logical value
ISNA	TRUE if value is #N/A error value
ISNONTEXT	TRUE if value is not text
ISNUMBER	TRUE if value is number
ISREF	TRUE if value is a reference
ISTEXT	TRUE if value is text

An IS function can be used to display error messages when invalid input occurs. For example, assume that cell C3 requires text input, as in Figure 10.1:

FIGURE 10.1

User input is required in column C.

Enter the following formula in D3:

```
=IF(ISTEXT(C3),"","Enter name.")
```

Translates to: If there is text in C3 then null text (two quotes), else message.

The following formulas are examples of various IS functions; they are used to validate data entered onto the worksheet pictured in Figure 10.1:

- The following formula displays a message if cell C5 does not contain a number:

```
=IF(ISNUMBER(C5),"","Enter a salary.")
```

- The following formula displays a message if cell C7 contains a non-text entry:

```
=IF(OR(ISBLANK(C7),ISTEXT(C7)),"","Enter position")
```

- The following formula displays an error message if cell C9 does not contain the logical values TRUE or FALSE:

```
=IF(ISLOGICAL(C9),"","Enter true or false")
```

Building Smart Templates

The remainder of this chapter is dedicated to the development of templates that can be easily reused in worksheet models. The broader sense of the word *template* is now being used, in that the techniques covered below are not specific to *official* templates. Essentially, the topic now becomes *how to construct modular building blocks*.

To illustrate modularity, a simple template will be constructed whose purpose is the analysis of data stored in a worksheet database. Step by step, features will be added that make the template applicable to a broader range of analysis situations. The business scenario is as follows:

- A computer company has two divisions: *Commercial* and *OEM*.
- Each division has three departments: *Hardware*, *Software*, and *Services*.
- The company sells into several regions worldwide—forecasts are tracked by division, department, and region.

- Accuracy of projections is vitally important: low forecasts result in too little inventory and lost sales; high forecasts result in overproduction.

- The purpose of the model is to compare the forecasts for any two regions.

The template will start off simple in Exercise One, and become successively more modular in Exercises Two through Four. To fully understand the process, you will need to understand names (Chapter 8), and the VLOOKUP function (Chapter 9).

Exercise One—Compare Regions within One Department

A forecast will be prepared for one department, *Hardware*, within the OEM division. The model will reside in one workbook containing two worksheets, which will contain:

- hardware forecast data by region

- formulas allowing any two regions to be compared side-by-side (think of this comparison sheet as a *template*)

NOTE The construction of this model is explained in tutorial format. It is not essential that you follow the tutorial precisely in order to understand it.

1. Create a new workbook with two worksheets; name the first sheet *Hardware* and name the second sheet *Compare*.

2. Enter the forecast database onto sheet *Hardware*:

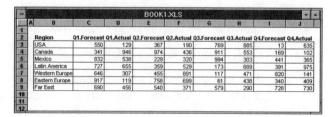

Region	Q1.Forecast	Q1.Actual	Q2.Forecast	Q2.Actual	Q3.Forecast	Q3.Actual	Q4.Forecast	Q4.Actual
USA	550	129	367	190	769	885	13	635
Canada	341	946	974	436	911	553	169	102
Mexico	832	538	229	320	994	303	441	365
Latin America	727	655	359	529	173	689	391	975
Western Europe	646	307	455	891	117	471	820	141
Eastern Europe	917	119	758	699	61	438	340	409
Far East	690	456	540	371	579	290	728	730

TIP

Here is a shortcut for quickly entering random integers: select cells C3:I9, enter the formula =INT(RAND( )*1000), and press Ctrl-Enter. Replace the formulas with values using Edit ➤ Copy followed by Edit ➤ Paste Special, then choose *Values*.

3. Name cells B3:J9 *Hardware*.

TIP

A meaningful naming strategy is a critical component in worksheet development.

4. Build the comparison sheet, intended to compare any two rows of the forecast data—Enter the following constants and formatting onto sheet *Compare*:

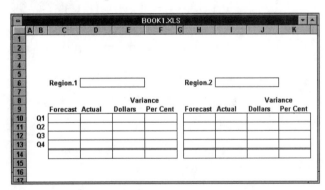

5. Name cell D6 *Region.1*—the first region being compared will be entered into this cell.

6. Name cell I6 *Region.2*—the second region being compared will be entered into this cell.

7. Enter the following formulas:

CELL(S)	FORMULA
C10	=VLOOKUP(Region.1,Hardware,2,FALSE)
C11	=VLOOKUP(Region.1,Hardware,4,FALSE)

CELL(S)	FORMULA
C12	=VLOOKUP(Region.1,Hardware,6,FALSE)
C13	=VLOOKUP(Region.1,Hardware,8,FALSE)
D10	=VLOOKUP(Region.1,Hardware,3,FALSE)
D11	=VLOOKUP(Region.1,Hardware,5,FALSE)
D12	=VLOOKUP(Region.1,Hardware,7,FALSE)
D13	=VLOOKUP(Region.1,Hardware,9,FALSE)
E10	=D10-C10
E11	=D11-C11
E12	=D12-C12
E13	=D13-C13
F10	=E10/D10
F11	=E11/D11
F12	=E12/D12
F13	=E13/D13
C14	=SUM(C10:C13)
D14	=SUM(D10:D13)
E14	=SUM(E10:E13)
F14	=E14/D14

8. Copy the Region.1 formulas to Region.2 section:

   - Copy cells C10:F14, and paste at cell H10.
   - Select cells H10:I13—replace every occurrence of *Region.1* with *Region.2*.

9. Enter valid regions into cells D6 and I6; if the model was constructed correctly, data for the two regions will display on the *Compare* sheet.

10. Save the workbook as OEM.XLS.

Exercise Two—Multiple Departments within the Workbook

So far, the compare template is not very modular. The comparison formulas are hard-wired to the *hardware* forecast database. (The only flexibility is the ability to choose which regions are being compared.) In Exercise Two, *software* and *services* databases will be added to the workbook, and the comparison template will be changed to work with any of the three databases.

1. Create two new department sheets:

   - Insert two new worksheets—name one *Software* and one *Services*.
   - Enter forecast data on the two new sheets (copy range B2:J9 from the Hardware sheet, then change the data).
   - On the Software sheet, name B3:J9 *Software*.
   - On the Services sheet, name B3:J9 *Services*.

2. Add Department to *Compare* sheet:

   - Enter **Department** into cell H4.
   - Name cell I4 *Department*—this cell will determine which forecast database the *Compare* sheet will refer to.

3. Define the name *Forecast* to refer to:

```
=IF(Department="Hardware",Hardware,IF(Department=
"Software",Software,Services))
```

NOTE   This named formula refers to the one of the three forecast databases based on the contents of cell *Department*.

4. On Compare sheet, use the Edit ➤ Replace command to change every occurrence of *Hardware* to *Forecast*.

To use the template, enter a valid department into I4, and valid regions into D6 and I6.

Exercise Three—Allow Analysis of More Than One Division

The *compare* template has now achieved a level of modularity—it is able to analyze data in one of three departments *within the OEM division*. In Exercise Three, the compare template will be placed in a stand-alone workbook so that it can work with the forecast for the OEM *and* Commercial divisions which reside in two different workbooks. The benefits to this architecture are:

- Since the divisional forecasts will reside in different workbooks, each division can work on its respective forecast concurrently.

- Since the comparison template will reside in its own workbook, any changes to the design of the template need only be made in place.

- The template can be easily used for new divisions in the future.

In addition, the template logic will be expanded to allow comparisons across departments (so that, for example, OEM/Hardware/Europe can be compared with OEM/Software/Europe).

NOTE In this data model, with only two divisions, the *compare* template could easily live inside both divisional workbooks. But picture a situation where there are dozens of divisions—a single compare template saves a huge amount of time in development and maintenance.

1. Create a new workbook—move the *Compare* sheet from OEM.XLS to the new workbook (see Chapter 2)—and save the new workbook as a template named COMPARE.XLT.

TIP

A shortcut for this task is to simply drag the Compare sheet and drop it outside of OEM.XLS, but not onto a different workbook. A new workbook is created automatically.

2. Create a workbook for the commercial division (save OEM.XLS as COM.XLS—change some numbers so that you will notice differences on the compare template).

3. Open OEM.XLS—all three workbooks (OEM.XLS, COM.XLS, and COMPARE.XLT) should now be open.

4. On COMPARE.XLT, enter the constants listed below:

CELL	ENTRY
C4	**Dept.1**
H4	**Dept.2**

5. Name the following cells:

CELL	NAME
D4	**Dept.1**
I4	**Dept.2**

6. On COMPARE.XLT, activate Compare sheet, and define the following names:

NAME	REFERS TO
Hardware	=OEM.XLS!Hardware
Software	=OEM.XLS!Software
Services	=OEM.XLS!Services
Forecast.1	=IF(Dept.1="Hardware",Hardware,IF(Dept.1="Software",Software,Services))
Forecast.2	=IF(Dept.2="Hardware",Hardware,IF(Dept.2="Software",Software,Services))

7. On COMPARE.XLT, select cells C10:D13 and replace every occurrence of *Forecast* with *Forecast.1*.

8. On COMPARE.XLT, select cells H10:I13 and replace every occurrence of *Forecast* with *Forecast.2*.

Using the Template

Here is how to use the Compare template at the end of Exercise Three:

- Use the Edit ➤ Links command to point the template to the desired workbook (OEM.XLS or COM.XLS).

- Enter valid departments into cells D4 and I4.

- Enter valid regions into cells D6 and I6.

- Workbooks containing source data do not have to be open— VLOOKUP works with closed workbooks.

Exercise Four—Allow Comparisons across Divisions

So far, the template is able to make comparisons *within* one division. One more twist will be added that allows the template to make comparisons *across* divisions (for example, OEM/Software/Europe versus Commercial/Software/Europe).

1. All three workbooks (OEM.XLS, COM.XLS, and COMPARE.XLT) should be open.

2. Enter the following constants onto COMPARE.XLT:

CELL	ENTRY
C2	**Div.1**
H2	**Div.2**

3. Name cell D2 as *Div.1*—name cell I2 as *Div.2*.

4. Insert a new worksheet into COMPARE.XLT, and name it *Divisions*.

5. Add the following to the Divisions sheet, then name cells B3:C4 *DivisionList*. (The purpose of this table is to maintain a cross-reference between "friendly" descriptions of the divisions, and the corresponding workbook names.)

	A	B	C	D	E	F	G
			BOOK2.XLS				
1							
2		DivisionList					
3		Commercial	COM.XLS				
4		OEM	OEM.XLS				
5							
6							
7							
8							
9							

6. On COMPARE.XLT, activate the Compare sheet, and define the following names:

NAME	REFERS TO
Forecast.1	=INDIRECT(VLOOKUP(Div.1,DivisionList,2,TRUE)&"!"&Dept.1)
Forecast.2	=INDIRECT(VLOOKUP(Div.2,DivisionList,2,TRUE)&"!"&Dept.2)

Using the Template

Here is how to use the Compare template at the end of Exercise Four:

- Enter either OEM or Commercial into cells D2 and I2.

- Enter valid departments into cells D4 and I4.

- Enter valid regions into cells D6 and I6.

- Workbooks containing source data must be open. (The INDIRECT function cannot be used to access closed workbooks.)

CHAPTER

11

Auditing and Protecting Your Work

fast TRACK

● **To turn on cell protection**   312

Activate the worksheet, choose Tools ➤ Protection ➤ Protect
Sheet, check *Contents*—all locked cells are then protected.

● **To enter or edit a cell note**   314

Select the cell, then choose Insert ➤ Note.

● **To trace cell dependents and precedents
with tracer arrows**   317

Display the auditing toolbar, then click the desired tools.

● **To search for files using various search criteria**   322

Choose File ➤ Find File.

TWO OF the biggest problems endemic to worksheet applications are security and maintainability. The most clever models are rendered useless if users are able to easily break them. Similarly, complex models that are difficult to support or modify will eventually collapse under their own weight. This chapter will provide you with these relatively simple security and auditing skills:

- *Prevent users from accidentally breaking worksheets by changing formulas and data that are not intended to be changed.*

- *Prevent users from accessing sensitive data and formulas.*

- *Allow workbooks to be effectively shared in a multi-user environment.*

- *Avoid the "spaghetti code" syndrome by documenting your work.*

- *Avoid getting lost when there are several levels of cell dependencies by learning to trace logic flow.*

- *Categorize files with file information settings.*

- *Search for files based on simple or advanced search criteria.*

File-Level Security

There are several levels of protection that can be applied to a workbook. The topmost level of protection is set on the file level. When a workbook is first saved, and any time you choose the File ➤ Save As command, the *Save As* dialog box is displayed.

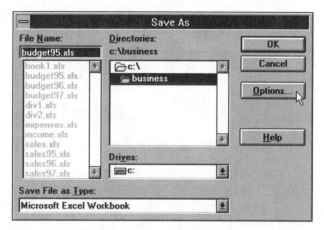

Click the Options button to display the Save Options dialog box (Figure 11.1)—this is where file-level security options are set.

FIGURE 11.1

Save Options

Requiring a Password to Open a Workbook

The *protection password* entered in the Save Options dialog box (see Figure 11.1) requires that a password be entered in order to open or access the workbook. In general, this password is used on workbooks requiring the highest possible level of security.

- The password can be up to 15 characters, can include special characters, and is case-sensitive.

- You will be prompted for the password when you try to open the workbook.

- You will be prompted for the password if a formula is entered into a different workbook that refers to cell(s) on the password-protected workbook (and the protected workbook is closed).

- If you forget the password, there is virtually nothing that can be done to recover the workbook—you will not get assistance from Microsoft technical support.

N O T E

Macros are able to specify a password when opening a password-protected workbook in order to avoid the password prompt. While this requires that the password be embedded in a module (or macro sheet), the module itself can be protected.

Requiring a Password to Save a Workbook

The *write-reservation password* entered in the Save Options dialog box (see Figure 11.1) requires that a password be entered in order to *save* the workbook. This allows users to open, view, and manipulate the workbook, but not save it under the same name without knowing the password. As with the protection password, the write-reservation password can be up to 15 characters long and is case-sensitive.

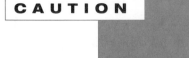

Scrutiny of the write-reservation password system reveals a critical shortcoming that you should be aware of: Application-managed file-level security is only as good as the underlying file system. You can open a file with a write-reservation password, change it, save it to a different name, and close it. Then copy the new file to the old file using File Manager or at the DOS prompt. Only security provided by the operating system can thwart this procedure.

Removing Protection and Write-Reservation Passwords

Follow this procedure to remove a protection password or write-reservation password:

1. Open the workbook.

2. Choose the File ➤ Save As command, then click the Options button.

3. Clear the password(s)—asterisks will display when there is a password.

4. Click OK to close the Save Options dialog box, then click OK to save the file.

5. Answer *Yes* when the following dialog box is displayed:

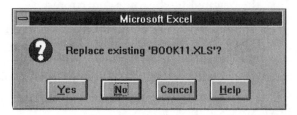

Read-Only Recommended

The *Read-Only Recommended* setting in the Save Options dialog box (see Figure 11.1) causes Excel to display the following dialog box when the file is opened:

The *Read-Only Recommended* setting is a handy solution for two scenarios:

- A workbook is used by more than one person; users should generally open it read-only in case somebody else needs to change it.

- Users are discouraged from accidentally changing a workbook that is not supposed to be changed on a day-to-day basis, yet periodically requires maintenance.

Always Create Backup

When checked, the *Always Create Backup* setting in the Save Options dialog box (see Figure 11.1) causes Excel to create a backup of the file every time it is saved. The backup file is saved with a *.BAK* extension in the same directory as the original file. Open the backup file if:

- the original file becomes corrupted

- you make mistakes, and do not realize it until *after* you have saved the file

Since files with a .BAK extension are not displayed in the File ➤ Open dialog box by default, you will have to type in the file name or change the filter. (See Chapter 2.)

CAUTION

Automatic backups are saved with a .BAK extension. If you have files named FINANCE.XLS and FINANCE.XLT in the same directory, and both files are set to create backups, both backups will be saved as FINANCE.BAK and thus overwrite one another.

Any File Can Be Opened Read-Only

Even when a write-reservation password is not defined, and *Read-Only Recommended* is not set, you can still open files read-only. Check the *Read-Only* setting in the lower right corner of the File ➤ Open dialog box.

Protection inside the Workbook

The remainder of the security options serve to restrict what a user can do *after* the workbook has been opened. Essentially, there are three levels of security:

- workbook level
- worksheet level
- object level (cells and graphical objects)

Workbook Protection

Choose the Tools ➤ Protection ➤ Protect Workbook command to display the Protect Workbook dialog box:

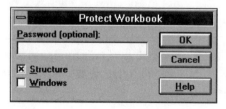

Password	Optional password up to 255 characters; it can include special characters and is case-sensitive.
Structure	If checked, prevents changes to worksheet structure; you are prevented from deleting, inserting, renaming, copying, moving, hiding, or unhiding sheets.
Windows	If checked, prevents changes to workbook's window; you are prevented from resizing the window—window controls (close, restore, minimize, maximize) are hidden.

Since a protected structure prevents users from inserting new sheets, there are several unexpected side effects that you should be aware of. When the structure is protected you are unable to:

- add a new chart sheet with ChartWizard

- record a macro onto a new module-sheet

- use the scenario manager to create a new scenario

- display source data for a cell in a pivot table

To unprotect a workbook, choose the Tools ➤ Protection ➤ Unprotect Workbook command. You will be prompted for the password if one was specified when the workbook was protected.

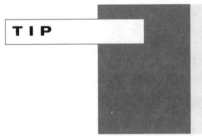

TIP

A workbook might only contain supporting data that is not intended to be changed, or even viewed. It can be hidden using the Window ➤ Hide command. If you quit Excel with a hidden workbook, and answer Yes when prompted to save it, the workbook will be automatically hidden the next time it is opened.

Worksheet Protection

Use worksheet protection to prevent users from changing the contents of a sheet. Choose the Tools ➤ Protection ➤ Protect Worksheet command to display the Protect Sheet dialog box:

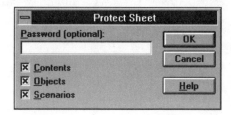

Password	Optional password up to 255 characters; it can include special characters and is case-sensitive.
Contents	Protects worksheet cells and chart items.
Objects	Protects graphic objects on worksheets (including embedded charts).
Scenarios	Prevents changes to scenario definitions.

To unprotect a worksheet, choose the Tools ➤ Protection ➤ Unprotect Worksheet command. You will be prompted for the password if one was specified when the worksheet was protected.

Another way to discourage users from changing cells is by hiding all or part of the sheet:

Hiding an Entire Sheet   Choose the Format ➤ Sheet ➤ Hide command to hide a sheet; it cannot be unhidden if you protect the workbook structure. To unhide, choose the Format ➤ Sheet ➤ Unhide command.

Hiding Rows   Select the rows you want to hide, then choose the Format ➤ Row ➤ Hide command.

Hiding Columns   Select the columns you want to hide, then choose the Format ➤ Column ➤ Hide command.

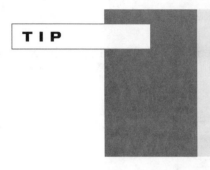
> **TIP**
>
> How do you unhide hidden rows or columns when you are unable to select them? To unhide a hidden row or column, select a contiguous range of cells that includes the hidden row or column, then choose the Format ➤ Row ➤ Unhide command, or the Format ➤ Column ➤ Unhide command. Alternatively, use the Name box to select a hidden cell, then unhide the row or column.

Cell Protection

Choose the Format ➤ Cells command, then select the Protection tab.

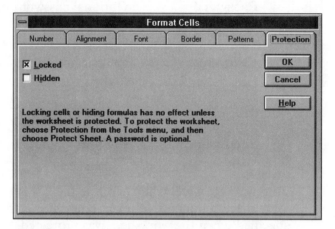

Locked	Cells can't be changed after sheet is protected.
Hidden	Hides formulas after sheet is protected.

Three simple facts can save you considerable confusion and frustration when working with cell protection:

- Inexplicably, Excel places the settings on the *Format* dialog box—it is easy to forget this fact.

- Cell protection does not take effect unless the worksheet is protected with Contents checked (think of sheet protection as a master breaker switch, and cell protection as a single outlet on the breaker).

- By default, *all* cells are locked—you must *unlock* the cells users are allowed to change before protecting the worksheet.

Object Protection

If objects placed on a worksheet are not protected, users are able to move them, resize them, or even delete them. To protect an object:

1. Select the object.

2. Choose the Format ➤ Object command, then select the Protection tab.

3. Lock the object and/or object text.

Keep these facts in mind when protecting objects:

- All objects have a protection setting called *Locked*; when checked, the object cannot be deleted, resized, moved, or formatted.

- Text boxes, buttons, and several controls have an additional setting called *Lock Text*; when checked, the text cannot be changed.

- Object protection does not take effect unless the worksheet is protected with *Objects* checked (think of sheet protection as a master breaker switch, and object protection as a single outlet on the breaker).

- By default, *all* objects are locked.

See Chapter 12 to learn about working with graphical objects on worksheets.

Documenting Your Work

Spreadsheet applications have a notorious "spaghetti code" reputation, and the blame falls directly on the shoulders of the people who build them. When spreadsheets were used solely for personal productivity, at least others weren't bearing the brunt of developers' bad habits. But spreadsheet programs have become popular tools used to create organizational solutions. Thorough documentation is vitally important—particularly in complex models.

TIP

Though it may be a practice that defies human nature, you are a lot better off if you document as you work. The formulas and logic are fresh in your mind, and a tedious task is not left for the end.

There are three primary means for documenting a worksheet model:

- cell notes
- text boxes and arrows
- meaningful naming conventions (see Chapter 8)

Cell Notes

Cell notes are an outstanding facility for documenting formulas, assumptions, and results. Choose the Insert ➤ Note command to display the Cell Note dialog box:

Cell	Indicates which cell note is being edited.
Text Note	There is no limit to the length of notes other than available memory; words automatically wrap; since pressing Enter closes the dialog box, use Ctrl+Enter to go to a new line.
Notes in Sheet	Lists all the worksheet's cells that have notes, and the first few characters of each note; click to edit the note.
Sound Note	Facility for annotating a cell with sound; requires special hardware and software.

N O T E   If you can't wait to liven up your worksheet with sound, remember that 30 seconds of speech can consume a couple of megabytes of disk storage!

Add	Adds the note, and leaves the dialog box displayed to edit other notes.
Delete	Deletes current note.
OK	Adds the note and closes the dialog box.

Viewing and Editing Notes

Cells with notes are indicated with a small red dot in the upper right corner of the cell. (Note indicators can be turned on and off using the *Note Indicator* setting on the Tools ➤ Options ➤ View dialog box.) Select a cell with a note, then use one of the following procedures:

- Click the Note tool on the Auditing toolbar.
- Choose the Insert ➤ Note command.
- If in-cell editing is turned off, double-click the cell.

Printing Notes

When a worksheet is printed using the normal procedures, cell notes are not included in the printout. Follow this procedure to print cell notes:

1. Choose the File ➤ Page Setup command, then select the Sheet tab.

2. Check the *Row and Column Headings* setting to print the cell references before each note.

3. Check the *Notes* setting, then print.

Clear Notes for Memory Efficiency

Sometimes cell notes are intended for the user of a worksheet to learn more about certain formulas or assumptions. Other times, notes are used by the developer, and are *not* intended for users. In the latter case, you may want to clear the notes (for memory efficiency) before deploying the workbook:

1. Save a copy of the workbook *with* notes for future reference.

2. Select all cells on the sheet (use the *Select All* button).

3. Choose the Edit ➤ Clear ➤ Notes command.

Documenting with Text Boxes

Sometimes it is desirable for notes to stand out boldly. Text boxes, combined with other on-sheet graphical objects, can add important information to a report, with style.

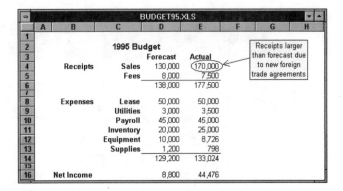

See Chapter 12 to learn more about text boxes and other graphical objects.

Auditing Worksheets

One of the most tedious tasks is troubleshooting complex worksheets. Excel 5 has added some powerful new features designed to simplify the process.

Dependent and Precedent Cells

Assume that cell B1 has the formula **=A1**.

- B1 is the *dependent* cell; it depends on A1.
- A1 is the *precedent* cell; it precedes B1.

On complex worksheets, there can be many levels of dependency, which makes it difficult to trace the flow. The auditing commands provide a graphical representation of cell relationships (see Figure 11.2).

FIGURE 11.2

Tracer arrows

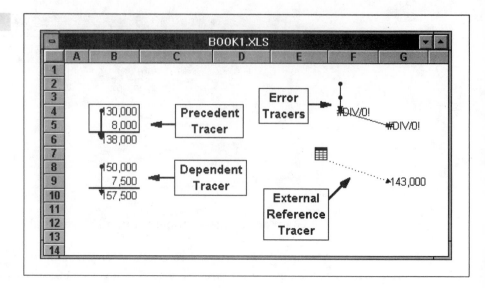

	Tracing Precedents	Select a dependent cell, then choose the Tools ➤ Auditing ➤ Trace Precedents command; arrows are displayed pointing from precedent to dependent cells.
	Tracing Dependents	Select a source cell, then choose Tools ➤ Auditing ➤Trace Dependents; arrows are displayed pointing from precedent to dependent cells.
	Tracing Errors	Select a cell containing an error value, then choose the Tools ➤ Auditing ➤ Trace Error command; arrows are drawn from the error value in the active cell to cells that might have caused the error.
	Removing Arrows	Choose the Tools ➤ Auditing ➤ Remove All Arrows command; all arrows on the worksheet are removed.

There are three types of tracer arrows:

- **Formula** tracers are solid blue arrows (solid black on black-and-white monitors).

- **Error** tracers are solid red arrows (short black dashes on black-and-white monitors) from precedent formulas, solid blue arrows from precedent values.

- **External reference** tracers are dashed black lines with a worksheet icon (long black dashes with an icon on black-and-white monitors).

Selecting Special Cells

Choose the Edit ➤ Go To command, then click the *Special* button to display the Go To Special dialog box pictured below.

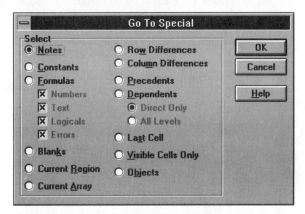

Notes   All cells containing notes

Constants   All cells containing constant values

Formulas   All cells containing formulas; you can then narrow the selection by choosing only certain types of data returned by the formulas. You can:

- Select formulas that return numbers.
- Select formulas that return text.
- Select formulas that return logical values (TRUE and FALSE).
- Select formulas that return error values.

Blanks   All blank cells

Current Region   A rectangular range of data (the active cell must be within the data before choosing the command)

Current Array   The entire array that the active cell resides in (if it is part of an array)

Row Differences   Cells in the same row as the active cell, whose contents are different from the active cell

Column Differences   Same as row differences, but in columns

Precedents   Cells referred to by the formula in the active cell

Dependents   Cells whose formulas refer to the active cell

- **Direct Only** selects only cells with direct references.
- **All Levels** selects cells with both direct and indirect references (the entire network of related cells).

Last Cell   The last cell in the worksheet (or macro sheet) containing data or formatting

Visible Cells Only   Only visible cells on the worksheet (so that changes will not affect hidden rows or columns)

Objects   All graphical objects (including embedded chart objects)

Once the desired cells are selected, you can use the Tab key to cycle through them.

If a range of cells is selected prior to choosing the Edit ➤ Go To command, only cells within the selected range will be searched.

TIP   Use the Edit ➤ Find command, covered in Chapter 3, to search for specific values or formulas. You can search cell values, formulas, or cell notes.

Learn Everything about a Cell at Once

The Info Window displays (almost) everything there is to know about the active cell:

1. Choose the Tools ➤ Options command, select the View tab, then check the *Info Window* setting to display the Info Window.

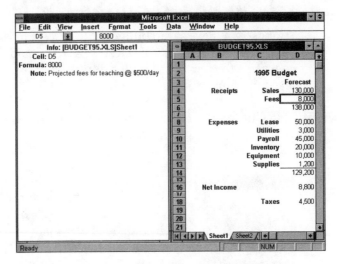

2. Use the Info menu (which only displays when the Info Window is active) to specify what information to include in the Info Window.

Searching for Files

Searching for files and categorizing files using *summary information* are important skills to help you organize your work.

Searching Based on the File Name

Suppose you have saved budget data by year in workbooks beginning with "BUDGET," such as BUDGET94.XLS and BUDGET95.XLS. You now want to view the files, but don't remember what directory they were saved in. This procedure will locate the files:

1. Choose the File ➤ Find File command (or click the Find File tool on the Workgroup toolbar).

NOTE   The very first time the File ➤ Find File command is chosen after Excel is installed, the Search dialog box will be displayed. After that, the File ➤ Find File command will display the Find File dialog box, which will list the files found in the last search.

2. Click the Search button to display the Search dialog box (see Figure 11.3).

3. Enter these search parameters in the Search dialog box:

   - In *File Name*, enter the file name, with optional wildcards— for example, enter **budget*.xls** to search for every file beginning with "BUDGET" and ending with ".XLS" (see Table 11.1 for a list of supported wildcard characters).

   - In *Location*, select a directory—use the drop-down list to specify the drive, then type a directory if desired.

   - To search all subdirectories of the *Location*, check *Include Subdirectories*.

4. Click OK—The Find File dialog box is displayed again, with the results of the search displayed in the *Listed Files* window (see Figure 11.4).

FIGURE 11.3

The Search dialog box

FIGURE 11.4

The files are listed on the left, and summary information for the selected file is displayed on the right.

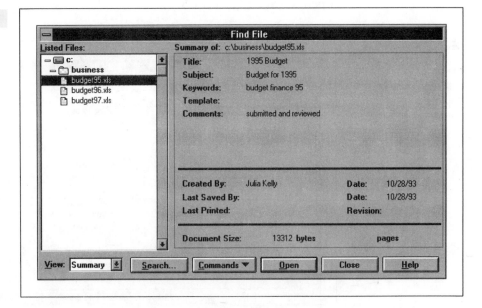

TABLE 11.1: Wildcard Characters for Searches

CHARACTER	MEANING
? (question mark)	Match single character
* (asterisk)	Match any number of characters
" " (double quotes)	Enclosed character is not wildcard (use to search for ?, *, &, etc.)
, (comma)	Indicates OR (search for information matching at least one item in list)
& (ampersand)	Indicates AND (search for information matching all items in list)
(space)	Same as &—Indicates AND (search for information matching all items in list)
~ (tilde)	Indicates NOT (exclude matching information from search)

To display a preview of the file, select *Preview* from the *View* drop-down list. This lets you quickly inspect the file before taking the time to actually open it. (See Figure 11.5.)

FIGURE 11.5

The upper left corner of the top sheet is displayed in the preview.

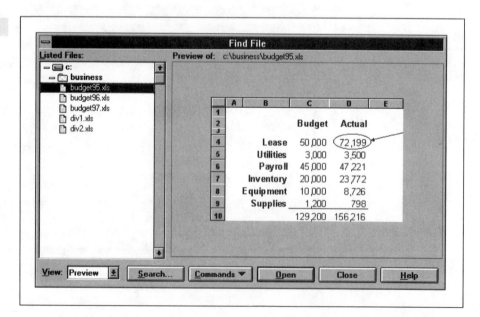

Click the Search button to conduct a new search. Click the Open button to open the file. When you click the Commands button, a drop-down menu is displayed.

Open Read Only opens selected workbook(s) read-only.

Print displays dialog box to select printing options for selected workbook.

Summary (Inexplicably, this command is never available.)

Delete deletes selected workbook.

Copy displays Copy dialog box, to copy files to another directory/drive or create new directory.

Sorting displays Options dialog box for choosing how listed files are sorted.

Performing an Advanced Search

There are several ways to search for files based on criteria other than the file name. For instance, your budget files may not always begin with "BUDGET." Before you can understand advanced searches, you need to understand how to enter summary information for a file.

Entering Summary Information

You can enter summary information for each workbook. The fields include title, author, subject, keywords, and comments. This information can help you locate workbooks, and is particularly useful in a workgroup environment. To enter summary information:

1. Open the workbook.

2. Choose the File ➤ Summary Info command.

3. Enter a title, subject, author name, comments, and any keywords that might be useful in a future search.

TIP To display the Summary Info dialog box every time a new worksheet is saved (or when the Save As command is used), choose the Tools ➤ Options command, select the General tab, and check the *Prompt for Summary Info* setting.

Keyword Search

The following exercise will search for files where the word "BUDGET" was entered as a keyword in summary information.

1. Choose the File ➤ Find File command. The results of the last search are displayed.

2. Click the Search button.

3. Click the Clear button (to clear all previous search parameters).

4. Enter ***.xls** in *File Name* (specifying all Excel workbooks).

5. Enter a *Location* (including a path to narrow the search).

6. Click the Advanced Search button.

7. Select the Summary tab

- Enter **budget** in *Keywords*.
- Select *Create New List* from the Options drop-down.

8. Click OK to close the Advanced Search dialog box, then click OK in the Search dialog box to begin the search.

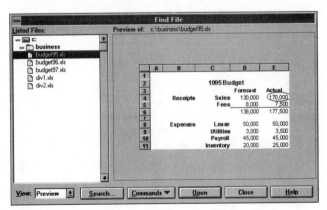

Saving the Search

Suppose this is a search that you want to perform regularly. Once a set of search criteria has been specified, it can be named and saved for future use. You can then perform the same search again at a later date without having to reenter the search parameters.

Follow these steps to name and save a search:

1. Specify the search criteria.

2. In the Search dialog box, click *Save Search As* (see Figure 11.3).

3. Type a name for the search in the *Search Name* edit box, and click OK.

To use a saved search, select it from the *Saved Searches* drop-down and click OK.

Table 11.1 explains the wildcard characters you can use in searches.

PART FOUR

Graphics and Charts

Working with Graphic Objects

f a s t TRACK

TRADITIONALLY, spreadsheet programs are used for number crunching. But Excel is a powerful graphics package in its own right. It allows graphic objects to be placed on worksheets, which lets you:

- *put your company logo on a worksheet*
- *use objects such as text boxes, arrows, and circles to emphasize information (with style!)*
- *enhance worksheets by using pictures of cells*

This chapter covers:

- *the different types of objects that can be created*
- *how objects are moved, sized, and formatted*
- *using the camera tool to create pictures*
- *how to protect objects*

See Chapter 25 to learn how to import and export graphics to and from other applications.

How to Draw Graphic Objects

Suppose you have a worksheet with information that needs explanation or emphasis.

A text box, circle, and arrow are used to explain a figure on the worksheet. These objects were drawn on the sheet using tools found on the drawing toolbar.

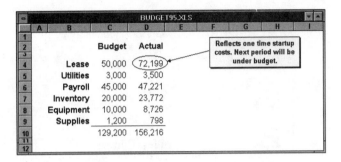

Objects such as circles, arrows, text boxes, and buttons are placed on worksheets by drawing them:

1. Display the Drawing toolbar—choose the View ➤ Toolbars command.

2. Click the tool for the object you want to draw—the mouse pointer becomes a crosshair.

3. Click on the worksheet, and drag the mouse.

4. Release the mouse button.

Table 12.1 explains the tools on the Drawing toolbar.

TABLE 12.1: Drawing Tools

TOOL	FUNCTION
	Line
	Arrow
	Freehand Line
	Filled Rectangle

TABLE 12.1: Drawing Tools (continued)

TOOL	FUNCTION
☐	Unfilled Rectangle
⬭	Filled Ellipse
◯	Unfilled Ellipse
◤	Filled Arc
◜	Unfilled Arc
◢	Filled Freeform Polygon
▱	Unfilled Freeform Polygon
▤	Text Box
▭	Create Button
▧	Drawing Selection (selects objects and controls)
▣	Bring To Front
▤	Send To Back
▦	Group
▦	Ungroup

TABLE 12.1: Drawing Tools (continued)

TOOL	FUNCTION
	Reshape (displays vertices on freehand lines and freeform polygons)
	Drop Shadow
	Pattern (drop-down, tear-off palette of patterns)

Drawing Several of the Same Object

Suppose that you want to draw several arrows. You can click the arrow tool and draw, then repeat the procedure for each arrow. But there is a quicker way—if you double-click a drawing tool it remains in effect until you are done:

1. Double-click a drawing tool.

2. Draw the object—the tool remains in effect—draw another object.

3. Single-click the tool when you are done drawing.

How to Select Objects

To format, move, resize, copy, or delete an object, it must first be selected. The procedure differs slightly depending on whether the object is *filled*:

Filled Objects A filled object is colored—it obscures the underlying cells, as pictured in Figure 12.1. (Some of the tools on the Drawing toolbar create filled objects that are colored white.) You can click anywhere on a filled object to select it. You will learn how to fill objects in the formatting section later in this chapter.

FIGURE 12.1

You can see gridlines behind the unfilled rectangle—you must click the border in order to select it. You can click anywhere on a filled object.

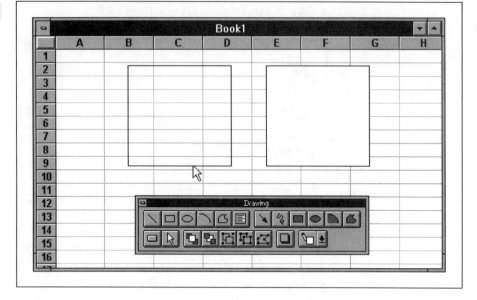

Unfilled Objects An unfilled object is an outline with no fill—you can see the cells behind the object. To select an unfilled object, you must click on the object's border.

To select an object, click on it. The name of the selected object displays in the Name box on the left of the formula bar.

A selected object has small markers on the border—these are called *handles*.

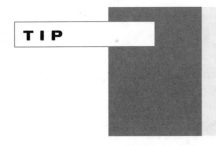

TIP

It is impossible to select a cell behind a filled object by clicking on the cell, because you will select the object instead. To select a cell behind a filled object, you can use the Name box or the Edit ➤ Go To command, or use the arrow keys to navigate to the cell behind a filled object.

Using the Object Shortcut Menu

When you click an object with the right mouse button, the object is selected and a shortcut menu is displayed, as in Figure 12.2.

The shortcut menu can save you several keystrokes when working with objects.

FIGURE 12.2

Click an object with the right mouse button to display the object shortcut menu.

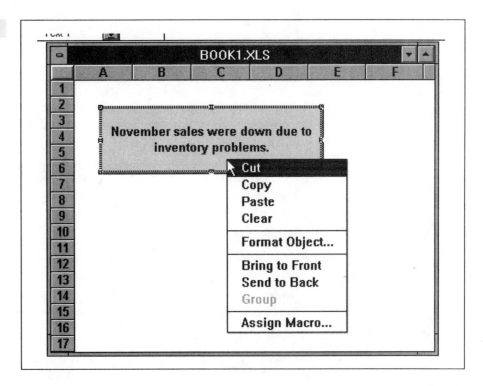

Manipulating Objects

In this section you will learn how to move, resize, copy, and delete graphic objects.

Moving and Resizing Objects

The mouse must be used to move and resize objects.

Moving an Object To move an object, select it with the mouse, then drag it across the worksheet. An outline of the object is displayed until you release the mouse button.

Resizing an Object To resize an object, select the object, then drag one of the handles. An outline of the new size is displayed until the mouse button is released.

Suppose you want to resize a rectangle, but retain the precise proportions. This is nearly impossible to do freehand. To resize an object while retaining its proportions, hold down the Shift key while dragging one of the corner handles.

Aligning Objects to the Worksheet Grid

A common problem is the task of perfectly aligning several objects, or making sure objects are the exact same size. When you do it freehand, no matter how careful you are, it is nearly impossible to align or size perfectly. When you look at a worksheet with imperfectly aligned objects, you may not be consciously aware of the imperfection. But the brain detects the imperfection anyway—something just doesn't look right.

If you hold down the Alt key while moving or resizing an object, the object is snapped to the worksheet grid—even if gridlines are not displayed.

Copying Objects

There are two ways to copy objects: by dragging and dropping, and with menu commands.

Using Drag and Drop The most efficient way to copy an object to a nearby location is to drag it and drop it:

1. Hold down the Ctrl key.

2. Select the object, then drag and drop it—a copy of the object is created.

Using Menu Commands To copy (or cut) an object using menu commands:

1. Select the object.

2. Choose the Edit ➤ Copy or Edit ➤ Cut command.

3. Select a cell where you want to paste.

4. Choose the Edit ➤ Paste command.

Alternatively, use the Cut, Copy, and Paste commands on the object shortcut menu.

Deleting Objects

To delete an object:

1. Select the object.

2. Press the Delete key (or choose the Edit ➤ Clear command).

Alternatively, use the Clear command on the object shortcut menu.

Formatting Objects

There are several different format settings that can be applied to objects. In addition, different objects have different format settings. For instance, only arrows have a formattable arrowhead. And only text boxes and buttons have formattable text.

In spite of the fact that some objects have unique formattable properties, all objects are formatted by displaying the Format Object dialog box pictured in Figure 12.3. There are three ways to display this dialog box:

FIGURE 12.3

The contents of the Format Object dialog box vary depending on the type of object.

- Double-click the object.
- Choose the Format Object command from the object shortcut menu.
- Select the object, then choose the Format ➤ Object command.

The following exercise will show how to format a text box using some visually effective formatting techniques:

1. Display the Drawing toolbar—use the Text Box tool to draw a text box.

2. Enter some text into the text box—press Esc when you are done entering text—the object will still be selected.

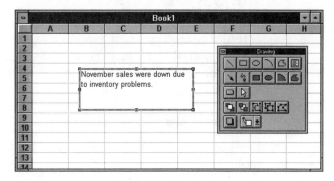

3. Select the Format ➤ Object command, then select the Patterns tab.

4. Check the Shadow setting, and select a yellow fill color.

TIP To tone down the bright yellow, use a pattern. Drop down the pattern list and choose white. Drop down the pattern list again, and choose a hatch pattern.

5. Select the font tab, and choose bold style.

6. Select the Alignment tab, and center horizontally and vertically.

7. Click OK.

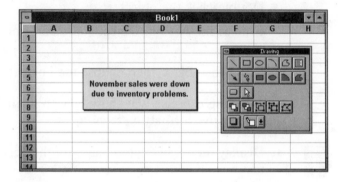

Use the Format Painter Tool to Quickly Format Several Objects

 The same formatting can be applied to several objects using the *Format Painter* tool (on the Standard toolbar). In the preceding exercise, seven steps were required to format the text box. Suppose you want to format several text boxes the same way—the *Format Painter* will let you do it quickly.

1. Select an object that is already formatted the way you want.

2. Double-click the *Format Painter* tool (located on the standard toolbar).

3. Click on each object you want format.

4. Click on the *Format Painter* to turn it off (or press Esc).

Understanding Object Properties

The Format Object dialog box has a tab called Properties (see Figure 12.4). This tab is identical for all types of objects.

FIGURE 12.4

The Properties tab controls object size and position relative to the underlying cells, and whether the object prints out.

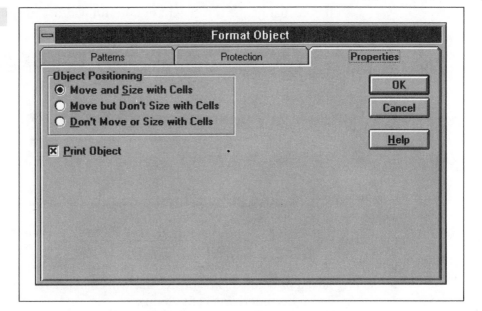

Controlling Object Size and Placement Relative to Underlying Cells

Suppose you draw a text box, enter some text, then manually size the text box:

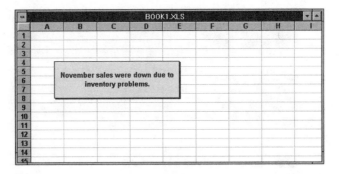

If you change the row height or column width of the underlying cells, the text box resizes accordingly:

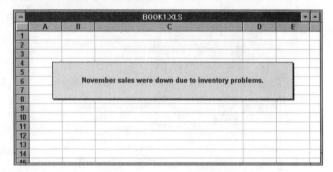

The *Object Positioning* options (see Figure 12.4) control this behavior:

Move and Size with Cells An object will move if rows/columns are inserted or deleted. The object size will change as the row height or column width of underlying cells changes.

Move But Don't Size with Cells An object will move with the underlying cells, but will not resize.

Don't Move or Size with Cells An object will not move with the underlying cells, and will not resize.

N O T E There is a global setting that determines if objects should cut, copy, and sort along with underlying cells. To access this setting, choose the Tools ➤ Options command, then choose the Edit tab.

Do You Want the Object to Print?

By default, all objects (except buttons) are included on the printout when the worksheet is printed. But some objects may be intended to display on the screen and not print. For example, a text box may instruct the user on how to enter data; this text box would be inappropriate on the printout. The *Print Object* setting (see Figure 12.4) determines whether an object will print.

Working with More Than One Object at a Time

More than one object can be selected at the same time, which lets you manipulate all of the selected objects at once. Suppose you want to move several objects, and retain their relative positions. You can select all of the objects and move them together, instead of moving them one by one.

Selecting Multiple Objects Using the Shift Key Hold down Shift while selecting objects with the mouse. This technique is probably the quickest if you need to select just two or three objects.

 Using the Drawing Selection Tool Click on the Drawing Selection tool (located on the Drawing toolbar), then draw a rectangle around the objects that you want to select. (When finished using the Drawing Selection tool, click it again to turn it off.)

Grouping and Ungrouping Objects

You have learned how to select more than one object in order to manipulate more than one object at once. But you may want to semi-permanently *group* objects together. When you group objects, a new object is created.

1. Draw a text box and an arrow.

 2. Select the text box and arrow, then choose the Format ➤ Placement ➤ Group command (or click the Group tool on the Drawing toolbar).

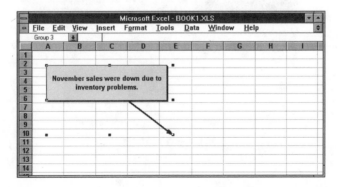

Notice that the two objects are now a single object, with a new name—Group 3.

You can choose to ungroup objects that have been previously grouped:

1. Select the group object.

2. Choose the Format ➤ Placement ➤ Ungroup command, or click the Ungroup tool.

Types of Objects

So far in this chapter, you have read about objects in general. This section will describe the unique properties of each type of object.

Rectangles, Ellipses, and Arcs

It is difficult, if not impossible, to draw perfect squares and circles free-hand. If you hold down the Shift key, you can draw squares and circles, rather than rectangles and ovals. Pressing Shift while drawing an arc will create a 90° arc.

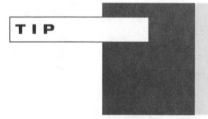

T I P

If you hold down the Shift key while clicking on an unfilled tool, it will draw a filled object. Likewise, if you hold down the Shift key while clicking on a filled tool, it will draw an unfilled object. See Table 7.3 for a list of other "reversible" tools.

Lines and Arrows

 An arrow is simply a line formatted with an arrowhead (see examples in Figure 12.5). The formatting dialog box lets you specify the arrowhead type, if any:

Lines can be drawn at perfect vertical, horizontal, and 45-degree angles by holding down Shift while drawing.

Text Boxes

A text box is a rectangle in which you can enter and format text. It is very useful for adding comments and explanations to worksheets and charts, especially when combined with arrows and circles to point to specific information.

FIGURE 12.5

Various lines and
arrowheads combined
to make arrows

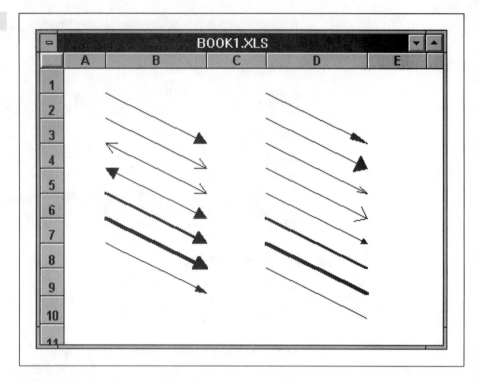

After you draw a text box, the text-insertion point will blink within the
box, ready for you to type text. Text boxes automatically wrap text (press
Enter to insert a hard break).

There are several format settings specific to text boxes:

- The *Alignment* and *Font* tabs are used to format the text.

- The *Automatic Size* setting on the Alignment tab causes the text box to size automatically based on the text.

- The *Lock Text* setting on the Protection tab prevents users from changing text. (The worksheet must also be protected for this setting to take effect—see Chapter 11 to learn about sheet protection.)

How can you place text inside an oval? Place a text box on top of the oval, then format the text box with no fill and no border.

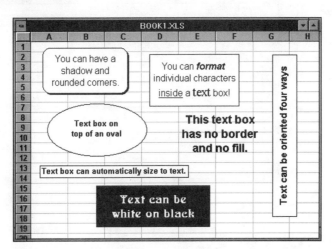

Linking a Text Box to Worksheet Cells

Suppose you want the contents of a text box to be variable. You can link a text box to a worksheet cell by entering a formula instead of a constant. Try this exercise:

1. On a new worksheet, enter the following formula into cell B2:

   =IF(ISNUMBER(B3),"You may now save the workbook.","Please enter a number into B3.")

2. Draw a text box.

3. Click in the formula bar and type **=B2**, then press Enter (see Figure 12.6).

CAUTION   A common mistake is entering the formula into the text box rather than into the formula bar.

4. Enter a number into B3 and watch the text box change.

FIGURE 12.6

When a linked text box is selected, the cell reference displays in the formula bar, where the cell reference can be changed.

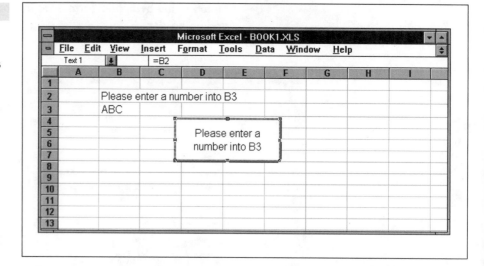

Linked Pictures

A linked picture is a picture of one or more worksheet cells that remains linked to the source cell(s). Put to creative use, linked pictures can greatly enhance reports and presentations.

 The camera tool is the easiest way to create a linked picture. It is not located on any of the built-in toolbars, so you will have to create a custom toolbar in order to use the camera tool. To create a linked picture using the camera tool:

1. Select source cell(s).

2. Click the camera tool.

3. Click on a worksheet—a picture of the source cells is created (see Figure 12.7).

To create a linked picture using menu commands:

1. Select the source cell(s).

2. Choose the Edit ➤ Copy command.

3. Hold down the Shift key, then choose the Edit ➤ Paste Picture Link command.

Here are some important properties of linked pictures:

- Any change to the source cells causes a linked picture to update.

- When a picture is first created, the picture object has its own border, independent of any borders or gridlines in the source cell(s)—use the Format ➤ Object command to remove the object border.

- The reference for the source cells displays on the formula bar when a linked picture is selected (see Figure 12.7).

- You can edit (or clear) the reference on the formula bar. If cleared, the link between the picture and the source cell(s) is broken and the picture becomes static.

FIGURE 12.7

When a linked picture is selected, the source cells are displayed on the formula bar.

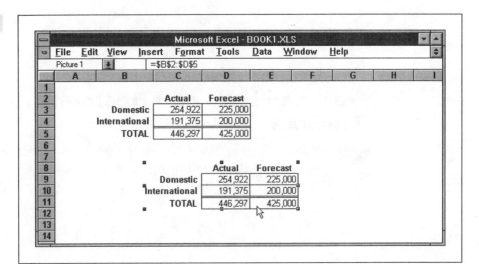

Consider the worksheet in Figure 12.8.

Application developers can derive two key benefits from linked pictures:

- Pictures can be placed on custom dialog boxes.

- When a linked picture is created, it refers to an absolute cell reference; however, a picture can refer to a named formula (see Chapter 8 to learn about named formulas). This lets user input dynamically change the picture source.

FIGURE 12.8

Some people prefer charts and others prefer tabular data. A linked picture placed on a chart sheet satisfies all.

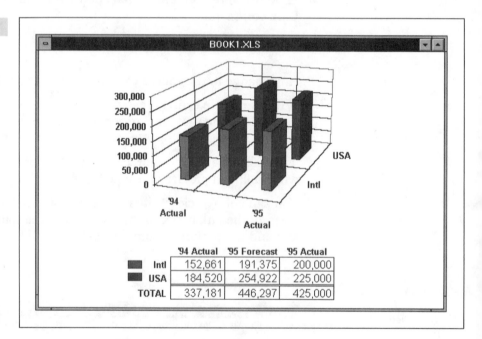

		'94 Actual	'95 Forecast	'95 Actual
■	Intl	152,661	191,375	200,000
■	USA	184,520	254,922	225,000
	TOTAL	337,181	446,297	425,000

Freehand Lines and Freeform Polygons

To draw a freehand line, click and drag the mouse. The mouse pointer becomes a pencil while drawing the line. When you release the mouse button, the line is completed.

Freeform polygons can combine straight lines and freehand lines. To draw straight lines, click at the endpoint of the line. You can make a polygon side vertical, horizontal, or a 45-degree angle by holding down Shift while clicking.

 To alter the shape of a freehand line after it is drawn, select the line and click the *Reshape* tool. Each vertex of the line will have a handle, and you can drag each handle with the crosshair to reshape the line. To turn the Reshape tool off, click the tool again, or click outside the object.

CHAPTER

13

Charting Basics

fast TRACK

To delete a data series from a chart   **377**

1. Activate the chart by double-clicking on it.

2. Select the series by clicking on it.

3. Press the Delete key.

To format a chart   **381**

Activate the chart by double-clicking on it, then double-click the element you want to format.

To draw inside a chart   **385**

Activate the chart, then use the Drawing tools to draw objects (the objects you draw "live" in the chart, not on the worksheet).

CHARTS are an effective way to present information. They allow a lot of information to be absorbed quickly, whereas a traditional columnar report might require considerable study and analysis. Excel includes a powerful built-in charting facility that makes it very easy to create a variety of charts.

This chapter covers:

- *how to create charts with the ChartWizard, including how to select the type of chart you want to create*
- *the difference between embedded charts and chart sheets*
- *adding data to an existing chart*
- *formatting charts for maximum impact*
- *an exercise that will show you how to create and format a chart*

Charts Are Easy

Creating a chart is (usually) quick and easy. Before you explore the many charting options covered later in this chapter, here is an exercise that will demonstrate how easy it is to create a chart.

1. Enter the following on a new worksheet:

	A	B	C	D	E	F
			BOOK1.XLS			
1						
2		Region	Actual	Forecast		
3		North	456	346		
4		South	562	854		
5		East	726	892		
6		West	851	238		
7						
8						
9						

2. Select cells B2:D6.

3. Click the ChartWizard tool (on the Standard toolbar).

4. Drag the mouse pointer across the worksheet to draw the chart frame (Figure 13.1).

5. When you release the mouse button, the ChartWizard (Step 1 of 5) dialog box will be displayed. Click the Finish button.

FIGURE 13.1

As you draw the chart, the chart outline is displayed.

	A	B	C	D	E	F	G	H	I
				BOOK1.XLS					
1									
2		Region	Actual	Forecast					
3		North	456	346					
4		South	562	854					
5		East	726	892					
6		West	851	238					
7									
8									
9									
10									
11									
12									
13									
14									
15									
16									
17									
18									
19									
20									

6. A chart using the default format is drawn on the worksheet (see Figure 13.2).

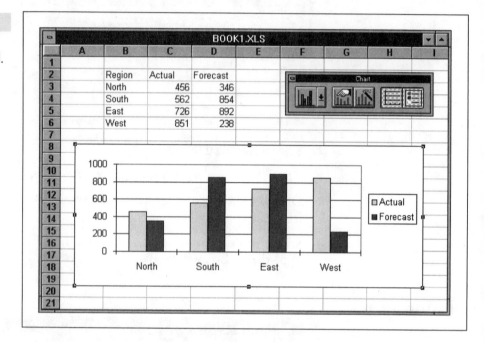

By default, charts are *linked* to the worksheet cells. To see this in action, change the source data in the worksheet—the chart will automatically re-draw accordingly.

When a chart is active, the menus change. The Data menu goes away, and chart-specific commands appear on the View, Insert, and Format menus. Also, the Chart toolbar is displayed. Table 13.1 describes the tools on the Chart toolbar.

TABLE 13.1: Tools on the Chart Toolbar

TOOL FACE	TOOL	FUNCTION
	Chart Type	Drops down tear-off palette of chart types
	Default Chart	Creates default embedded chart without ChartWizard
	ChartWizard	Starts ChartWizard
	Horizontal Gridlines	Toggles display of horizontal gridlines on/off
	Legend	Toggles display of legend on/off

Embedded Charts vs. Chart Sheets

The chart created in the previous exercise is an *embedded* chart. Charts can also reside on *chart sheets*.

About Embedded Charts

An embedded chart is a graphic object that lies on a worksheet. It can be moved, resized, and deleted just as you would other graphical objects, such as text boxes. (See Chapter 12 to learn about graphical objects.)

The primary advantage of embedded charts is that they can be viewed (and printed) side-by-side with worksheet data. You can place more than one embedded chart on a worksheet.

An embedded chart must be activated before you can format it or make changes to it. Double-click an embedded chart to activate it. A heavy border is displayed around an active chart, as shown in Figure 13.3.

FIGURE 13.3

An embedded chart is activated by double-clicking on it. A heavy border is displayed.

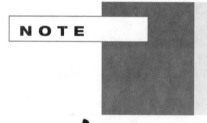

NOTE

An embedded chart is *selected* by single-clicking it with the mouse, as with all graphic objects. When selected, it can be moved, resized, or deleted. Do not confuse *selecting* with *activating*—you must double-click an embedded chart to *activate* it.

About Chart Sheets

Chart sheets are like worksheets, except there are no cells. A chart sheet is a separate page in a workbook—it contains one chart (see Figure 13.4). To create a chart sheet:

1. Select the data you want to chart.

2. Choose Insert ➤ Chart ➤ As New Sheet—the ChartWizard is started. (Or press F11 to create a new chart sheet, and circumvent the ChartWizard.)

FIGURE 13.4

Column chart on a
chart sheet

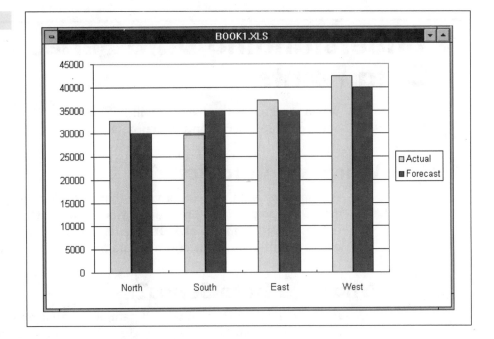

Chart sheets can be renamed, moved, copied, and deleted just as you
would a worksheet. (See Chapter 2 to learn how to manage sheets.)

The primary advantages of chart sheets are they can be made to be full
size without manual sizing, and when printed do not include any worksheet data.

Also, there is a command that is available only for chart sheets: The View
► Sized with Window command controls whether the size of the chart is
dependent on the size of the window. By default, this command is unchecked. If checked, the chart is automatically sized to fit the window.
(This setting has no effect on how the chart will appear when printed.)

N O T E   In previous versions of Excel, it was impossible to place
graphical objects on chart sheets. The restriction has
been removed.

Understanding Data Series and Data Points

When working with charts, it will help if you understand the difference between a data series and data points.

What Is a Data Point?

A *data point* is an individual value that originated in a single worksheet cell. Data points are represented by columns, bars, dots, slices, or other shapes called *data markers*. In Figure 13.3, North-Actual is one data point; South-Forecast is another data point.

What Is a Data Series?

A *data series* is a group of related data points that represents a single row or column of data. Each series is distinguished by a unique color or pattern. In Figure 13.3, Forecast is one data series and Actual is the other data series—each series consisting of four data points.

Using the ChartWizard

 In the previous exercise, the ChartWizard was used to create an embedded chart. But the exercise asked you to immediately click the Finish button, which skipped over most of the ChartWizard options. In this section, the five major ChartWizard steps will be thoroughly explained.

Starting the Chart Wizard

To begin creating a chart, select the data to be charted (including labels for columns and rows), then do one of the following:

- Click the ChartWizard tool if you want to create an embedded chart, then use the mouse to draw the chart object on the worksheet.

- Choose Insert ➤ Chart ➤ On This Sheet (same as the ChartWizard tool).

- Choose Insert ➤ Chart ➤ As New Sheet to create a new chart sheet.

The ChartWizard is displayed (see Figure 13.5). Each step of the ChartWizard includes Cancel, Back, Next, and Finish buttons:

- Click Cancel to stop the ChartWizard—no chart will be created.

- Click Back to go back to the previous step.

- Click Next to proceed to the next step.

- Click Finish when you are done specifying chart properties—the chart will be created immediately.

FIGURE 13.5

Step 1 of the ChartWizard displays the range that the chart will be based on, and lets you override it.

Step 1 confirms that the selected range contains the data you want included in the chart (see Figure 13.5). If the range displayed is not correct, change it by typing a new reference or by selecting a different range.

The chart data does not have to come from the active worksheet; you can specify a different worksheet, or even a different workbook:

If Data Is on a Different Worksheet Display the ChartWizard Step 1 dialog box. Select the worksheet, then select the range of cells containing the data. Click the Next button.

If Data Is in a Different Workbook Be sure the workbook containing the data (Book1, for example) is open, and the workbook where the chart will be drawn (Book2) is active. Display the ChartWizard Step 1 dialog box. Select Book1 from the Window menu, then select the worksheet and the range of cells containing the data. Click the Next button.

Include row and column headings if you want them to appear as labels in the chart. When the range is correct, click Next.

N O T E You can change the properties of the default chart. This procedure is described in Chapter 14.

Step 2 of 5—Choose the Type of Chart

Step 2 lets you choose the type of chart. In Figure 13.6, a column chart has been selected.

Step 3 of 5—Select a Type Format

Each type of chart has several different formats from which to choose. Step 3, pictured in Figure 13.7, lets you choose the chart format.

FIGURE 13.6

Choose the type of chart you want to create.

FIGURE 13.7

Choose the chart format.

Step 4 of 5—Orient the Chart

Step 4, pictured in Figure 13.8, displays a preview of the chart, and lets you specify how the data on the chart is oriented:

Data Series in: Rows   This means that each data series is plotted from a row of data.

Data Series in: Columns   If this option is selected, each data series will be plotted from a column of data.

Use First X Row(s)   This setting lets you specify how many top rows contain X-axis labels.

Use First X Column(s)   This setting lets you specify how many left-hand columns contain the legend entries.

N O T E   Multiple rows and columns can be selected for X-axis labels and legend text because Excel is capable of charting multi-level categories.

FIGURE 13.8

The ChartWizard guesses how the data should be oriented, but you can override these settings.

Step 5 of 5—Enter Titles and Legend

Step 5 lets you specify legend, chart title, and axis titles. (See Figure 13.9.)

- If you don't want a legend, choose *No*—you can always add one later by clicking the Legend tool on the Chart toolbar.

- Type chart and/or axis titles if you want them—if left blank, titles can be added later with the Insert ➤ Titles command.

Click Finish to create the chart, as in Figure 13.10.

FIGURE 13.9

Choose chart and axis titles and a legend display.

Changing a Chart Using the ChartWizard

The ChartWizard can be used to change an existing chart. However, when changing a chart, only two of the original five steps are available.

1. If the chart is an embedded chart, select it (click it with the mouse); if it is a chart sheet, activate the sheet.

2. Click the ChartWizard tool.

FIGURE 13.10

Completed column
chart created with
ChartWizard

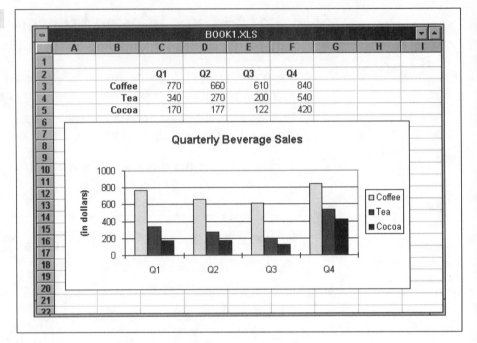

| Step 1 | Same as step 1 when creating a new chart |
| Step 2 | Same as step 4 when creating a new chart |

Changing a Chart to a Different Type

There are several built-in chart types to choose from (see Figure 13.6). Each type of chart has several basic formats, sometimes referred to by Excel as subtypes. For example, a 2-D column chart has three subtypes.

The previous exercise explained how to change a chart using the ChartWizard. There are several other ways to change a chart from one type to another, or change the subtype.

Changing the Chart Type Using the Main Menu Activate the chart, then choose Format ➤ Chart Type and select a new chart type.

 Changing the Chart Type Using the Chart Type Tool The Chart Type tool (on the Chart toolbar) contains a drop-down palette of chart types. These tools are faster to use than the Format ➤ Chart Type command, but do not offer the variety of subtypes that the command offers. To use the tools, select the chart (no need to activate it), then select a chart type from the palette.

TIP The Chart Type tool has a tear-off palette. See Chapter 1 to learn how to use tear-off palettes.

Changing the SubType Using AutoFormat To use an AutoFormat, activate the chart, then choose Format ➤ AutoFormat. Select a type from the *Galleries* list, then choose a format from the *Formats* options. If you don't like the result, choose Edit ➤ Undo to undo the AutoFormat, or choose a different AutoFormat.

TIP
You can create your own user-defined chart AutoFormats. See Chapter 14 to learn how.

Adding, Deleting, and Changing Chart Data

Once created, a chart does not need to be recreated in order to add data, delete data, or reorganize the data.

Adding Data to a Chart

There are several ways to add new data to an existing chart:

- using Drag and Drop (embedded charts only)
- using the Edit ➤ Copy and Edit ➤ Paste commands
- using the Insert ➤ New Data command

Drag and Drop New Data onto an Embedded Chart

You can add a new data series, or new data points, using drag-and-drop.

Drag and Drop New Data Series To add a new series with drag-and-drop, select the cells containing the data and drag and drop it onto the chart.

Drag and Drop New Data Points To add new points to an existing series, select the points and drag and drop them onto the chart.

After you drag and drop, if Excel is unable to determine whether you are adding a series or data points, a dialog box is displayed which lets you specify the type of data being added.

Suppose you have a worksheet that tracks sales by region and charts the data. At the end of each month, data is added to the sheet and needs to be added to the chart.

To add the new data to the chart in Figure 13.11:

1. Select F2:F4.

2. Drag and drop the cells onto the chart. (Drag the cells as if you were moving them, and drop them anywhere on the chart.)

Adding Data Using Copy and Paste

New data can be added by copying from the worksheet and pasting onto the chart. This works for embedded charts and chart sheets.

1. Select the data you are adding to the chart.

2. Choose Edit ➤ Copy.

FIGURE 13.11

The new data points are added at the end of each data series—it doesn't matter where on the chart you drop the cells.

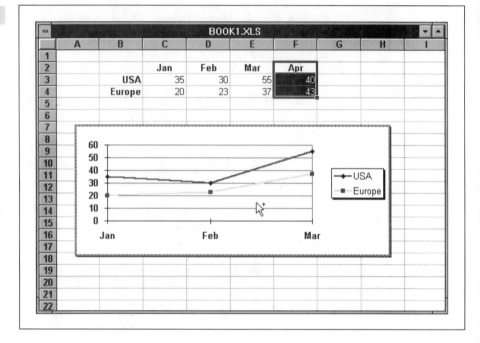

3. Activate the chart:

   • If it is an embedded chart, select it with the mouse.

   • If it is a chart sheet, activate the sheet.

4. Choose Edit ➤ Paste.

Adding Data Using Insert ➤ New Data

The Insert ➤ New Data command is available only when a chart is active. This technique works for both embedded charts and chart sheets.

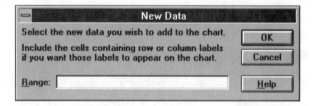

Enter a cell reference, or use the mouse to point-and-click the range, then click OK.

TIP

A chart can include data that comes from more than one worksheet, and even from more than one workbook.

Deleting Data from a Chart

A data series can be deleted directly from a chart, and there is no impact on the underlying worksheet data.

1. Activate the chart.

2. Select the series you want to delete by clicking a data marker within the series.

3. Choose Edit ➤ Clear ➤ Series (or press the Delete key).

Changing a Data Series

Suppose that after you create a chart, you want to change the source for one of the data series. In Figure 13.12, the budget and Y-T-D columns (C and D) are charted. Revised budget figures have been entered into column F, and the budget data series needs to point to the revised budget instead of the original budget.

1. Activate the chart.

2. Select the budget data series by single-clicking any data point in the series—in Figure 13.13 the budget data series is selected.

TIP

The first time you click a data point, the entire data series is selected. If you click the data point a second time, just the single point is selected.

FIGURE 13.12

The budget data series points to C3:C4. It needs to be changed to F3:F4.

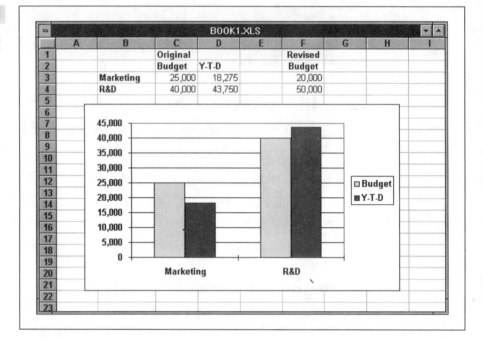

FIGURE 13.13

The S1 on the left part of the formula bar indicates that data series one is selected.

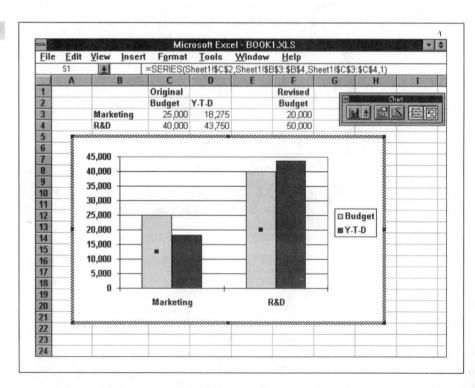

3. Choose Format ➤ Selected Series, then select the Name and Values tab (Figure 13.14).

4. Change the Y Values to: **=Sheet1!$F$3:$F$4** (you can type this in, or you can point-and-click on the worksheet to fill it in).

5. Click OK.

Changing Data Orientation

Suppose you want to change the orientation of the chart in Figure 13.11 so that the months are data series (on the legend) and the regions are categories (on the horizontal axis). The ChartWizard makes it easy to change the data orientation:

1. Activate the chart and click the ChartWizard tool.

FIGURE 13.14

The Name and Values tab in the Format Data Series dialog box

CHARTING BASICS

2. Click Next on the Step 1 of 2 dialog box.

3. In the Step 2 of 2 dialog box, use the *Data Series In* options to specify columns instead of rows.

Charting Noncontiguous Ranges

On Figure 13.15, suppose you want to chart only the TOTAL rows:

1. Select cells C2:F2.

2. Hold down Ctrl, then select cells C5:F5 and C9:F9.

3. Create the chart with ChartWizard.

Figure 13.15 illustrates charted noncontiguous data ranges.

FIGURE 13.15

Only the two TOTAL rows and labels are included in the chart.

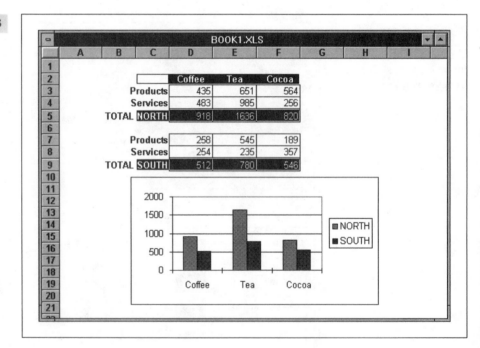

Deleting Charts

Here is how to delete embedded charts and chart sheets:

Embedded Charts

Deleting an embedded chart from the worksheet is the same as deleting any other object: Select the chart object and press Delete. (Or right-click the chart and choose the Clear command from the shortcut menu.)

Chart Sheets

Deleting a chart sheet is just like deleting any other sheet in a workbook: Activate the sheet, and choose Edit ➤ Delete Sheet. (Or right-click the sheet tab and choose the Delete command from the shortcut menu.)

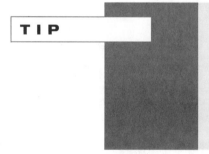

T I P

If you want to print a worksheet that contains an embedded chart, but don't want to include the chart in the printout, you need not delete the chart. Instead, select the chart and choose the Format Object command, select the Properties tab, and uncheck the *Print Object* setting. (See Chapter 12 to learn more about object properties.)

Formatting Charts

Formatting charts is not difficult. The topic seems complex only because there are so many different elements of a chart, each with unique formatting properties, as identified in Figure 13.16.

FIGURE 13.16

Chart elements

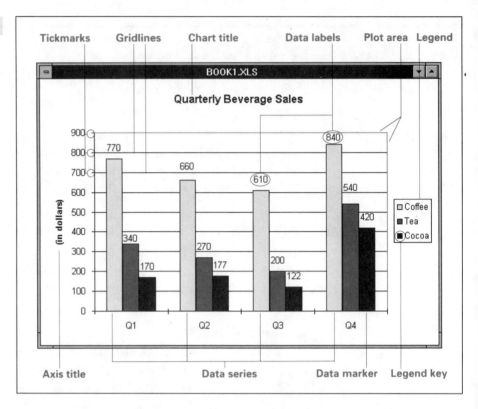

There are certain rules and procedures that apply regardless of which chart element you are formatting:

- The chart must be active in order to format it. Activate embedded charts by double-clicking the chart; activate chart sheets by clicking the sheet tab.

- Double-click the chart element you want to format (or you can right-click the chart element, and select the format command from the shortcut menu). The name of the selected element displays in the Name box on the left part of the formula bar.

Sometimes it is hard to select the right chart element. The element you want to select may not be visible, or another element may overlap it. A sure way to select an elusive chart element is to select any element, then use the left or right arrow keys to cycle through all of the elements.

To delete a chart element, select the element and press Delete (or choose Clear from the shortcut menu).

Using Formatting Tools on Chart Elements

Most of the tools on the Formatting toolbar can be used to format chart elements. Follow these steps to format axis text to bold:

1. Display the Formatting toolbar (use the View ➤ Toolbars command).

2. Activate the chart.

3. Select an axis.

 4. Click the Bold tool.

Formatting an Embedded Chart Object

You just read about formatting the elements inside a chart. Embedded charts are just like other graphic objects, and the *chart object* itself can be formatted (as opposed to the elements inside the chart). In fact, the formatting options are identical to a rectangle. (See Chapter 12.) Formatting the *chart object* has nothing to do with formatting the chart elements that live inside the chart.

Think of an embedded chart object as a boring box full of interesting stuff. Formatting the chart object makes the box a little bit more interesting, but has no bearing on the interesting stuff inside the box.

To format an embedded chart, select it and choose Format ➤ Object. (Remember, *selecting* is just one click, whereas *activating* requires a double-click.)

Figure 13.17 shows several embedded charts with different formatting.

TIP

Embedded charts with no fill and no border are most effective on a worksheet with no gridlines.

FIGURE 13.17

The only difference between these embedded charts is the formatting of the chart object.

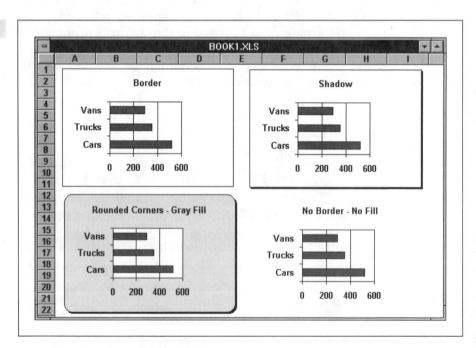

Shortcut Menus

Many of the elements within a chart have shortcut menus providing context-sensitive commands. To use a shortcut menu, right-click on the chart element and choose a command. Here is a list of the elements within an active chart that can be right-clicked to display a shortcut menu:

Chart	Plot Area	Axis
Legend	Legend Entry	Legend Key
Data Series	Data Marker	Gridlines
Chart Title	Axis Title	Data Label
Trendline	Error Bars	Droplines
Series Lines	High-Low lines	Up-Down bars
Walls (3-D)	Floor (3-D)	Corner (3-D)

Drawing inside a Chart

In Chapter 12 you learned how to draw objects on a worksheet. Similarly, you can draw objects *inside* a chart. The procedure is the same as when you draw on a worksheet, except the chart must be active:

1. Display the Drawing toolbar.
2. Activate the chart.
3. Click the drawing tools, and draw on the chart.

The objects that you draw in a chart live inside the chart. The chart must be activated to move, resize, or format the objects. The chart in Figure 13.18 includes a text box and an arrow.

FIGURE 13.18

A text box and an arrow are drawn on the chart.

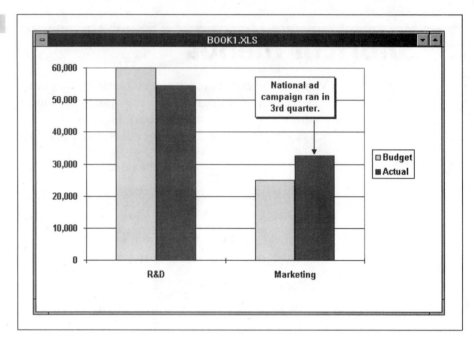

Charting Exercise

In this exercise you will apply many of the skills learned in this chapter to create and format a chart.

Step 1. Enter Data and Create a Chart

Enter the data in Figure 13.19 on a new worksheet, and use the ChartWizard to create a chart using default formatting (click Finish in the ChartWizard Step 1 dialog box).

Step 2. Change the Colors of the Data Series

1. Right-click on one of the markers (notice that the whole series is selected, and a shortcut menu is displayed).

2. Choose the Format Series command, then select the Patterns tab.

3. Select a different color from the color palette, and click OK.

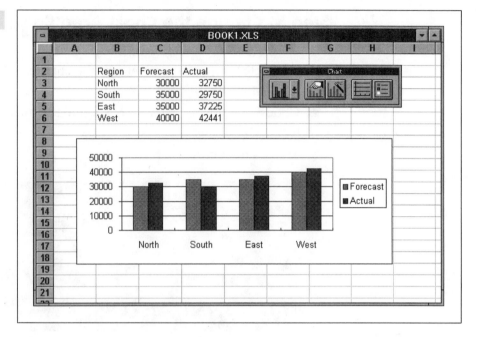

4. Repeat the process to change the color of the other series.

TIP

The Color tool on the Formatting toolbar can be used to color chart elements.

Step 3. Change the Forecast Series Chart Type from Column to Area

1. Right-click on one of the Forecast series markers.

2. Choose the Chart Type command, then select Area and click OK.

Step 4. Remove the Plot Area Color

1. Right-click on the plot area.

2. Choose Format ➤ Plot Area, then select the Patterns tab.

3. Select *Area—None,* then click OK.

Step 5. Change the Chart Area Color to Dark Grey

1. Right-click near the perimeter of the chart to select the Chart area and display the shortcut menu.

2. Choose the Format Chart Area command, then select the Patterns tab.

3. Select a dark grey color, then click OK.

Step 6. Change Axis Text to Bold and White

1. Right-click one axis and choose the Format Axis command.

2. Select the Font tab.

3. Select settings for bold and white, and click OK.

4. Select the other axis and choose Edit ➤ Repeat.

Step 7. Format Numbers on the Y-Axis to Display in Thousands

1. Right-click the Y-axis and choose the Format Axis command.

2. Select the Number tab, and type **#,###,** in the Code edit box (be sure to type both commas). See Chapter 5 to learn more about custom number formats.

3. Leave the Format Axis dialog box displayed for the next procedure.

Step 8. Change Scale on the Y-Axis to Reduce Gridline Clutter

1. Select the Scale tab.

2. Type **10000** in the *Major Unit* edit box.

3. Click OK to close the Format Axis dialog box.

NOTE   Depending on how large you drew the chart, the default major unit may already be 10,000.

Step 9. Format the Legend

1. Right-click the legend and choose the Format Legend command.

2. Select the Patterns tab, and select a light grey color and the border *Shadow* setting.

3. Select the Font tab and choose bold. Click OK to close the dialog box.

Step 10. Add and Format a Chart Title

1. Choose Insert ➤ Titles, and check the *Chart Title* setting.

2. Double-click the title text to select it, then type **Sales**. Press Esc to deselect the title text.

3. Right-click the new title and choose the Format Chart Title command.

4. Format the title color, border, and text to match the legend.

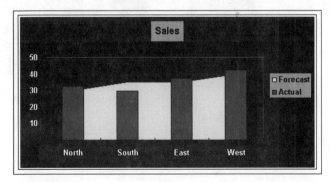

Step 11. Reshape the Legend and Plot Area to Reduce Empty Space

1. Move the chart title over to the left side of the plot area, and move the legend to the top of the chart.

2. Reshape the legend (drag handles) to be wide and shallow, with the legend entries side-by-side.

3. Select the plot area. Drag the right-side handle to the right side of the chart, to fill in the empty space.

Step 12. Apply a Shadowed Border to the Chart

1. Click a worksheet cell to deactivate the chart.

2. Right-click the chart and choose the Format Object command.

3. Select the Patterns tab. Select a fill color for the chart object that is the same as you chose for the chart area.

4. Select a light grey, medium-weight border, and check the *Shadow* and *Round Corners* settings.

Now, turn off the gridlines on the worksheet, and the chart should look something like this:

CHAPTER

14

Advanced Charting

f a s t TRACK

To change the 3-D view   **404**

Click on a corner of the 3-D chart, and drag the corner to rotate the view (hold down Ctrl while dragging to display the marker outlines).

To add drop lines, series lines, high-low lines and up-down bars   **409**

1. Right-click the series you want to add lines or bars to, and choose the Format Group command.

2. Select the Options tab, and select the options you want to apply.

To separate pie slices   **412**

- To separate all slices, select the entire pie and drag a slice away from the center.

- To separate a single slice, select just the marker and drag it away from the center.

- To rejoin separated slices, drag a slice into the center of the pie.

To create a picture chart   **420**

1. Copy a picture.

2. Select the series to be replaced by pictures.

3. Choose Edit ➤ Paste.

To chart data dynamically   **429**

A dynamic chart is created from cells that contain formulas. Those formulas point dynamically to different sets of data, based on user input.

IN the previous chapter we covered the basics of working with charts. Once you have mastered the basics, this chapter will provide you with the advanced skills needed to create and format charts that are not of the everyday variety:

- *creating custom AutoFormats, and changing the default chart*
- *creating combination charts*
- *forecasting with trendlines*
- *creating picture charts*
- *the most important advanced skill: charting data dynamically*
- *advanced tips and tricks*

Custom AutoFormats Can Save Time and Create Consistency

If you often create charts with similar formatting, you can save a lot of time by creating one or more custom AutoFormats. In addition to time savings, AutoFormats can help you create a consistent, professional look for reports and presentations.

Suppose that you frequently chart two types of data using the same chart type, with the same colors, fonts, and other formatting—for example:

- comparing budgeted expense versus actual expense
- comparing sales to sales forecasts

One custom AutoFormat can be used for both of these charts. Here are the basic steps for creating a custom AutoFormat:

1. Create a chart (embedded chart or chart sheet)—apply all formatting such as fonts, gridlines, color, legend, etc.

2. Activate the chart, and choose Format ➤ AutoFormat.

3. Select the *User-Defined* option, then click the Customize button.

4. Click the Add button.

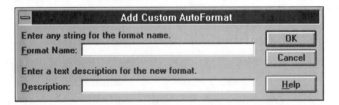

5. Type a name for the custom AutoFormat (and a brief identifying description, if desired), then click OK.

6. Close the User-Defined AutoFormats dialog box.

Applying a Custom AutoFormat

Once you have created a custom AutoFormat, follow these steps to apply it:

1. Create a new chart using default formats.

2. Select and activate the chart.

3. Choose the AutoFormat command.

4. Click *User-Defined*.

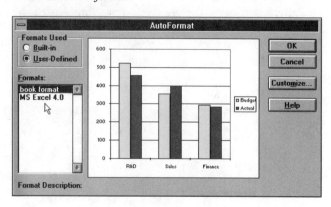

5. Select the custom AutoFormat from the *Formats* list—the Auto-Format is previewed in the dialog box—click OK.

The chart in Figure 14.1 was built, formatted, and then custom AutoFormatted using this chart as the basis.

This AutoFormat can be applied to charts that are not identical to the original chart, as shown in Figures 14.2 and 14.3.

FIGURE 14.1

The title and legend have shadows, and are positioned to allow a large plot area. The fonts are bold. The colors are customized.

FIGURE 14.2

The AutoFormat is applicable even when there are more (or fewer) data series.

FIGURE 14.3

The AutoFormat is now applied to Forecast/Sales instead of Budget/Actual.

How to Change the Default Chart

Once you have created one or more custom AutoFormats, it is easy to configure Excel to use one of them as your default chart. Just follow these steps:

1. Choose Tools ➤ Options, then select the Chart tab (Figure 14.4).

2. Select your custom AutoFormat from the *Default Chart Format* drop-down list.

3. Alternatively, if a chart is active, you can click the *Use the Current Chart* button to use the active chart as the default chart.

To reset the default chart back to the original default, select *(Built-in)* from the list of default chart formats.

FIGURE 14.4

The settings inside the Active Chart group, and the Use Current Chart button, are available only when a chart is active.

Other Chart Options

The Active Chart settings, pictured in Figure 14.4, are also important to understand:

SETTING	FUNCTION
Not Plotted	A gap is left in the chart when a plotted cell is blank.
Zero	Blank cells are treated as zero value.
Interpolated	Fills in lines by interpolating a value.
Plot Visible Cells Only	Only visible cells are plotted—hidden cells are ignored (particularly useful in conjunction with outlining).
Chart Sizes with Window	This setting pertains to chart sheets—when checked, the chart automatically sizes according to size of the window (same as the View ➤ Sized with Window command).

Creating Combination Charts

Suppose you have charted actual and projected sales for a period. A combination chart may emphasize the relationship between the two data series better than a single chart type, as illustrated in Figure 14.5.

Follow these steps to create a combination chart:

1. Activate the chart and select the data series that you want to change.

2. Choose Format ➤ Chart Type and select a type from the Chart Type dialog box.

ADVANCED CHARTING

FIGURE 14.5

The combination chart on the right combines a column chart and line chart.

Unlike previous versions, Excel 5 is not limited to two chart types in a combo chart—as you can see in Figure 14.6.

More facts about combination charts:

- 3-D charts cannot be combined.

FIGURE 14.6

Combination charts are particularly effective when printed on a black-and-white printer, where it can be difficult to distinguish gray scales.

- You can create any combination of area, column, line, and scatter charts.

- You can include bar, pie, doughnut, or radar types in a combo chart, but only one series can be formatted using these types.

Working with 3-D Charts

3-D charts are a mixed blessing. They are visually appealing, and sometimes allow complex data to be presented in a way that is easier to absorb than a 2-D chart. On the other hand, they present certain problems. For instance, a data series in a 3-D column chart might obscure another data series. But used judiciously, 3-D charts can enhance your reports and presentations.

Visual Appeal

Some 3-D chart types and formats are essentially the same as their 2-D counterparts. The benefit is visual appeal, as illustrated in Figure 14.7.

Practical Application

The benefits of 3-D charts are not limited to aesthetics. The 3-D column chart provides a result that would be difficult to achieve using 2-D.

Viewing a 3-D Chart from Different Angles

For some 3-D chart formats, such as the column chart in Figure 14.8, it is possible for a data series to obscure another data series. When a 3-D chart is active, you can choose Format ➤ 3-D View to change the view angle.

FIGURE 14.8

Terminology for manipulating 3-D column charts

As you click the elevation, perspective, and spin buttons, the preview box gives you a general idea of how you are viewing the chart.

- Click OK to accept the view.

- Click Close to cancel the view changes.

- Click Apply to apply the view settings to the chart, but leave the dialog box displayed for more changes.

- Click Default to go back to the default 3-D view.

Another way to change the 3-D view is by direct manipulation of the chart using the mouse. Follow these steps:

1. Activate the chart—select the corners by clicking any corner of the chart.

2. Click a corner again and hold down the mouse button—the mouse becomes a crosshair.

3. Drag the corner (hold down Ctrl while dragging the corner if you want to display outlines of the data markers while changing the view, as pictured in Figure 14.9).

FIGURE 14.9

Holding down Ctrl displays the marker outlines while dragging a corner.

Create and Format a 3-D Chart

In this exercise, you will create and format a 3-D column chart.

1. Enter Data and Create a Chart

1. Enter the following on a new worksheet:

	A	B	C	D	E	F
1						
2		Region	Hardware	Software	Services	
3		North	654	352	245	
4		South	871	325	235	
5		Central	322	212	121	
6						
7						
8						
9						

BOOK1.XLS

2. Choose Insert ➤ Chart ➤ As New Sheet to create a chart sheet—choose these options in the ChartWizard:

   - Select the 3-D column chart in Step 2.
   - Select format #6 in Step 3.
   - Select no legend in Step 5.

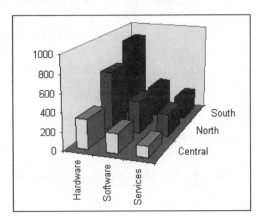

2. Change the Floor Color

1. Double-click the floor (or right-click the floor and choose Format Floor from the shortcut menu).

2. Choose a light gray color from the Format Floor dialog box.

TIP You can change the color of any chart element using the Color tool palette from the Formatting toolbar, and text color can be changed using the Font Color tool palette.

3. Change the Size and Spacing of Columns

1. Choose the Format 3-D Column Group command, then select the Options tab.

2. Change the *Gap Depth* setting to 280.

3. Change the *Chart Depth* setting to 300.

4. Change the *Gap Width* setting to 350.

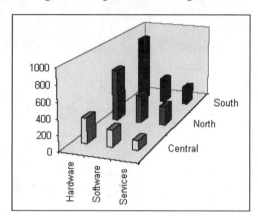

Special Formatting

This section will explain how to add special lines, such as droplines and up-down bars, and how to separate pie wedges.

Adding Lines and Bars

You can add droplines, series lines, high-low lines, and up-down bars to some charts. They are all added the same way:

1. Select the chart, plot area, or series.

2. Choose the Format Group command (this will display as Format ➤ Line Group in a line chart, Format ➤ Area Group in an area chart, etc.).

3. Select the Options tab.

4. Check the setting for *Drop Lines, Series Lines, High-Low Lines,* or *Up-Down Bars.*

Droplines

Droplines are vertical lines that emphasize the location of the data point on the X-axis. They are applicable to area and line charts only.

Series Lines

Series lines connect the series in stacked bar and column charts. They highlight the amount of value change between data points.

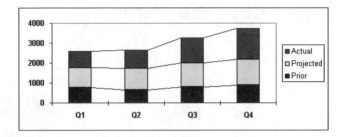

High-Low Lines

High-low lines emphasize the difference between the high and low data points within each category. They can be applied to line charts only, and are particularly useful on stock market charts.

Up-Down Bars

Up-down bars highlight the performance of one data series relative to another data series. Suppose you have charted forecast vs. actual sales over several periods. In periods where actual exceeds forecast, the up-down bars display the variance in one color. When actual is less than forecast, the up-down bars display the variance in another color. Up-down bars can be placed only on line charts with at least two series.

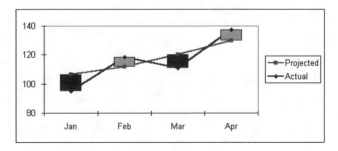

Separating Pie Slices

Slices of pie charts can be separated from the rest of the pie for emphasis. A single slice can be separated, or all of the slices can be separated.

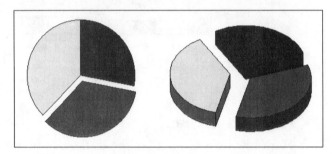

- To separate all of the slices, select the series (single-click any slice) and drag it away from the center of the pie.

- To separate only one slice, select the slice (single-click the slice, then single-click it again) and drag it away from the center of the pie.

- To join separated slices, drag the slice(s) back to the center of the pie.

Changing Worksheet Values by Manipulating the Chart

Some charts let you change underlying worksheet data by manipulating the chart with the mouse. This is a useful technique when doing what-if analysis. Only 2-D bar, 2-D column, and 2-D line charts allow direct manipulation of data markers. Try the following exercise:

1. Enter the following on a worksheet, then create a 2-D column chart:

	A	B	C	D	E
1					
2		Region	Actual	Forecast	
3		North	456	346	
4		South	562	854	
5		East	726	892	
6		West	851	238	
7					
8					

2. Select the **North Actual** marker by single-clicking it twice (not a double-click).

3. Drag the handle on top of the marker up or down (Figure 14.10), and notice that the value in cell C3 changes.

FIGURE 14.10

While dragging the marker, the mouse pointer becomes an up-down arrow. The underlying cell changes as soon as you release the mouse button.

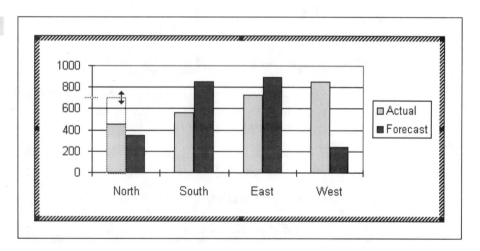

What If the Chart Is Based on a Cell Containing a Formula?

If you directly manipulate a data marker that points to a cell containing a formula, something different happens. Excel will not change the formula.

Rather, it changes one of the cells that the formula depends on. The Goal Seek dialog box is displayed, allowing you to specify which cell should be changed.

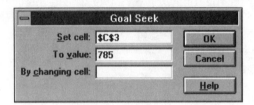

You are required to enter a cell reference that the charted cell depends on. (See Chapter 23 to learn more about Goal Seek.)

Changing the Way Data Is Plotted

Once you have created a chart, there are several ways to change how the data is plotted.

Reversing the Plot Order

There are two common reasons for reversing the plot order for an axis: You may want to look at the data differently, or you may have created the chart incorrectly in the first place.

In Figure 14.11, the data in B3:C7 is sorted by sales in descending order. Yet the bar chart goes from small to large.

Follow these steps to reverse the plot order:

Activate the chart.

FIGURE 14.11

An instance of the
data sheet and bar
chart being oriented
in reverse order

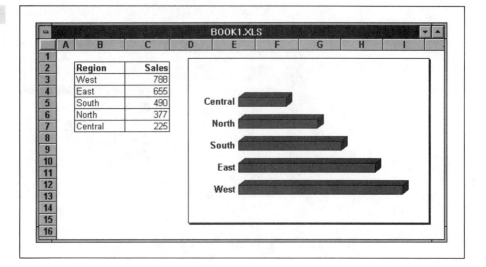

2. Select the axis to reverse, and choose Format ➤ Axis—select the
   Scale tab.

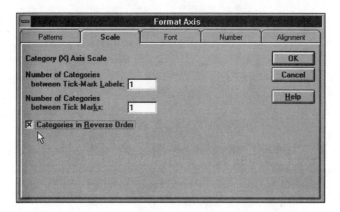

3. Check the *Categories in Reverse Order* setting, then click OK.

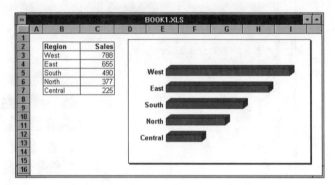

Changing the Series Order

Suppose you have created a column chart with a data series for Y-T-D sales, and a data series for prior year sales.

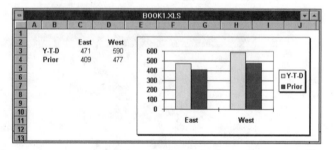

It might make more sense to place Prior to the left of Y-T-D. Follow these steps:

1. Activate the chart.

2. Choose the last command on the Format menu (the command will change based on the type of chart, e.g., Format ➤ Pie Group or Format ➤ Column Group)—select the Series Order tab.

3. Select a series in the *Series Order* box, then click Move Up or Move Down to rearrange the order of the series, then click OK.

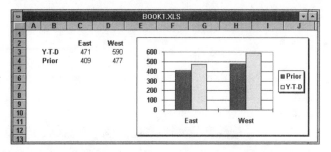

Using a Secondary Axis to Display Two Value Scales

Suppose you want to chart two series with different value scales on the same chart. For example, one chart needs to show average home sales price and number of homes sold. The average sales price will be over $100,000, whereas the number of homes sold for a given period will be less than 100. Figure 14.12 shows an example of this.

To create a new chart with a secondary axis using the ChartWizard:

1. Select a combination chart in ChartWizard Step 2.

FIGURE 14.12

A secondary axis typically requires a combination chart in order to create a meaningful result.

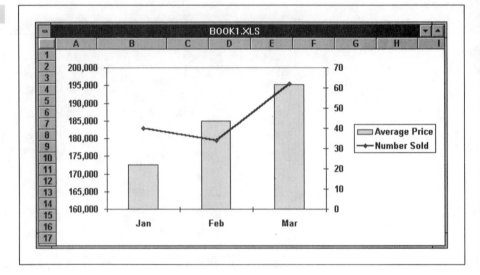

2. Select a format in ChartWizard Step 3 that includes a secondary axis.

To add a secondary axis to an existing chart:

1. Activate the chart.

2. Select the data series that is being placed on a secondary axis.

3. Choose Format ➤ Selected Series, then select the Axis tab.

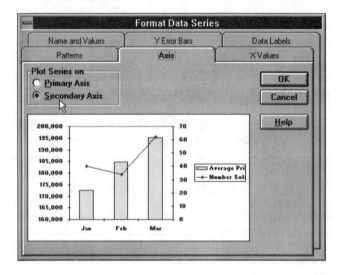

4. Select the *Secondary Axis* option, then click OK.

Charting Multi-Level Categories

You can get more useful information onto a single chart with Excel 5's new multi-level category capability. Suppose you want to chart data on sales of the same three products in four different regions of the country.

	A	B	C	D	E	F
1						
2		Sex		East	West	
3		Men	Tennis	402	744	
4			Running	544	721	
5			Hiking	350	412	
6		Women	Tennis	355	564	
7			Running	346	449	
8			Hiking	281	366	
9						
10						

BOOK1.XLS

If all of the category labels (columns B and C) are included in the charted range, Excel creates multi-level category labels by default.

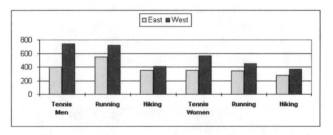

If you want to use only the first column (column B) as category labels, select the chart and click ChartWizard. On the Step 2 dialog box, change the *Category (X) Axis Labels* setting to *Use First 1 Column*.

Special Types of Charts

In this section, you will learn about picture charts, trend lines, error bars, and surface charts.

Creating Picture Charts

You can replace the normal data markers used in various 2-D charts with pictures that are imported from a graphics program, or drawn with Excel's built-in drawing tools. The result can be very appealing when used in reports and presentations (see Figure 14.13).

FIGURE 14.13

This picture was pasted into the chart from the Microsoft Powerpoint clip-art library.

The procedure for using pictures in charts is simple. Follow these steps to use a picture in an existing chart:

1. Copy a picture to the Clipboard:

    - Copy a graphic from another application.
    - Create a picture using Excel's drawing tools, then select it and choose Edit ➤ Copy.

2. Activate the chart.

3. Select the data series (or individual data point) that you want to replace with a picture.

4. Choose Edit ➤ Paste.

Formatting Picture Markers

There are formatting styles for picture markers. Select the marker, and choose Format ➤ Selected Series (or if a single point, Format ➤ Selected Point). Then click the Patterns tab.

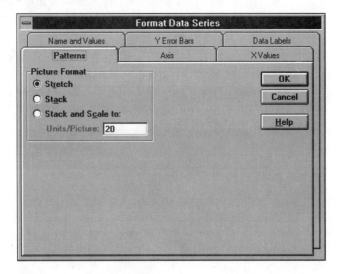

The picture in Figure 14.13 is stretched. The Stack option causes the picture to be stacked to the appropriate height:

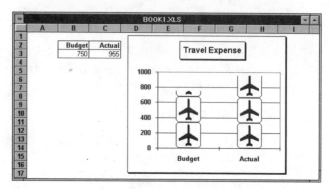

The Stack and Scale option lets you specify the size of the picture, in the same unit of measure as the chart axis.

More Facts about Picture Markers

- More than one picture can be used in a chart (for example, a chart showing statistics for USA, Mexico, and Canada could use the flag of each nation).

- To remove picture formats from a series, select the series and choose Edit ➤ Clear ➤ Formats—don't accidentally delete the entire data series by using the Edit Clear command on the short-cut menu.

- Charts with pictures can be saved as custom AutoFormats.

Using Trendlines

In previous versions of Excel, if you wanted to plot a trend, the trend had to be calculated on the worksheet. Now, a chart is able to examine a set of data, and plot a trendline based on that data—without adding formulas to the worksheet to calculate the trend. Here are some potential applications:

- Forecast sales for the next six months based on the previous 18 months.

- A chemical analysis based on a standard curve can be validated with a linear regression.

- Chart the half-life of a radioactive compound into the future.

- Smooth out the daily fluctuations in stock prices to see performance trends more clearly.

Trendlines can extrapolate data backwards as well as forwards, and can be based on five different regression equations or on a moving average. Using a moving average, each average is calculated from the specified number of preceding data points.

Trendlines can be added to area, column, line, bar, and scatter charts, and are formatted and deleted just like other chart elements. They cannot be added to 3-D charts. Multiple trendlines can be added to the same data series.

Adding a Trendline to a Data Series

Here are the steps to add a trendline to a data series:

1. Activate the chart.

2. Select the series you want to add the trendline to, then choose Insert ➤ Trendline.

3. Select the Type tab, and choose the type of trend you want to chart.

- For polynomial regression, specify the highest power for the independent variable in the *Order* edit box (must be an integer between 2 and 6).

- For a moving average, specify the number of periods the moving average is based on in the *Period* edit box.

4. Use the Options tab to name the trendline, and set the other options described in Table 14.1.

Table 14.1 explains the options available for applying trendlines.

TABLE 14.1: Trendline Options

SETTING	FUNCTION
Trendline Name	Displays in legend
Forecast	Selects number of periods forward and backward for trend forecast
Display Equation on Chart	Displays regression equation (can be formatted, moved)
Display R-squared Value on Chart	Displays R-squared value (can be formatted, moved)
Set Intercept	Changes Y-intercept value

Using Error Bars

Error bars are used to display a degree of uncertainty (a plus/minus factor) surrounding a given data series, as shown in Figure 14.14. Error bars can be added to these 2-D chart types: line, column, area, bar, and scatter charts. They cannot be used on 3-D charts. In scatter charts, error bars can be added to both axes. If the series values change, the error bars will be automatically adjusted.

FIGURE 14.14

This shows the predicted rate of return for three portfolios, and uses error bars to plot one standard deviation.

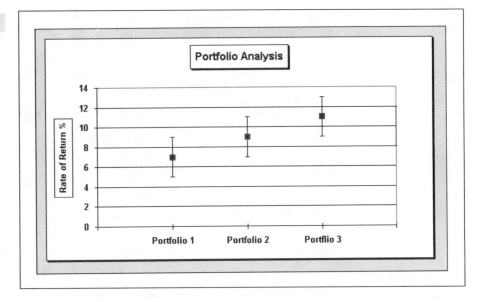

Here are the steps to add an error bar to a data series:

1. Activate the chart and select the data series that you want to add error bars to.

2. Choose Insert ➤ Error Bars.

Table 14.2 explains the options available for applying error bars.

TABLE 14.2: Error Bars Options

SETTING	FUNCTION
Display	Error bar can display above and/or below the data point.
Fixed Value	Constant value used to plot the error bar.
Percent	Error bar is based on percentage calculated from each data point.
Standard Deviation	Enter the number of standard deviations from the data points.
Standard Error	The standard error of the plotted values is displayed as the error amount.
Custom	A worksheet range containing the same number of values as there are data points in the series.

Using Surface Charts

A surface chart is a graph that shows one variable as a function of two other variables. Surface charts are often used for scientific data, but are also applicable for certain business requirements.

For a surface chart to make sense, the two variables need to represent continuous data. For instance, an axis may represent temperature, a continuous measurement, in 10-degree increments—there are temperatures that lie between the 10-degree increments. But *product code* would be an illogical variable—it is not a continuous measurement.

Case Study

The following case study will use a surface chart to help a company establish a retail price for a new product, and establish a marketing budget.

- The company is in the business of making electronic toys—a new product is being introduced, with a retail price between $20 and $40.

- A marketing budget must be established between $500,000 and $2,500,000.

- Historical sales and profit data have been gathered for similar products where price and marketing expenditures were within the above parameters (see Figure 14.15).

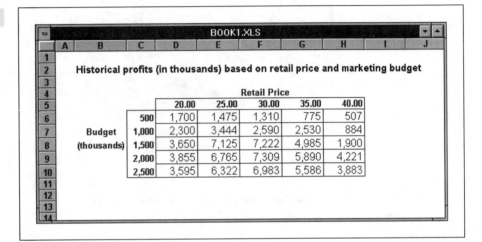

		BOOK1.XLS							
	A	B	C	D	E	F	G	H	I	J

Historical profits (in thousands) based on retail price and marketing budget

		Retail Price				
		20.00	25.00	30.00	35.00	40.00
	500	1,700	1,475	1,310	775	507
Budget	1,000	2,300	3,444	2,590	2,530	884
(thousands)	1,500	3,650	7,125	7,222	4,985	1,900
	2,000	3,855	6,765	7,309	5,890	4,221
	2,500	3,595	6,322	6,983	5,586	3,883

- The historical data will be analyzed to determine a retail price and marketing budget most likely to yield maximum profitability (since marketing expenditures reduce profit, a point of diminishing returns must be determined).

One horizontal axis of the chart will represent list price. The second horizontal axis will represent marketing budget. The two axes define a horizontal plane equivalent to a flat map. To create a surface chart based on the data in Figure 14.15:

1. Select cells C5:H10.

2. Use the ChartWizard—specify 3-D Surface at Step 2, then click Finish. The result is shown in Figure 14.16.

The contour reveals that a product priced in the $25 to $30 range, with a marketing budget of $1.5 to $2 million, is apt to produce the greatest profitability. As might be expected, a forty-dollar product with a marketing budget under one million is apt to fare poorly.

Historical profitability based on similar products.

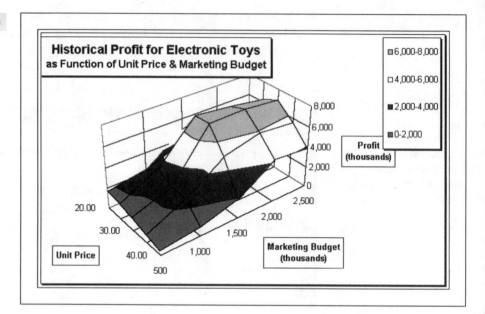

Historical Profit for Electronic Toys
as Function of Unit Price & Marketing Budget

- 6,000-8,000
- 4,000-6,000
- 2,000-4,000
- 0-2,000

Profit (thousands)

8,000
6,000
4,000
2,000
0

2,500
2,000
1,500
1,000
500

20.00
30.00
40.00

Unit Price

Marketing Budget (thousands)

TIP

A printed report of a 3-D surface chart might actually include two or three different charts based on the same data. Each chart could be set up from a different angle so that all areas of the contour can be viewed.

Protecting a Chart

Here are the procedures (and implications) for protecting charts:

Embedded Charts

Protecting an embedded chart is exactly the same as protecting any graphic object (see Chapter 12). Select the chart object, choose Format ➤ Object, select the Protection tab, and check the *Locked* setting. The lock does not take effect until the worksheet containing the chart is protected.

Chart Sheets

Protecting a chart sheet is exactly the same as protecting a worksheet (see Chapter 11). Activate the sheet, and choose Tools ➤ Protection ➤ Protect Sheet.

Protecting a chart prevents users from deleting, resizing, or otherwise manipulating the chart.

Charting Data Dynamically

In a spreadsheet environment, there are often many sets of data with similar structures. For example, you may store budgeting data on a division, department, or cost-center level. The data may be stored in one workbook or many workbooks. But there is always a *budget* column and an *actual* column.

One of the most common design problems is one of chart proliferation. Different charts are created for the division budget, department budget, cost-center budget, etc. This causes a problem in terms of maintenance and consistency. When your organization decides that all budget charts need to be modified to show original and revised budgets, you have a maintenance problem on your hands if there are dozens of similar charts floating around.

By applying a variety of Excel skills, you can learn what is arguably the most important charting skill: how to use a single chart on multiple data sets. In other words, dynamically bring data to your chart, as is represented in Figure 14.17, instead of "marrying" a given chart to a particular set of data. This is accomplished in several ways:

- Chart cells containing formulas—user input drives the formulas, causing different data sets to be charted (typically, this will entail the use of functions like INDEX, VLOOKUP, OFFSET, MATCH, SUMIF, and the so-called D functions.)

- Use file links (controlled with the Edit ➤ Links command) to link a workbook to different workbooks (see Chapter 4).

- Use dynamic names, covered in Chapter 8, to point to different data sets based on user input.

FIGURE 14.17

A well-designed
charting model can
dynamically chart
different sets of data.

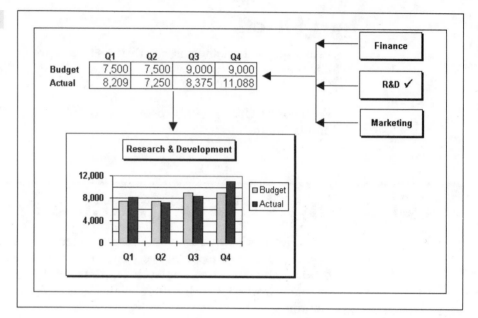

- Create charts based on Pivot Tables (see Chapter 17).

- Use workbook templates and chart templates to create reusable
  models (see Chapter 10).

Tools Not Found on the Built-in Toolbars

There are a number of charting tools that are not on the Charting toolbar.
In order to use these tools, you have to add them to a built-in toolbar, or
create a custom toolbar. (See Chapter 26.)

Most of the tools described in Table 14.3 are AutoFormat shortcuts.
These tools, like the Chart Type tools, let you draw a specific type of chart.

N O T E   Chapter 26, "Advanced Tips and Techniques," includes a section on charting.

TABLE 14.3: Special Charting Tools

TOOLFACE	TOOL	FUNCTION
	Vertical Gridlines	adds/deletes vertical gridlines
	Line/Column Chart AutoFormat	combination line/column chart
	Stacked Column Chart AutoFormat	stacked column chart
	3-D Perspective Column Chart AutoFormat	3-D perspective column chart
	Pie Chart AutoFormat	pie chart, percentage labels
	3-D Pie Chart AutoFormat	3-D pie chart, percentage labels
	Doughnut Chart AutoFormat	doughnut chart, category labels
	Volume/Hi-Lo-Close Chart AutoFormat	combination chart for stock prices

PART FIVE

Database Power

CHAPTER

15

Basics of Internal Databases

fast TRACK

To remove filters　　　　　　　　　　　　　　　　**449**

Choose Data ➤ AutoFilter (to remove the checkmark next to the AutoFilter command).

To total a filtered database　　　　　　　　　　　　**449**

Use the SUBTOTAL function—it ignores rows which are hidden as a result of filtering.

To edit a database using the built-in data form　　**451**

1. Choose Data ➤ Form, and select the desired record.

2. Edit the field values.

3. Click the New button to update the database.

To use a data form to display records matching search criteria　　　　　　　　　　　　　　　　　　**451**

1. Choose Data ➤ Form, and click the criteria button.

2. Enter criteria in the edit box next to the field you want to filter.

AS far as Excel is concerned, there are two distinct types of databases. There are external databases, such as Access, dBASE, Paradox, FoxPro, SQL Server, and Oracle, and there are *internal databases*—databases that reside in worksheets. You will learn how to work with external databases in Chapters 17 and 18. This chapter will show you how to work with internal databases. You will learn:

- *the pros and cons of internal databases*

- *why internal database skills are vital—even if you don't permanently store databases in Excel*

- *how to build an internal database*

- *how to sort data*

- *how to filter a database (i.e., to view a subset of the data based on user-specified criteria)*

Database Skills Are Important for All Users

Many users have been put off by Excel's database features simply because the term *database* implies something complex and hard to learn. This perception was reinforced by the fact that database management in previous versions of Excel actually *was* hard to learn. In Excel 5, database features have been greatly simplified, and provide very powerful functionality for managing and analyzing data.

NOTE The extraordinary level of confusion about databases in general, and Excel databases in particular, prompted Microsoft to practically abandon the term *database* altogether. The Excel manuals and on-line help instead refer extensively to *list management*.

There is another category of users who have avoided internal databases—people who use a "real" database management system (DBMS). An internal Excel database lacks certain features possessed by the simplest DBMS. Knowing this, DBMS aficionados skip over Excel's database features. Just because a range of cells is treated as a database doesn't mean that the worksheet is necessarily the permanent home for the data. Excel is an extraordinary tool for analyzing data stored in a DBMS, and the internal database features play an important role in this process. Here are a few reasons to become familiar with how Excel manages its internal databases:

- Much of Excel's database functionality is easy to learn.

- Most of the database functionality is *important* to learn, even if the problems you are solving are not, on the surface, database management problems.

- Even if your data is stored in an external DBMS, Excel database features can help you dissect, analyze, and report.

- Most tables of data on worksheets can be treated as databases.

Limitations of Spreadsheet Databases

Excel provides outstanding facilities for entering, editing, analyzing, and manipulating data. But there are limitations inherent to all spreadsheet programs that you should be aware of before choosing Excel as the place to store your data:

- A worksheet is limited to 16,384 rows and 256 columns.

- Only one user can have write access to an internal database at a time.

- Enforcing data integrity (for example, by disallowing text in numeric columns) requires custom macros and dialog boxes.

- The entire database must be in memory (unless you are accessing an external database—see Chapter 18).

- Data stored on worksheets tends to consume more disk space than data stored in external databases (a worksheet stores formulas, formatting, graphics, etc.; a DBMS stores raw data).

Remember, even if your data is stored in an external DBMS, Excel is an outstanding tool for analyzing, manipulating, and reporting on external data.

For Users of Earlier Versions of Excel

Excel's database features have been drastically improved. Many of the old commands are missing from the menu system, which may give you the *misconception* that there has been a loss of functionality. Here are some key differences and similarities between Excel 4 and Excel 5:

- Named ranges *Database*, *Criteria*, and *Extract* are no longer required, which is why the SET DATABASE, SET EXTRACT, and SET CRITERIA commands are no longer on the menu.

- Instead of relying on a named range *Database*, Excel automatically detects when the active cell is located within a range of data.

- There is a simplified interface for defining simple criteria and performing extracts (covered in this chapter).

- For complex problems, you can still define criteria and perform extracts the old way; see Chapter 16 to learn the Excel 5 nuances.

- Pivot Tables, covered in Chapter 17, are a dramatic improvement over Excel 4's crosstab facility.

Setting Up a Database

Setting up a database is quite simple. First, it will help if you understand these three terms:

Field	column within a database
Record	row within a database
Field Name	the top row of a database usually contains *field names*; a field name consists of unique text describing the field (there is no need to actually name the cells)

In the example shown in Figure 15.1,

- Cells B2:H2 contain field names.

- There are 10 records (or rows) in the database; B3:H3 is the first record.

- There are 7 fields (columns) in the database.

Field names are not required to use some database features, such as sorting. But to use all database features, you must enter field names. Unlike Excel 4, there are no particular rules for field names; they can contain spaces and special characters.

Setting up a database is extraordinarily simple: enter field names and data onto a worksheet. It is likely that you have already performed this task countless times.

FIGURE 15.1

An internal database consists of fields, field names, and records (or rows).

	A	B	C	D	E	F	G	H
				BOOK1.XLS				
1								
2		Client No	Name	Category	Region	MTD Sales	YTD Sales	Last Year
3		101	Argus Industries	Manufacturing	North	9,569	13,775	14,723
4		102	LEX Software	Services	South	3,527	10,534	12,887
5		103	National Bank	Financial	South	1,472	8,123	10,022
6		104	Kinsman & Nelson	Services	East	3,717	12,374	9,221
7		105	Northwest Investments	Financial	North	3,315	18,656	11,044
8		106	Nica Corporation	Manufacturing	West	6,542	58,229	52,559
9		107	MDC Enterprises	Manufacturing	East	8,167	23,613	25,733
10		108	Wilson & Roth CPA	Services	West	4,026	11,786	9,225
11		109	JK Associates	Financial	South	12,391	71,805	23,490
12		110	T.K. James Inc.	Services	North	3,146	19,104	11,373
13								
14								
15								
16								
17								

NOTE

You may want to create the database pictured in Figure 15.1 so you can follow along; this database is referred to throughout this chapter.

TIP

For rapid data entry into a range of cells, select the range, then use the Tab key to navigate the range. (Use Shift+Tab to move backwards.)

Sorting a Database

Here is the procedure for sorting a database:

1. Select any one cell within the database range.
2. Choose the Data ➤ Sort command.

3. The *Sort By* drop-down displays all fields in the database—choose the field you want to sort by.

4. Use the option buttons to specify ascending or descending order.

5. The two *Then By* inputs are optional; they allow two more sort fields to be specified (up to three total).

6. Excel tries to determine if the database has a header row (field names), and sets the *Header Row* or *No Header Row* setting accordingly. Override this setting if required.

7. Click OK to sort.

CAUTION

If the database has a header row, but you specify no header row, the headings (field names) will be sorted into the database as if the header row was a data record. Excel will make a guess concerning header/no header correctly 99% of the time, causing users not to pay attention to this setting. If you sort incorrectly, the sort can be undone using Edit ➤ Undo.

Assume you want to sort the database pictured in Figure 15.1 by *Category*, and by *YTD Sales* within category from highest to lowest sales:

1. Select a cell inside the database, then choose Data ➤ Sort.

2. Select the **Category** field from the *Sort By* list; choose ascending order.

3. Select **YTD Sales** as the second sort field, and choose descending order.

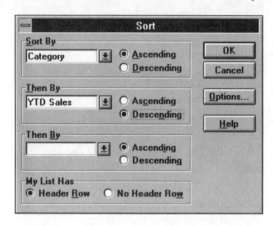

4. Click OK to sort the data as follows:

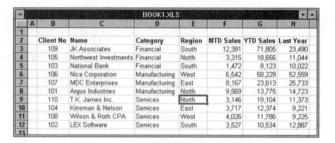

See Chapter 16 to learn how to sort by more than three fields.

More Facts about Sorting

- Sorts are performed according to underlying cell value, not the formatted appearance of the cell.

- Logical value FALSE comes before TRUE in an ascending sort.

- All error values are considered the same.

- Blanks sort last for both ascending *and* descending sorts.

- Avoid text and numbers in the same field (it is generally a bad practice anyway).

Filtering a Database Using AutoFilter

Sometimes you will want to view only database records that meet certain criteria. This is accomplished by *filtering* the database. There are two types of filters:

- *AutoFilters*, covered in this chapter
- *advanced filters*, covered in Chapter 16

Follow these steps to filter your database:

1. Select any cell in the database, then choose the Data ➤ Filter ➤ AutoFilter command—drop-down controls are placed on top of the field names.

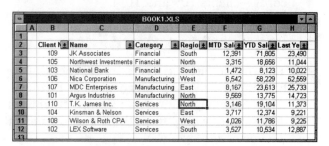

	Client N	Name	Category	Region	MTD Sal	YTD Sal	Last Ye
3	109	JK Associates	Financial	South	12,391	71,805	23,490
4	105	Northwest Investments	Financial	North	3,315	18,656	11,044
5	103	National Bank	Financial	South	1,472	8,123	10,022
6	106	Nica Corporation	Manufacturing	West	6,542	58,229	52,559
7	107	MDC Enterprises	Manufacturing	East	8,167	23,613	25,733
8	101	Argus Industries	Manufacturing	North	9,569	13,775	14,723
9	110	T.K. James Inc.	Services	North	3,146	19,104	11,373
10	104	Kinsman & Nelson	Services	East	3,717	12,374	9,221
11	108	Wilson & Roth CPA	Services	West	4,026	11,786	9,225
12	102	LEX Software	Services	South	3,527	10,534	12,887

2. Click a drop-down control to apply a filter to the field. The contents of a drop-down list are dictated by the contents of the field. For example, the *Category* drop-down will contain each unique data item found in the field, plus four other choices:

- Select one of the categories, such as *Financial*, to display only those records where the category is equal to **Financial**; when the filter is applied, the drop-down control turns blue as an indicator that the filter is in effect (the row numbers also turn blue).
- Select *(All)* to turn off a filter for a given field (remember, you are turning off the filter for the one field only—filters for other fields are left in place).
- Select *(Blanks)* to display only those rows where the field is blank.
- Select *(NonBlanks)* to display only those rows where the field is not blank.
- Select *(Custom...)* to set a custom AutoFilter (covered below).

You can filter more than one field at a time. In this example, if you add a filter for *Region* equals **South**, you will be viewing all records where *Category* equals **Financial** AND *Region* equals **South** (a total of two records—clients 109 and 103).

Setting Custom AutoFilters

The simple filters covered in the previous exercise are based on what a field is *equal* to (i.e., category *equals* financial, region *equals* south). Custom AutoFilters allow relationships other than *equal* to be specified. If you choose *(Custom...)* from the drop-down list, the Custom AutoFilter dialog box is displayed.

- The narrow drop-down lets you specify the relational operator (see Table 15.1).

TABLE 15.1: Custom AutoFilter Operators

OPERATOR	MEANING
=	equal to
>	greater than
<	less than
>=	greater than or equal to
<=	less than or equal to
<>	not equal

- The wide drop-down lets you specify the field value; you can select an item from the list or type in a value (wildcard characters can be included).
- The *And Or* options are used if you want to apply two comparison criteria.
    - Select *And* to display rows that meet both criteria.
    - Select *Or* to display rows that meet either criteria.
- The bottom two (optional) drop-downs are used to specify a second comparison criterion.

Using the database in Figure 15.1, assume that you want to analyze the north and east regions. Within those regions, you want to display only the larger clients—those with YTD sales greater than 15,000.

1. Choose Data ➤ Filter ➤ AutoFilter.
2. Click the *Region* drop-down.
3. Select Custom.

4. From the drop-downs, select **= north,** *or,* **= east** (as pictured below), then click OK.

5. Click the *YTD Sales* drop-down.

6. Select Custom.

7. In the upper drop-downs, select **>** and enter **15000** (as pictured below).

When the filtering exercise is complete, the worksheet will look like this:

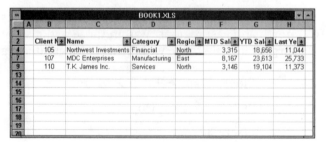

Removing All Filters at Once

If one or more filters are set, use the Data ➤ Filter ➤ AutoFilter command to remove the filter(s). The command is unchecked, the drop-down controls are removed from the worksheet, and all records are displayed.

Totaling Fields of a Filtered Database

Suppose that you want to see column totals for a filtered database. There are three things you need to know about totaling filtered data:

- Use the SUBTOTAL function (covered in Chapter 9); unlike SUM, it ignores rows that are hidden as a result of filtering.

- The AutoSum button, used on a cell directly beneath a database field, will place a SUBTOTAL function in the cell instead of SUM—but only if the database is filtered.

- If you calculate totals by placing SUM formulas on the row directly beneath the database, the Totals row will be treated as a database record—avoid this practice by using the SUBTOTAL function instead (see Chapter 9 to learn about SUBTOTAL).

For a short example of totaling fields of a filtered database, perform the following steps, using the worksheet pictured in Figure 15.1:

1. Filter the database to show region *North* only.

2. Select cells F13:H13.

3. Click the AutoSum button.

The results are shown in Figure 15.2.

TIP

For clarity and aesthetics, you may be tempted to place the word TOTALS in cell C13 or E13. However, this causes Excel to treat row 13 as a database record, and thus hide it when filters are applied. Skip a row, and place the totals on row 14 instead—it will not be treated as a database record.

FIGURE 15.2

Filtered database with
column totals

A	B	C	D	E	F	G	H
			BOOK1.XLS				
1							
2	Client N	Name	Category	Regio	MTD Sal	YTD Sal	Last Ye
4	105	Northwest Investments	Financial	North	3,315	18,656	11,044
8	101	Argus Industries	Manufacturing	North	9,569	13,775	14,723
9	110	T.K. James Inc.	Services	North	3,146	19,104	11,373
13					16,030	51,535	37140
14							
15							
16							
17							
18							
19							
20							

Implications of Working with a Filtered Database

As you apply AutoFilters to a database, Excel is simply hiding the rows that do not match the filter criteria. However, rows that are hidden as a result of filtering are not the same as rows that are hidden using the Format ➤ Row ➤ Hide command. By and large, this is a very good thing. You should be aware of the following points concerning cells hidden as a result of a filter:

- They are unaffected by AutoFills.

- They are unaffected by formatting commands.

- They are not included in newly created charts, as is the case with "manually" hidden cells (though this can be overridden on a per-chart basis using the *Plot Visible Cells Only* setting in the Tools ➤ Options ➤ Chart dialog box).

- They are unaffected by the Clear command.

- They are not copied with the Copy command.

- They are not deleted by the Delete Row command.

- They are unaffected by sorting.

- They are included in SUM functions—and are not included in SUBTOTAL functions.

- They are not printed (compare with manually hidden cells).

Using the Built-in Data Form

Typically, databases are entered and maintained by typing directly onto a worksheet. However, you could use a built-in *data form* instead. This form

- displays one record at a time;
- can be used to add new records and edit existing records;
- lets you view records matching specified criteria.

To display a data form, select a cell inside your database, then choose Data ➤ Form. The field names from the database are used as titles inside the form:

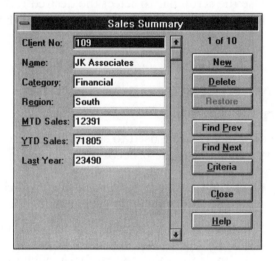

Adding New Records

Follow these steps to add a new record to a database using a data form:

1. Click the New button to clear the form for a new record—*New Record* is displayed in the upper right corner of the dialog box.

2. Fill in the field values.

3. Click the New button to add a record (new records are placed at the bottom of database).

Editing Records

Here is how to edit database records using a data form:

1. Use the scroll bar to select the desired record—the record number is displayed in the upper right corner of the dialog box.

2. Edit the field values.

3. Click the New button to update the database.

Deleting Records

To delete database records with a data form:

1. Use the scroll bar to select the desired record—the record number is displayed in the upper right corner of the dialog box.

2. Click the Delete button.

Displaying Records Matching Search Criteria

The data form can be used to search for records that match criteria that you specify. Here is the procedure:

1. Click the Criteria button—the form will clear and *Criteria* is displayed in the upper right corner of the dialog box.

2. Enter criteria in the edit box next to the field you want to filter:

   - Enter the value to search for, such as **West**.
   - Or, precede the value with relational operator (see Table 15.1), such as **<>West**.
   - You can enter criteria for any number of fields.

3. Click the *Find Prev* or *Find Next* button.

Using the database pictured in Figure 15.1, the following criteria would display every record where region is equal to north, month-to-date sales is not equal to zero, and year-to-date sales is greater than 10000:

To clear the criteria, click the Criteria button, then manually clear the criteria from each edit box, and click the Form button.

More Facts about Data Forms

- Values from calculated fields (cells with formulas) are displayed in the form, but cannot be edited.

- Hidden columns are not displayed.

- As new records are added, the data form will not overwrite data located underneath the database—it will disallow new records from being added.

CHAPTER

16

Getting More Power from Databases

f a s t TRACK

● To use D-functions   479

D-functions perform calculations on a specified column within a specified database, and use a criteria range to determine which records to include in the calculation. All D-functions have the same syntax. For example, the DSUM syntax is DSUM(Database.Range,Field,CriteriaRange).

● To insert subtotals into a database   482

Select a cell within the database range, and choose Data ➤ Subtotals.

● To create friendly-looking databases   484

1. Enter legal field names on the header row of the database.

2. Enter field descriptions on the row(s) above the header row.

3. Hide the first row of the database (the header row).

THE previous chapter covered the basics of internal databases. This chapter will teach you more advanced techniques for working with internal databases:

- *special database sorting techniques*
- *defining criteria ranges*
- *using advanced filters*
- *using the so-called "D functions"—the family of database functions beginning with the letter D*
- *placing embedded totals in a database*

Special Sorting Problems

Chapter 15 explains how to address common sorts using up to 3 fields to sort rows in ascending or descending order. This section covers several other sorting requirements.

Sorting by More Than Three Fields

Consider the database in Figure 16.1.

FIGURE 16.1

Sample database

Client No	Name	Category	Region	Last Call	MTD Sales	YTD Sales	Last Year
107	MDC Enterprises	Mfg	East	1/30/94	8,167	23,613	25,733
104	Kinsman & Nelson	Services	East	2/7/95	3,717	12,374	9,221
110	T.K. James Inc.	Services	North	8/11/94	3,146	19,104	11,373
105	Pacific Investments	Financial	North	12/1/93	3,315	18,656	11,044
101	Argus Industries	Mfg	North	1/10/95	9,569	13,775	14,723
109	JK Associates	Financial	South	3/1/94	12,391	71,805	23,490
102	LEX Software	Services	South	4/23/94	3,527	10,534	12,887
103	National Bank	Financial	South	6/1/94	1,472	8,123	10,022
106	Nica Corporation	Mfg	West	2/25/94	6,542	58,229	52,559
108	Wilson & Roth	Services	West	11/1/93	4,026	11,786	9,225

NOTE

The database in Figure 16.1 is the same database used in Chapter 15, but with the *Last Call* field inserted. You may want to create this database on your system, as it will be referred to throughout this chapter.

Suppose that you want to sort the database using four fields: *Region, Last Call, Category*, and *Name*. Here are two ways to work around the three-field limit of the Data ➤ Sort command:

Method One

Sort the data twice, starting with the least significant fields:

1. Choose Data ➤ Sort.

2. Select *Last Call, Category*, and *Name*.

3. Click OK to sort.

4. Choose Data ➤ Sort.

5. Select *Region* as the first field.

6. Select *(none)* as the second and third fields.

7. Click OK to sort.

TIP

Dates and times, when sorted in ascending order, sort from oldest to newest. Sort order is based on the *underlying cell value*, not the formatted appearance.

Method Two

Create a field that combines other fields:

1. Add a new field in column J using the field name *Region - Last Call*.

2. Place the following formula in cell J3, then fill it down through cell J12:

```
=LEFT(E3&"     ",5)&F3
```

There are five spaces within the quotations. The LEFT function is padding the region field to five characters (assuming a maximum region length of five characters). Padding is only required when a field within a calculated sort field is not the last one, and is variable in length.

3. Choose Data ➤ Sort.

4. Select *Region - Last Call* as the first sort field.

5. Select *Category* and *Name* as the second and third sort fields.

6. Click OK to sort.

Note that with calculated sort fields, you lose the ability to specify ascending or descending order for the individual fields within the calculated field. What if you want to combine Region=ascending with YTD Sales=descending in column K? Use a formula in K3 such as:

```
=LEFT(E3&"     ",5)&TEXT(1000000-H3,"0000000")
```

Sorting Columns Instead of Rows

The columns in the following database are sorted alphabetically by region name. Assume that you want to sort the columns according to total sales in descending order:

	A	B	C	D	E	F	G
1							
2			East	North	South	West	
3		Q1	374	426	568	512	
4		Q2	750	236	682	875	
5		Q3	410	475	797	775	
6		Q4	409	225	450	922	
7		Total	1,943	1,362	2,497	3,084	
8							
9							
10							

BOOK1.XLS

1. Select cells C2:F7 (so as not to sort the row labels with the data).

2. Choose Data ➤ Sort.

3. Click the Options button to display the Sort Options dialog box.

4. Select the *Sort Left to Right* option.

5. Click OK.

6. Sort by *Row 7* (row number on worksheet, not row number within database).

7. Select the *Descending* option.

8. Click OK to sort the database as follows:

	A	B	C	D	E	F	G
			BOOK1.XLS				
1							
2			West	South	East	North	
3		Q1	512	568	374	426	
4		Q2	875	682	750	236	
5		Q3	775	797	410	475	
6		Q4	922	450	409	225	
7		Total	3,084	2,497	1,943	1,362	
8							
9							

T I P

The Sort Options dialog box lets you specify case-sensitive sorts. An ascending case-sensitive sort will go *aAbBcC*, etc.

Using Custom Sort Orders

There are times when you may want to sort data using a sort order that is neither ascending nor descending. For example, your organization may sort regions on printed reports in roughly the order they appear on a map, rather than alphabetically. Or you may want to sort a list of vendors with the most frequently used vendor on top.

On the following worksheet, the months are listed in date sequence.

	A	B	C	D
		BOOK1.XLS		
1				
2			Service	
3		**Month**	**Calls**	
4		January	51	
5		February	78	
6		March	49	
7		April	37	
8		May	34	
9		June	75	
10		July	69	
11		August	45	
12		September	65	
13		October	58	
14		November	63	
15		December	72	
16				

Suppose that your company has a fiscal year that begins October 1 and ends September 30. You can cut and paste to get the data in the right sequence, or you can use a custom list to determine the sort order.

Creating Custom Lists

Follow these steps to create a custom list for an October-through-September fiscal-year sort:

1. Enter the data on a worksheet in the desired sequence.

	A	B	C	D
1				
2		October		
3		November		
4		December		
5		January		
6		February		
7		March		
8		April		
9		May		
10		June		
11		July		
12		August		
13		September		
14				

BOOK1.XLS

2. Select B2:B13.

3. Choose Tools ➤ Options, then select the Custom Lists tab (Figure 16.2).

4. Click the Import button.

5. Click OK.

You only to have to create a custom list once. Since the list is not stored in a workbook, it is available globally.

TIP

Custom lists are also used by Excel's AutoFill feature. See Chapters 7 and 26 to learn more about performing AutoFills.

FIGURE 16.2

The Tools ➤ Options,
Custom Lists tab

Using a Custom List to Drive a Sort

Once you have created a custom list, it is easy to use it to sort data. Follow these steps to sort using the October-September sort order defined in the previous exercise:

1. Select a cell inside the database, then choose Data ➤ Sort.

2. Select *Month* as the Sort By setting.

3. Click the Options button to display the Sort Options dialog box.

4. Use the *First Key Sort Order* drop-down, and select the item reading *October, November, December,* etc.

5. Click OK to close the Sort Options dialog box, then click OK again to sort.

Working with Criteria Ranges

An important construct in advanced database manipulation is the *criteria range*—a range of cells that defines a database filter. Criteria ranges are used in two ways:

- They are used by advanced database filters—to display only those records that meet the criteria.

- They are used by *D functions*, a special category of function that uses a criteria range to determine which database records to use in calculations.

Using a criteria range requires two steps:

1. Define the criteria range.

2. Use the criteria range when performing an advanced filter, or in a D function—the criteria range by itself does nothing.

N O T E

Learning about criteria ranges requires some patience. There is a lot of ground to cover before you will see how to put them to use. In this chapter we will present the basics of criteria ranges, proceed to the topic of computed criteria, and then move on to advanced filters and D functions. Initially, you might want to read just the basics of criteria ranges and then skip ahead to see how they are used in advanced filters before you finish the presentation of criteria ranges.

Parts of a Criteria Range

A criteria range consists of two parts:

- a header row—containing field names that must identically match the database field names

- one or more criteria rows

The following criteria range is used to filter the database in Figure 16.1:

The criteria range in cells B2:C3 means: All records where the *Category* is equal to **Services** AND *YTD Sales* are greater than **15000**. If this criteria range were used to filter the database shown in Figure 16.1, only row 5 would display.

T I P

If you are familiar with Structured Query Language (SQL), then you may recognize that a criteria range is the equivalent of a simple *where* clause.

Parts of the Criteria

Criteria specifications are identical to criteria entered in a data form. There is an optional relational operator, followed by a value. Table 16.1 defines the relational operators that can be used.

TABLE 16.1: Relational Operators

OPERATOR	MEANING
=	equal to
>	greater than
<	less than
>=	greater than or equal to
<=	less than or equal to
<>	not equal

Table 16.2 contains examples of criteria, as they would be entered into the criteria range.

TABLE 16.2: Criteria Examples

CRITERION	MEANING
=East	equal to East
>B	greater than B
<Jones	less than Jones
>=West	greater than or equal to West
<=West	less than or equal to West
<>West	not equal to West
Smith	starts with Smith (Smith, Smithe, Smithsonian)
*Smith	ends with Smith (Jane Smith, John Smith, Smith)
<>*Smith	every value that does not end with Smith
car	every value containing car (Carson, scare, car)
?ON	finds Ron and Jon, but not Stone
=10	equal to 10
>100	greater than 100
<100	less than 100
>=25	greater than or equal to 25
<=25	less than or equal to 25
<>0	not equal to zero
100	equal to 100

N O T E The criteria examples in Table 16.2 that begin with an equal sign are not formulas; they are text constants beginning with an equal sign. However, when the first character entered into a cell is an equal sign, Excel assumes the entry is a formula. Precede the equal sign with an apostrophe to indicate a text entry.

Multiple Criteria

Multiple criteria can be specified in two forms:

AND   Records that match all criteria (where Region equals west *and* YTD Sales are greater than 15000). Place the criteria on one row.

OR   Records that match one of several criteria (where Region equals west *or* Sales are greater than 15000). Place the criteria on different rows.

The examples shown in Figure 16.3 apply to the database pictured in Figure 16.1.

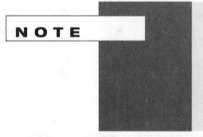

N O T E If you have never used a criteria range before, the topic may seem abstract at this point. This is a good time to jump ahead to advanced filters, where you will learn how to apply criteria ranges. Come back to computed criteria once you have a more solid understanding of the uses of criteria ranges.

Computed Criteria

Criteria specifications can be complex, especially if they include multiple criteria with relational operators. Picture a worksheet model with a database, a complex criteria range, and various D functions (covered later in this chapter). By changing the data in the criteria range, you can ask different

FIGURE 16.3

Examples of multiple criteria used with the database shown earlier in the chapter (in Figure 16.1)

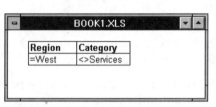

Where Region equals West and Category does not equal Services

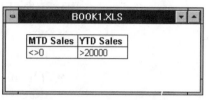

Where MTD Sales does not equal zero and YTD Sales is greater than 20000

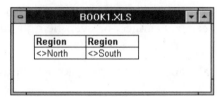

Where Region does not equal North and Region does not equal South

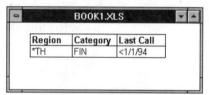

Where Region ends with TH and Category starts with FIN and Last Call is prior to 1/1/94

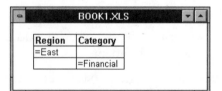

Where Region equals East or Category equals Financial

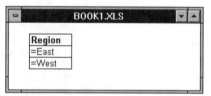

Where Region equals East or Region equals West

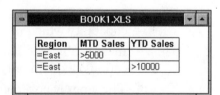

Where Region equals East and MTD Sales > 5000 OR where Region equals East and YTD Sales > 10000

questions of the database. This provides a lot of power, but also presents two problems:

- When you change the criteria you run the risk of "breaking" the model with a typographical error.

- The model may be intended for use by people in your organization who neither understand criteria ranges nor wish to understand them.

Computed criteria can be used to solve these problems. They allow user input to be incorporated into a criteria range without the user of the model knowing about criteria ranges, or even being aware that a criteria range exists.

There are several important things to know about computed criteria:

1. The term *computed criteria* tends to confuse people because of the unusual use of the word *computed*. Formulas can be entered into a criteria range, and these formulas *calculate* results, just like any formula. A computed criterion is just a criteria range that has formulas in it.

2. Computed criteria are very powerful, and *vitally* important for serious worksheet development.

3. The topic is widely misunderstood because there are two ways to express computed criteria: *Method One* is a logical extension of what you have learned so far; *Method Two* is somewhat idiosyncratic:

   - Method One is more powerful and easier to learn than Method Two, though Method Two does have one unique capability which makes it worth learning.

   - Inexplicably, the Excel manuals (and most third-party publications) explain only Method Two.

   - The lengthy coverage of Method Two here is not intended to place emphasis—it just requires more explanation.

4. The two methods are *not* mutually exclusive.

Computed Criteria—Method One

Very simply, you are *not limited to constant values* in a criteria range. You can also use formulas which calculate the criteria. Using the database in Figure 16.1, suppose you want to ask the question, "How many clients had YTD Sales exceeding X (a user-specified threshold)?" The next exercise shows how to build a criteria range that incorporates variables:

1. Create the following worksheet:

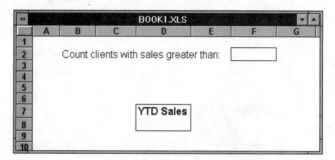

2. Enter this formula into D8: **=">"&F2**

3. Enter a number into F2; the formula in D8 causes the criteria to change—see Figure 16.4. (Performing the count requires the use of the DCOUNT function, covered later in this chapter.)

Perhaps you also want the ability to count the number of clients with MTD (Month-to-Date) Sales exceeding a user-specified threshold. Any cell within a criteria range can include a formula instead of a constant. Add the following to your model:

B4	**Enter M for M-T-D, or Y for Y-T-D**
D7	**=IF(F4="M","MTD Sales","YTD Sales")**

Computed Criteria—Method Two

The second way of expressing computed criteria is the method that is taught in the Excel manual, and in most third-party publications. Though some find this method more complicated to use, it nonetheless provides an important capability that cannot be achieved with Method One: the ability to compare a field to one or more fields in the same record.

FIGURE 16.4

The user input in cells
F2 and F4 is driving
the criteria range
D7:D8.

> **N O T E**
>
> Remember, Methods One and Two are not mutually exclusive. Both techniques can be employed in the same criteria range.

The database in Figure 16.5 is used to measure the efficiency of regional customer service departments for a fictional utility company.

Suppose that you want to create a criteria range that will be used to display only those regions where the number of calls received in 1995 exceeded the number of calls in 1994. Using the database and criteria range in Figure 16.5, entering the following formula in cell D5:

$$=E8>C8$$

would cause an advanced filter (covered later in this chapter) to display only rows 8, 9, and 11—the rows where 1995 calls exceeded 1994 calls. The rules for constructing this type of relative comparison are:

- The formula must return logical values TRUE or FALSE.
- The field name used in the criteria range (i.e., cell D4 in Figure 16.5) must *not* match a field name in the database—in fact, it can be left blank.

FIGURE 16.5

The *Calls 94* and *Calls 95* fields contain the number of incoming calls for 1994 and 1995 respectively. Fields *OK 94* and *OK 95* contain the number of those calls resolved to the customer's satisfaction.

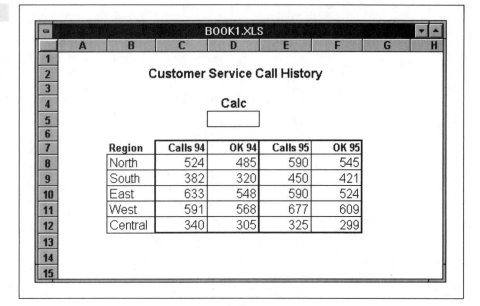

- The cell references in the formula are relative, and point to the first record of the database (you can use absolute references, but not to compare fields within each record).

- Like Method One, the criteria range can contain more than one column.

Here are some more examples of Method Two criteria using the database in Figure 16.1. Each formula goes into cell D5:

Example 1:

Filter	Display every record where the total calls for 1994 and 1994 are greater than 1000.
Formula	=C8+E8>1000
Display	Rows 8, 10, and 11

Example 2:

Filter	Display every record where the percentage of successful call resolutions in 1995 is worse than 1994.
Formula	=(F8/E8)<(D8/C8)
Display	Rows 8 and 11

Example 3:

Filter	Display every record where the percentage of successful resolutions in 1995 is worse than 90%.
Formula	=(F8/E8)<.9
Display	Rows 10 and 11

Example 4:

Filter	Display every record where the percentage of successful resolutions in 1994 is better than the percentage contained in cell $F$5.
Formula	=(D8/C8)>$F$5 (Note the absolute reference $F$5; it is not contained in the database— an absolute comparison is being performed).
Display	Depends on cell F5—if F5 contains 90%, rows 8 and 11 are displayed.

Using Advanced Filters

AutoFilters, covered in Chapter 15, allow simple data filters to be defined with ease, and provide an outstanding interface for specifying filter criteria. Custom AutoFilters provide a little more flexibility, but even they are limited. *Advanced filters* are able to ...

- use an unlimited number of criteria per field (using criteria ranges, covered earlier in this chapter)

- use variables as part of the criteria (using computed criteria, covered earlier in this chapter)

Filtering "In Place"

When you filter in-place, all records that do not meet a criteria specification are hidden, and all other records are displayed (in the same way that AutoFilters do). Here are the steps required to perform an advanced filter in-place:

1. Create a criteria range.

2. Select a cell within the database range.

3. Choose Data ➤ Filter ➤ Advanced Filter (Figure 16.6).

4. Select the *Filter the List in-place* option.

5. Enter the *Criteria Range* (you can type a cell reference, or point-and-click on the worksheet).

6. Click OK to filter.

7. To filter again with new criteria:

- Enter new value into criteria range (on worksheet).
- Then choose Data ➤ Filter ➤ Advanced Filter and click OK (the Advanced Filter dialog box remembers the settings from the last AutoFilter).

FIGURE 16.6

Advanced AutoFilter dialog box

Copying Records to a New Location

So far, every filter in this chapter (and the previous chapter) has filtered data in-place. As an alternative, filtered rows can be copied to a new location. Use the same steps as in the previous exercise, but with the following options:

- Choose the *Copy to Another Location* setting (see Figure 16.6)—this will make the *Copy To* setting available.

- Enter a *Copy to* range (type in a cell reference, or point-and-click on the worksheet).

Every record meeting the criteria specification is copied to the specified location.

Often, when you copy records to a new location, it is desirable to copy them to a different worksheet or a different workbook. There is a trick to this—you must activate the destination workbook/worksheet before choosing the Data ➤ Filter ➤ Advanced Filter command.

N O T E

In previous versions of Excel, the process of copying a record to a new location was referred to as a *data extract*.

Copying Only Specified Fields

If you do not want to extract all fields from a database, an *extract range* must be defined. An extract range serves three purposes:

- It specifies which fields to copy.

- It specifies the field order.

- It optionally limits the number of rows copied.

An extract range consists of field names that match the field names used in the database. The following exercise will copy records from the database in Figure 16.1:

1. Build a criteria range:

CELL	ENTRY
B14	**Region**
B15	**North**

2. Build an extract range:

CELL	ENTRY
C17	**Name**
D17	**YTD Sales**

3. Select a cell inside the database range, then choose Data ➤ Filter ➤ Advanced Filter. Excel will automatically detect the list (database) range $B$2:$I$12 (see Figures 16.7 and 16.8).

4. Select the *Copy to Another Location* option.

5. Enter a *Criteria Range* of **B14:B15**. (If you point-and-click the cells on the worksheet, the sheet name is automatically included as part of the range.)

6. Enter a *Copy to* range of **C17:D17**. (If you point-and-click the cells on the worksheet, the sheet name is automatically included as part of the range.)

7. Click OK.

TIP After setting an advanced filter, and copying to another location, the header row (field names) of the copied data is named *Extract*, and the criteria range is named *Criteria*.

FIGURE 16.7

This advanced filter will copy only the Name and YTD Sales fields.

	Client No	Name	Category	Region	Last Call	MTD Sales	YTD Sales	Last Year
3	107	MDC Enterprises	Mfg	East	1/30/94	8,167	23,613	25,733
4	104	Kinsman & Nelson	Services	East	2/7/95	3,717	12,374	9,221
5	110	T.K. James Inc.	Services	North	8/11/94	3,146	19,104	11,373
6	105	Pacific Investments	Financial	North	12/1/93	3,315	18,656	11,044
7	101	Argus Industries	Mfg	North	1/10/95	9,569	13,775	14,723
8	109	JK Associates	Financial	South	3/1/94	12,391	71,805	23,490
9	102	LEX Software	Services	South	4/23/94	3,527	10,534	12,887
10	103	National Bank	Financial	South	6/1/94	1,472	8,123	10,022
11	106	Nica Corporation	Mfg	West	2/25/94	6,542	58,229	52,559
12	108	Wilson & Roth	Services	West	11/1/93	4,026	11,786	9,225
14	Region							
15	North							
17		Name	YTD Sales					

FIGURE 16.8

The criteria range caused only those records in region North to be copied. The extract range caused only the fields Name and YTD Sales to be copied.

	Client No	Name	Category	Region	Last Call	MTD Sales	YTD Sales	Last Year
3	107	MDC Enterprises	Mfg	East	1/30/94	8,167	23,613	25,733
4	104	Kinsman & Nelson	Services	East	2/7/95	3,717	12,374	9,221
5	110	T.K. James Inc.	Services	North	8/11/94	3,146	19,104	11,373
6	105	Pacific Investments	Financial	North	12/1/93	3,315	18,656	11,044
7	101	Argus Industries	Mfg	North	1/10/95	9,569	13,775	14,723
8	109	JK Associates	Financial	South	3/1/94	12,391	71,805	23,490
9	102	LEX Software	Services	South	4/23/94	3,527	10,534	12,887
10	103	National Bank	Financial	South	6/1/94	1,472	8,123	10,022
11	106	Nica Corporation	Mfg	West	2/25/94	6,542	58,229	52,559
12	108	Wilson & Roth	Services	West	11/1/93	4,026	11,786	9,225
14	Region							
15	North							
17		Name	YTD Sales					
18		T.K. James Inc.	19,104					
19		Pacific Investments	18,656					
20		Argus Industries	13,775					

Using the D Functions

The database functions, or D functions, are different from most other functions because:

- They perform calculations on a specified column within a specified database (or any range of cells with a header row containing valid field names—see Chapter 15 to learn how to set up a database).

- They use a criteria range to determine which records to include in the calculation (criteria ranges are explained earlier in this chapter).

The D functions are all structured identically. Once you understand DSUM, you will be ready to use all of the D functions.

NOTE

For most D functions, there is a non-database equivalent. For example, there is a DSUM function and a SUM function.

DSUM Syntax

The DSUM syntax is:

```
DSUM(DatabaseRange,Field,CriteriaRange)
```

DatabaseRange	range of cells containing database—must include header row with unique field names (covered in Chapter 15)
Field	field within *DatabaseRange* used in calculation
CriteriaRange	range of cells containing criteria specification (covered earlier in this chapter)

In Figure 16.9, DSUM is used to calculate MTD Sales for all clients in region *North*.

FIGURE 16.9

As you can see from the DSUM arguments, the database is at B2:I12, the field being summed is *MTD Sales*, and the criteria range is at B14:B15.

	B	C	D	E	F	G	H	I
	Client No	Name	Category	Region	Last Call	MTD Sales	YTD Sales	Last Year
3	101	Argus Industries	Mfg	North	1/10/95	9,569	13,775	14,723
4	102	LEX Software	Services	South	4/23/94	3,527	10,534	12,887
5	103	National Bank	Financial	South	6/1/94	1,472	8,123	10,022
6	104	Kinsman & Nelson	Services	East	2/7/95	3,717	12,374	9,221
7	105	Pacific Investments	Financial	North	12/1/93	3,315	18,656	11,044
8	106	Nica Corporation	Mfg	West	2/25/94	6,542	58,229	52,559
9	107	MDC Enterprises	Mfg	East	1/30/94	8,167	23,613	25,733
10	108	Wilson & Roth	Services	West	11/1/93	4,026	11,786	9,225
11	109	JK Associates	Financial	South	3/1/94	12,391	71,805	23,490
12	110	T.K. James Inc.	Services	North	8/11/94	3,146	19,104	11,373
13								
14	Region							
15	North		16030					

BOOK1.XLS

Contains formula:
=DSUM(B2:I12,"MTD Sales",B14:B15)

Here are some variations on the DSUM formula in Figure 16.9. All four of these examples are based on the criteria range B14:B15, which specifies region *North*.

An example summing *YTD Sales*:

```
=DSUM(B2:I12,"YTD Sales",B14:B15)
```

An example summing *Last Year* (assuming that the database range is named *SalesData*, and the criteria range is named *SalesCriteria*):

```
=DSUM(SalesData,"Last Year",SalesCriteria)
```

Now, assume that the text **Last Year** has been entered into C14. This formula demonstrates that the second argument, *field*, can be a variable:

```
=DSUM(B2:I12,C14,B14:B15)
```

Any worksheet function that requires range arguments can use embedded functions to calculate the range. The D functions are no exception. In the next example, the OFFSET function points to cells B14:B15 (see Chapter 9 to learn about OFFSET). While the next formula does not require the use of the OFFSET function, it still demonstrates a powerful capability: Since the arguments for OFFSET can be variables, user input can be used to dynamically point to different criteria ranges:

```
=DSUM(B2:I12,"MTD Sales",OFFSET(B13,1,0,2,1))
```

Table 16.3 contains all of the D functions. They all use the same arguments as DSUM, but perform different types of calculations.

TABLE 16.3: D Functions

FUNCTION	DESCRIPTION
DAVERAGE	calculates average
DCOUNT	counts cells containing numbers
DCOUNTA	counts nonblank cells
DGET	gets a single field from a single record
DMAX	calculates maximum value
DMIN	calculates minimum value
DPRODUCT	multiplies values
DSTDEV	calculates standard deviation based on sample
DSTDEVP	calculates standard deviation based on entire population
DSUM	sums values
DVAR	calculates variance based on sample
DVARP	calculates variance based on entire population

TIP

There are two functions in addition to the D functions that use criteria ranges: SUMIF and COUNTIF. Both are covered in Chapter 9.

Inserting Embedded Subtotals in a Database

The ability to embed subtotals into a range of data, in a semi-automated fashion, is an important new Excel 5 capability. This feature (and Pivot Tables, the subject of the next chapter) has significantly enhanced Excel's overall capability as a reporting tool.

Using the database pictured in Figure 16.1, assume you want to add subtotals and a grand total for the MTD Sales and YTD Sales fields by region. Here's how you could do it:

1. Sort the database by Region.

2. Select a cell within the database range.

3. Choose Data ➤ Subtotals to display the dialog box in Figure 16.10.

4. Choose *Region* from the *At Each Change In* list (subtotals will be inserted each time the region changes).

5. Select the SUM function from the *Use Function* list (see SUBTOTAL in Chapter 9 for explanation of each function).

6. The *Add Subtotal To* list is used to specify which fields to subtotal—check *MTD Sales*, *YTD Sales*, and *Last Year*.

7. Check the *Page Break Between Groups* setting to insert a page break after each subtotal.

8. If *Summary Below Data* is checked, the subtotal row is placed beneath the data; otherwise it is placed on top.

9. Click OK to insert subtotals (pictured in Figure 16.11).

TIP

Use Format ➤ AutoFormat to format a range that contains subtotals. The built-in formats detect the subtotals, and format accordingly for optimal readability.

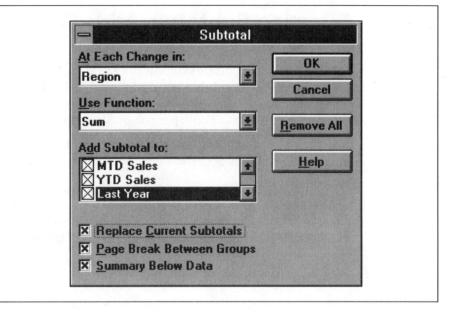

FIGURE 16.10

The Data ➤ Subtotals dialog box

FIGURE 16.11

Database with subtotals

Figure 16.10 contents:

Subtotal

A̲t Each Change in:
Region

U̲se Function:
Sum

A̲dd Subtotal to:
☒ MTD Sales
☒ YTD Sales
☒ Last Year

☒ Replace C̲urrent Subtotals
☒ P̲age Break Between Groups
☒ S̲ummary Below Data

OK
Cancel
R̲emove All
Help

Figure 16.11 contents — BOOK1.XLS:

	Client No	Name	Category	Region	Last Call	MTD Sales	YTD Sales
3	107	MDC Enterprises	Mfg	East	1/30/94	8,167	23,613
4	104	Kinsman & Nelson	Services	East	2/7/95	3,717	12,374
5				East Total		11,884	35,987
6	110	T.K. James Inc.	Services	North	8/11/94	3,146	19,104
7	105	Pacific Investments	Financial	North	12/1/93	3,315	18,656
8	101	Argus Industries	Mfg	North	1/10/95	9,569	13,775
9				North Total		16,030	51,535
10	109	JK Associates	Financial	South	3/1/94	12,391	71,805
11	102	LEX Software	Services	South	4/23/94	3,527	10,534
12	103	National Bank	Financial	South	6/1/94	1,472	8,123
13				South Total		17,390	90,462
14	106	Nica Corporation	Mfg	West	2/25/94	6,542	58,229
15	108	Wilson & Roth	Services	West	11/1/93	4,026	11,786
16				West Total		10,568	70,015
17				Grand Total		55,872	247,999

Inserting Subtotals Adds Outlining to the Sheet

Notice the outline symbols in Figure 16.11. Outlining is an automatic by-product when subtotals are inserted using Data ➤ Subtotals.

- To expand/collapse the outline, click the outline symbols.
- To hide/unhide outline symbols, use the Options ➤ Tools command, select the View tab, then use the *Outline Symbols* checkbox.

Outlining is covered in depth in Chapter 22.

Removing Embedded Subtotals

There are two ways to remove embedded subtotals that were inserted using Data ➤ Subtotal:

- To remove all embedded subtotals, choose the Data ➤ Subtotals command, and click *Remove All*.
- To add different subtotals to the same range, and remove the old subtotals at the same time, check the *Replace Current Subtotals* setting (see Figure 16.10).

Creating Friendly Looking Databases

Since field names must be unique, you often wind up with field names which, from a user perspective, are not very friendly. Figure 16.12 contains two databases, each with a different type of problem.

The 1994 database duplicates the field names *Budget* and *Actual*, which causes problems for many database operations. In addition, the Q1–Q4 descriptive labels above the database confuse Excel—when you sort this database, Excel will attempt to include rows 2 and 3 in the data area.

FIGURE 16.12

The 1994 database does not have unique field names. The field names in the 1995 database are not user-friendly.

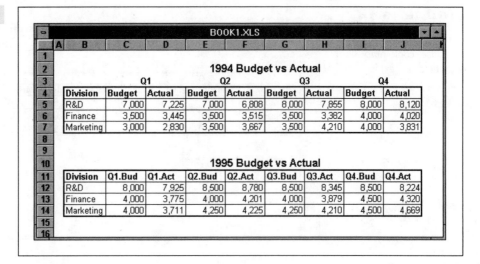

BOOK1.XLS

1994 Budget vs Actual

Division	Q1		Q2		Q3		Q4	
	Budget	Actual	Budget	Actual	Budget	Actual	Budget	Actual
R&D	7,000	7,225	7,000	6,808	8,000	7,855	8,000	8,120
Finance	3,500	3,445	3,500	3,515	3,500	3,382	4,000	4,020
Marketing	3,000	2,830	3,500	3,667	3,500	4,210	4,000	3,831

1995 Budget vs Actual

Division	Q1.Bud	Q1.Act	Q2.Bud	Q2.Act	Q3.Bud	Q3.Act	Q4.Bud	Q4.Act
R&D	8,000	7,925	8,500	8,780	8,500	8,345	8,500	8,224
Finance	4,000	3,775	4,000	4,201	4,000	3,879	4,500	4,320
Marketing	4,000	3,711	4,250	4,225	4,250	4,210	4,500	4,669

The 1995 database uses unique field names—it is perfectly legal. But the field names are aesthetically displeasing, and potentially confusing to others.

There is a way to design your databases to combine the friendliness of the 1994 database with the correctness of the 1995 database. Consider Figures 16.13 and 16.14.

FIGURE 16.13

The database is at B5:J8. Rows 3 and 4 are for clarity only.

BOOK1.XLS

Division	Q1		Q2		Q3		Q4	
	Budget	Actual	Budget	Actual	Budget	Actual	Budget	Actual
Division	Q1.Bud	Q1.Act	Q2.Bud	Q2.Act	Q3.Bud	Q3.Act	Q4.Bud	Q4.Act
R&D	8,000	7,925	8,500	8,780	8,500	8,345	8,500	8,224
Finance	4,000	3,775	4,000	4,201	4,000	3,879	4,500	4,320
Marketing	4,000	3,711	4,250	4,225	4,250	4,210	4,500	4,669

FIGURE 16.14

The first row of the database, containing legal field names, is hidden.

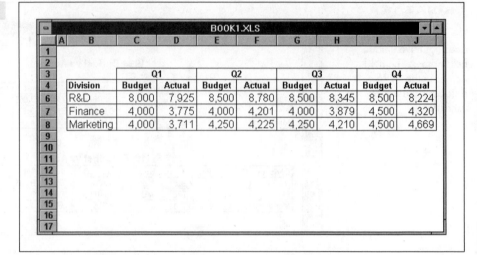

Division	Q1		Q2		Q3		Q4	
	Budget	Actual	Budget	Actual	Budget	Actual	Budget	Actual
R&D	8,000	7,925	8,500	8,780	8,500	8,345	8,500	8,224
Finance	4,000	3,775	4,000	4,201	4,000	3,879	4,500	4,320
Marketing	4,000	3,711	4,250	4,225	4,250	4,210	4,500	4,669

Here is how you can create this database:

- Enter legal field names on the header row of the database.
- Enter field descriptions on the row(s) above the header row.
- Hide the first row of the database (the header row).

CHAPTER

17

Pivot Tables

fast TRACK

To control how a data field is calculated   508

1. Select a cell inside the data area of the pivot table.

2. Choose Data ➤ PivotTable Field.

3. Choose the type of calculation in the *Summarize By* list box.

To perform a custom calculation   509

1. Select a cell inside the data area of the pivot table.

2. Choose Data ➤ PivotTable Field, then click Options.

3. Choose from the *Summarize By* list.

To base a pivot table on an external database   516

Select *External Data Source* at Step One of the PivotTable Wizard.

To refresh a pivot table   520

Select a cell inside the table, then choose Data ➤ Refresh Data.

ONE of the biggest challenges in the real world is the need to derive important information from large quantities of raw data. *Pivot tables* provide a way to easily summarize and analyze data using special direct manipulation techniques. They are called pivot tables because you can change their layout by *pivoting* the row and column headings. Pivot tables are arguably the most important new feature in Excel 5, and are well worth the time to learn and master. This chapter covers:

- *how to create a pivot table from a worksheet database*
- *how to change the layout of a pivot table*
- *creating pivot tables from external databases*
- *creating pivot tables from multiple consolidation ranges*

Example Database

Through much of this chapter, a database will be used that is located in a sample workbook that comes with Excel. The workbook is named PRODUCTS.XLS, and can be found in the EXCELCBT directory, inside your Excel directory. The database is stored on the worksheet named **Products** (Figure 17.1).

If you want to follow the exercises in the chapter, you may want to copy this data to a new workbook so as not to accidentally change PRODUCTS.XLS, which is used in Excel's online Examples and Demos.

The database contains sales history for a fictitious company that sells produce and dairy products to supermarkets. Sales are tracked by product category, period (year and month), salesperson, and region.

FIGURE 17.1

Database of sales history

	A	B	C	D	E	F	G	H	I
1	Product	Year	Month	Sales	Units	Salesperson	Region		
2	Dairy	1992	Dec	7,686	5,563	Davolio	North		
3	Produce	1993	Sep	2,956	1,242	Buchanan	West		
4	Produce	1992	Oct	8,165	983	Buchanan	South		
5	Dairy	1993	Jan	4,448	3,833	Buchanan	North		
6	Dairy	1993	Sep	75	3,216	Buchanan	East		
7	Produce	1993	Feb	4,923	8,160	Davolio	South		
8	Dairy	1993	Dec	2,733	2,790	Davolio	West		
9	Produce	1993	Apr	450	9,265	Davolio	East		
10	Produce	1992	Jul	797	3,868	Buchanan	North		
11	Dairy	1993	Mar	8,751	1,773	Buchanan	West		
12	Dairy	1993	Mar	2,741	6,290	Davolio	North		
13	Produce	1993	Dec	7,047	9,888	Davolio	West		
14	Produce	1992	Oct	7,191	39	Davolio	North		
15	Dairy	1992	Jun	5,575	9,970	Davolio	East		
16	Dairy	1992	Jul	7,612	3,656	Buchanan	South		
17	Dairy	1992	Aug	4,873	2,730	Buchanan	North		
18	Dairy	1993	Feb	8,076	3,670	Davolio	South		
19	Dairy	1992	Oct	3,338	1,695	Davolio	West		
20	Dairy	1993	Jan	6,544	9,550	Davolio	West		
21	Produce	1993	Oct	6,955	8,722	Buchanan	East		
22	Produce	1993	Feb	4,138	4,661	Davolio	East		
23	Produce	1992	Aug	8,447	8,056	Buchanan	East		
24	Dairy	1993	May	8,516	5,954	Davolio	West		

Creating a Simple Pivot Table from an Internal Database

There is a PivotTable Wizard that makes the job of creating pivot tables simple. The following exercise will walk you through the steps required to create a simple pivot table using the Products database pictured in Figure 17.1.

1. Starting the PivotTable Wizard

Follow these steps to start the PivotTable Wizard:

1. Open the products workbook.

2. Select a cell anywhere inside the database.

3. Choose the Data ➤ Pivot Table command—Step One of the Pivot-Table Wizard, pictured in Figure 17.2, is displayed.

4. Since the source data is stored in an internal database, select the *Microsoft Excel List or Database* option.

5. Click Next to proceed to Step Two.

2. Confirming the Database Range

Step Two of the PivotTable Wizard lets you confirm the database range.

FIGURE 17.2

Step One lets you specify where the source data is located.

If the active cell is inside a database when you choose the Data ➤ Pivot Table command, the Wizard automatically detects the boundaries of the database. You can enter a different range, or you can use the mouse to point, click, and drag a range of cells.

- If the source data is on a different worksheet, click the sheet tab, then select the database range.

- If the source data is in a different (open) workbook, use the window menu to activate the workbook, then select the database range.

- If the source data is stored in a workbook that is not open, click the Browse button to choose the workbook.

Click Next to proceed to Step Three.

3. Laying Out the Pivot Table

Step Three (Figure 17.3) is the heart of the pivot table.

FIGURE 17.3

The database fields are displayed as buttons on the right part of the dialog box. The pivot table in the dialog box is a preview of the actual table that will be placed on a worksheet.

The data fields are represented by a set of buttons at the right of the dialog box. You can select whichever buttons you want as row and column heads—and whichever ones you want as the data inside the pivot table. The layout is created by dragging and dropping the field buttons onto the pivot table. There are four places where you can drop a field button:

Row	Field(s) used as row titles
Column	field(s) used as column titles
Page	field(s) used to show data for one item at a time
Data	the actual data that will be inside the pivot table (typically numeric fields)—at least one field must be placed in the data area

Using the Products database, suppose you want to see how each salesperson has performed within each region—by product. Follow these steps, referring to Figure 17.4.

1. Drag the **Salesperson** field into the Row area.

2. Drag the **Region** field into the Column area.

3. Drag the **Product** field into the Page area.

4. Drag the **Sales** field into the Data area.

This example positions one data field at each of the four places that a field can be positioned: row field, column field, page field, and data field. However, you are not limited to one field per location—you can place more than one field at each of the four areas.

TIP

If you place the wrong field onto the pivot table, it can be removed by dragging it anywhere outside of the table.

Click Next to proceed to the last step.

FIGURE 17.4

Drag and drop field
buttons onto the pivot
table.

4. Finishing the Pivot Table

Step Four (Figure 17.5) lets you specify where the pivot table will be placed, and several other options.

FIGURE 17.5

You can position the
table and choose
miscellaneous options
in Step 4.

1. Specify where the pivot table goes using the *Pivot Table Starting Cell*:

   - If you do not specify a starting cell, the pivot table will be placed on a new worksheet that is inserted into the active workbook.

   - You can place the pivot table anywhere in the active workbook—click on any sheet tab, and select a cell.

   - To place the pivot table on a workbook other than the active workbook, use the Window menu to activate the book, click a tab, and select a cell.

2. The pivot table is named automatically—you can override the name if desired.

3. Set the pivot table options:

   - Check *Grand Totals for Columns* to place totals at the bottom of each column.

   - Check *Grand Totals for Row* to place totals at the end of each row.

   - By checking *Save Data with Table Layout*, the data behind the pivot table is saved in a hidden cache—this allows the pivot table to be changed without the source data being open (the implications of this setting are discussed later in this chapter).

   - Check *AutoFormat Table* to format the pivot table—the columns are sized and borders added to the table.

4. Click Finish—Figure 17.6 shows a finished pivot table.

The pivot table in Figure 17.6 shows how each salesperson performed within each region. The layout, specified in Step Three of the PivotTable Wizard (see Figure 17.3), determines the level of summarization. In the example just described, a database containing over fifty records (rows) was summarized into an informative, concise format.

You cannot edit the cells inside a pivot table. However, in the next section, you will learn how to change the layout of a pivot table using special simple, direct manipulation techniques. First, notice that two changes to the workspace have occurred:

- If no starting cell was specified at Step 4 of the PivotTable Wizard (see Figure 17.5), the pivot table is placed on a new worksheet inserted next to the sheet containing the source data.

FIGURE 17.6

You can change the table layout by dragging the field buttons on the worksheet, without using the PivotTable Wizard.

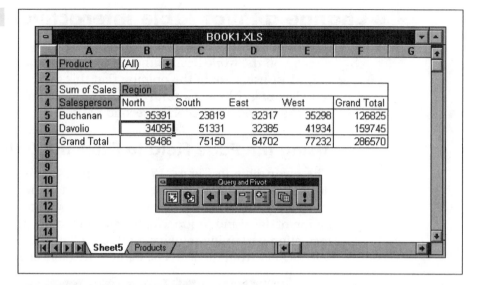

- The *Query and Pivot* toolbar is displayed (it is displayed anytime you activate a worksheet containing a pivot table, not just when the table is first created).

TIP

There is no limit, other than available memory, to the number of pivot tables that can be defined in the same workbook—or even on the same worksheet.

Changing the Layout of a Pivot Table

Once a pivot table has been created, there are two ways to change the layout: interacting directly with the table on the worksheet, or using the PivotTable Wizard.

Change a Pivot Table Interactively

One of the best aspects of pivot tables is that you can manipulate them directly on the worksheet, without having to restart the PivotTable Wizard. Most users are of the opinion that this method for changing a pivot table layout is the most intuitive—once you become familiar with pivot tables, the interaction becomes second nature.

Using the Page Field to Filter the Data

The pivot table in Figure 17.6 has a page field—**Product**. This drop-down control lets you filter the data displayed in the pivot table. By default, when a pivot table is first created, the page will be set to *(All)*, a combination of dairy and produce products. Suppose you only want to view information pertaining to dairy products. Click the drop-down arrow, and select Dairy from the list. The data in the table changes accordingly.

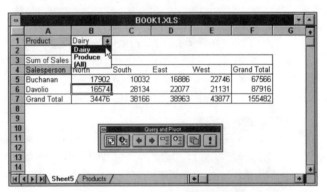

Now, suppose you want to print two separate reports, one for dairy and one for produce. First, use the page button to switch back to *(All)*. Then follow these steps:

1. Select a cell anywhere inside the pivot table.

2. Click the Show Pages tool on the Query and Pivot Toolbar. Depending on your layout, there can be more than one page field. The Show Pages dialog box is displayed, letting you select which field will determine the page breaks.

3. Select Product from the list, and click OK. Figure 17.7 shows the result.

Notice in Figure 17.7 that two new worksheets have been inserted into the workbook—one for *Produce* and one for *Dairy*.

Changing the Layout by Moving Field Buttons

As you saw in Figure 17.6, the field buttons are placed on the pivot table. This allows you to change your view of the data by dragging the buttons on the sheet, without having to redisplay the PivotTable Wizard.

For instance, using the pivot table in 17.6, suppose you want to see sales by product for each sales rep—just click the *Product* button, and drag it

FIGURE 17.7

For each page, a new worksheet is inserted into the workbook.

just beneath the *Salesperson* button. The pivot table will recalculate, as pictured in Figure 17.8.

The best way to learn about pivot tables is through experimenting. Try positioning each button as a row category, column category, and page break—the pivot table will reveal different information about the underlying data with each layout.

FIGURE 17.8

Sales by region by product by salesperson.

			BOOK1.XLS				
	A	B	C	D	E	F	G
1							
2							
3	Sum of Sales		Region				
4	Salesperson	Product	North	South	East	West	Grand Total
5	Buchanan	Dairy	17902	10032	16886	22746	67566
6		Produce	17489	13787	15431	12552	59259
7	Buchanan Total		35391	23819	32317	35298	126825
8	Davolio	Dairy	16574	28134	22077	21131	87916
9		Produce	17521	23197	10308	20803	71829
10	Davolio Total		34095	51331	32385	41934	159745
11	Grand Total		69486	75150	64702	77232	286570
12							

Sheet5 / Products

Removing a Field from a Pivot Table

To remove a field from a pivot table, simply drag the field button outside the pivot table range. When a large × displays, as shown in Figure 17.9, release the mouse button.

Remember, removing a field from a pivot table does not affect the underlying data, nor does it affect the hidden cache.

Drilling Down into the Detailed Data

When viewing summary data in a pivot table, you may observe a number that requires explanation. You can double-click any value within the data area, including subtotals and totals, to view the detailed data behind the number. For instance, using the pivot table in Figure 17.6, suppose you

FIGURE 17.9

Drag a field button
outside of the pivot
table to remove it from
the table.

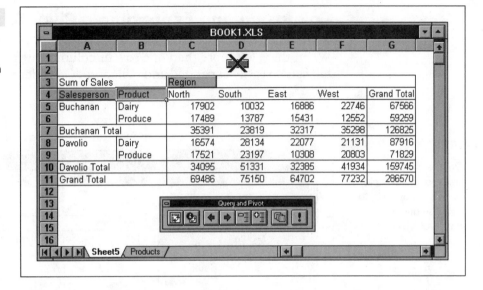

FIGURE 17.9

Drag a field button
outside of the pivot
table to remove it from
the table.

want to see what factors contributed to Davolio's high sales in region
South: Simply double-click cell C6. A new worksheet is inserted into the
workbook, and every record (row) from the source database where salesperson is equal to Davolio, and region is equal to South, is displayed (see
Figure 17.10).

FIGURE 17.10

Double-click a cell in
the data area of a
pivot table to view the
detail behind the
number.

Collapsing and Expanding a Pivot Table

Sometimes, within a pivot table, you may want to view more or less detail. When there are more than one row or column categories, the level of detail can be easily expanded and collapsed. Consider the pivot table in Figure 17.11.

The pivot table in Figure 17.11 is still small, but suppose there are dozens of regions instead of only four—the data for a single salesperson may not fit in the window. Double-click the salesperson row categories, cells A5 and/or A10, to collapse the pivot table. Figure 17.12 shows the pivot table after cell A5 has been double-clicked.

FIGURE 17.12

The Buchanan rows
have been collapsed,
leaving only the
Buchanan total row.

By double-clicking A5 again, the Buchanan rows are unhidden.

The database includes sales history from 1992 and 1993. Suppose, using the pivot table in Figure 17.11, you want to see the breakdown of 1992/1993 sales for Dairy and/or Produce. Double-click the Dairy column heading (cell C4). Since Excel is not sure how you want to expand the pivot table, the Show Detail dialog box is displayed.

Select *Year* from the list, then click OK. A breakdown of 1992/1993 is added to the pivot table for Dairy and Produce, even though it is only displayed for Dairy (see Figure 17.13). Double-click the Produce column heading (cell F3) to show the 1992/1993 breakdown. Also, notice that the field button *Year* has been added to the table.

FIGURE 17.13

Double-click the Dairy column heading, cell C4, to expand and collapse the pivot.

	A	B	C	D	E	F	G	H
1								
2								
3	Sum of Sales		Product	Year				
4			Dairy		Dairy Total	Produce	Grand Total	
5	Salesperson	Region	1992	1993				
6	Buchanan	North	9883	8019	17902	17489	35391	
7		South	7612	2420	10032	13787	23819	
8		East	15164	1722	16886	15431	32317	
9		West	7592	15154	22746	12552	35298	
10	Buchanan Total		40251	27315	67566	59259	126825	
11	Davolio	North	7752	8822	16574	17521	34095	
12		South	13029	15105	28134	23197	51331	
13		East	7016	15061	22077	10308	32385	
14		West	3338	17793	21131	20803	41934	
15	Davolio Total		31135	56781	87916	71829	159745	
16	Grand Total		71386	84096	155482	131088	286570	
17								

BOOK1.XLS

Sheet5 / Products /

Changing a Pivot Table Using the PivotTable Wizard

Another way to change a pivot table is with the PivotTable Wizard. Follow these steps:

1. Select a cell inside the pivot table.

NOTE If the active cell is not inside the pivot table when you choose the Data ➤ Pivot Table command, Excel assumes that you want to create a new pivot table. There can be more than one pivot table on a worksheet.

2. Start the PivotTable Wizard using the Data ➤ Pivot Table command, or click the corresponding tool (pictured to the left) on the Query and Pivot toolbar.

3. The wizard is displayed starting at Step Three (see Figure 17.3). The procedure for changing the layout is the same as when the pivot table was first created.

Use Names to Simplify Synchronization

When the source for a pivot table is an Excel database, or multiple consolidation ranges, you will likely specify a cell reference as the source data (e.g., $A$1:$E$99). Later, if you add records to the source database (or delete records), the pivot table definition needs to be changed using these steps:

1. Select a cell inside the pivot table, then choose Data ➤ PivotTable.

2. Step Three of the wizard is displayed. Click Back to display Step Two.

3. Change the range, then click Finish.

However, there is a much better way to synchronize the pivot table with the source data using names:

1. Name the source data range, e.g., **MyData**.

2. When you create the pivot table, at Step Two of the wizard, refer to the source data by name.

When rows are deleted from the source data range, the named range contracts automatically. If you insert one or more rows into the source range, the name expands automatically. (If you add a row beneath the named range, you will have to redefine the name.) In all cases, the pivot table refreshes correctly after choosing Data ➤ Refresh Data. (See Chapter 8 to learn about names.)

Controlling How Data Fields Calculate

When a data field inside a pivot table is numeric, then, by default, the numbers in the data area are summations of fields from the source database. (If the data field is text, a count is performed by default.) However, there are many other types of calculations that can be performed.

Using the Wizard Double-click the value field button on Step Three of the PivotTable Wizard, then choose the type of calculation in the *Summarize By* list box. (The different types of calculations are described in Table 17.1.)

On the Worksheet Select a cell inside the data area of the pivot table, then choose Data ➤ PivotTable Field. Choose the type of calculation in the *Summarize By* list box. (The different types of calculations are described in Table 17.1.)

TABLE 17.1: Calculations That Can Be Performed in a PivotTable Value Field

USE...	TO CALCULATE...
Sum	sum (total) of the values
Count	number of records (rows)
Average	average value in underlying data
Max	maximum value in underlying data
Min	minimum value in underlying data
Product	product of the underlying data
Count Nums	number of records (rows) containing numbers
StdDev	estimated standard deviation of population where the underlying data represents the sample
StdDevp	standard deviation of population where the underlying data represents the entire population
Var	variance of population where underlying data represents the sample
Varp	variance of population where underlying data represents entire population

Performing Custom Calculations

In a pivot table, you can perform certain custom calculations where a value is compared in one of several ways to another value. For example, using Figure 17.6, suppose you want to see each sales rep's percentage of total sales rather than dollars. Follow these steps:

1. Select a value cell inside the data area of the pivot table, then choose Data ➤ PivotTable Fields.

2. From the the PivotTable Field dialog box, click Options to expand the dialog box.

3. From the *Show Data As* list, choose **% of Total**, then click OK.

The results are demonstrated in Figure 17.14.

You can also define custom calculations from Step Three of the Pivot-Table Wizard. Double-click the value field button, then repeat steps 2 and 3 of the previous exercise.

FIGURE 17.14

Every value cell is represented as a percentage of the grand total—cell F7.

Sum of Sales	Region				
Salesperson	North	South	East	West	Grand Total
Buchanan	12.35%	8.31%	11.28%	12.32%	44.26%
Davolio	11.90%	17.91%	11.30%	14.63%	55.74%
Grand Total	24.25%	26.22%	22.58%	26.95%	100.00%

Customizing a Pivot Table

Pivot tables are flexible, and you can change field labels, set number formats, and control how data is grouped.

Changing Field Button Labels

The text that is used on the field buttons is determined by the field names in your database. These names may not be very friendly, so you may want to change them—without changing the source database.

Using the Wizard Double-click the field button on Step Three of the PivotTable Wizard. Change the *Name* in the PivotTable field dialog box.

On the Worksheet Click the field button—the button text displays on the formula bar. Use the formula bar to edit the text, just as you would edit the contents of a cell. (Or, double-click the field button, and change the *Name* in the PivotTable Field dialog box.)

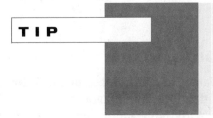

TIP

When you create a pivot table from multiple consolidation ranges (covered later in this chapter), generic button labels are automatically created (e.g., *Column* and *Row*). It is likely you will want to change these button labels.

Formatting Numbers in the Data Area

You can apply number formats to the cells in a pivot table just as you would format any cell. But, if you change the layout, the formatting does not automatically adjust. Instead, use one of the following procedures.

Using the Wizard Double-click the field button on Step Three of the PivotTable Wizard, then click the Number button. Select a format from the Format Cell dialog box, pictured in Figure 17.15.

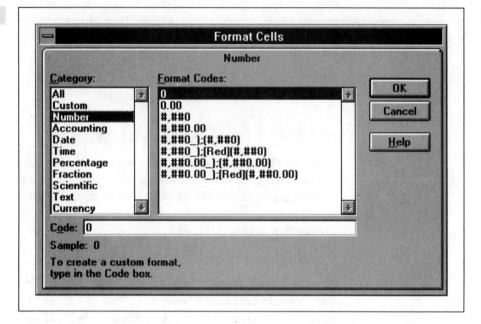

On the Worksheet Select a cell inside the data area of the pivot table, then choose Data ➤ PivotTable Field. Click the Number button to display the Format cell dialog box, pictured in Figure 17.15.

Grouping and Ungrouping Data

There are times when the source database is structured in a way that does not fit the way you want to group the data in the pivot table. A good example of this problem can be seen with dates. Consider Figure 17.16.

Suppose you want to design a pivot table that shows the sales reps, Smith and Jones, on separate rows, and their total sales for each month in columns. The pivot table in Figure 17.17 uses **Rep** as a row category, **Date** as a column category, and **Amount** as a data value. As you can see, each discrete date in the source database occupies a separate column.

Follow these steps to group the dates by month:

1. Select any of the date-column heading cells.

2. Click the Group tool, or choose the Data ➤ Group and Outline ➤ Group command.

FIGURE 17.16

Invoice Database to be used as source for pivot table

	A	B	C	D	E	F	G
			BOOK1.XLS				
1							
2		Invoice	Date	Rep	Amount		
3		1001	1/5/95	Jones	275		
4		1002	1/5/95	Jones	1,045		
5		1003	1/11/95	Smith	770		
6		1004	1/14/95	Jones	835		
7		1005	1/23/95	Smith	108		
8		1006	2/4/95	Smith	388		
9		1007	2/11/95	Jones	572		
10		1008	2/21/95	Smith	1,336		
11		1009	3/2/95	Jones	260		
12		1010	3/9/95	Jones	449		
13		1011	3/20/95	Smith	820		
14							
15							
16							
17							

FIGURE 17.17

The date columns are too detailed—the goal is to see totals for each month.

	A	B	C	D	E	F	G	H	I	J	K
					BOOK1.XLS						
1											
2	Sum of Amount	Date									
3	Rep	1/5/95	1/11/95	1/14/95	1/23/95	2/4/95	2/11/95	2/21/95	3/2/95	3/9/95	3/20/95
4	Jones	1320	0	835	0	0	572	0	260	449	
5	Smith	0	770	0	108	388	0	1336	0	0	82
6	Grand Total	1320	770	835	108	388	572	1336	260	449	82
7											
8											
9					Query and Pivot						
10											
11											
12											
13											
14											

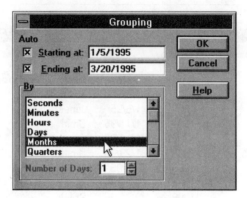

3. Select *Months*, then click OK. The date columns are rolled up into months, as pictured in Figure 17.18.

Follow these steps to ungroup the columns:

1. Select any of the date (month) column heading cells.

 2. Click the Ungroup tool. Or, choose the Data ➤ Group and Outline ➤ Ungroup command.

FIGURE 17.18

You can group dates by any number of days (such as weeks), months, quarters, or years.

	A	B	C	D	E	F	G	H	I	J	K
1											
2	Sum of Amount	Date									
3	Rep	Jan	Feb	Mar	Grand Total						
4	Jones	2155	572	709	3436						
5	Smith	878	1724	820	3422						
6	Grand Total	3033	2296	1529	6858						
7											
8											
9											
10											
11											
12											
13											
14											

BOOK1.XLS

Query and Pivot

Sorting a Pivot Table

You can sort the data inside a pivot table, using the Data ➤ Sort command, and the logical organization of the data within the table will be left intact. Consider the pivot table in Figure 17.11. Suppose that within the data for salesperson Buchanan, you want to list the regions in order of how well Buchanan performed—in descending order (from best to worst). Follow these steps:

1. Select any cell in the Grand Total column that corresponds to Buchanan (E5:E8).

2. Choose Data ➤ Sort.

3. Choose the *Descending* option, then click OK. Figure 17.19 shows the sorted pivot table.

Figure 17.19 also illustrates a problem you should be aware of when you sort a pivot table. Notice that Davolio's regions were placed in the exact same order as Buchanan's—even though Davolio's sort is illogical. There is no way to override this behavior. (See Chapters 15 and 16 to learn more about sorting.)

FIGURE 17.19

Buchanan's regions are sorted in descending order based on the Grand Total column.

Creating a Pivot Table from an External Database

So far in this chapter, you have learned how to create a pivot table based on a database that resided on a worksheet. You can also create pivot tables based on an external database, such as Access, dBASE, Paradox, Oracle, or SQL Server.

NOTE The databases you can access depend on the ODBC drivers installed on your system, and the appropriate network connections to the database. See Chapter 18 to learn more about accessing external databases.

What Is Microsoft Query?

Creating a pivot table from an external database requires that you use *Microsoft Query*. Microsoft Query is a separate program that comes with Excel that serves two purposes:

- It is a stand-alone program that can be used to query databases— a separate manual for Microsoft Query is included in the Excel retail package.

- It is used by Excel to retrieve data from external databases. In this capacity, it acts as an intermediary between Excel and the external database.

When you originally installed Excel, installing Microsoft Query was optional. If it is not installed on your system, you will be unable to create pivot tables from external databases. You must run the Excel setup program to add Microsoft Query, and associated files, to your system.

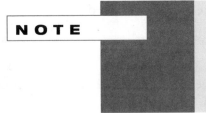

NOTE Microsoft Query is included with Microsoft products other than Excel. Even if you chose not to install it when you installed Excel, it may be on your system anyway. It is usually located under the MSAPPS directory, which is inside your Microsoft Windows directory.

Performing the Database Query

Step One of the PivotTable Wizard (see Figure 17.2) has an option called *External Data Source*. When you choose this option, then click Next, Step Two of the PivotTable Wizard is displayed. But this is different than the Step Two when creating a pivot table from a worksheet database.

Notice that the text in the dialog box states "No data retrieved." Click the *Get Data* button—Microsoft Query is started, and you will now define a query.

Defining the Query

You are now working inside Microsoft Query. In this discussion, only the basic steps are provided. However, Chapter 18 includes a more detailed discussion on how to define a query—refer to the heading entitled "Using Microsoft Query to Define a Query" within Chapter 18.

1. Select a data source.

2. Add one or more tables where the data is stored.

3. Add the fields to the query.

4. Optionally, add a criterion.

5. From the Microsoft Query menu, choose the File ➤ Return Data to Microsoft Excel command.

NOTE   You do not have to save the query definition in Microsoft Query. When the data is returned to Excel, the SQL statement generated by Microsoft Query is stored in the Excel workbook, though it is hidden.

Back to Excel

Step Two of the PivotTable Wizard is again displayed. If you successfully defined a query in Microsoft Query, the text in the dialog box will read "Data Retrieved."

Until it says data retrieved, you will be unable to proceed. Click the Next button.

Step Three of the PivotTable Wizard is displayed. Use it the same as when defining a pivot table from an Excel database (covered previously in the chapter). Click Next when you are done designing the pivot table layout.

Step Four of the Pivot Table Wizard is displayed. As with Step Three, it works just the same as when you created a pivot table from an Excel database. Click Finish to complete the pivot table.

Working with a Pivot Table Created from External Data

Once the pivot table is placed on a worksheet, working with it is very similar to working with pivot tables created from an Excel database. You can:

- Drag the field buttons to change your view of the data.
- Double-click data cells inside the pivot table to display detailed source records.
- Double-click row or column headings to expand and contract the pivot table.
- Select a cell inside the table, and choose Data ➤ Pivot Table to change the table.

Refreshing the Pivot Table

The detailed data that came from Microsoft Query is stored in the workbook in a special hidden cache. When you change the layout of the pivot table, the cache is driving the table, not the source database.

Suppose that you save the workbook containing the pivot table, then reopen it days or weeks later. What if the source database is a transaction file that changes daily? Your pivot table will not be in sync with the source database. Choose the Data ➤ Refresh Data command to refresh the pivot table from the source database. Behind the scenes, Excel will re-query the database, refresh the hidden cache, and then refresh the pivot table.

TIP

When you refresh a pivot table created from an external database, Excel uses an XLL (a special Excel DLL) to re-query the database—not Microsoft Query. This makes the query go faster, and uses less of your system's memory.

Changing the Source Data

There are several circumstances when you may want to change the database query behind a pivot table. You may want to...

- add new fields
- add or change the query criteria
- completely redefine the query

Follow these steps to change the query that is driving a pivot table:

1. Select a cell inside the pivot table.

2. Choose Data ➤ Pivot Table—Step Three of the PivotTable Wizard is displayed.

3. Click the Back button to display Step Two.

4. Click the Get Data button—Microsoft Query is started with the original query loaded.

5. Change the query, or choose File ➤ New Query and create a new query.

6. Choose File ➤ Return Data to Microsoft Excel.

Step Two of the PivotTable Wizard is displayed—follow the normal procedures to complete the table layout.

Creating a Pivot Table from Multiple Consolidation Ranges

Suppose your organization, a distributor of electronic goods, has several regional offices, and each office submits a sales forecast by product. It is your job to create a report that consolidates these forecasts. Consider the workbooks in Figure 17.20.

With the four workbooks open, follow these steps to consolidate the information onto a new workbook:

1. Choose File ➤ New to create a new workbook.

2. Choose Data ➤ Pivot Table—Step One of the PivotTable Wizard is displayed.

FIGURE 17.20

Four regional sales forecasts that need to be consolidated

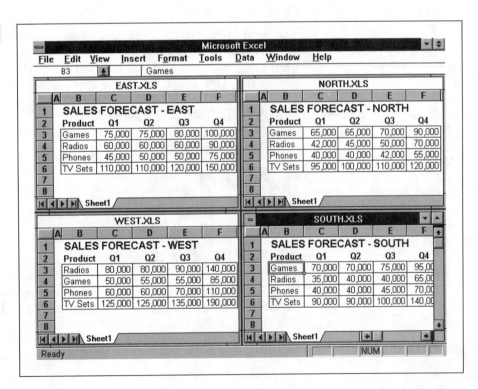

3. Select Multiple Consolidation Ranges, then click Next. Step 2a of the PivotTable Wizard, pictured in Figure 17.21, is displayed.

4. Select the option *Create a Single Page for Me*, then click Next to proceed to Step 2b of the PivotTable Wizard (pictured in Figure 17.22).

NOTE   When you select the option *Create a Single Page for Me*, the wizard creates a separate page for each consolidated range. The option *I will Create the Page Fields* lets you override the default pagination.

5. Enter the range by pointing and clicking on the workbooks—click on WEST.XLS, and select cells B2:F6, then click Add.

6. Repeat step 5 above for EAST.XLS, NORTH.XLS, and SOUTH.XLS, then click Next to proceed to Step Three of the PivotTable Wizard (Figure 17.23).

7. The field button in the data area must read *Sum of Value*. If it doesn't (the PivotTable Wizard is somewhat unpredictable as to what type of calculation will be used as the default), double-click the button, and select Sum from the *Summarize By* list.

8. Click Next to proceed to Step Four. Check all four options, then click Finish to create the pivot table pictured in Figure 17.24.

Step 2a is a special
step that applies only
when consolidating
multiple consolidation
ranges.

Step 2b lets you
specify the ranges to
be consolidated.

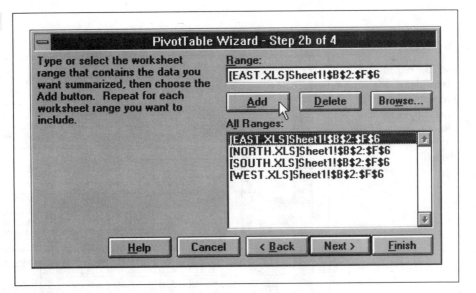

FIGURE 17.23

Double-click the field buttons to customize them. For aesthetic reasons only, you may want to change the name *Page1* to *Region*, *Row* to *Product*, and *Column* to *Quarter*.

FIGURE 17.24

The four regions are consolidated. The drop-down lets you select any of the four regions, or all of them (*All* is chosen by default).

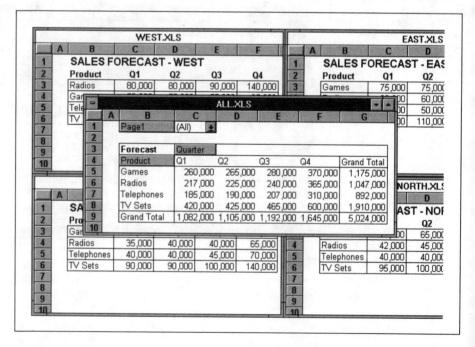

There is one key fact to keep in mind when creating a pivot table from multiple consolidation ranges: The consolidation is based on the column labels (field names), and the row labels (the values in the first column of each range). Matching labels are consolidated, though the position of the label within the range is not a factor.

Creating a Pivot Table from Another Pivot Table

So far, you have learned how to create pivot tables based on three different data sources: an Excel database, an external database, and multiple consolidation ranges. A pivot table can also be based on another pivot table.

If you choose Data ➤ PivotTable when there is already a pivot table defined in the active workbook (and if the active cell is not inside the existing pivot table), Step One of the PivotTable Wizard makes the *Another Pivot-Table* option available (see Figure 17.2). After clicking Next, Step Two lets you pick which existing pivot table you want to use.

Choose a pivot table from the list, then click Next to proceed to Step Three of the PivotTable Wizard.

TIP

When you create a new pivot table, Step Four of the PivotTable wizard lets you override the default name assigned by the wizard. Meaningful names can come in handy if you create more than one pivot table in a workbook, then create a new pivot table based on an existing table. With meaningful names, you can distinguish the tables from one another.

In fact, when a pivot table uses another pivot table as its source, then both tables are driven by the same hidden cache. If you uncheck the *Save Data with Table Layout* option in Step Four (see Figure 17.5) for *either* table, both tables are impacted.

Save Data with Table Layout?

Step Four of the Pivot Table Wizard, pictured in Figure 17.5, has a setting called *Save Data With Table Layout*. When checked, the source data is saved, inside the workbook, in a special hidden cache. It is useful to understand the implications of this setting.

- When checked, the pivot table can be changed without having to access the source data. This can save you the trouble of opening up workbooks, or the time it takes to query an external database.

- When checked, you need to make sure the hidden cache is not out of sync with the source data. (The Data ➤ Refresh Data command refreshes the cache, and, accordingly, the pivot table itself.)

In general, you will get better performance by saving the data with the table layout. But you pay a memory usage penalty, and must be mindful of data synchronization.

Charting a Pivot Table

You can create charts using the data in a pivot table. The procedure is no different than charting any other worksheet data. (See Chapter 13 to learn the basics of charting.) In Figure 17.25, the source data for the chart is B5:D8.

FIGURE 17.25

When a different region is selected from the page drop-down, the chart re-draws accordingly. The chart title is linked to cell C2.

Figure 17.26 is the same worksheet as Figure 17.25. However, the pivot table layout has been changed. The **Year** field has been repositioned as a page field. The **Region** field has been repositioned as a column heading. The chart has automatically redrawn accordingly.

FIGURE 17.26

The chart redraws after the pivot table layout is changed.

The Pivot Table Shortcut Menu

If you click anywhere in a pivot table using the right mouse button, a shortcut menu is displayed.

This is the same shortcut menu that is displayed when you right-click a normal cell, but with six commands added that are specific to pivot tables.

 Refresh Data Same as Data ➤ Refresh Data. Updates the pivot table from the source data.

 Show Pages Places each page of a multi-page pivot table onto a separate worksheet.

Group and Outline Displays a submenu that lets you hide detail, unhide detail, group data, and ungroup data.

 Add Field This command lets you add column fields, row fields, or data fields to the pivot table—depending on which type of cell is selected when the command is chosen.

PivotTable Displays the PivotTable Wizard.

 PivotTable Field Lets you customize a field. Same as the Data ➤ PivotTable Field command.

More Facts about Pivot Tables

Here are some more facts about pivot tables that are important to know.

Pivot tables are a replacement for *crosstabs*, which were introduced in Excel 4. The menu commands that were used in Excel 4 to create crosstabs have been replaced with the pivot table commands. Follow these steps to convert an Excel 4 crosstab to a pivot table:

1. Open the Excel 4 worksheet.

2. Select a cell inside the crosstab range, and choose Data ➤ Pivot Table.

3. Step Three of the PivotTable Wizard is displayed.

4. Click Finish.

Once you save the file, the crosstab is permanently converted to an Excel 5 pivot table. You will no longer be able to open the file under Excel 4.

When the Source Database Is Filtered

If you create a pivot table from an Excel database that has been filtered (using Data ➤ Filter), the filtering is ignored. Therefore, you may want to remove the filter before creating the pivot table.

When the Source Database Includes Embedded Subtotals

If you create a pivot table from an Excel database that has embedded subtotals (for either rows or columns), the subtotal rows are treated as separate records in the database. Accordingly, you *must* remove embedded subtotals to get meaningful results in the pivot table. (If the embedded subtotals were inserted using Data ➤ Subtotals, then choose Data ➤ Subtotals, and click Remove All.)

Freezing a Pivot Table

Suppose that you include a pivot table in a report, and want to keep an exact copy. Since you may inadvertently refresh the pivot table at a later date, follow these steps to make a frozen copy:

1. Select the entire table.

2. Choose Edit ➤ Copy.

3. Select a cell where you want to place the copy, then choose Edit ➤ Paste Special.

4. Select the *Values* option, then click OK.

The copy of the pivot table is not an actual pivot table. It cannot be pivoted, or changed with the PivotTable Wizard.

Two Calculation on One Data Field

Suppose that you want to calculate the sum of a data field, and calculate the average of the same field. The same field can be placed into the data area more than once.

CHAPTER

18

Accessing External Databases

fast **TRACK**

To change a query definition   **549**

1. Select any cell inside the data, then choose Data ➤ Get External Data.

2. Click Edit Query—change the query in Microsoft Query.

To format a column of data retrieved by a query   **550**

Format the entire column—the next time the query is performed, more rows may be retrieved.

To perform queries without Microsoft Query   **551**

1. Load the ODBC add-in (XLODBC.XLA).

2. Use the SQL.REQUEST worksheet function.

To access a dBASE file   **553**

If small enough, dBASE files can be opened using File ➤ Open. Or, they can be queried as an external database.

IN Chapters 16 and 17 you learned how to manage and manipulate databases residing on a worksheet. But in a corporate environment, source data is typically stored in an external database, such as Access, dBASE, Paradox, SQL Server, Oracle, or DB2. Accessing such data is one of the biggest obstacles faced by corporate users, and a lot of time is spent manually entering data into worksheet models when, ideally, data would be imported into worksheets electronically.

There is a separate program that comes with Excel called *Microsoft Query*, which makes the process of querying external databases relatively simple. Microsoft Query uses a technology called *Open Database Connectivity* (*ODBC*) to access data. This chapter will explain:

- *the various ways you can get external data into your worksheets*
- *how to perform queries using Microsoft Query*
- *how to place query results onto a worksheet*
- *performing queries with the SQL.REQUEST function*

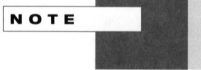

NOTE The Excel retail package includes an entire manual on Microsoft Query. This chapter is intended to provide a condensed primer to get you up and running quickly.

When you originally installed Excel, you were provided the option of installing Microsoft Query. (It will have been installed in the MSAPPS\MSQUERY directory which is located in the Microsoft Windows directory.) If Microsoft Query is not installed, you may want to use the Excel setup program to install it before reading this chapter.

NOTE   Microsoft Query is also included with Microsoft applications other than Excel. Even if you did not install it when you installed Excel, it might already be on your system.

There Are Several Ways to Get External Data into Excel

There are a number of ways to get external data into your worksheets. This chapter will show you how to issue queries to an external database using Microsoft Query (and using the SQL.REQUEST function), which in turn uses a Microsoft technology called ODBC, which stands for Open Database Connectivity. ODBC provides access to many types of databases. However, you may want to access a database for which there is no ODBC driver. Or, your organization may not have the required networking infrastructure in place to support a direct "conversation" between Excel and a certain database. You should be aware of the alternatives:

Opening dBASE Files

You can use the File ➤ Open command to open a dBASE file (or compatible files created with xBASE programs such as Fox and Clipper). You can even edit and save the data. However, the size of the file may not exceed Excel's limit of 16,384 rows and 256 columns. See Chapter 25 for more information on the types of files that can be opened directly.

Importing Text Files

If your mainframe application is capable of outputting text files, you can import them into Excel with the File ➤ Open command. (The various options are explained in Chapter 25.)

Exporting Excel Worksheets from Your Database Application

Some database applications, such as Microsoft Access, have the ability to save data in Excel format. Then, there is nothing special to be done on the Excel end—you just open the file that was output from the database application.

Pivot Tables

Pivot tables, covered in Chapter 17, provide a powerful, intuitive interface for accessing and viewing external (and internal) databases. (Pivot tables require the use of Microsoft Query, and thus ODBC.)

Definition of Terms

It is relatively simple to perform database queries, and to place the results of a query onto a worksheet. But with two different applications involved, Microsoft Excel and Microsoft Query, there are a number of ways to perform queries. To fully understand the options, it will help if you understand the various pieces of the puzzle. Here are some of the terms that will be referred to in this chapter.

Structured Query Language There is an industry-standard language used to communicate with databases which is called *Structured Query Language*, or *SQL* (generally pronounced "sequel"). When you perform queries from Excel or from Microsoft Query, whether you know it or not, the query is translated into SQL.

Microsoft Query This program is a stand-alone application that is included with Excel. It provides an interface that lets you create SQL statements without having to know (or even see) SQL. You can use MS Query to perform queries, then paste the results onto an Excel worksheet. (You can even paste a query *definition* onto an Excel worksheet, in which case the query can be fired directly from Excel, even though MS Query is doing the real work behind the scenes.)

ODBC Manager ODBC stands for Open Database Connectivity, a Microsoft technology that allows different applications, such as Excel and MS Query, to communicate with a variety of database types. Whenever you perform a query from Excel (or MS Query), a SQL statement is sent to the ODBC manager—it acts as an intermediary between the application and the database. This means that the same query syntax can be used to query a database server, such as SQL Server and Oracle, and "flat" files such as dBASE and Paradox.

ODBC Driver The ODBC Manager does not actually "talk" directly to a database. Rather, it communicates through *drivers*. Included in the Excel package are drivers for Access, dBASE, FoxPro, Paradox, SQL Server, Oracle, Excel worksheets, and text files. Additional drivers can be purchased from database vendors, or from third-party companies that publish ODBC drivers. (To learn how to install ODBC drivers, refer to Appendix B of the Microsoft Query manual.)

Data Sources When performing a query, it is not enough to know what type of database you are accessing. A *Data Source*, defined in the ODBC manager, tells the ODBC manager the type of data, where to find the database, and in some cases, how to connect to the data. For example, you may have several different dBASE databases on your computer, each of which is considered a discrete data source.

ODBC Add-In This Excel add-in, named XLODBC.XLA, allows Excel to talk to the ODBC manager directly, circumventing MS Query. The SQL.REQUEST worksheet function, covered later in this chapter, is a service provided by the ODBC add-in. In addition, the ODBC add-in provides an API for application developers.

Microsoft Query Add-In This Excel add-in, named XLQUERY.XLA, serves to integrate Excel with Microsoft Query. It adds two commands to Excel's Data menu, and one command to MS Query's File menu. These commands make it easier to work with the two programs. (See Chapter 24 for more information on add-ins.)

NOTE

When installing Excel, if you did not choose to install the data-access components, the ODBC add-in and the Microsoft Query add-in will not be in your system. They are required if you want to apply the skills discussed in this chapter. You can use the Excel setup program to install them.

The NorthWind Traders Database A sample database is included with MS Query for a fictitious company called Northwind Traders. The data is in dBASE format, and is defined as data source *NWind*. Exercises in this chapter will query this database.

Retrieving Data from an External Database

The query add-in helps to integrate Excel with Microsoft Query, and simplify the process of retrieving data from an external database. In this section, you will learn how to:

- load the query add-in
- define a query
- place the query results, and query definition, on a worksheet
- refresh the query at a later date without having to redefine it in MS Query

Loading the Query Add-In

The query add-in, XLQUERY.XLA, is an Excel add-in that appends a special command to Excel's Data menu:

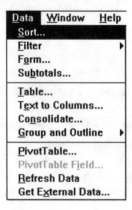

If the command *Get External Data* is not on your Data menu, then the query add-in is not loaded. Use the File ➤ Open command to open XLQUERY.XLA—it is located in the LIBRARY\MSQUERY directory, located in the directory where you installed Excel.

T I P   The add-in manager, displayed with the Tools ➤ Add-Ins command, can be used to configure Excel so that the query add-in loads automatically every time you start Excel. (See Chapter 24 to learn more about add-ins.)

Starting Microsoft Query

 Once the query add-in is loaded, choose the Data ➤ Get External Data command to start Microsoft Query, or click the Get External Data tool which is on the Query and Pivot toolbar.

Since Microsoft Query is a separate application, you can run it by double-clicking its icon from Program Manager, but the Data ➤ Get External Data command does two special things: It adds a command to the Microsoft Query menu that returns you to Excel after the query is defined, and it leaves Excel in a state where it is ready to complete the process once you return from Microsoft Query. Thus, the Data ➤ Get External Data command makes things a lot easier.

Using Microsoft Query to Define a Query

After choosing the Data ➤ Get External Data command, you will be working inside Microsoft Query. This chapter will walk you through the basic steps involved in defining a query. Remember, a separate manual on Microsoft Query comes in the Excel package.

Selecting a Data Source

Once inside Microsoft Query, the first step is to select a data source—see Figure 18.1.

FIGURE 18.1

Microsoft Query—
select a data source.

The precise meaning of *data source* differs somewhat depending on the type of database you are accessing. Table 18.1 describes several commonly used database types, and the corresponding meaning of *data source*.

TABLE 18.1: Meaning of *Data Source* in Various Types of Databases

TYPE OF DATABASE	MEANING OF *DATA SOURCE*
dBASE, FoxPro, and Paradox	a group of related files stored in a discrete directory
Excel	an Excel workbook with a *Database* range defined
Text	a text file containing records and fields
SQL Server and Oracle	a database defined on a server—the data source specifies the server, the network containing the server, and other information required to make the connection to the database

Select the *NWind* data source (the sample Northwind database included with MS Query), then click the Use button. Refer to the Microsoft Query manual to learn how to define new data sources.

Choosing the Tables

Next, you must specify which tables (files) you wish to retrieve data from. The Add Tables dialog box lists all of the dBASE files in the NorthWind database:

NOTE   If the .DBF files are not displayed in the *Table Name* list, use the dialog box to navigate your way to the Microsoft Windows directory, then to the MSAPPS\MSQUERY directory that is contained within your Windows directory—this is where the NWind data should be stored on your system.

Select *product.dbf* from the list of tables, then click Add (Figure 18.2). A query can retrieve data from more than one table. We are going to start with a simple query, so click the Close button to close the Add Tables dialog box.

FIGURE 18.2

The product table has been added to the query definition.

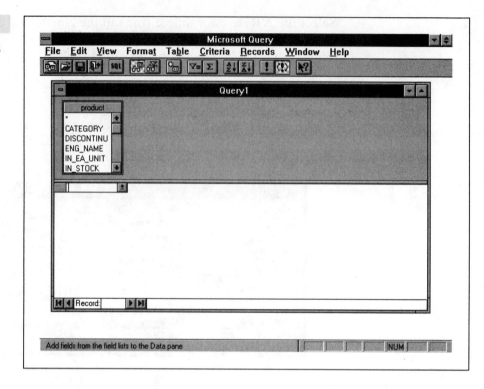

Choosing the Fields

Next, you must specify which fields you want to include in the query. There are several ways to add fields to the query:

- Double-click the field names.

- Select one or more fields (use the Ctrl or Shift keys to select more than one field), then drag and drop them onto the bottom part of the window.

- Use the * (asterisk) to add all fields to the query.

Use one of these techniques to add the fields PRODUCT_ID, PROD_NAME, CATEGORY, IN_STOCK, and UNIT_PRICE to the query (see Figure 18.3).

The query results are
displayed in the query
window.

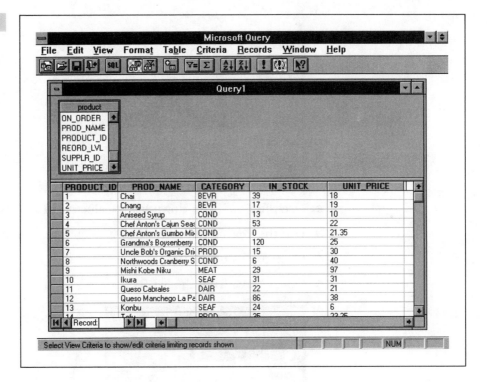

TIP

Each time you add a field to the query, the query is
re-issued. You can use the Records ➤ Automatic Query
command to control this behavior.

Adding Criteria

If you want to retrieve a subset of the records, you must add a criterion.
Follow these steps to select only those products in the *beverage* category:

1. Choose the Criteria ➤ Add Criteria command, which displays the
   Add Criteria dialog box.

2. Use the *Field* drop-down list to select **CATEGORY**.

3. Use the *Operator* drop-down list to choose **equals**.

4. Click the Values button.

5. Select **Bevr** from the list (beverages).

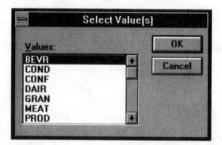

6. Click OK to close the Select Value dialog box.

7. Click the Add button—a criteria grid is added to the query window (see Figure 18.4).

NOTE

The criteria grid is almost identical to an advanced criterion defined on a worksheet. See Chapter 16 to learn how to apply advanced criteria to worksheet databases.

8. Click the Close button to close the Add Criteria dialog box.

FIGURE 18.4

Behind the scenes, the criterion causes a *where clause* to be added to the SQL statement.

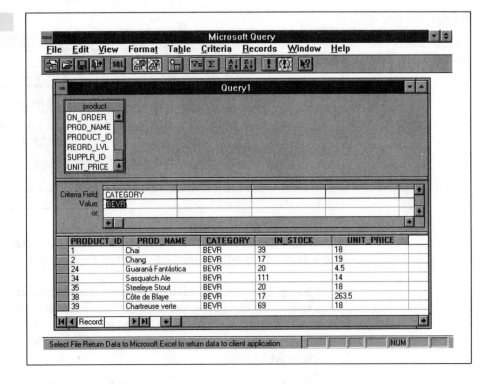

The query window will now display only those products in the beverage category.

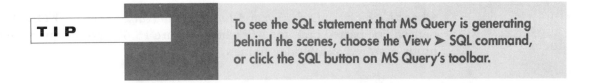

TIP

To see the SQL statement that MS Query is generating behind the scenes, choose the View ➤ SQL command, or click the SQL button on MS Query's toolbar.

Placing the Data onto an Excel Worksheet

Now that there is data in the query window, choose the File ➤ Return Data to Microsoft Excel command (from the MS Query menu). Excel takes over, and displays the Get External Data dialog box (Figure 18.5).

FIGURE 18.5

The Get External Data dialog box

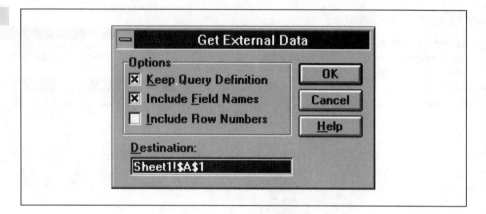

Remember, the *Return Data to Microsoft Excel* command only appears on the File menu if MS Query was started from Excel.

Keep Query Definition causes the query definition to be stored on the active worksheet (the data source, and the SQL statement generated by MS Query), which in turn allows the query to be processed in the future without having to reconstruct it in MS Query.

Include Field Names causes the field names to be pasted onto the worksheet, in addition to the data.

Include Row Numbers adds sequential row numbers to the records (once they are pasted onto the worksheet).

Check *Keep Query Definition* and *Include Field Names*, then click OK. The data will be pasted onto the worksheet (Figure 18.6), and the query definition is stored as a hidden name.

Refreshing a Query

Once query results are placed on a worksheet, you may want to refresh the query at a later date. Otherwise, if the source data changes, the worksheet will not be synchronized with the source data. This is the reason for checking the *Keep Query Definition* option (see Figure 18.5)—it allows the

FIGURE 18.6

The data is pasted onto the active worksheet.

	A	B	C	D	E	F	G
1	PRODUCT_ID	PROD_NAME	CATEGORY	IN_STOCK	UNIT_PRICE		
2	1	Chai	BEVR	39	18		
3	2	Chang	BEVR	17	19		
4	24	Guaraná Fantástica	BEVR	20	4.5		
5	34	Sasquatch Ale	BEVR	111	14		
6	35	Steeleye Stout	BEVR	20	18		
7	38	Côte de Blaye	BEVR	17	263.5		
8	39	Chartreuse verte	BEVR	69	18		

Book1 — Sheet1 / Sheet2 / Sheet3 / Sheet4 / Sheet5

query to be refreshed without having to redefine the query. If *Keep Query Definition* was checked, you can use this procedure to refresh the query:

1. Make sure the query add-in (XLQUERY.XLA) is loaded.

2. Select any cell within the range of data retrieved from the previous query.

3. Choose the Data ➤ Refresh Data command—the database is re-queried and the results are placed on the worksheet. (Or click the Refresh Data tool which is found on the Query and Pivot toolbar.)

Changing a Query

If you keep a query definition, as described above, follow these steps to change the query:

1. Make sure the query add-in (XLQUERY.XLA) is loaded.

2. Select any cell within the range of data retrieved from the previous query.

3. Choose Data ➤ Get External Data—since a query was already defined, the Get External Data dialog box is displayed.

4. Click Edit Query—MS Query is started.

5. Change the query in MS Query, and choose File ➤ Return Data to Microsoft Excel (from the MS Query menu).

6. Click OK at the Get External Data dialog box.

Querying an Excel Database

One of the external data sources that you can Query is Excel files. This is a cause of considerable confusion for many users, since an Excel file is not an external database. But in fact, when you query an Excel file, it is treated like an external data source. The file must have a database defined on it, and the database range must be named *Database*. Behind the scenes, the query is processed much like a query of a dBASE file—records are retrieved from the file from the disk.

Except under special circumstances, there is no compelling reason to query Excel files as external databases. Here are several reasons why:

- The file can just be opened, without the extra overhead required to query it like an external database.

- Excel files are an inefficient mass-storage medium, unlike a "real" database which stores only raw data. (Excel files store formatting, formulas, etc.)

- It is impossible to index an Excel database.

Working with Query Results

Often, retrieving data onto a worksheet is just the first part of the job. You may want to format the data, or use Excel to further analyze the data. Here are some ideas:

How to Quickly Format the Data Select a cell within the data, and choose Format ➤ AutoFormat to apply a built-in table format.

How to Apply a Number Format Look at the UNIT_PRICE column in Figure 18.6. The numbers are not properly formatted as dollars and cents. You could format the range E2:E8. But, when you refresh the query at a later date, more rows may be retrieved—the additional rows will *not* be formatted. Instead, apply the number format to the entire column (as long as there is no other numeric data in the same column elsewhere on the worksheet using a different format).

Manipulating the Data on the Worksheet The Data ➤ Filter command can be used to filter the data on the worksheet. The Data ➤ Sort command can be used to sort the data. (See Chapters 15 and 16 for more information.)

Build a Pivot Table Use the Data ➤ Pivot Table command to build a pivot table based on the retrieved data.

Using the SQL.REQUEST Worksheet Function

The SQL.REQUEST function provides a different way of retrieving data from an external database. It uses the ODBC add-in (XLODBC.XLA), which allows Excel to communicate directly with the ODBC Manager, circumventing MS Query. There are pros and cons to this approach:

PROS:

- User input can be dynamically incorporated into the SQL statement.
- It will take less time to perform a query.

CONS:

- The SQL.REQUEST function must be entered as an array formula that anticipates the maximum number of rows that may be retrieved—plus, array formulas are limited in size.
- The data source must be known, and the SQL statement must be entered manually (though it can be pasted from MS Query).
- Column widths are not automatically adjusted.

Loading the ODBC Add-In

Before you can use the SQL.REQUEST function, the ODBC add-in must be loaded. (If you enter a formula with SQL.REQUEST and get a #NAME! error, the add-in is not loaded.) Use the File ➤ Open command to open XLODBC.XLA, stored in the LIBRARY\MSQUERY directory, under the Excel directory. (See Chapter 24 to learn how to load add-ins automatically.)

Function Syntax

The SQL.REQUEST function accepts the following arguments:

Connection_String   text string specifying the data source name (used by the ODBC manager), and other information required to make connection to the database (user ID, password, server, database). Samples based on database type:

dBASE	DSN=NWind
Text	DSN=My Text Data
Excel	DSN=My Excel Data
Oracle	DSN=My Oracle Data; DBQ=MYSERVER; UID=Jane; PWD=Password
SQL Server	DSN=My SQL Server; UID=Jane; PWE=123; Database=Pubs

Output_Ref   cell reference (or name) where the completed connection string is to be placed—if omitted, no connection string returned

Driver_Prompt   specifies if the ODBC manager dialog box (or boxes) is displayed, and which options are available to the user (defaults to 2 if omitted)

1	Always display dialog box.
2	Only display dialog box if Connection_String does not provide enough information to make connection.

3   Only display dialog box if Connection_String does not provide enough information to make connection—options that are not required are disabled.

4   If connection cannot be made, no dialog box is displayed and an error is returned.

SQL_Statement   SQL text, such as: SELECT Product, Qty FROM Products WHERE Qty<>0

Field_Names   logical (TRUE or FALSE) specifies whether to return field names with query—if omitted defaults to FALSE

Array-Entering the Formula

One of the biggest disadvantages of SQL.REQUEST is that you must *array-enter* the formula into a range of cells that anticipates the maximum number of rows and columns that will be retrieved. If the retrieved data does not fill the range, the remainder of the range is filled with blanks.

Follow these steps to retrieve 2 fields, and up to 20 rows (plus field names), from the *product* master file in the Northwind sample data. Only those products where quantity in stock is less than 5 will be retrieved.

1. Make sure XLODBC.XLA is loaded.

2. Select B2:C22.

3. Enter the following formula (but do not press Enter)—use the precise upper/lower case specified.

```
=SQL.REQUEST("DSN=NWind",,2,"SELECT PROD_NAME, IN_STOCK FROM
product.dbf WHERE IN_STOCK<5",TRUE)
```

4. To array-enter the formula, hold down Ctrl+Shift keys, then press Enter—Figure 18.7 shows the result.

NOTE   When you array-enter a formula, brackets are placed around the formula. You cannot type the brackets—you must "Ctrl+Shift+Enter" the formula. (See Chapter 26 to learn more about array formulas.)

FIGURE 18.7

Five products have stock less than 5—the last argument TRUE causes field names to be placed on the sheet.

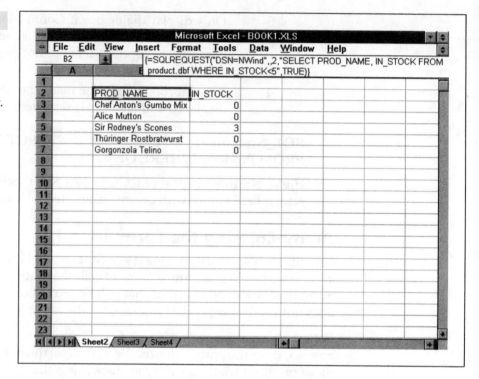

Incorporating Variables into the SQL Statement

An important benefit of the SQL.REQUEST function is the ability to dynamically incorporate variables into the SQL statement. In the previous example, the SQL statement is hard-coded into the formula. The only way to change the query is by changing the array formula, which is awkward.

The **where** clause of the SQL statement specifies a threshold (5) that determines which products will be retrieved. Suppose that you want to be able to enter this threshold easily—without changing the array formula. The following steps allow you to use a cell, E2, to enter the threshold.

1. Enter the number 10 into cell E2.

2. Select cells B2:C22.

TIP

You cannot edit a portion of an array—the entire array must be selected before revising the formula. A shortcut for selecting an array is to select a cell within the array, then choose the Edit ➤ Go To command, click Special, then choose the *Current Array* option.

3. Edit the formula to read as follows—remember, don't press Enter.

```
=SQL.REQUEST("DSN=NWind",,2,"SELECT PROD_NAME, IN_STOCK FROM
product.dbf WHERE IN_STOCK<"&E2,TRUE)
```

4. Press Ctrl+Shift+Enter to array-enter the formula—Figure 18.8 shows the result.

5. Enter the number **20** into cell E2 and watch the data change.

FIGURE 18.8

Cell E2 determines the threshold for quantity in stock.

	Microsoft Excel - BOOK1.XLS					
	File	Edit	View	Insert	Format	Tools	Data	Window	Help

B2   `{=SQLREQUEST("DSN=NWind",,2,"SELECT PROD_NAME, IN_STOCK FROM product.dbf WHERE IN_STOCK<"&E2,TRUE)}`

	A					
1						
2	PROD_NAME	IN_STOCK		10		
3	Chef Anton's Gumbo Mix	0				
4	Northwoods Cranberry Sauce	6				
5	Alice Mutton	0				
6	Sir Rodney's Scones	3				
7	Thüringer Rostbratwurst	0				
8	Gorgonzola Telino	0				
9	Mascarpone Fabioli	9				
10						
11						
12						
13						
14						
15						
16						
17						
18						
19						
20						
21						
22						
23						

Sheet2 \ **Sheet3** / Sheet4

6. Remember these important facts:

- The dimensions of the array formula limit the number of rows and columns that will be retrieved—in the previous example, no matter how large a number you enter into cell E2, the data will stop at C22. (Don't hesitate to create large arrays to avoid this problem.)

- If the value in cell E2 results in an invalid SQL statement, caused by text in cell E2, for example, the cell returns an error.

When a SQL Statement Requires Embedded Quotation Marks

A SQL statement **where** clause that performs a numeric comparison might read:

```
WHERE IN_STOCK < 100
```

But when comparing a text value, the text must be quoted using single quote marks (apostrophe). The **where** clause might read:

```
WHERE CATEGORY = 'BEVR'
```

If the **where** clause contains variables, as with the previous exercise, and a formula is constructing the SQL statement, the formula must place the single quotes around the text string. Such formulas are difficult to read and edit, due to the proliferation of double quotes and single quotes. Notice how difficult it is to discern the single and double quotes at the end of the following formula:

```
="SELECT * FROM product.dbf WHERE CATEGORY = '"&B2&"'"
```

A trick that simplifies the job of entering and editing such formulas is to define a named constant that is equal to a single quote, then use the name in your formulas. Try this exercise:

1. Use Insert ➤ Name ➤ Define to create the name **Q**—it refers to a single quotation mark (see Chapter 8 to learn more about named constants).

2. Enter **BEVR** into cell B2.

3. Enter the following formula into a cell:

```
="SELECT * FROM product.dbf WHERE CATEGORY = "&Q&B2&Q
```

4. This formula will result in:

```
SELECT * FROM product.dbf WHERE CATEGORY = 'BEVR'
```

Working with Long SQL Statements

Text strings in Excel are limited to 255 characters. This is a severe restriction because SQL statements can be quite long. To overcome this limit, the SQL statement can be placed in a range of cells. The following example combines a long SQL statement with some creative use of variables.

On a blank worksheet, define the name **Q** to refer to a single quote (see previous example). Then enter the following:

In cell B2 **Enter Category:**

In cell C2 **BEVR**

In cell B4 **select PROD_NAME, CATEGORY, IN_STOCK, REORD_LVL, SUPPLR_ID from product.dbf** (and enter a trailing space after product.dbf)

In cell B5 **where IN_STOCK < (REORD_LVL + 100)** (and enter a trailing space)

In cell B6 **=IF(ISBLANK(C2),"","and CATEGORY = "&Q&C2&Q&" ")**

In cell B7 **order by CATEGORY, PROD_NAME**

In cell B9:F50 **=SQL.REQUEST("DSN=NWind",,2,B4:B7, TRUE)** (array-enter the formula)

All products in the beverage category are retrieved. Change cell C2 to COND, and all products in the condiment category are retrieved (Figure 18.9). Clear cell C2, and all products are retrieved.

This demonstrates the following points.

FIGURE 18.9

The SQL statement referred to by the SQL.REQUEST function can reside in a range of cells, overcoming the 255-character limit for a cell.

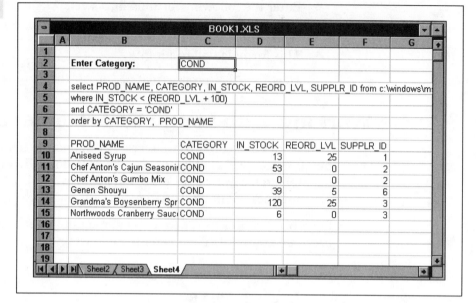

- The formula in B6 appends the **where** clause only if a value is entered in C2.

- When the SQL statement is sent to the ODBC manager, the values in B4:B7 are concatenated into one long string—without the trailing spaces, the query would fail.

For Users of Earlier Versions of Excel

Earlier versions of Excel used a utility called Q+E to perform queries. Microsoft Query takes the place of Q+E, and most users will find it to be a considerable improvement. If you have written macros to perform queries using Q+E, there are two important facts to be aware of.

- The DDE interface to MS Query is compatible with Q+E. In your macro code, all you have to do is change the name of the executable from QE.EXE to MSQUERY.EXE.

- Previously, the interface between Excel and Q+E was simplified by an add-in named QE.XLA. An add-in of the same name is included with Excel 5. It works just like the old QE.XLA, except it works with MS Query instead of Q+E. This means that if you have written macros that call routines on QE.XLA, the macros should work properly under Excel 5 without modification.

- If for some reason you want to continue to use Q+E, Excel 5 is still capable of sending DDE commands to Q+E.

PART SIX

Customizing Excel

Controls and Custom Dialog Boxes

fast **TRACK**

The items displayed in a listbox can be changed nonprogrammatically   **579**

by using a named formula as the input range.

To rename a control   **590**

Select the control and change the name in the Name box.

Any graphic object can be placed on a dialog sheet   **590**

including charts and pictures of cells taken with the Camera tool.

Dialog box properties can be controlled programmatically   **596**

- You can hide and unhide objects.
- You can disable and enable objects.
- You can change the text associated with the control.
- You can change the dialog box caption.

USERS are drawn to spreadsheet products in large part because of the openness of the spreadsheet environment. However, this same openness is one of the biggest obstacles when trying to deploy bulletproof solutions. Validating user input, and performing certain actions based on user input, are among the most common development tasks. This chapter covers the two primary techniques used to control user input:

- *enhancing the user interface by placing controls, such as list boxes and checkboxes, directly on worksheets*

- *creating custom dialog boxes when bulletproof programmatic control is required*

Understanding Custom Controls

A *control* is a special type of object that is placed on a worksheet or dialog sheet. They are used to facilitate user input. For example, one type of control is a list box—it allows you to make selections from a list rather than typing in a response. Controls are placed on worksheets and dialog sheets by drawing them, just as you would draw a graphic object such as a rectangle. (See Chapter 12 to learn about graphic objects.)

The most important thing to understand about controls is that there is much similarity between controls on worksheets and controls on dialog sheets:

- All of the controls that can be used on a worksheet can also be used on a dialog sheet.

- Most controls are *active*—when clicked, something happens.

- Some controls are passive; they are not interacted with—for instance, you do not interact with a group box.

- Controls have many traits in common with other graphical objects, such as text boxes and drawing objects (see Chapter 12)—they can be formatted, locked, sent to back, brought to front, or hidden.

On the other hand, dialog sheets support several controls that cannot be used on worksheets.

The Forms Toolbar

The tools that are used to draw controls are found on the Forms toolbar.

The Forms toolbar is displayed automatically when a dialog sheet is active. (Dialog sheets are explained later in this chapter.) When a worksheet is active, use the View ➤ Toolbars command to display the Forms toolbar.

Table 19.1 lists all of the drawing tools on the Forms toolbar. The table specifies which controls can be placed on worksheets, and also specifies which controls are passive (in other words, they are not clicked or otherwise interacted with).

Several controls (checkbox, option button, list box, drop-down list box, scrollbar, spinner) can be linked to a worksheet cell. These controls...

- can be linked to only one cell (though a cell can have multiple controls linked to it);

- are typically linked to a cell in the same workbook, but can also be linked to a cell in a different workbook (in which case the workbook must be open for the control to work);

- when selected, and the Format ➤ Object command has been chosen, have a tab called *Control* which allows the cell link to be defined (this dialog box differs somewhat from control to control).

TABLE 19.1: Drawing Tools on the Forms Toolbar

TOOL	DESCRIPTION	USABLE ON WORKSHEETS?	PASSIVE?
Aa	label (text)	yes	yes
ab	edit control	no	no
[XYZ]	group box	yes	yes
▢	button	yes	no
☒	check box	yes	no
◉	option button	yes	no
list box icon	list box	yes	no
drop-down list box icon	drop-down list box	yes	no
list box linked icon	list box linked to edit control	no	no
combination icon	combination drop-down / edit control	no	no
scrollbar icon	scrollbar control	yes	no
spinner icon	spinner control	yes	no

Controls on Worksheets

Effective user interfaces can be created with controls on worksheets. You can make it easier for users to interact with your model, and also avoid data entry errors.

- Controls can be linked to cells—certain data entry is simplified, and data integrity enforced.

- Adding controls to a worksheet is easy—knowledge of macros is not required.

- When combined with advanced naming techniques (see Chapter 8) and the macro recorder (see Chapter 20), advanced functionality can be added to a worksheet model with relative ease.

To Place a Control on a Worksheet

Follow these steps to draw a control on a worksheet:

1. Display the Forms toolbar using View ➤ Toolbars.

2. Click a tool on the Forms toolbar (one of the tools designated in Table 19.1 as usable on worksheets)—the mouse pointer becomes a crosshair.

3. Draw the object on the worksheet using the mouse (as you would draw any graphic object).

NOTE Excel will not let you to draw a control on a worksheet if it is not allowed on a worksheet—Excel just beeps when you click one of these tools.

Formatting Controls

The term *format*, when applied to controls, encompasses all of the control's properties, not just the visual format. This discussion will explain how to access the formatting dialog box for controls.

Unlike "normal" graphic objects, active controls perform an action when clicked. Follow these steps to format them.

Select the object by holding down the Ctrl key while clicking the object.

Choose the Format ➤ Object command.

You do not have to hold down Ctrl while clicking a passive control.

TIP Any graphic object can have a macro assigned to it. When the object is clicked, the macro runs. To select such objects on a worksheet, hold down the Ctrl key, then click the object.

Another way to format a control is to click it with the right mouse button, then choose the Format Object command from the shortcut menu pictured below.

Cut
Copy
Paste
Clear
Edit Object
Format Object.
Bring to Front
Send to Back
Group
Assign Macro...

Setting Control Properties

Active controls have *control properties*. This is where cell linkage is defined, as well as other behavioral settings. (Later in this chapter, each type of control will be discussed.) Regardless of the type of control, here are two ways to access the control properties:

• Follow the procedures for formatting the control (described above), then select the Control tab.

- Select the control, and click the Control Properties tool (located on the Forms toolbar).

Moving and Resizing Controls

Controls are simply graphic objects, though they possess special properties. They are moved and resized using the same procedures for moving and resizing other types of objects.

Worksheet Controls

The controls discussed in this section can all be used on worksheets (and on dialog sheets).

Labels

Labels are used for text, and they are passive. They are of little value on worksheets because they are less flexible than text boxes. Unlike a text box, a label cannot be formatted, nor can a formula be used. (The text format on labels is automatically the same as the text on built-in dialog boxes.)

Checkboxes

Checkboxes are used to toggle between logical values TRUE and FALSE (for inputs that require a yes/no answer). To create a checkbox linked to a cell:

1. Draw a checkbox on a worksheet.

2. With the checkbox object still selected, choose the Format ➤ Object command, then select the *Control* tab.

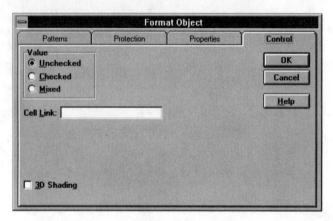

3. Enter a cell reference or cell name into *Cell Link* (this is a range edit—you can point and click on the worksheet to specify the cell).

The current value setting is not particularly useful for controls on worksheets; it is used to set default values for controls on dialog sheets. This is true of all the controls which allow an initial value to be set.

4. Click OK, then test the checkbox. It will enter TRUE or FALSE into the linked cell (Figure 19.1).

It is common for the linked cell to be located out of view. There is no particular reason for the user to see the TRUE/FALSE value, even if the cell is referenced by other cells in the model.

Scrollbars

Scrollbars are used to control an integer value in a cell (Figure 19.2).

- *Minimum* and *Maximum* values constrain the cell value—these values can be no less than zero and no greater than 30000 (meaning that the cell must contain a number from 0 to 30000).

FIGURE 19.1

The checkbox is linked to cell B6. When checked, B6 is set to TRUE. When unchecked, B6 is set to FALSE.

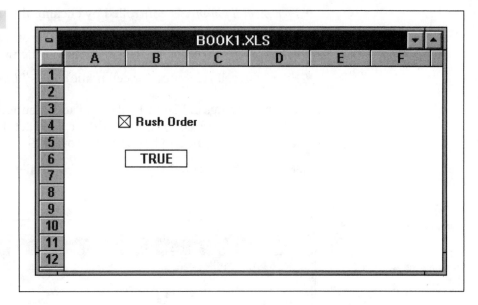

FIGURE 19.2

Scrollbars control the integer value in a cell.

- *Incremental Change* is controlled by clicking the up or down arrows.

- *Page Change* is controlled by clicking the scroll bar itself, or by dragging the scroll box—the box between the up and down arrows.

- Enter the cell reference (or cell name) in *Cell Link*.

The scrollbar settings in Figure 19.2 would add or subtract one from cell A1 when the arrows are clicked, and add or subtract 10 when the bar is clicked. The cell will not go below 1 or above 999.

Scrollbars can be oriented vertically or horizontally (Figure 19.3).

FIGURE 19.3

Scrollbars can be oriented vertically or horizontally.

Spinners

 Spinners are identical to scrollbars, except there is no *Page Change* setting, and they can only be oriented vertically.

Option Buttons

 Option buttons are used to select one option from a list of two or more exclusive choices. Option buttons are sometimes called radio buttons because they work the same way as the buttons on a car radio—since you can only listen to one station at a time, the choices are mutually exclusive.

The worksheet in Figure 19.4 includes three option buttons, all linked to the same cell. However, the linkage only needs to be set for one of the option buttons—the other buttons are automatically linked.

 Option buttons can be placed inside of a *Group Box*. The group box not only groups the buttons visually—it also groups them logically (see Figure 19.5).

FIGURE 19.4

All of the option buttons are linked to cell D5. When the first button is chosen, D5 is set to 1. When the second button is chosen, D5 is set to 2, etc.

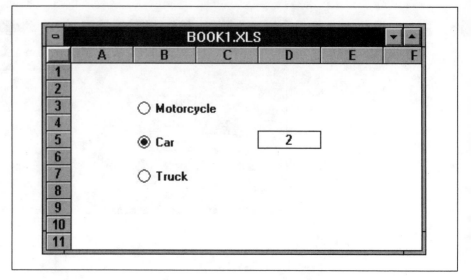

FIGURE 19.5

The option buttons in the Media group box are linked to B7. The option buttons in the Category group box are linked to D7.

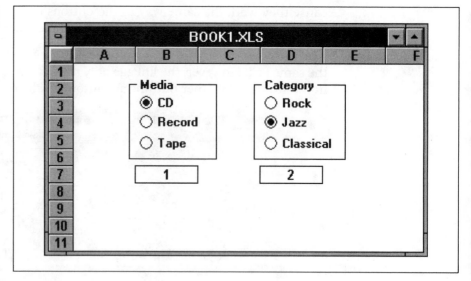

Here are some important facts to remember about the behavior of option buttons and group boxes:

- All option buttons on a worksheet that are *not* inside a group box are part of the same logical group. When you link any of them to a cell, all of the others are automatically linked to the same cell.

- All options buttons within a group box are part of the same logical group. When you link any of them to a cell, all of the others are automatically linked to the same cell.

- There can be more than one group box on a sheet containing option buttons. And, on the same sheet, there can be option buttons that are not inside a group box.

- If you resize a group box so that an option button that was previously not inside the box is now inside, the new member automatically becomes part of the logical group. Conversely, if you resize a group box so that one of the option buttons is no longer in the box, the "orphaned" option button ceases to be a member of the logical group.

- Other controls, such as checkboxes and list boxes, can be placed inside a group box (see Figure 19.6). The sole purpose is aesthetics—there is no logical side effect.

FIGURE 19.6

Controls other than option buttons can be placed in a group box, with no effect on the behavior of the controls. Group boxes only affect the behavior of option buttons.

List Boxes

List boxes let the user select an item from a list, and place a result in a linked cell. They require two separate cell linkages:

- an input range—the range of cells that contains the list of choices
- a cell link—when an item is selected in the list box, this cell contains the position within the list of the selected item

Here are the control properties for the list box in Figure 19.7.

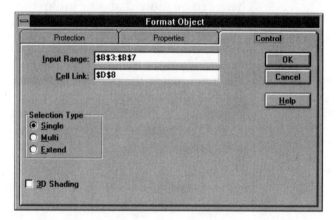

FIGURE 19.7

The input range for the list box is B3:B7. The cell link is D8. Since the second item in the list is selected, D8 contains the number 2.

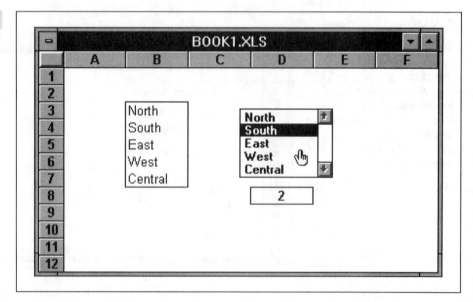

You can use names in place of cell addresses for the list box cell linkages. For example, in Figure 19.7, you could name B3:B7 *Regions*, then enter *Regions* as the input range.

T I P

For *all* controls that are linked to cells, a cell name can be entered for the link. When the control and the linked cell are in the same workbook, the benefit is clarity. But if the control and linked cell are on separate workbooks, the benefit is integrity—it is very important to refer to cells by name in this circumstance.

Drop-down List Boxes

 Drop-down list boxes are identical to standard list boxes, except you must specify how high the list box is, measured in lines, when dropped down.

Buttons

 The sole purpose of a button is to run a macro—buttons are not linked to cells. When you draw a button, a dialog box displays allowing you to assign a macro.

At this stage, there are three ways to assign a macro:

- Select an existing macro from the list.

- Click New to write a new macro—a shell for a new macro will be placed on a VBA module, and displayed so that you can write the actual macro.

- Click Record to record a macro—the Record New Macro dialog box is displayed.

Chapter 20 provides more information on how to assign macros to buttons, and how to record macros.

TIP   Any graphic object can have a macro assigned to it, not just "official" buttons. Just select the object and choose Tools ➤ Assign Macro. As with official buttons, when the object is clicked the macro is run.

In terms of formatting, buttons are similar to text boxes (see Chapter 12). You can format the font, and set the text alignment. Figure 19.8 shows some buttons with different formatting.

FIGURE 19.8

Examples of buttons
with different
formatting

By default, buttons do not print (whereas by default, all other controls do). This can be changed using the *Print Object* setting, on the Properties tab of the Format Object dialog box.

Design Techniques

Here are some tips to help you design effective user interfaces using controls:

- Use option buttons when there are only a few choices, and the choices are relatively static. Otherwise, a list box is probably a better bet. Adding more choices to a list box only involves expanding the input range, as opposed to redesigning the sheet to accommodate more option buttons. Figures 19.9 and 19.10 show some examples using option buttons and list boxes.

- Technically, one checkbox can serve the same purpose as a group of two option buttons. But sometimes two option buttons provide more clarity, as shown in Figure 19.11.

- Group boxes are not limited to grouping option buttons—all related controls can be grouped together, as pictured in Figure 19.12. In fact, a group box might contain no option buttons.

- A worksheet can be made to look similar to a "real" custom dialog box. Color the cells grey and remove gridlines from the sheet, as pictured in Figure 19.13.

FIGURE 19.9

List boxes require less maintenance than option buttons when the contents of the list changes, since they are data driven. And when the list is long, list boxes are more aesthetic.

FIGURE 19.10

Option buttons are very effective when there are few choices, and the choices are relatively static. List boxes with only two or three choices are not aesthetically appealing.

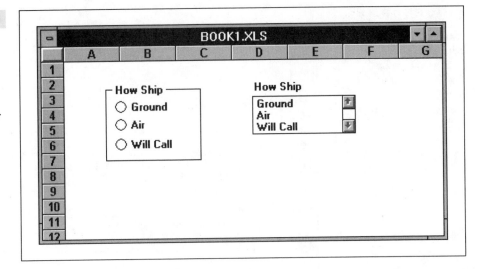

FIGURE 19.11

The one checkbox can perform the same logical function as the two option buttons. But in this example, the option buttons provide more clarity because the meaning of each choice is spelled out.

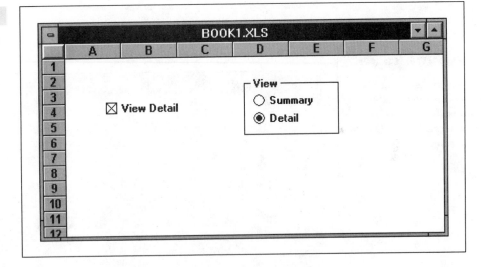

FIGURE 19.12

You can place controls other than option buttons in a group box. The *Ordered By* input is not a control—it is a cell with a border.

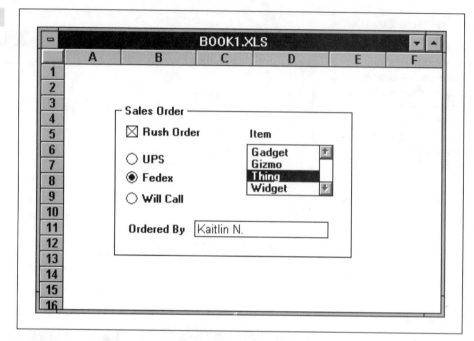

FIGURE 19.13

A worksheet formatted to look like a dialog box. The controls are formatted with 3-D shading.

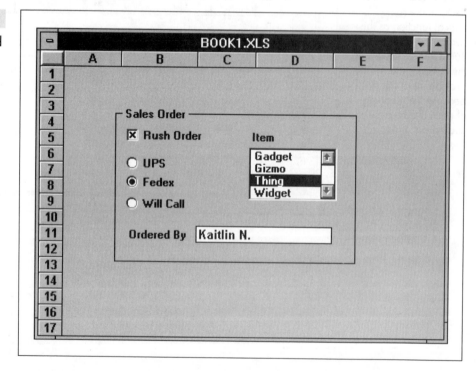

Dynamic List Boxes

Here is an advanced technique that combines named formulas (covered in Chapter 8) with list boxes. This exercise uses named formulas to dynamically change the contents of a list box—without having to write custom macros.

1. On a new worksheet, enter these values in range B2:D15:

2. Name the ranges indicated on the worksheet.

3. Define the name **CourseList** referring to:

```
=INDIRECT("List."&DeptChoice)
```

4. Add grouped option buttons to the worksheet:

- Draw the group box.
- Draw four option buttons inside the group box, and link one of them to cell **DeptChoice** (the rest will be linked automatically).

5. Add a list box to the worksheet:

- input range: **CourseList**
- cell link: **CourseChoice**

> **TIP**
>
> The formula =OFFSET(CourseList,CourseChoice-1,1,1,1) will return the code for the course selected in the list box.

Another common problem is a list with a variable number of rows. For example, a list may be built by querying an external database, and the number of rows may vary from time to time. The standard approach to this problem is to programmatically (or manually!) define a named range after performing the query. Alternately, the list box can use a name that dynamically calculates the number of rows in the list. Consider the following worksheet:

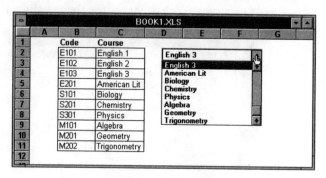

- The name **CourseList** is defined as:

  `=OFFSET($C$1,1,0,COUNTA(OFFSET($C$1,1,0,999,1)),1)`

  (This formula assumes a maximum of 999 rows.)

- The Input range for list box is **CourseList**.

- If new rows of data are added to bottom of list, the drop-down list box automatically includes the new rows.

Custom Dialog Boxes

So far, this chapter has covered how to place controls directly on worksheets. Custom dialog boxes provide greater programmatic control of events, and are a key component in application development.

- Custom dialog boxes are *modal*, whereas worksheet dialog boxes are not. Modal dialog boxes retain the focus until the dialog box is dismissed.

- Worksheet controls do not support *accelerator* (shortcut) keys, or tab order.

- Custom dialog boxes must be displayed programmatically.

- All controls that can be placed on worksheets can be placed on dialog sheets; dialog sheets support several additional controls.

Creating a New Dialog Box

To create a new dialog box, insert a dialog sheet into your workbook: Choose the Insert ➤ Macro ➤ Dialog command. When you insert a new dialog sheet, you will notice that two things happen (see Figure 19.14):

- The Forms toolbar displays automatically.

- A dialog box frame containing two buttons (OK and Cancel) is placed on the new dialog sheet.

The Dialog Frame

The dialog frame (see Figure 19.14) is a separate object. It can be moved, resized, and the caption can be changed. To select the dialog frame, click anywhere on its title or outer border.

Moving and Sizing Controls

The procedures for moving and resizing controls on dialog boxes differ somewhat from controls on worksheets. When gridlines are displayed, controls automatically snap to the gridlines when the control is drawn,

FIGURE 19.14

A new dialog sheet includes three objects: a dialog frame, an OK button, and a Cancel button.

moved, or resized. This behavior can be overridden in two ways:

 • Turn off gridlines using the toggle gridlines tool (located on the Forms toolbar).

TIP The toggle gridlines tool can also be used to toggle gridlines on a worksheet.

• Hold down the Alt key while moving/sizing to temporarily override snap to grid.

Edit Boxes

 An *edit box* is used to enter text or numeric data, and can also be used to enter a cell reference. Here are the steps to draw an edit box, and then set its properties:

1. Click the edit box tool, and draw the object inside the dialog box frame.

2. With the edit box still selected, click the Control Properties tool.

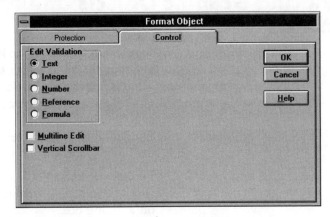

Text	up to 255 characters can be entered
Integer	limits input to values from –32,765 to 32,767
Number	any valid number
Reference	requires valid cell reference—allows input by pointing and clicking on worksheet
Multiline Edit	causes input to wrap within the control
Vertical Scrollbar	places vertical scrollbars beside the control when the dialog box is run

Combination List-Edit

A combination list-edit (or combo list-edit) box is actually two separate controls that work together—a list box and an edit box. The edit box is automatically linked to the list box. When an item is chosen from the list box, the text is automatically placed in the edit box. You can also type directly into the edit box (the entry does not have to match an item in the list).

Drop-down combo list-edits are identical to combo list-edits, except the list is a drop-down.

Placing Graphic Objects on Dialog Boxes

You are not limited to the controls found on the Forms toolbar when placing objects on a dialog box. Any graphic object can be placed on a dialog box, including pictures, charts, text boxes, and any of the drawing objects. There are specific benefits to using these objects:

Text Boxes	Unlike labels, text boxes can be formatted, and can contain a formula.
Pictures	Pictures linked to cells are a convenient way of displaying formatted, tabular data on a dialog box.
Charts	Just like charts embedded on worksheets, chart objects on dialog boxes remain linked to source cells.

Use Meaningful Names for Controls

When you draw objects on a worksheet, they are automatically named by Excel using the object type, followed by a sequential number. Controls drawn on dialog sheets are automatically named the same way. For example, a new dialog sheet contains three objects:

- Dialog Frame 1
- Button 2 (OK button)
- Button 3 (Cancel button)

If you add an edit box, it will be named **Edit Box 4**. Add a label after that, and it will be named **Label 5**, and so on. You can rename the controls using meaningful names that will make your macros more readable. To rename a control:

1. Select the control.
2. Overwrite the name in the Name Box.

For example, in Figure 19.15, Edit Box 4 has been renamed **Company Name**.

FIGURE 19.15

Rename a control by selecting it and overwriting its name in the Name Box.

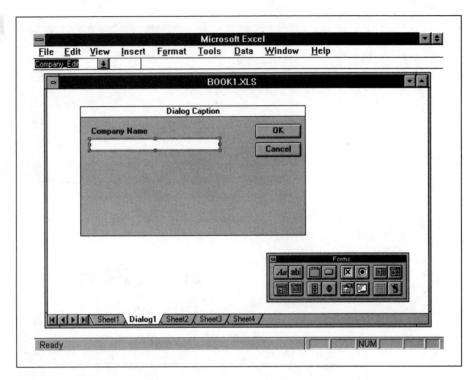

CAUTION

If macros refer to a control named, say, *List Box 7*, then you rename the list box to *ListRegions*, the macros must be edited accordingly.

Setting the Tab Order

When a dialog box is displayed, the tab key moves the focus from control to control. By default, the tab order of a custom dialog box is determined by the order in which the controls were created. To change the tab order, choose the Tools ➤ Tab Order command (or click the dialog box frame with the right mouse button and select Tab Order from the shortcut menu).

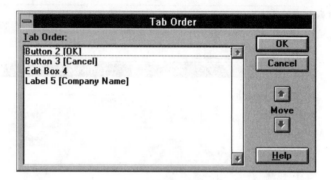

Select an item in the list, and click the up/down arrows to move it up or down.

Assigning Accelerator Keys

Accelerator keys are shortcuts that let you move to a specific control in a dialog box. They are used in conjunction with the Alt key. For example, in the *Go To* dialog box (displayed by pressing F5), you press Alt+R to move to the *Reference* box. You can define accelerator keys in your custom dialog boxes. To assign an accelerator key, select the control, and click the *Control Properties* tool. Then select the *Control* tab.

Buttons, checkboxes, option buttons, labels, and group boxes can have accelerator keys assigned. You can use any letter, number, or special character; however, user-interface conventions dictate that you use a letter that appears in the text associated with the control.

Controlling Events

Custom dialog boxes are able to run macros when three types of events occur: when the dialog box is displayed (*on-show*), when a control is clicked (*on-click*), or when a control is changed (*on-change*).

On-Show

You can assign a macro to run automatically when the dialog box is initially displayed. On-show macros are often used to set default values for dialog box controls. To create an on-show macro, select the dialog box frame, then use one of the following two procedures:

- If the macro does not exist, click the Edit Code tool; a new macro (procedure) will be placed on a VBA module (see Figure 19.16). Place your VBA code between the **Sub** and **End Sub**. (If there is no module in the workbook, a new module is inserted.)

- If the macro already exists, choose the Tools ➤ Assign Macro command; a list of macros will be displayed from which to choose.

FIGURE 19.16

A new macro (procedure) is created. Place the code between the *Sub* and *End Sub*.

NOTE When you create a new macro (procedure) using the Edit Code tool, Excel automatically names the macro. The name of the object is included as part of the macro name. There is no special meaning to these names; they can be overridden with a name of your choosing.

TIP If a macro is already assigned to a control, the Edit Code tool will display the macro.

On-Click

An *on-click* macro is run when it is clicked by the user. You can assign an on-click macro to the following controls:

- button
- checkbox
- option button
- any graphic object

Buttons have some special properties that determine their behavior. Draw a button on a dialog frame, select it, then click the *Control Properties* tool, then select the Control tab.

Default	Sets button as the default—when checked, pressing Enter on the keyboard is the equivalent of clicking the button
Cancel	Determines if the button is triggered when the dialog box is canceled
Dismiss	Determines if the button will close the dialog box when clicked
Help	Determines if the button is triggered when F1 is pressed while the dialog box is displayed

On-click macros are created, assigned, and edited the same way as on-show macros.

On-Change

An on-change macro is run when user input occurs. You can assign an on-change macro to the following controls:

- edit box
- list box
- combo edit-list

In the case of edit boxes, the macro is run each time a character is typed, deleted, or changed. On-change macros are created the same way as on-show macros.

Testing the Dialog Box

 Choose the Tools ➤ Run Dialog command, or click the Run Dialog tool, to test the dialog box. All event macros are run (as events dictate) when the dialog box is tested in this manner.

Running the Dialog Box for Real

A dialog box is displayed from a VBA macro (procedure) using the *Show* method. The following code sample assumes that a dialog box resides on a dialog sheet named **EnterStats**, and the VBA module resides in the same workbook as the dialog sheet:

```
Sub ProcessStats()
    DialogSheets("EnterStats").Show
End Sub
```

Typically, a macro will take different action if an OK button dismisses the dialog box rather than a Cancel button. The following code sample tests for this condition:

```
Sub ProcessStats()
    If  DialogSheets("EnterStats").Show Then
     MsgBox "You clicked the OK button"
    End If
End Sub
```

If an on-click macro were assigned to the OK button on the **EnterStats** dialog box, events would occur in the following sequence when OK is clicked:

1. On-click macro runs (not shown above)

2. Dialog box closes

3. In-line code is processed (message box displayed)

When Not to Link Controls to Cells

Controls that are linked to cells edit the cell immediately. This causes two often undesirable side-effects:

- Cells are edited regardless of whether OK or Cancel is pressed.

- Each change to a cell can trigger a worksheet recalculation.

Thus, controls on dialog boxes are often *not* linked to cells, which requires cell updates to be handled programmatically.

Controlling Dialog Box Properties Programmatically

The controls on a dialog sheet can be manipulated programmatically from VBA. They can be disabled or enabled, have their text changed—virtually any of the properties can be set from VBA code. The code samples below manipulate properties of the dialog box pictured in Figure 19.17. The dialog box resides on a dialog sheet named **StudentInfo**.

FIGURE 19.17

Student information
dialog box

Disabling a Control

The following code disables the checkbox:

```
Sub DisableCheckBox()
    DialogSheets("StudentInfo").CheckBoxes(1).Enabled = False
End Sub
```

CheckBoxes(1) refers to the first checkbox in the dialog box. Here is another way to disable the checkbox, this time referring to it by name (Check Box 10):

```
Sub DisableCheckBox()
    DialogSheets("StudentInfo").CheckBoxes("Check Box
10").Enabled = False
End Sub
```

TIP

Macros are easier to read if you rename controls with meaningful names. For example, VBA code that refers to a control as "Tutor CheckBox" makes more sense than "Check Box 10."

Conditionally Disable/Enable a Control

Using the dialog box in Figure 19.17, if a student is not available to tutor, the dialog box needs to prohibit entry into the *Skills* edit box (the second edit box). In addition, the label **Skills** (the second label) will also be enabled/disabled in order to provide the user with a visual cue as to the status of the edit box. The following macro, which is run when the checkbox is clicked, disables the edit box and the label when the checkbox is unchecked, and vice-versa when checked:

```
Sub HandleEditBox()
    Dim Check As Integer
    Check = DialogSheets("StudentInfo").CheckBoxes(1).Value
    If Check = 1 Then
     DialogSheets("StudentInfo").Labels(2).Enabled = True
     DialogSheets("StudentInfo").EditBoxes(2).Enabled = True
    Else
     DialogSheets("StudentInfo").Labels(2).Enabled = False
     DialogSheets("StudentInfo").EditBoxes(2).Enabled = False
    End If
End Sub
```

The use of a **With** statement makes the same macro somewhat less verbose:

```
Sub HandleEditBox()
    With DialogSheets("StudentInfo")
     Dim Check As Integer
     Check = .CheckBoxes(1).Value
     If Check = 1 Then
         .Labels(2).Enabled = True
         .EditBoxes(2).Enabled = True
     Else
         .Labels(2).Enabled = False
         .EditBoxes(2).Enabled = False
     End If
    End With
End Sub
```

Setting Dialog Box Properties

The dialog frame is an object whose properties can be set programmatically. The following macro changes the caption of the StudentInfo dialog box:

```
Sub SetCaption()
 DialogSheets("StudentInfo").Dialog Frame.Caption = "Hello!"
End Sub
```

This macro sets the focus to Edit Box 12:

```
Sub SetFocus()
     DialogSheets("StudentInfo").Focus = "Edit Box 12"
End Sub
```

Creating a Functional Dialog Box

The following exercise walks you through the creation of a full-featured, functional dialog box that...

- sets default values using an on-show macro;
- accepts user inputs, and disables controls based on certain conditions;
- validates user input when OK is clicked;
- places user inputs onto a worksheet.

The dialog box will be used to enter information for job applicants. Input to the supervisor edit box can occur only if the applicant was previously employed at the company, and a name must be entered.

This exercise uses the worksheet and dialog box pictured in Figures 19.18 and 19.19.

1. Create a new workbook with a worksheet named **Apply**; insert a dialog sheet and name it **DataEntry**.

2. Build the Apply worksheet, as pictured in Figure 19.18. Name the cells as indicated.

3. Draw the controls pictured in Figure 19.19 (on dialog sheet DataEntry).

FIGURE 19.18

The dialog box will be used to edit cells C4 (Applicant), C6 (Department), C8 (WorkedHere), and C10 (Supervisor).

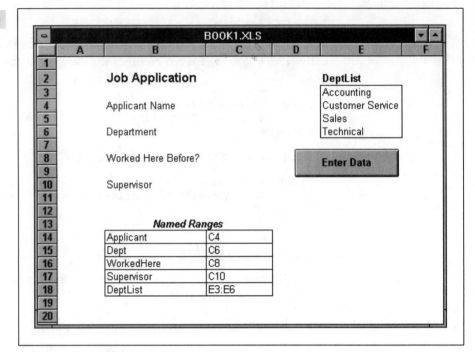

4. The controls that will be referred to from macro code will be renamed for clarity; rename them as follows:

CONTROL	NAME
name edit box	**Edit_Name**
department list box	**List_Dept**
checkbox	**Check_Prev**
supervisor label	**Label_Super**
supervisor edit box	**Edit_Super**

5. Assign an input range for the list box of **Apply!DeptList** (the named range on worksheet *Apply*).

FIGURE 19.19

Job applicant
data-entry dialog box.

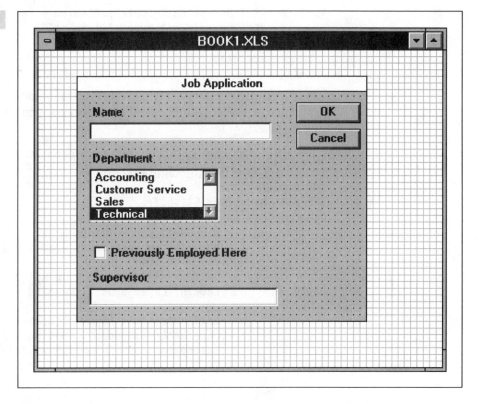

6. An on-show macro will set default values so that the dialog box does not retain values from the last time it was used. Since most applicants apply for technical positions, the department will default to *technical*; edit boxes will be set to *null*, the checkbox unchecked, and the supervisor edit box disabled:

   - Select the dialog frame, then click the Edit Code tool.
   - Enter the following macro:

```
Sub Frame_Show()
    With DialogSheets("DataEntry")
    Dim Check As Integer
    .EditBoxes("Edit_Name").Text = ""
    .ListBoxes("List_Dept").Value = 4
    .CheckBoxes("Check_Prev").Value = False
    .Labels("Label_Super").Enabled = False
```

```
    .EditBoxes("Edit_Super").Enabled = False
    .EditBoxes("Edit_Super").Text = ""
    .Focus = "Edit_Name"
    End With
End Sub
```

7. When the checkbox is checked, the supervisor edit must be enabled; when it is unchecked the supervisor must be cleared and disabled:

   • Select the checkbox, then click the Edit Code tool.

   • Enter the following macro:

```
Sub Check_Prev_Click()
    Dim Checked As Integer
    With DialogSheets("DataEntry")
     Checked = .CheckBoxes("Check_Prev").Value
     If Checked = 1 Then
         .EditBoxes("Edit_Super").Enabled = True
         .Labels("Label_Super").Enabled = True
     Else
         .EditBoxes("Edit_Super").Enabled = False
         .Labels("Label_Super").Enabled = False
         .EditBoxes("Edit_Super").Text = ""
     End If
    End With
End Sub
```

8. Change the OK button so that it does *not* dismiss the dialog box (verification that a name was entered must occur, and an on-click event will decide whether to dismiss the dialog box).

9. Define an on-click macro for the OK button:

   • Select the OK button then click the Edit Code tool.

   • Enter the following macro:

```
Sub Button2_Click()
    Set Dial = DialogSheets("DataEntry")
    If Dial.EditBoxes("Edit_Name").Text = "" Then
     MsgBox "You must enter a name."
     Dial.Focus = "Edit_Name"
    Else

   Set Sheet = Worksheets("Apply")
```

```
Sheet.Range("Applicant").Value =
 Dial.EditBoxes("Edit_Name").Text

Sheet.Range("Dept").Value =
 Sheet.Range("DeptList")(Dial.ListBoxes("List_Dept").Value)

Dim Worked As String

If Dial.CheckBoxes("Check_Prev").Value = 1 Then Worked =
 "Yes" Else Worked = "No"

Sheet.Range("WorkedHere").Value = Worked

Sheet.Range("Supervisor").Value =
 Dial.EditBoxes("Edit_Super").Text

Dial.Hide
End If

End Sub
```

10. Test the dialog box using the Run Dialog tool

11. Write the macro to initially show the dialog box:

- Activate the module.
- Enter the following macro:

```
Sub EnterApplicantData()
    DialogSheets("DataEntry").Show
End Sub
```

12. Draw a button to display the dialog box:

- Draw a button on worksheet Apply.
- Assign the macro *EnterApplicantData*.

Your dialog box should be ready to go. Click the new button on worksheet *Apply to try it.*

CHAPTER

20

Macro Basics

fast TRACK

To assign a macro to any graphic object   626

1. Select the object.
2. Choose Tools ➤ Assign Macro.
3. Select a macro from the list in the Assign Macro dialog box

To assign a macro to a tool   626

1. Display the toolbar containing the tool.
2. Choose View ➤ Toolbars.
3. Click the Customize button.
4. Click the tool (on the toolbar) you want to assign the macro to.
5. Choose Tools ➤ Assign Macro.

To create a custom menu system   627

Activate a module and choose Tools ➤ Menu Editor.

To run a macro automatically when a workbook is opened   628

Name the macro **Auto_Open**.

THERE are two types of people who create macros: everyday users (nonprogrammers), who can use the *macro recorder* to automate simple tasks, and application developers, who create complete custom applications. This chapter provides some useful information for both ends of the spectrum, but with an emphasis on skills for the nonprogrammer:

- *programming Excel overview*
- *recording macros*
- *running macros*
- *user-defined functions (function macros)*

Programming Excel Overview

Excel is the first application to support VBA—Microsoft's *Visual Basic, Applications Edition*—a language based on the popular Visual Basic programming language. Microsoft intends VBA to be the common macro language used in all of its programmable applications, making it strategically important for application developers. Eventually, VBA will be the programming language for Microsoft Access, Microsoft Word, and other Microsoft products. VBA code (and knowledge) is easily transferable between Microsoft applications.

- The old macro language, referred to as *XLM*, is still supported and has been extended to support features that are new in Excel 5. You can run your old macros, and continue to write XLM macros if so desired.

- Future versions of Excel will continue to support XLM, but will not extend the functionality of XLM. Microsoft has made it very clear that VBA is where the future lies. Accordingly, the focus of this chapter is VBA.

- VBA macros can call XLM macros, and vice-versa. This allows users with an investment in XLM code to gradually transition to VBA.

- Excel is able to run Lotus 1-2-3 macros, without the need to translate them. See Chapter 25 for more information on Lotus compatibility.

- Macros can be protected using Excel 5's improved add-in facility.

- For serious programmers, VBA provides scoped variables and debugging facilities—features that were sorely lacking in XLM.

- Excel macros are compatible across Windows *and Macintosh* platforms. If your organization uses Windows and Mac, you can create applications that run on both.

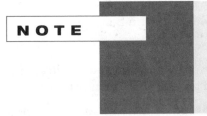

NOTE This chapter does not attempt to teach the details of how to program in VBA. That is an exhaustive topic that requires a lot of coverage to do it justice. Instead, it will provide a general orientation for you to build upon. Refer to the *Visual Basic User's Guide* for more information.

All macros reside in workbooks: VBA macros reside on *modules*, and XLM macros reside on *XLM sheets*. There is no limit, other than available memory, to the number of modules and/or XLM sheets in a workbook.

NOTE The Excel documentation uses the terms *macro* and *procedure* interchangeably, as does this book.

The Macro Recorder

The *macro recorder* is a tool that translates your actions into macro code, without the need to understand the underlying macro syntax. It works like a tape recorder: When you turn the recorder on, it "records" everything you do. Later, you can play back (run) the macro, and the actions that you previously recorded are repeated. The macro recorder provides two primary benefits:

- Simple, repetitive tasks can be automated without the need to know VBA.

- The recorder is an excellent tool for learning VBA.

When used in conjunction with general Excel know-how, surprisingly complex tasks can be reliably automated. But using the recorder *effectively* requires that you understand its limitations, and carefully plan a course of action before you start recording. Here are some typical tasks that could be automated with recorded macros:

- Format a range of cells as bold font, with borders.

- Open a workbook, print it, then close it.

- Open a text file that was output by a mainframe application, sort the data, insert subtotals and grand totals, then print the report.

- Open several workbooks, consolidate information onto a new workbook, then save the new workbook.

- Perform a query, then chart the results.

As you can see from these examples, creating reports is a task that is ideally suited for automation by recording macros.

How to Start Recording a Macro

Here are the steps to begin recording a new macro.

1. Plan exactly what you want to accomplish, and how to go about it. In fact, you should run through the precise keystrokes that you plan on recording before actually recording them.

2. Turn on the recorder using the Tools ➤ Record Macro ➤ Record New Macro command.

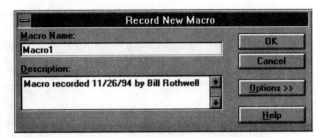

If there are no visible workbooks at the time you plan to start recording, then the *Tools* menu does not display. In this case, start recording with the File ➤ Record New Macro command.

3. Enter a meaningful Macro Name. The name can be up to 255 characters in length, consisting of letters, numbers, and underscores. There can be no spaces or other punctuation marks. (It is common to use underscores or proper case to separate words.) The name must begin with a letter.

VALID NAMES	INVALID NAMES	REASON
MyMacro	My Macro	contains a space
Sales_Report	Sales.Report	contains a period
Summary95	95Summary	starts with a number
Get_YTD_Info	Y-T-D	contains illegal characters

4. By default, the *Description* will include your name and the date—this text is placed above the actual macro in the VBA module, as comments. You can add additional comments to explain the purpose of the macro.

At this point, you can click OK to begin recording. But there are additional settings that are made available by clicking the Options button.

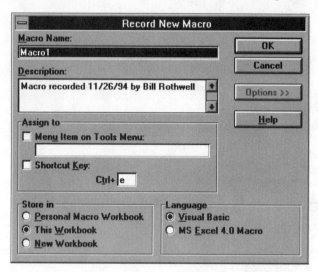

Menu Item on Tools Menu Check this option if you want to add the macro to Excel's built-in *Tools* menu. The text that you enter in the box beneath the checkbox is used as the command text on the *Tools* menu.

Shortcut Key Check this option if you want to assign a shortcut key for the macro you are about to record. Then, enter a key that is to be used in conjunction with the Ctrl key to run the macro. If you check *Shortcut Key*, and enter **x** as the *Ctrl+* key, then after the macro is recorded, pressing Ctrl+x will run the macro.

Store In These options specify where the soon-to-be-recorded macro will be placed.

> **Personal Macro Workbook** This workbook, named PERSONAL.XLS, is automatically opened, and hidden, each time you start Excel. This is a good place to store macros that you want available at all times. (It is discussed later in this chapter.)
>
> **This Workbook** Places the macro in the active workbook. If there is no active workbook, this option is not available.
>
> **New Workbook** A new workbook will be created, and the macro will be recorded in it.

Language Specifies which language the macro will be recorded in. Visual Basic is the default choice—choose *MS Excel 4.0 Macro* if you want to record a macro in the old XLM language.

Recording Your Actions

As soon as you click OK on the *Record New Macro* dialog box, every action you take is recorded (including mistakes!). The word *Recording* is displayed on the status bar, and a Stop tool is displayed (see Figure 20.1).

Click the Stop tool to stop recording. The tool also serves as a visual reminder that you are recording a macro.

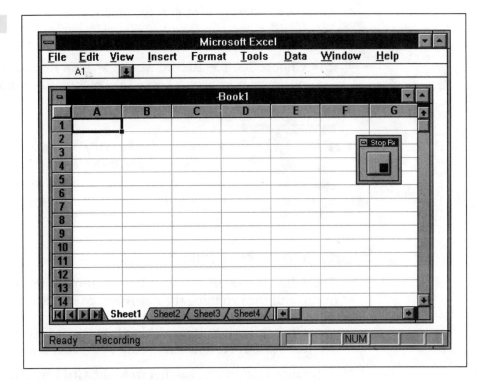

At this point, you simply perform the actions that you want to record. For example, you might open a workbook, create a chart, and then print the workbook.

NOTE The recorder tries not to record wasted actions. Suppose you select cell A2, then realize you made a mistake, and then immediately select B2. The selecting of cell A2 will not be recorded. Or, suppose you display the wrong dialog box. If you click Cancel, the action will not be recorded.

Stopping the Recorder

There are two ways to stop recording:

- Click the Stop tool.
- Choose Tools ➤ Record Macro ➤ Stop Recording. (Or, if there is no active workbook, choose File ➤ Stop Recording.)

CAUTION A common mistake many users make is to forget they are recording, and then unwittingly record a huge, useless macro. As the macro becomes larger and larger, your computer will start to slow down.

From Start to Finish

The following exercise will walk you through the steps of recording a macro and then running the newly recorded macro:

1. Choose Tools ➤ Record Macro ➤ Record New Macro to display the Record New Macro dialog box. Enter a name for your macro.

2. Click Options, and assign **m** as the Ctrl key. Then choose to store the macro in a new workbook (so as not to pollute your personal workbook with this learning exercise). Click OK to start recording.

3. Perform the following actions:
   - Choose File ➤ New.
   - Enter some data onto the new workbook.
   - Apply some formatting.

4. Stop the recorder by choosing Tools ➤ Record Macro ➤ Stop Recording.

Before running the macro, close the workbook where you entered and formatted data (no need to save it). Then, press Ctrl+m to run the macro. Just like the first time, a new workbook is created, data is entered, and formatting is applied.

TIP

It is wise to save your work, including the workbook containing the newly recorded macro, before running the macro. Until a macro is tested, it should be considered capable of undesired consequences.

Viewing the Macro

In the previous exercise, you recorded a macro into a new workbook. This means there is a new, unsaved workbook, named Book2 or Book3 (or Book whatever) in memory. Use the Window menu to locate the workbook—it will have a sheet in it named *Module1*. Click the Module1 tab to view the macro. Figure 20.2 shows a newly recorded macro named *Enter_Then_Format*.

Even if you don't understand macro syntax, you can usually distinguish some of your actions in the macro code. Observe the following:

- The description entered in the *Record New Macro* dialog box are placed on the module, above the macro. (Any line that starts with an apostrophe is a comment line, and has no effect on the macro.)

- As you might deduce, the statement **Range("B2").Select** selects cell B2.

- When you enter anything into a cell, an **ActiveCell.FormulaR1C1** command is recorded.

- Look at the command that enters a SUM formula—even though the workspace is set to A1 reference style, an R1C1 reference is recorded.

FIGURE 20.2

Macros (procedures) reside in a special kind of sheet called *modules*.

```
' Enter_Then_Format Macro
' Macro recorded 11/26/93 by Bill Rothwell
'
'

Sub Enter_Then_Format()
    Range("B2").Select
    ActiveCell.FormulaR1C1 = "10"
    Range("B3").Select
    ActiveCell.FormulaR1C1 = "20"
    Range("B4").Select
    ActiveCell.FormulaR1C1 = "=SUM(R[-2]C:R[-1]C)"
    Range("B2:B4").Select
    Selection.Font.Bold = True
End Sub
```

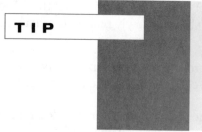

TIP

Macros created with the recorder are not very efficient. Where the recorder creates two lines of code, one line will often do the job. For example, a handwritten macro can place a formula into a cell without selecting the cell first. Once you understand macro syntax, you can edit your recorded macros to make them more efficient.

What Can Go Wrong?

The initial feeling of empowerment provided by the macro recorder can quickly vanish as you try to solve real-world problems. Users get into trouble because of four common problems:

Ambiguous Intent Many actions that you record can be interpreted in several ways. For example, assume cell B2 is the active cell, the macro recorder is on, and you select cell B3. Do you really mean B3? Or do you mean the top row of a database? Or did you mean to move down one row?

Things Happen Picture an automobile with a trip recorder. You want to automate the task of getting to work each day, so you get in the car, turn on the recorder, drive to work, then turn off the recorder. But everything goes wrong when the macro is played back the next morning. The problem stems from the fact that things are different when you play back the macro: a bike is in the driveway, the traffic light is red, and there is a traffic jam. The same type of obstacles may be encountered when you play back your recorded macros.

Over-Recording Many recorded macros start out with a blank slate—unnecessarily. By using templates (covered in Chapter 10) you can simplify macro recording. Templates can be pre-formatted, and they can contain pre-defined names, styles, and formulas that make the job easier.

Inherent Limitations The macro recorder is pretty good at automating everyday tasks. But if you want to create serious applications, you will need to learn how to write macros yourself.

Recording in Relative or Absolute Reference Mode

By default, the macro recorder records absolute cell references. Sometimes, you will want to record relative references. Use the Tools ➤ Record Macro ➤ Use Relative References command to switch to relative recording. (This command is a toggle—use the same command to switch back to absolute recording.) The following example illustrates the usefulness of this option.

Suppose you want to record a macro that adds the active cell and the number above the active cell. The macro will place a formula in the cell beneath the active cell (see Figure 20.3).

Create the worksheet in Figure 20.3, then record a macro the wrong way:

1. Select B3.

2. Start the recorder. (Make sure you are recording absolute references—the Tools ➤ Record Macro ➤ Use Relative References command should *not* have a checkmark.)

3. Select B4. Enter the formula **=B2+B3**.

4. Stop recording.

FIGURE 20.3

The macro needs to act relative to the active cell at the time the macro is run. If B3 is active, the formula should be placed in B4. If D3 is active, the formula should be placed in D4.

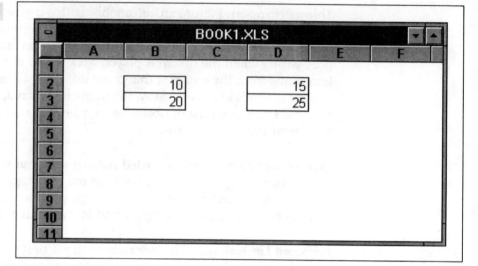

To see how it worked, clear B4. Then select D3 and run your new macro. Since you were in absolute mode when the macro was recorded, the formula is placed in B4, not in D4. Regardless of which cell is active, the macro will always place the formula in B4.

Now, record the same macro again. This time switch to relative reference mode before you do step 3. After you are done recording, test the new macro:

- Clear B4 and D4.
- Select B3 and run the macro.
- Select D3 and run the macro.

Since you recorded the macro in relative mode, the macro enters formulas relative to the active cell.

TIP

You can switch back and forth between absolute reference mode and relative reference mode at any time while recording a macro.

- When you record in absolute reference mode, Excel records the absolute reference of every cell you select.

- When you record in relative reference mode, and you select one or more cells, Excel records the selection relative to the previously selected cell.

Recording Macros That Work As Intended

As you use the macro recorder, you will discover that it often misinterprets your intent. Sometimes the only way to make it right is by manually editing the recorded macro. But there are some specific techniques you can use to cause the recorder to correctly interpret your actions.

Selecting Variable Size Ranges

Suppose that every month you are responsible for creating a report based on data that is output from a mainframe. (See Chapter 25 to learn more about importing data.) The mainframe outputs a text file in CSV format (comma separated values). The data needs to be copied into another workbook, which contains related information. Figure 20.4 shows the text file, opened in Excel.

FIGURE 20.4

Sales data output as text file from mainframe. The number of rows varies from month to month.

	A	B	C	D	E	F
1	Product	Forecast	Actual			
2	Decals	1000	1178			
3	Handlebars	10000	10602			
4	Horns	2750	2619			
5	Packs	3500	3450			
6	Seats	8000	9900			
7	Wheels	20000	23250			
8						
9						
10						
11						
12						
13						

DATA.CSV

The plan of action for recording the macro is:

1. Start recording.

2. Open the workbook where the source data needs to be copied (REPORT.XLS).

3. Open the text file—by default, A1 is the active cell.

4. Select the data, and copy it to the Clipboard.

5. Activate REPORT.XLS and select destination cell.

6. Paste.

7. Print.

8. Stop recording.

There is one small, yet typical, problem that you must deal with: The number of rows in the text file is variable. It does no good to record the selection of A1:C7 as an absolute reference, because next month, the data may reside in A1:C10. Therefore, the task of selecting the data to be copied (step 4) presents a problem.

The solution is to use a command that selects the *current region*, rather then using the mouse to select A1:C7. At step 4, choose Edit ➤ Go To, then click Special, to display the *Go To Special* dialog box.

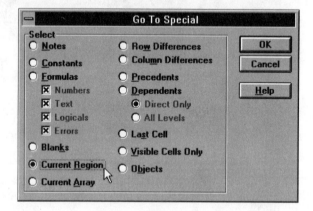

Choose Current Region, then click OK. (Easier yet, click the Select Current Region tool.) A1:C7 is selected, but the recorded macro is different than if you had selected A1:C7 with the mouse.

The following is the command that is recorded when you select an absolute range:

```
Range("A1:C7").Select
```

The following is the command that is recorded when you select Current Region:

```
Selection.CurrentRegion.Select
```

Formatting a Column of Numbers

Figure 20.5 is a slight variation of Figure 20.4. There is a column for units (an integer value), and dollars (currency).

	A	B	C	D	E
			DATA.CSV		
1	Product	Units	Dollars		
2	Decals	320	1178.55		
3	Handlebars	299	10602.2		
4	Horns	266	2619.75		
5	Packs	309	3450.03		
6	Seats	245	9900.8		
7	Wheels	504	23250.32		
8					
9					
10					
11					
12					
13					

The recorded macro must apply a currency format to the *Dollars* column. You can't select the current region, as in the previous problem, because you would mistakenly format the *Units* column. The solution is simple: Select the entire column C before applying the currency format. It doesn't matter that a number format will be applied to C1—the format has no effect on text.

Charting a Variable Number of Rows

Suppose that you want to record a macro that charts the data in Figure 20.4. Remember, the number of rows varies from month to month. Don't use the ChartWizard to create the chart—no matter how you go about it, recording the ChartWizard results in a macro that charts an absolute range. Here is a procedure that works:

1. Start recording.

2. Open the file.

3. Select the current region (using the Current Region tool, or the commands presented in previous group of steps).

4. Create the chart using one of these techniques:

   • Press F11 to create a chart sheet.

   • Use the default chart tool (not the Chart Wizard) to draw an embedded chart.

5. Stop recording.

Summing a Column with a Variable Number of Rows

Using the data in Figure 20.5, suppose that your recorded macro must add a total to the bottom of column C. This presents two problems:

   • How do you select the cell at the bottom of column C? (Remember, the number of rows is variable.)

   • How do you write the formula? Regardless of the reference mode, the AutoSum tool will record the wrong formula.

Follow these steps to record a macro that will work regardless of the number of rows:

1. Start recording.

2. Open the file.

3. Select C1.

4. Hold down the End key, then press the down arrow key (selects the last number in the column).

5. Switch to relative reference mode.

6. Press down arrow (moving the active cell to C8).

7. Enter the formula **=SUM(OFFSET($C$1,1,0,ROW()-2))**.

8. Stop recording.

In English, the formula reads: Sum the range of cells beginning one cell beneath C1, and include the number of rows equal to the row number containing the formula, minus two (accounting for the header row). The OFFSET and ROW functions are among the most useful worksheet functions—they are both covered in Chapter 9.

Running Macros

There are several ways to run a macro. Earlier in this chapter, you learned how to assign a shortcut key to a recorded macro. In this section, you will learn how to run a macro...

- using the Excel menu
- from a button
- from a tool
- from a custom menu
- when a workbook is opened or closed
- when a worksheet is activated or de-activated

Running a Macro Using Menu Commands

Choose the Tools ➤ Macro command to display the Macro dialog box.

Macros that are contained on all currently open workbooks are displayed in the list. To run a macro, select it from the list and click Run. The Macro dialog box provides several additional capabilities:

Step	Click this button to run the macro step-by-step. Stepping through a macro is useful for debugging purposes.
Edit	The module containing the macro is activated, and the macro is displayed for editing purposes.
Delete	Deletes the selected macro. (You can also delete macros by activating the module and clearing the macro.)
Options	Lets you assign a shortcut key, add a command to Excel's Tools menu that runs the macro, and change the description of the macro.

Assigning a Macro to a Button

You can assign a macro to a button (or any graphic object). When the button is clicked, the macro runs. Follow these steps to create a new button, and assign a macro to it:

1. Display the Forms toolbar.

2. Click the Button tool, then draw the button on the worksheet. (Drawing a button is just like drawing other objects—see Chapter 12 to learn about graphic objects and drawing tools.)

3. The Assign Macro dialog box is displayed.

4. Select a macro from the list, and click OK.

If you want to record a new macro to assign to the button, click the Record button. Click Edit to display the module containing the macro.

Follow these steps to change the macro assignment of an existing button:

1. Hold down the Ctrl key, and click the button.

2. Choose Tools ➤ Assign Macro.

Follow these steps to assign a macro to any graphic object:

1. Select the object.

2. Choose Tools ➤ Assign Macro

Here are two important implications of assigning macros to buttons:

- If the macro is in a different workbook than the button, a link is established to the workbook containing the macro. (The workbook will display in the Edit ➤ Links dialog box.) If the workbook containing the macro is closed, and you click the button, the workbook containing the macro is opened automatically, and the macro runs.

- If you delete a button that is assigned to a macro, the macro is not deleted.

Assigning a Macro to a Tool

When a macro is assigned to a button on a worksheet, it is only available when the worksheet containing the button is active. Macros assigned to button tools (on toolbars) are available whenever the toolbar is displayed.

Typically, you will assign macros to custom tools. But in fact, you can assign macros to any of Excel's built-in tools, which overrides the tool's built-in functionality. Follow these steps to assign a macro to any tool that already exists on a toolbar. (See Chapter 26 to learn how to customize toolbars.)

1. Display the toolbar containing the tool using the View ➤ Toolbars command.

2. Choose View ➤ Toolbars, then click Customize.

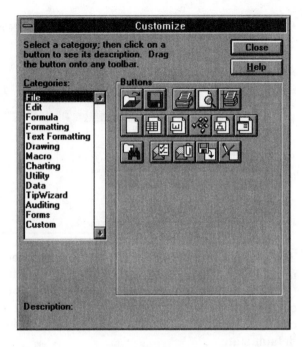

3. Click the tool that you want to assign a macro to. (Be sure to click the tool on the actual toolbar, not a tool inside the Customize dialog box.)

4. Choose Tools ➤ Assign Macro.

5. Select a macro from the list, and click OK.

6. Close the Customize dialog box.

Here are some general guidelines to decide whether to assign a macro to a button on a worksheet, or to a tool on a toolbar:

- Use buttons on worksheets when the macro is specific to the worksheet.

- Use tools (on toolbars) when the macro must be available globally.

Creating a Custom Menu System

With a module active, choose the Tools ➤ Menu Editor command to create a custom menu system, or to modify the built-in menus.

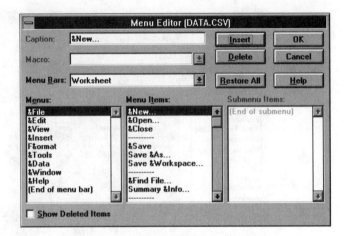

There is one important fact to understand about the menu editor: The menus that you modify and create are specific to the active workbook (and stored in the active workbook). When you open a workbook with a custom menu system, the custom menu system takes over. When you close the workbook, Excel's built-in menus take over, and revert to their default state.

Running Macros Automatically When a Workbook Is Opened or Closed

You can create special macros (procedures) that run automatically when a workbook is opened or closed. This is accomplished by placing macros in the workbook that are named using special reserved names:

Auto_Open	If there is a macro named Auto_Open in a workbook, it runs automatically when the workbook is opened.
Auto_Close	If there is a macro named Auto_Close in a workbook, it runs automatically *before* the workbook is closed.

Suppose that you want to suppress an Auto_Open or Auto_Close macro from running. How do you do it? Just hold down the Shift key while you open or close the workbook.

NOTE Auto_Open and Auto_Close macros do *not* run when a workbook is opened or closed programmatically, though your macro can explicitly run them if desired.

Running Macros Automatically When a Worksheet Is Activated or De-Activated

Macros can be automatically triggered when a worksheet is activated or deactivated. These macros will run when you activate or de-activate a worksheet by using any of these methods:

- Clicking worksheet tabs
- Pressing Ctrl+Page Up or Ctrl+Page Down
- Changing the active workbook

These activate and de-activate macros are defined using special names that are placed on the worksheet. To cause a macro named *CreateReport* to run when a sheet named *MySheet* is activated:

1. Activate the worksheet *MySheet*.
2. Choose Insert ➤ Name ➤ Define.
3. Enter the name: **MySheet!Auto_Activate**
4. Enter **refers to: =CreateReport**

You can use the same steps to create a de-activate macro, except the name is defined as **MySheet!Auto_Deactivate**.

T I P

If the macro is located in a different workbook, the book name must be included, using the syntax =BOOK1.XLS!ModuleName.MacroName.

More Events That Can Run Macros

Here are the other events in Excel that can cause a macro to run. (See the Visual Basic User's Guide to learn how to implement these event-handling facilities.)

OnTime Method Causes a macro to run at a specified time.

OnWindow Property Runs a macro when a specified window is activated.

OnKey Method Runs a macro when a specified key is pressed.

OnCalculate Property Runs a macro when a worksheet recalculation occurs.

OnEntry Property Runs a macro when an entry occurs into a worksheet cell.

OnData Property Runs a macro when data is received from another application via dynamic data exchange (DDE).

OnRepeat Method Runs a macro when user chooses Edit ➤ Repeat (or clicks Repeat tool).

OnUndo Method Runs a macro when user chooses Edit ➤ Undo (or clicks Undo tool).

User-Defined Functions

Excel includes hundreds of built-in functions, such as SUM, PRODUCT, and INDEX. You can write your own functions using VBA, and use them on a worksheet in much the same way that you refer to built-in functions like SUM.

NOTE

Previous versions of Excel have referred to user-defined functions as *function macros.*

All user-defined functions have two common characteristics:

- They accept one or more arguments.
- They return a result.

Don't let the terminology confuse you—this is no different than a built-in function. For instance, SUM takes an argument (a range of cells), and returns a result (the sum of the range). The only difference is that you get to define the arguments and the calculation that produces the result.

Consider the worksheet pictured in Figure 20.6. On this example invoice, Column E requires a formula that multiplies column C by column D, then adds a 7% sales tax.

FIGURE 20.6

A user-defined function can be used to calculate the extension, plus sales tax.

	A	B	C	D	E	F
					BOOK1.XLS	
1						
2				Unit	Extension	
3		Item	Qty	Price	(Plus Tax)	
4		Gadgets	5	20.00		
5		Gizmos	10	6.00		
6		Things	3	100.00		
7		Widgets	7	8.50		
8						
9						
10						
11						
12						
13						
14						

N O T E

This problem does not require a user-defined function—it can be solved with a relatively simple worksheet formula. Therein lies the paradox of user-defined functions: the ones that are easy to write are usually not needed!

The following exercise will walk you through all of the steps to create, and apply, a user-defined function.

1. In a new workbook, enter the data in Figure 20.6.
2. Insert a VBA module by choosing the Insert ➤ Macro ➤ Module command. A new module is inserted (see Figure 20.7).

FIGURE 20.7

A new VBA module is inserted in the workbook, and the Visual Basic toolbar is automatically displayed.

3. Enter the following three lines in the module:

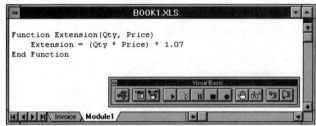

```
Function Extension(Qty, Price)
    Extension = (Qty * Price) * 1.07
End Function
```

As you can see, there are three parts of a user-defined function:

- The first line defines the name of the function, and the arguments it will receive. The above function is named *Extension*, and it receives two arguments: *Qty* and *Price*. Arguments are separated by commas.

- The last line of the function is a terminator. All functions must end with *End Function*.

- In the middle, the actual calculation occurs. In this simple example, the calculation only requires one line of code. But there is virtually no limit to the length of the function. Notice the use of the three variables: the function name and the two arguments. The variable name *Extension* calculates the final result.

Next, the function is entered on the worksheet in the same way you enter a built-in function:

1. Activate the Invoice worksheet.

2. Enter the formula **=Extension(C4,D4)** into E4. (Notice the sequence of the two arguments corresponds to the first line of the function on the module.)

3. Copy E4 to E5:E7.

The Personal Macro Workbook

When you read about recording macros, earlier in this chapter, you learned how to record macros into a *personal macro workbook* named

PERSONAL.XLS. When you first install Excel, the personal macro workbook does not exist. PERSONAL.XLS is created the first time you record a macro into it. It is stored in the XLSTART directory (located in the directory where you installed Excel).

TIP

All workbooks in the XLSTART directory are automatically opened each time you start Excel. You can also place templates in XLSTART, which is covered in Chapter 10.

PERSONAL.XLS is a good place to store macros that are used on an everyday basis. Here are some important things you should know about it:

- It is automatically opened each time you start Excel, and it is hidden.

- You can manually edit PERSONAL.XLS. Use the Window ➤ Unhide command to view it.

- Since it is opened every time you start Excel, you may want to avoid placing large macros on it that are not used regularly.

Turn to Chapter 21 to see how to create a custom application from start to finish.

CHAPTER

21

Creating an
Application

fast TRACK

To make a chart insensitive to the amount of data   656

Link the chart to a named range.

To suppress screen updates while a macro is running 670

Place the line *Application.ScreenUpdating = False* at the start of your macro.

To bulletproof an application   671

- Create a custom menu system.

- Protect the workbook and the worksheets.

THIS chapter will walk you through all of the steps to create a powerful custom application—a *decision support system* (DSS) used to analyze the performance of a fictitious company that sells bicycle parts. Skills that you have learned throughout the book will be utilized, and several new techniques will be introduced along the way. The application will include:

- *powerful worksheet functions like INDEX, OFFSET, and COUNTA*
- *pivot tables*
- *recorded macros (you do not need to understand macros to create this application, though you should be familiar with the macro recorder)*
- *controls (list boxes and option buttons)*
- *criteria ranges and the DSUM function*
- *advanced naming techniques*

The Business Requirement

The management of *Western BikeStuff* needs to track actual sales performance against forecast.

- The company carries four product lines: helmets, handlebars, seats, and racks. More may be added in the future, so the application must be insensitive to the number of product lines.
- Products are sold in two markets: USA and Europe. Even if new markets are added in the future, management will combine all foreign markets into one for analysis purposes.
- Sales and forecast data is tracked per market, per product, per month.

- As is typical of decision support systems, the program is read-only. It analyzes existing data.

- The program must start off by displaying a high-level summary, and then allow the users to "drill down" to a greater level of detail.

Getting Started

Create a directory to house the application. It doesn't matter where the directory is located. Then create a new workbook, and save it in the application directory—name it DSS.XLS.

To start with, DSS.XLS will contain six worksheets. (More will be created later.) Name the worksheets: **Home**, **Trend**, **Breakdown**, **Data**, **Settings**, and **Products** (see Figure 21.1).

FIGURE 21.1

To rename a worksheet, choose Format ➤ Sheet ➤ Rename (or click the tab with the right mouse button, and choose Rename from the shortcut menu).

	A	B	C	D	E	F	G	H	I
1									
2									
3									
4									
5									
6									
7									
8									
9									
10									
11									
12									
13									
14									
15									

DSS.XLS

Home / Trend / Breakdown / Data / Settings / Products

NOTE

The instructions in this chapter do not instruct you to save your work. Needless to say, you should save the workbook periodically.

Building the Database

The database driving the application is 97 rows by 6 columns. Fortunately, there are some shortcuts that will make it easy to enter this data:

1. On worksheet *Data*, enter the following information:

2. Copy range A2:C5, and paste at the bottom of the data (A6). Then change the number in C6:C9 to a **2** (for period 2).

3. Repeat step 2 ten more times, for periods 3 through 12. (When this step is complete, the data will extend to row 49.)

4. Copy range A2:A49, and paste starting at A50. Then change A50:A97 to Europe.

5. Select D2:F97 and enter: **=INT(RAND()*10000)** Enter the formula into the selected range by pressing Ctrl+Enter.

N O T E   The formula places random numbers into the range, which will probably create some illogical data. You can edit the data later if desired.

6. With D2:F97 still selected, choose Edit ➤ Copy, then Edit ➤ Paste Special. Choose *Values*. (This replaces the formulas with the underlying values, so that the random numbers don't constantly recalculate.)

Name the Range Using a Named Formula That Counts the Rows

The database range will be named to facilitate some of the formulas that will be used later on. At the end of this exercise, the data will be saved as a dBASE file, and a query will be performed to retrieve the data onto the worksheet. In the real world, you won't know how many rows are contained in the database. Accordingly, the database range will be named using a formula that dynamically calculates the number of rows.

With worksheet Data active, choose Insert ➤ Name ➤ Define. Create a name **Database** that refers to:

```
=OFFSET(Data!$A$1,0,0,COUNTA(OFFSET(Data!$A$1,0,0,9999)),6)
```

T I P   The name *Database* will automatically expand or contract based on the number of values in column A. Since a named formula is not a "real" named range, it will not display in the name box. However, press F5 and type *Database*—the range will be selected. (Named formulas are covered in Chapter 8.)

Name the Product List

There are several places in the application where the user will select from a list of products. In two cases, pivot tables will do the work for you. But there is one instance where the list must reside in a range of cells. Activate the Products sheet, and enter the information shown below:

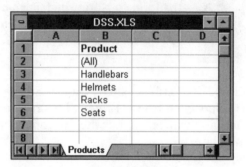

Remember, the application is supposed to be insensitive to the number of products. (Later, you will learn how to create this list by performing a query.) So the named range must use the same technique as was used for the *Database* range. In addition, two different names will be created—one that includes *(All)* and one that does not (in case there is a need to display both lists).

Activate worksheet *Products*, then follow these steps:

1. Define the name **Products.Plus.All** referring to:

   ```
   =OFFSET($B$1,1,0,COUNTA(OFFSET($B$1,1,0,999,1)))
   ```

This name counts the number of products, allowing for a maximum of 999.

2. Define the name **Product.List** referring to:

   ```
   =OFFSET(Products.Plus.All,1,0,ROWS(Products.Plus.All)-1)
   ```

This name uses **Products.Plus.All**, less the first row.

To test the names, press F5 to display the Go To dialog box, then type the name into the reference box.

Setting Up the Globals

Most applications include various settings and calculations that are used by worksheets throughout the application. You can save a lot of time by defining such settings one time only—on a worksheet whose sole purpose is to store *global* settings. The BikeStuff DSS application, as designed, has only one such setting. Still, it is worthwhile to set up the globals worksheet as a learning exercise.

In this application, the sheet named *Settings* is being used to store globals. Activate Settings, and follow these steps:

1. Name cell C2 **Current.Year**.

2. Enter the formula **=YEAR(NOW())** into C2 to calculate the current year.

Building the Home Worksheet

The worksheet named *Home* will be the first sheet displayed when the application is started. (The finished sheet is displayed in Figure 21.2.) It provides a very high-level summary, from which the user can "drill down" into a greater level of detail.

FIGURE 21.2

Completed Home worksheet

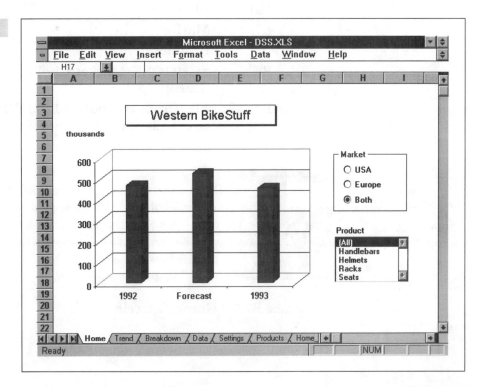

Place the Supporting Data on a Separate Worksheet

In order to create the chart, several calculations have to be performed first. The user doesn't have to see these interim calculations, so they will be placed on a separate sheet that will eventually be hidden from view. Insert a new worksheet, and name it *Home_Hide*. This name will serve as a reminder that the sheet contains calculations supporting the *Home* sheet, and that it needs to be hidden later.

Activate Home_Hide and follow these steps:

1. Name C2 **Market.Choice** and name cell C3 **Product.Choice**. (The controls on Home will be linked to these cells.) The quickest way to name these cells is by placing labels in B2 and B3 (see Figure 21.3), then use Insert ➤ Name ➤ Create. (See Chapter 8 to learn about creating names.)

2. Build the criteria range by entering the following onto Home_Hide:

CELL	ENTRY
B7	**Market**
C7	**Product**
B8	**=CHOOSE(Market.Choice,"USA", "Europe","")**
B9	**=IF(Product.Choice=1,"",INDEX(Product.List,Product.Choice-1))**

TIP

This is a criteria range that uses formulas which, based on user input, calculate the second row of the criteria range—this type of criteria range is sometimes called a *computed criteria*. See Chapter 16 to learn about computed criteria.

3. Name B7:C8 **Home.Criteria**

4. Build the range of data that the final chart is based on—add the following to Home_Hide:

CELL	ENTRY
B12	**=Current.Year-1**
C12	**=DSUM(Database,"Prior", Home.Criteria)/1000**
B13	**Forecast**
C13	**=DSUM(Database,"Forecast", Home.Criteria)/1000**
B14	**=Current.Year**
C14	**=DSUM(Database,"Current", Home.Criteria)/1000**

TIP The DSUM formulas divide by 1000 because the chart is based on thousands—this is done for aesthetic purposes. See Chapter 16 to learn about DSUM, and other so-called D functions.

5. Name B12:C14 **Home.Chart.Range**

Adding a Title and Creating the Chart

Now that the supporting data is ready, the chart on the Home sheet can be built. Activate Home, and follow these steps.

1. Draw a text box, and enter the company name. The text box pictured in Figure 21.2 has a border and a shadow.

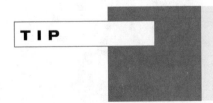

TIP A text box gives you control of text position—when text is placed in cells, you have to fight the worksheet grid when designing the sheet. See Chapter 12 to learn about text boxes, and other graphic objects.

FIGURE 21.3

Completed
Home_Hide worksheet

2. Click the ChartWizard tool, and draw the chart border on the worksheet. (Chapter 13 covers the ChartWizard.)

3. At Step 1 of the wizard, specify range as **=Home.Chart.Range**.

4. At Step 2 of the wizard, choose 3-D column chart.

5. At Step 3 of the wizard, choose format #4.

6. At Step 4 of the wizard, set *Data Series In* to Columns, and *Use First Column(s)* to 1.

7. At Step 5 of the wizard, set *Add a Legend* to No.

Figure 21.2 shows the finished chart. Some extra formatting has been performed, so it will not look identical to the chart that you create.

Adding Controls

Worksheet controls will let the user specify what data to chart. (See Chapter 19 to learn about controls.) With the Home sheet active, follow these steps:

1. Display the Forms toolbar (View ➤ Toolbars).

2. Draw a group box, and place three option buttons inside it. Change the text on the group box and option buttons as shown in Figure 21.2.

3. Ctrl+Click the first option button, choose Format ➤ Object, and link it to cell **Market.Choice**.

TIP The other two option buttons inside the group box are automatically linked to cell Market.Choice.

4. Draw a list box. With the list box still selected, choose Format ➤ Object. Specify an input range **Products.Plus.All**. Specify cell link **Product.Choice**.

Test the controls. As you click different options, the chart should change. If not, verify the settings for the controls, and verify the entries on Home_Hide.

Comparing the Current Year to the Prior Year

The *Home* sheet displays a high-level summary. Now, you will build the *Trend* worksheet, which compares current-year sales to prior-year sales using a line chart. (The finished Trend sheet is pictured in Figure 21.6.) A pivot table will be used to organize the data for charting. (See Chapter 17 to learn about pivot tables.)

Creating the Pivot Table

Activate Trend, then follow these steps:

1. Choose Data ➤ Pivot Table to start the PivotTable Wizard.

2. At Step 1 of the wizard, choose *Microsoft Excel List or Database.*

3. At Step 2 of the wizard, enter **Database** for the range. (Since the name Database is already defined in the workbook, Step 2 should default to Database.)

4. At Step 3 of the wizard, drag the field buttons to the locations shown in Figure 21.4.

5. The text labels **Sum of Prior** and **Sum of Current** are not very friendly. Still at Step 3 of the wizard, double-click these field buttons, and change the names (text) to **Last Year** and **This Year** respectively.

6. At Step 4 of the wizard, change the starting cell to **=$B$2** (to leave some space above the table, for aesthetic purposes). Only the setting *Save Data With Table Layout* should be checked. See Figure 21.5.

FIGURE 21.4

A pivot table can have multiple page fields, and multiple data fields.

FIGURE 21.5

The finished pivot table. Don't worry about the appearance—the chart is going to obscure most of the pivot table.

Creating the Chart

The pivot table has organized the data exactly the way the soon-to-be-created line chart requires. But there are still a couple of problems:

- If the user moves the Data or Period buttons (see Figure 21.5), the pivot table layout changes, in which case the chart changes as well. Sometimes this is desirable. But in this case, the application dictates that chart layout not change. To discourage the user from changing the pivot table layout, the chart will be placed on top of the pivot table.

- The chart won't be large enough to cover all 13 columns of the pivot table.

Follow these steps to create the chart:

1. Set the width of columns D through N to **1**. The pivot table will then be small enough to be covered by the chart.

2. Use the ChartWizard to draw a line chart. Cover the data area of the pivot table, but leave the **Market** and **Product** page buttons showing, so the user can change the data being charted (See Figure 21.6).

Change the market and product using the two drop-down lists, and watch the chart change.

Creating the Product Breakdown

The *Breakdown* worksheet will use a pie chart to show how the products have performed within each market, or for both markets combined. (The finished worksheet is shown in Figure 21.9) As with the *Trend* sheet, a pivot table will organize the data for the chart.

Creating the Pivot Table

Activate *Trend*, and follow these steps:

1. Choose Data ➤ PivotTable.

FIGURE 21.6

Completed Trend sheet. The user is discouraged (though not completely prevented) from changing the pivot table layout.

2. At Step 1 of the wizard, choose *Microsoft Excel List or Database*.

3. At Step 2 of the wizard, enter **Database** for the range. (Since the name Database is already defined in the workbook, Step 2 should default to Database.)

4. At Step 3 of the wizard, drag the field buttons to the locations shown in Figure 21.7.

5. At Step 4 of the wizard, change the starting cell to **=$B$2** (to leave some space above the table, for aesthetic purposes). Only the setting *Save Data With Table Layout* should be checked. Figure 21.8 shows the finished pivot table.

FIGURE 21.7

A pivot table does not require a column field.

FIGURE 21.8

This pivot table will be used to create a pie chart.

	A	B	C	D	E	F	G	H
1								
2		MARKET	(All)					
3								
4		Sum of Current						
5		PRODUCT	Total					
6		Handlebars	112976					
7		Helmets	137522					
8		Racks	96084					
9		Seats	110556					
10								
11								
12								
13								
14								
15								
16								
17								
18								

Home / Trend \ **Breakdown** / Data / Settings / Products /

What If Products Are Added?

Since the application must be insensitive to the number of products, the chart will be based on names that dynamically expand and contract, rather than on the absolute reference $B$6:$C$9. With *Breakdown* active, define the following two names:

1. Define the name **Pie.Labels** referring to:

   `=OFFSET($B$5,1,0,COUNTA(OFFSET($B$5,1,0,999,1)))`

2. Define the name **Pie.Data** referring to:

   `=OFFSET($C$5,1,0,COUNTA(OFFSET($C$5,1,0,999,1)))`

Test the names: Press F5 and enter the names—Pie.Labels should select B6:B9, and Pie.Data should select C6:C9.

Creating the Pie Chart

With *Breakdown* still active, follow these steps to create the pie chart:

1. Select B6:C9, then draw the chart using the ChartWizard tool— do not override the range at Step 1 of the wizard.

2. At Step 2 of the wizard, choose 3-D Pie.

3. At Step 3 of the wizard, choose format #7.

4. At Step 4 of the wizard, choose *Data Series in Columns*, and *Use First 1 Column*.

5. At Step 5 of the wizard, enter a chart title. (The text doesn't matter, because it will replaced with a formula later.)

6. Size the chart to cover the data region of the pivot table, but leave the market drop-down showing. (The finished chart shown in Figure 21.9 has been formatted, and won't look identical to the one you created.)

Now, the chart needs to be modified to use the two named formulas:

7. Double-click the chart object to activate it. Then, single-click any pie wedge. The entire data series (S1) will be selected.

8. Carefully change the formula (in the formula bar) to read:

`=SERIES(,Breakdown!Pie.Labels,Breakdown!Pie.Data,1)`

9. Change the chart title to refer to the drop-down selection at cell $C$2: Single-click the title, and enter the following formula on the formula bar:

`=Breakdown!$C$2`

Deselect the chart, and test it: place some text in B10, and a number in C10—the pie should automatically add a fifth wedge. Use the market drop-down to change the pivot table—the chart title should change accordingly. (Remember to clear B10:C10 when done testing.)

The pie chart (see Figure 21.9) shows the percentage of each product's contribution to the whole pie. But how big is the pie? Add the following to the *Breakdown* sheet to let the user know how big the pie is:

CELL	ENTRY
E2	**Total:**
F2	**=SUM(Pie.Data)**

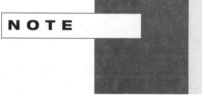

NOTE One of the original assumptions was insensitivity to the number of products. However, pie charts have an inherent limitation: When there are too many wedges, the pie loses its impact.

Moving the Data to an External Database

The data that resides on the *Data* worksheet will now be moved to an external database—a dBASE file. The application will be set up to query the

FIGURE 21.9

The finished
Breakdown sheet

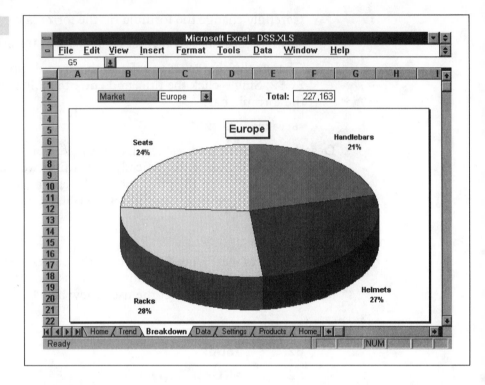

database each time it is started, so that it is always working with current data. Before you can proceed with this step, there are two requirements:

- Microsoft Query must be installed on your system. (Chapter 18 explains how to determine if this is the case.)

- The Excel query add-in, which provides the interface between Excel and Microsoft Query, must be installed on your system. (The file XLQUERY.XLA must be on your system, loaded under your Excel directory in LIBRARY\MSQUERY.)

These components can be installed using the Excel setup program.

N O T E   If your system is not set up properly, or if you do not want to store the data in an external database, skip ahead to the section *Recording the Startup Macro.*

Saving the Data in dBASE Format

Follow these steps to save the database as a dBASE file. (See Chapter 25 for more information on this topic.)

1. Activate the worksheet named *Data*.

2. Arrange the workspace so that you can see the Excel desktop, as pictured in Figure 21.10.

3. Hold down the Ctrl key, then drag the Data worksheet tab onto the Excel desktop—a new workbook is created with a copy of the Data sheet.

4. Select a cell in the database range, then choose File ➤ Save As. Select dBASE IV file type, and name the file **BIKES.DBF**.

5. Close the file. (Answer *No* when asked again if you want to save the file.)

Defining the Query

In this section, the query will be defined that retrieves the data from the dBASE file and places it onto the Data worksheet. (See Chapter 18 to learn more about this topic.)

Starting Microsoft Query

Follow these steps to start Microsoft Query:

1. Make sure the query add-in is loaded. (If it is loaded, there will be a command called *Get External Data* on the Data menu.) If not loaded, open the file XLQUERY.XLA located under your Excel directory, under LIBRARY\MSQUERY.

2. Select cell A1, then choose Data ➤ Get External Data—Microsoft Query is started.

Defining an ODBC Data Source

Follow these steps to define an ODBC data source for BIKES.DBF:

1. At the Select Data Source dialog box, click *Other*.

2. At the ODBC Data Sources dialog box, click *New*.

3. At the Add Data Source dialog box, select **dBASE Files**, and click *OK*.

4. At the ODBC dBASE Setup dialog box, enter data source name **BikeStuff**, and any description you want.

5. Click *Select Directory*. The directory should be set to the application directory, and BIKES.DBF should display in the list of files. (If not, use this dialog box in the same way you use a File ➤ Open dialog box to navigate to the application directory.) Click OK.

6. The ODBC dBASE Setup dialog box will display the name of the application directory. Click OK.

7. At the ODBC Data Sources dialog box, select **BikeStuff** from the list, then click *OK*.

8. At the Select Data Source dialog box, select **BikeStuff**, and click *Use*.

T I P

There is one good piece of news about this tedious procedure: it only needs to be performed once for a given data source. Any application that uses ODBC can then utilize the same ODBC data source.

CREATING AN APPLICATION

Completing the Query Definition

Follow these steps to complete the query definition in Microsoft Query, and then place the results onto the Data worksheet:

1. At the Add Tables dialog box, select **bikes.dbf**, and click *Add*. Then click *Close*.

2. In the Bikes table, at the top of the query window (see Figure 21.11), double-click the asterisk to add all of the fields to the query.

3. Choose File ➤ Return Data to Microsoft Excel. Control is transferred back to Excel.

4. At the Get External Data dialog box, check *Keep Query Definition* and *Include Field Names*. Then click OK.

NOTE

Since the sales data was already on the *Data* sheet,
you may wonder why all this work, and with no visible
change as a result: The query definition is now stored
on the worksheet, hidden, and the data can be
painlessly refreshed.

To test the query, clear several cells inside the database on the Data worksheet. Then choose Data ➤ Refresh Data. The data will be retrieved from
the dBASE file, and the cells that you cleared should contain data.

Querying the List of Products

The list on the *Products* worksheet needs to be refreshed each time the application is run. In the real world, it is likely that there would be a product
master file. Without a master file, the list can still be derived from
SALES.DBF. The inclusion of *(All)* at the top of the list introduces a
wrinkle.

Activate the *Products* worksheet, and follow these steps to define the query:

1. Select cell B3, then choose Data ➤ Get External Data.

2. At the Select Data Source dialog box, pick **BikeStuff**, then click Use.

3. At the Add Tables dialog box, pick **bikes.dbf**, then click Add. Then click Close.

4. In the Bikes table, at the top of the query window (see Figure 21.11), double-click the Product field to add it to the query.

5. Choose View ➤ Query Properties, and check *Unique Values Only*, then click OK.

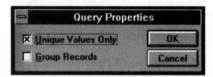

6. Choose Records ➤ Sort. Pick *Ascending*, click Add, then click Close.

NOTE   Even though the products may be sorted correctly, there is no guarantee that they will remain sorted as the database changes.

7. Choose File ➤ Return Data To Microsoft Excel. Control is transferred back to Excel.

8. At the Get External Data dialog box, check only the *Keep Query Definition* setting, then click OK.

CAUTION

It is critical that you do not check *Include Field Names*. Otherwise, the word *Product* will be included in the product list.

Recording the Startup Macro

Next, you will record a macro that will automatically be run every time the application is started (by opening the workbook). The macro will perform two major tasks:

- Pivot tables do not refresh automatically. The macro must make sure these tables contain current data.

- In the real-world scenario, the source database (BIKES.DBF) is constantly changing. The macro needs to refresh the database on worksheet *Data* by querying BIKES.DBF.

NOTE　Querying the dBASE file requires the use of the query add-in, XLQUERY.XLA. Excel can be configured to automatically open the add-in using Tools ➤ Add-Ins (covered in Chapter 24). However, if the application is being deployed to other desktops in your organization, you may not want to make the assumption that these desktops are properly configured.

Starting the Recorder

Recording a complex macro requires advance planning. All of your actions—including mistakes—are recorded. (See Chapter 20 to learn about recording macros.) Create a plan, and perform each step carefully. Before you begin recording:

- Make sure the query add-in is loaded (unless you chose not to save the data in a dBASE file).

- Activate the *Home* worksheet.

Follow these steps to start the recording process:

1. Choose Tools ➤ Record Macro ➤ Record New Macro.

2. Enter the macro name **Auto_Open,** then click Options. The macro must be stored in *This Workbook*.

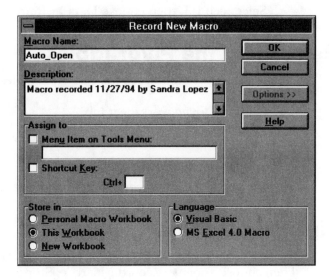

3. Click OK—you are now recording.

4. Make sure the Tools ➤ Record Macro ➤ Use Relative References command is *not* checked.

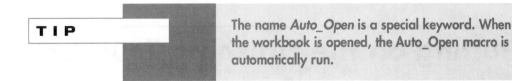

T I P

The name *Auto_Open* is a special keyword. When the workbook is opened, the Auto_Open macro is automatically run.

Refreshing the Data

Follow these steps to refresh the database. (Skip this section if you chose not to store the data in a dBASE file.)

1. Click the *Data* worksheet tab.

2. Select cell A1, then choose Data ➤ Refresh Data.

That takes care of the database stored on worksheet *Data*. But now, the product list must be refreshed:

3. Click the *Products* worksheet tab.

4. Select cell B3, then choose Data ➤ Refresh Data.

Refreshing the Pivot Tables

Follow these steps to refresh the two pivot tables:

1. Click the *Trend* worksheet tab.

2. Select cell C2, then choose Data ➤ Refresh Data.

3. Click the *Breakdown* worksheet tab.

4. Select cell C2, then choose Data ➤ Refresh Data.

Finishing Up

There's only one more step to record: Click the *Home* worksheet tab. Then choose Tools ➤ Record Macro ➤ Stop Recording. The new macro resides on a VBA module that was inserted into the workbook by the macro recorder. It is shown in Figure 21.12.

You can test the macro by choosing the Tools ➤ Macro command, picking Auto_Open from the list, and clicking Run.

Putting on the Finishing Touches

There are two more steps required to complete the application.

1. Remove gridlines and remove row and column headings (on all the visible sheets) using Tools ➤ Options, then select the View tab. You can also remove the horizontal and vertical scrollbars, since the information on each sheet fits in the window. See Figure 21.13.

NOTE   The scrollbar settings are not specific to a given worksheet. They apply to the entire workbook.

2. Activate Home, and save the workbook.

FIGURE 21.12

Even if you are unfamiliar with VBA syntax, you can still recognize the recorded actions.

```
' Auto_Open Macro
' Macro recorded 11/27/94 by Sandra Lopez
'
'
Sub Auto_Open()
    Sheets("Data").Select
    Range("A1").Select
    Application.Run "QueryRefresh", Range("Data!$A$1")
    Sheets("Products").Select
    Range("B3").Select
    Application.Run "QueryRefresh", Range("Products!$B$3")
    Sheets("Trend").Select
    Range("C2").Select
    Application.ActiveCell.PivotTable.RefreshTable
    Sheets("Breakdown").Select
    Range("C2").Select
    Application.ActiveCell.PivotTable.RefreshTable
    Sheets("Home").Select
End Sub
```

FIGURE 21.13

Choose Tools ➤ Options, and select the View tab, to remove gridlines, row and column headings, and scrollbars.

Comments and Caveats

Here are some comments about the application, some ideas on how to improve it, and some thoughts about application development in general.

Suppressing Screen Updates While Macros Run

When you open the workbook, the Auto_Open macro runs automatically. You can watch the various sheets being activated, and charts being repainted. This slows down the macro, and some people consider it unaesthetic.

Insert the following VBA command at the beginning of the Auto_Open macro to suppress the screen display while the macro is running. (Once the macro stops, the screen updates as usual.)

```
Application.ScreenUpdating = False
```

There is a trade-off involved. When screen update is suppressed...

- The macro runs faster.
- The user is looking at an hourglass, instead of being entertained by watching the macro work.

In other words, you have to weigh the difference between *actual* elapsed time, and *perceived* elapsed time.

Prototyping vs. Real-World Development

If you examine the effort that went into the development of this simple application, you will see that many of the tasks were dictated by the requirement that the application be insensitive to the number of products in the database. Therein lies one of the biggest differences between prototyping and developing truly data-driven applications.

It may be relatively easy to grind out prototype quality applications. But such applications require constant maintenance. Changes to the underlying data require that the application be modified. A well-designed, data-driven application takes more time to develop up front, but is worth the effort in the long run.

Using Microsoft Query

The application uses Microsoft Query to retrieve data from the dBASE file. As a result, there are two issues to consider:

- Microsoft Query is left in memory after you run the application, which could be confusing to users. To solve this problem, you can modify the macro to shut down Microsoft Query.

- There is a faster way to perform queries. There is an add-in included with Excel that provides an API to the ODBC manager, circumventing Microsoft Query. The add-in is named XLODBC.XLA. (This add-in also provides the SQLREQUEST worksheet function, covered in Chapter 18.)

Hiding the Formula Bar

This application does not require that the formula bar be displayed, because there is no data entry taking place. You could hide it when you record the Auto_Open macro, but this introduces a problem: This is a global setting, and Excel "remembers" it from session to session. If the Auto_Open macro hides the formula bar, it will remain hidden until it is manually unhidden (using View ➤ Formula Bar)—even in future Excel sessions. This is not a big problem when you are the only user, but it can be a support problem if the application is being deployed to many desktops.

The solution is to record an Auto_Close macro, which restores the formula bar.

Bulletproofing the Application

The more people who use an application, the more important it is for the application to be *bulletproof*. In other words, no matter what the user does, they cannot cause an error, harm the data, or change the program.

NOTE Bulletproofing is a matter of degree. It is kind of like the temperature absolute zero—you can get very close, but it is ultimately unachievable. You need to weigh the development cost of each bulletproofing measure against the benefits realized (reduced support cost, and overall user satisfaction).

Here are some things you can do to bulletproof the application:

Create a Custom Menu System An application is not even remotely bulletproof if the built-in menus are displayed. There are too many commands that will break the application.

Trapping Keyboard Shortcuts Even with a custom menu system, the user can still use keyboard shortcuts to perform all kinds of disruptive tasks. You can write a macro to trap every insidious keystroke.

Protecting the Worksheets Minimally, the worksheets should be protected so that users cannot delete the objects (embedded charts and controls). You can also protect cells, but this has many side-effects that you should be aware of. For instance, you can't manipulate a pivot table on a worksheet where the cells are protected. (See Chapter 11 to learn more about protection.)

Protecting the Workbook If you protect the workbook structure, users will not be able to unhide hidden worksheets, or delete worksheets. (See Chapter 11 to read more about this topic.)

Save the File as Read-Only With the data stored in an external database, there is no reason for users to be able to change the workbook. Use File ➤ Save As, then click Options, to save the workbook as a read-only file (using the write-reservation password).

PART SEVEN

Solving Real-World Problems

CHAPTER
22

Consolidating and Outlining

f a s t **TRACK**

In a multi-level linked consolidation, when data is changed on the lowest level   696

The highest level won't recalculate until the middle level is recalculated.

To create an automatic outline   698

Choose Data ➤ Group And Outline ➤ Auto Outline.

To expand and collapse an outline   700

- Click the level tools in the upper left corner of the worksheet to hide or show entire levels of detail.
- Click the show or hide details symbols in the top and left margins of the worksheet to expand or collapse groups.

To hide outline symbols   700

- Click the Show Outline Symbols tool.
- Choose Tools ➤ Options, select the View tab, and uncheck the *Outline Symbols* setting.

To remove outlining   704

Choose Data ➤ Group And Outline ➤ Clear Outline.

CONSOLIDATING information from multiple sources is a task often performed using spreadsheet software. This chapter is going to show how to use Excel's consolidation features to create a multi-level budgeting model. You will learn how to:

- *use the Data* ➤ *Consolidate command*
- *link the consolidation to source data*
- *outline consolidated data*
- *solve a real-world business problem using consolidation*

The second subject covered in this chapter is outlining. Several commands in Excel, such as Consolidate, create worksheet outlines as an automatic by-product. You can also create your own outlines. You will learn how to:

- *create automatic outlines*
- *use outline symbols to expand and collapse outlines*
- *create "manual" outlines*

Consolidating Data

In a sense, many of the formulas placed on a worksheet serve to consolidate data, using a broad definition for this term. But this section covers a specific command: Data ➤ Consolidate.

Data consolidations are used to roll-up and summarize data from more than one source. For example, suppose that you have workbooks storing population statistics for each county within a state, with one workbook for each county. You need to take the information from the county workbooks and create a state-wide report that summarizes all of the counties. You can painstakingly open each workbook, copy the information to a new workbook, and then write formulas to summarize the information.

Better yet, you can use Excel's built-in consolidation capabilities to simplify this process. Using the Data ➤ Consolidate command, you can:

- Consolidate information stored on different worksheets within the same workbook.
- Consolidate information stored on different workbooks (without the need to open the workbooks).
- Consolidate multiple ranges on the same worksheet.
- Consolidate data on the basis of row and column labels, regardless of position on the worksheet.
- Use different calculations when you consolidate, such as sum, count, and average.
- Link the consolidation to the source data.

NOTE

Pivot tables, covered in Chapter 17, provide a powerful, flexible way to analyze data. They are capable of consolidating data from multiple sources, summarizing detailed data, and creating multi-level outlines. If you need to perform consolidations, pivot tables rank as a *must learn* topic.

The Business Problem

In this section, you will learn how to perform a two-level consolidation for a fictitious company, Electronic Gizmos Corp. (EGC), that distributes electronic products nationwide.

- EGC has four distribution centers, which are designated as A through D.

- Two distribution centers, A and B, are in the eastern region. Centers C and D are in the western region. There is a regional manager for each of the two regions.

- Every year, during the 4th quarter, the distribution centers prepare a proposed budget for the following year and submit it to the regional manager for approval.

- The regional managers submit consolidated budgets for their respective regions to the VP of Finance for approval.

Using a Template for Conformity

To simplify the consolidation process, a template will be used that forces the distribution centers to enter data in the same format. The budget template is shown in Figure 22.1.

FIGURE 22.1

Budgets are submitted for four departments. Notice that the row labels (B6:B10) and column labels (C5:F5) are unique.

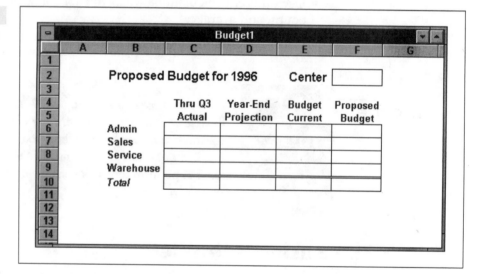

Follow these steps to create the template pictured in Figure 22.1:

1. Create a new workbook—delete every worksheet except Sheet1.

2. Enter the row and column labels shown in Figure 22.1.

3. Hide the gridlines (using Tools ➤ Options, View tab).

4. Apply borders as shown in Figure 22.1. (See Chapter 5 to learn about cell formatting.)

TIP Place the double border on the top of row 10 rather than the bottom of row 9. Later, when you copy D6 to D7:D9, the double border won't get overwritten.

5. Enter the following formulas:

D6	**=C6*1.33**
C10	**=SUM(C6:C9)**

NOTE The distribution centers submit budget proposals for the upcoming year during the 4th quarter—before 4th quarter data is available. The formula in D6 is intended to predict 4th quarter expenses on the basis of the previous three quarters.

6. Copy the formula in D6 to D7:D9.

TIP Use the fill handle to AutoFill D6 down through D9. (AutoFill is discussed in Chapter 7.)

7. Copy the formula in C10 to D10:F10.

8. Name the range B5:F10 **Budget_Area**.

TIP To suppress the display of zero values, choose Tools ➤ Options, click the View tab, and uncheck *Zero Values*.

9. Choose File ➤ Save. Enter the file name **BUDGET**. Using the *Save File as Type* drop-down, choose *Template*.

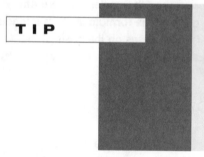

TIP

If you want to prevent users from overwriting formulas, all cells where data entry is allowed should be unlocked, and all other cells should be locked. (All cells are locked by default.) The cell lock takes effect when the worksheet cells are protected using Tools ➤ Protection ➤ Protect Worksheet. (See Chapter 11 to learn about protecting worksheets.)

The template is complete. When you close it and re-open it, a copy of the template is loaded into memory, instead of the original. (See Chapter 10 to learn about templates.)

TIP

To open an original template rather than a copy, hold down the Shift key while you open the template.

Using a File Naming Convention

For reasons you will discover later, a file naming convention is vitally important when performing workbook consolidations. EGC has chosen the following conventions:

- Distribution center workbook names begin with the name of the parent region, followed by an underscore, followed by the one character distribution center ID. For example, center C, which is in the western region, will create a budget workbook named **WEST_C.XLS**. Center A, in the eastern region, will create a workbook named **EAST_A.XLS**, and so on.

- The regional managers create workbooks beginning with REG, followed by an underscore, followed by the region. These two workbooks will be named **REG_EAST.XLS** and **REG_WEST.XLS**.

- The corporate summary workbook will be named CORP.XLS, though the name of this workbook is not critical as are the names of the lower level workbooks.

Consolidating by Position or Category

Before creating a consolidation, there is an important issue to consider: The Data ➤ Consolidate command lets you consolidate on the basis of position or on the basis of row/column categories.

Consolidating by Position

Consolidation based on position requires that the data be structured identically, relative within each data source:

- Each cell being consolidated must reside in the same relative position within the source range, as is the case with the EGC model.

- The row and column heading in the source range(s) are ignored, even if they are included as part of the consolidation range.

- Data ➤ Consolidate lets you consolidate multiple ranges from the same worksheet. Therefore, the *relative* position of cells within each range is critical—not the absolute position on the worksheet. (See Figure 22.2.)

FIGURE 22.2

F7:G8 is a consolidation of the two source ranges, C4:D5 and C11:D12.

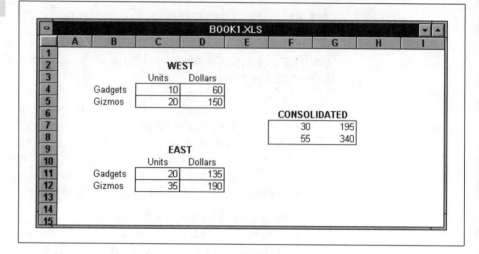

- Since the row and column headings are not part of the source data (and are not copied to the consolidation even if included), the source data and the consolidation are often based on a template.

Generally, consolidating by position is a risky proposition. A minor change to source data can cause erroneous results.

Consolidating by Category

When you consolidate on the basis of category, the row and/or column labels are used to determine how to perform the consolidation. Accordingly, the source data ranges do not have to be structured identically.

- The source ranges can contain a varying number of rows or columns.

- The sequence of the row and/or column labels doesn't matter.

Figure 22.3 shows a consolidation by category, with the source ranges and the consolidation located on the same worksheet.

Consolidating by category provides greater data integrity and more flexibility than consolidating by position.

FIGURE 22.3

F7:H10 is a consolidation of the two source ranges, B3:D6 and B12:D14. Consolidation by category allows the source ranges to differ.

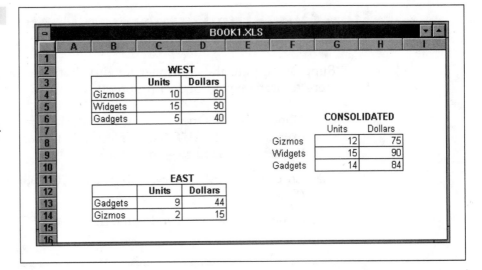

To Link or Not to Link

The second major choice you are presented with when consolidating is whether to link the consolidation to the source data ranges.

When to Link A consolidation that is linked to source data recalculates automatically, when links are refreshed. Linking is a good idea if the source data is subject to change, and the consolidation needs to stay in sync with the source data. For instance, using the EGC model, suppose that the budgeting process is iterative. A distribution center submits a proposal. The manager reviews the numbers and sends it back for revision. The center makes changes, the manager reviews again, and so on. In this scenario, the workbooks will remain in sync without manual effort.

When Not to Link You should not link if the consolidation is a one-time process—the consolidation will be a "frozen" report, with no formulas pointing back to the source data. Otherwise, you run the risk of the consolidation inadvertently changing because of a change in the source.

Step One—The Distribution Center Budget

Suppose you are the controller for distribution center C. Follow these steps to prepare your budget proposal:

1. Choose File ➤ Open to open the template created in the previous exercise—**BUDGET.XLT**. (Notice that a copy of the template is loaded into memory—not the original.)

2. Enter **C** into F2. Enter numbers into C6:C9, E6:E9, and F6:F9. (See Figure 22.4.)

3. Choose File ➤ Save, and name the file **WEST_C.XLS**.

FIGURE 22.4

The completed budget proposal for distribution center C.

	A	B	C	D	E	F	G
2		Proposed Budget for 1996			Center	C	
4			Thru Q3	Year-End	Budget	Proposed	
5			Actual	Projection	Current	Budget	
6		Admin	15,291	20,337	19,000	21,500	
7		Sales	9,224	12,268	13,500	16,000	
8		Service	11,404	15,167	16,000	18,000	
9		Warehouse	21,793	28,985	30,000	35,000	
10		*Total*	57,712	76,757	78,500	90,500	

In the next step, the western region manager will consolidate centers C and D. You can repeat the previous steps for center D, or take a shortcut: Save **WEST_C.XLS** as **WEST_D.XLS**, then change a few numbers so that the workbooks can be distinguished later, then save again.

Step Two—The Regional Consolidation

Suppose you are the western regional manager for EGC. It is your job to consolidate the proposed budgets submitted by the distribution centers within your region. The structure of the template will allow a consolidation by position. However, the personnel at center D are known to break the rules from time to time, so the safest bet is a consolidation by category. Follow these steps:

1. Close **WEST_C.XLS** and **WEST_D.XLS**.

TIP The source workbooks do not have to be open in order to perform a consolidation. This is an important feature, especially when there are dozens of source workbooks instead of only two.

2. Create a new workbook.

NOTE When performing a consolidation by category, the row and column headings are part of the source data ranges. As such, the template provides marginal value, as the consolidation process will copy row and column headings for you.

3. Select B2 (the upper left corner of the consolidation range) and choose Data ➤ Consolidate. The Consolidate dialog box is shown in Figure 22.5.

4. Enter **WEST_?.XLS!Budget_Area** in the *Reference* box, then click Add.

5. Check *Top Row* and *Left Column,* which causes the consolidation to be based on category, rather than position. Check *Create Links to Source Data.*

FIGURE 22.5

The Data ➤
Consolidate
dialog box.

6. Click OK to perform the consolidation. The result is shown in Figure 22.6.

7. Name the range B2:G17 **Budget_Area** (this will be used for the corporate consolidation).

FIGURE 22.6

When you create links
to the source data, the
sheet is automatically
outined.

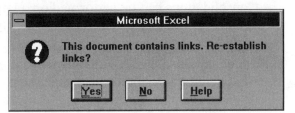

		A	B	C	D	E	F	G	H
	1								
	2				Actual	Projection	Current	Budget	
+	5		Admin		27,516	36,596	36,000	41,500	
+	8		Sales		19,368	25,759	26,500	31,000	
+	11		Service		22,067	29,349	31,000	34,000	
+	14		Warehouse		39,633	52,712	55,000	62,000	
+	17		Total		108,584	144,417	148,500	168,500	
	18								
	19								
	20								
	21								
	22								
	23								

REG_WEST.XLS

Refreshing a Linked Consolidation

A linked consolidation behaves just like any workbook that is linked to
one or more source workbooks. When the file is opened, the following dialog box is displayed.

Microsoft Excel

This document contains links. Re-establish
links?

[Yes] [No] [Help]

Press OK to recalculate the links. New values are retrieved from the
source workbooks, even if they are closed.

TIP

If you want dependent workbooks to update links
without a prompt, choose Tools ➤ Options, click the Edit
tab, and uncheck *Ask to Update Automatic Links*. This is
a global setting that pertains to all workbooks.

Using Wildcards and Named Ranges

Two vitally important techniques were used in the previous exercise, the benefits of which can not be over-estimated if you intend to perform, and rely upon, consolidations.

Using Wildcards in the File Name

You can include asterisks and question marks in the file name as wildcard characters. The use of wildcards adheres to software conventions: The asterisk is used as a place marker for any number of characters, and the question mark is used as a place marker for any one character. The EGC file naming convention, discussed earlier in this chapter, is intended to support this wildcard-based consolidation methodology.

The file name **WEST_?.XLS** will consolidate from all files in the current directory with a prefix of **WEST_**, any character in the sixth position, and a suffix of **.XLS** (i.e., WEST_C.XLS, WEST_D.XLS, WEST_Z.XLS). The benefit may not be obvious with the EGC model, consisting of two source workbooks, but consider the following:

- Consolidations can be performed on a large number of workbooks, without the tedious effort of specifying each source range.

- If a new workbook is added to the directory and the name of the workbook matches the wildcard specification, it will be included automatically the next time the consolidation workbook recalculates.

CAUTION

When using wildcards, the source data must be contained on the first worksheet in the source workbook(s).

Referring to the Source Data by Name

The second vital technique used in the previous exercise was the reference to a named range, **Budget_Area**. (Earlier in the chapter, when the template was created, the name was defined.) By using a name:

- When creating links to source data, the name helps ensure the integrity of the external reference. (Refer to Chapter 8 to learn more about names.)

- New categories can be inserted into one or more source data ranges. The name expands automatically, and the next time the consolidation recalculates, everything stays in sync.

Automatic Outlining

The worksheet shown in Figure 22.7 contains outline symbols, which are an automatic by-product when you create links to source data. When you click the outline symbols in the left margin, the outline expands. (Outlining is covered in depth later in this chapter.)

FIGURE 22.7

On the detail rows, Column C contains the workbook prefix indicating which row comes from which source.

REG_WEST.XLS

	A	B	C	D	E	F	G	H
1								
2				Actual	Projection	Current	Budget	
3			West_C	15,291	20,337	19,000	21,500	
4			West_D	12,225	16,259	17,000	20,000	
5		Admin		27,516	36,596	36,000	41,500	
8		Sales		19,368	25,759	26,500	31,000	
11		Service		22,067	29,349	31,000	34,000	
14		Warehouse		39,633	52,712	55,000	62,000	
17		Total		108,584	144,417	148,500	168,500	
18								
19								
20								
21								

The numbers on the detail rows contain formulas that refer to the source workbooks.

Entering Source References

In the previous exercise, the source reference was entered manually. But there are several other ways to enter this information.

- If the source workbook is open, you can point and click the source range.

- Click the Browse button (see Figure 22.5) to select a closed workbook, then type the sheet name and source range following the workbook name.

- Use a single 3-D reference to consolidate source areas that are identically positioned on different sheets in the same workbook. (See Chapters 4 and 8 to learn more about 3-D references.)

Using Category Labels in the Consolidation Range

In the previous exercise, one cell (B2) was selected when the Data ➤ Consolidate command was chosen. However, if you select more than one cell when you choose Data ➤ Consolidate, and the range contains category labels, the labels control what data is consolidated. The following exercise demonstrates the technique:

1. On a new workbook, build the worksheet shown in Figure 22.8.

2. Select F8:G10 and choose Data ➤ Consolidate.

3. With the Consolidate dialog box displayed, select B3:D6 (which enters the range into the *Reference* in the consolidate dialog box), then click Add.

4. Add the second source range: Select B12:D14 and click Add.

5. Check *Top Row* and *Left Column*.

FIGURE 22.8

A consolidation will be created of the East and West data.

NOTE When the consolidation is on the same sheet as the source data, you cannot create a link to the source.

Click OK to perform the consolidation. Figure 22.9 shows the result.

FIGURE 22.9

Product *Gizmos* and column *Units* were excluded from the consolidation.

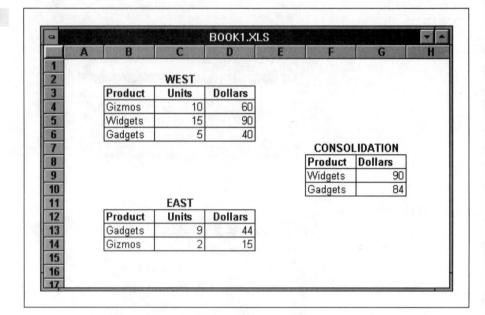

Since category labels were included in the selected range when Data ➤ Consolidate was chosen, the labels controlled which data was consolidated.

Using Wildcards in the Categories

There is an interesting and powerful variation to the technique described above. If the categories in the consolidation range include wildcards, all categories matching the wildcard are summarized. Consider the worksheet in Figure 22.10.

When the consolidation in Figure 22.10 was created, F9:H11 was selected. The asterisk caused all bikes, and all trikes, to be summarized.

FIGURE 22.10

Category labels inside
the consolidation
range can include
wildcard characters.

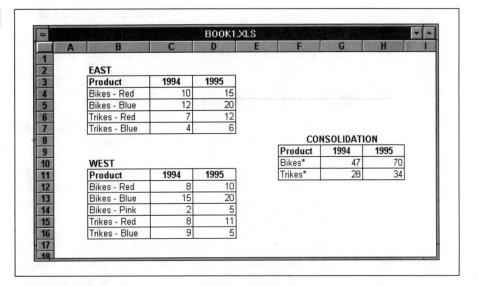

Consolidation Functions

While consolidation is most often performed to sum data, you can also perform consolidations that use other functions:

Count	counts cells containing a value—text or number (equivalent to COUNTA function)
Count Nums	counts numbers (equivalent to COUNT function)
Average	calculates average
Max	finds the maximum value
Min	finds the minimum value
Product	calculates the product
StDev	calculates the standard deviation of a sample
StDevP	calculates the standard deviation of the population

Var	calculates the variance of a sample
VarP	calculates the variance of the population

Multi-Level Consolidations

There are some important things to understand about multi-level consolidations. Let's re-visit the EGC model.

At step two, the western region consolidation was completed, and saved as **REG_WEST.XLS**. Suppose that the eastern region consolidation was also performed and saved as **REG_EAST.XLS**. (Remember, both of these consolidations are linked to the distribution center source data.)

Consolidating the two regions into a corporate total involves the same basic procedure as when the regional consolidations were created. (The only difference is the file name.) Here are the implications of EGC's two-level linked model:

- The regional budgets are linked to the distribution center budgets. When the regional budgets are opened, the links are (optionally) recalculated.

- The corporate budgets are linked to the regional budgets. When the corporate budget is opened, the links are (optionally) recalculated.

- Link recalculation only goes down one level. Suppose a change is made to a distribution center (bottom level) budget. Then, the corporate (top level) workbook is opened. The change at the bottom level will not flow to the top level. The workbooks must be recalculated in reverse order of the hierarchy.

More Facts about Consolidation

- Only one consolidation can be defined on a (destination) worksheet.

- Consolidation settings are persistent—the same consolidation model can be used repeatedly without setting it up from scratch each time.

- Destination cells are formatted using the number formats in the first source selected for consolidation.

- An unlinked consolidation can be reversed by choosing Edit ➤ Undo immediately following the consolidation.

- A linked consolidation cannot be reversed with Edit ➤ Undo. (It can be reversed by closing the workbook without saving the consolidation.)

- If the source and destination areas are on the same worksheet, you cannot create a linked consolidation.

Worksheet Outlining

An outlined worksheet lets you easily and quickly view various levels of detail—for rows and/or columns. Figure 22.11 shows a worksheet with outlining.

FIGURE 22.11

The outline symbols in the left and top margins let you expand and collapse the outline.

There are several operations in Excel that create outlines for you automatically:

- Data ➤ Subtotals (see Chapter 16)
- Data ➤ Consolidate, when the *Link To Source* option is chosen (covered earlier in this chapter)
- a summary report created with Solver (see Chapter 23)

This section will explain how to create your own outlines, and how to use outlining symbols—regardless of how the outline was created.

Creating Automatic Outlines

The easiest way to create an outline is with the Data ➤ Group And Outline ➤ Auto Outline command. Excel looks for formulas on the active sheet, and on the basis of the formulas, determines where the summary and detail rows/columns are located. Consider the outlined worksheet in Figure 22.12.

FIGURE 22.12

Automatic outlining was applied to this worksheet.

	A	B	C	D	E	F	G	H
1				Jan	Feb	Mar	Q1 Total	
2		North	Tennis	75	88	152	315	
3			Running	125	132	138	395	
4			Hiking	224	234	254	712	
5			**North Total**	424	454	544	1422	
6		South	Tennis	355	437	564	1356	
7			Running	346	425	589	1360	
8			Hiking	385	489	521	1395	
9			**South Total**	1086	1351	1674	4111	
10								
11								
12								

The outline symbols in the left and top margins indicate where the summary rows and columns are located. Since row 5 sums rows 2 through 4, and row 9 sums rows 6 through 8, rows 5 and 9 become summary rows in the outline. Since column G sums columns D through F, it becomes a summary column.

Using the Outline Symbols

The plus and minus symbols in the top and left margins of an outlined worksheet are used to expand or collapse sections of the outline selectively. Using the worksheet pictured in Figure 22.12, suppose that you want to collapse the data for region *North*. Figure 22.13 shows the sheet after the symbol to the left of row 5 is clicked—rows 2 through 4 are hidden.

FIGURE 22.13

The symbols in the top and left margins are used to collapse sections of the outline selectively.

The symbols in the top left corner of the sheet are used to expand and collapse the entire outline at once. Figure 22.13 shows two buttons for changing the row outline, and two buttons for changing the column outline. The number of buttons depends upon the number of levels in the outline.

Figure 22.14 shows the same worksheet, after pressing both of the level one buttons in the corner of the sheet.

FIGURE 22.14

Use the symbols in the upper left corner to expand and collapse the entire outline at once.

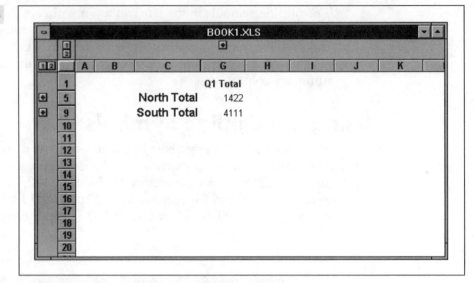

Using Menu Commands to Expand and Collapse Outlines

Menu commands can be used in lieu of the outline symbols to expand or collapse an outline. Follow these steps to collapse a section of an outline using menu commands:

1. Select a summary cell for the group you want to collapse.

2. Choose Data ➤ Group And Outline ➤ Hide Detail.

To expand an outline group (display details) using menu commands:

1. Select a summary cell for the group you want to expand.

2. Choose Data ➤ Group And Outline ➤ Show Detail.

Hiding the Outline Symbols

Suppose you are distributing an outlined worksheet to co-workers, and you do not want the outline symbols displayed. Follow these steps to hide the symbols:

1. Choose Tools ➤ Options, and select the View tab.

2. Uncheck the *Outline Symbols* setting, and click OK.

You can also use the Show Outline Symbols tool to toggle outline symbols, or from the keyboard, press Ctrl+8.

NOTE   Hiding the outline symbols does not remove the underlying outline from the worksheet. The outline is still in place, and can still be manipulated with menu commands.

Creating Manual Outlines

Automatic outlining is convenient because it does all the work for you. But sometimes you may want more control over the outline, in which case you must define the outline manually. Here are several scenarios in which manual outlining might be used:

- If there are no formulas on the worksheet (for example, data downloaded from a mainframe)
- To outline just a portion of the worksheet
- If the data is not organized for automatic outlining (for instance, one section has summary data above detail data, and another section has summary data below detail data)

Consider the worksheet in Figure 22.15:

Suppose you want the ability to collapse just the East section.

1. Select the rows you want to outline (rows 3:9).

2. Choose Data ➤ Group And Outline ➤ Group (or click on the Group tool). The results are shown in Figure 22.16.

Formatting Worksheet Outlines

You can manually format an outline, as you would any range of cells. But there are two more effective techniques: styles and table AutoFormats.

You can outline just the East section of the worksheet by creating a manual outline.

	A	B	C	D	E	F	G
1							
2				1994	1995		
3		East	Wages	120000	120000		
4			Rent	5000	5000		
5			Utilities	395	450		
6			Insurance	300	300		
7			Advertising	200	250		
8			Supplies	250	270		
9			Repairs	50	75		
10			**Total East**	126195	126345		
11							
12		**West**	Wages	50000	50000		
13			Utilities	450	300		
14			**Total West**	50450	50300		
15							
16			**Grand Total**	176645	176645		
17							
18							

The manual outline created for region East has been collapsed.

	A	B	C	D	E	F	G
1							
2				1994	1995		
10			**Total East**	126195	126345		
11							
12		**West**	Wages	50000	50000		
13			Utilities	450	300		
14			**Total West**	50450	50300		
15							
16			**Grand Total**	176645	176645		
17							
18							

Applying Styles to Outlines

You can apply built-in styles to different levels of an outline, as shown in Figure 22.17. As with cell styles, if you change a style definition, every outline level using the given style will be automatically reformatted.

FIGURE 22.17

Outline with styles defined for each of three levels

To apply automatic styles to an outline, the Automatic Styles option must be selected before creating the outline. To select the Automatic Styles option:

1. Choose Data ➤ Group and Outline ➤ Settings.
2. Check the Automatic Styles setting.

Then, when an automatic outline is created, the outline styles are automatically applied. To change the definition of a style:

1. Choose Format ➤ Style.
2. Select the style from the *Style Name* list (the styles are named RowLevel_1, ColLevel_1, and so on).
3. Click the Modify button and make your changes, then click OK. (See Chapter 5 to learn more about styles.)

The new style definition is automatically applied.

Applying Table AutoFormats to Outlines

You can apply AutoFormats to a worksheet before or after outlining the data. The AutoFormat feature is "smart"—it detects summary and detail levels using the formulas. Follow these steps to apply an AutoFormat:

1. Select a cell within the data range.

2. Choose Format ➤ AutoFormat.

3. Select an AutoFormat from the list of *Table Formats*.

NOTE If only one cell is selected when the Format ➤ AutoFormat command is chosen, the format will be applied to all contiguous data. If the range you want to AutoFormat contains blank rows or columns, you must select the entire range before choosing the command.

TIP By default, charts created from outlined data automatically change when the outline is expanded or collapsed.

Removing an Outline

You can remove outlining from an entire worksheet, or from selected rows or columns.

To remove outlining from the entire worksheet:

1. Select any cell on the worksheet.

2. Choose Data ➤ Group And Outline ➤ Clear Outline.

To remove outlining from a group of rows or columns:

1. Select the rows or columns you want to remove outlining from.

2. Choose Data ➤ Group And Outline ➤ Ungroup (or click on the Ungroup tool)

CHAPTER

23

What-If Analyses

fast TRACK

● **Use Scenario Manager** 724

> to create and save different sets of input values with their results.

● **To create a scenario** 725

> 1. Choose Tools ➤ Scenarios.
> 2. Click the Add button to add new scenarios with different input values.

● **To create scenario summary reports** 728

> Click the Summary button on the Scenario Manager dialog box, and select the *Scenario Summary* option.

● **To merge scenarios** 729

> 1. Open all workbooks to be merged, and activate the worksheet to which the scenarios will be merged.
> 2. Choose Tools ➤ Scenarios, and click the Merge button.
> 3. On the Merge Scenarios dialog box, select the workbooks and worksheets to be merged.

GENERALLY, a worksheet with simple SUM functions is performing *what-if* analysis. When you change a cell, you can see what happens as a result. This means that almost everything you do with worksheets can be characterized as what-if analysis, using a broad definition of the term. This chapter, however, explains three specific tools to help with *complex* what-if analysis:

- *Goal Seek, which determines the input required to produce a desired result.*

- *Solver, which finds the optimum solution to complex problems involving multiple variables and constraints.*

- *Scenario Manager, which allow you to create and save sets of input values that produce different results.*

NOTE
The Excel manual and various third-party publications include *data tables* when discussing what-if analysis. There is virtually nothing that can be done in a data table that cannot be done using "normal" worksheet formulas—and you don't have to learn a new construct.

Solving Simple Problems Using Goal Seek

Essentially, *Goal Seek* solves formulas backwards. Use Goal Seek when you know the result you want, but need to determine how much to change a single input to get that result. For example, here are two typical problems that can be solved with Goal Seek:

- You want to take out a loan to buy a car, but the maximum payment your budget will allow is $300 per month. What is the most expensive car you can afford?

- You are taking a course in Biology, and the final grade is based on the weighted average of six exams. You have taken five of the six exams, and want to know the minimum score you need on the sixth exam in order to get a B for the course.

To use Goal Seek, select a cell containing a formula, then choose the Tools ➤ Goal Seek command.

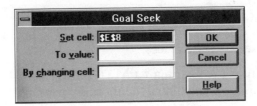

- *Set Cell* must be a cell which contains a formula—it defaults to the active cell.

- *To Value* must be a constant value (not a cell reference).

- *By Changing Cell* must be a cell containing a constant value, and must be directly or indirectly referenced by the cell specified in *Set Cell*. The reference can be several levels away, and can be located in another worksheet or another workbook.

Goal Seek—Case One

Suppose you want to buy a new car. Here's what you know:

- You can get a bank loan at 9%.
- The loan requires a 20% down payment.
- The maximum monthly payment you can afford is $300.

What's the most expensive car you can afford? Follow this exercise, using the PMT function and Goal Seek, to find out:

1. Enter the following on a new worksheet:

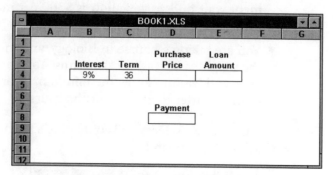

2. In cell E4, enter the formula **=D4*0.8** (the loan amount is 80% of the purchase price).

3. Enter the formula **=PMT(B4/12,C4,-E4)** in cell D8 (the PMT function calculates the monthly payment).

4. With cell D8 selected, choose Tools ➤ Goal Seek. Fill in the dialog box as shown below.

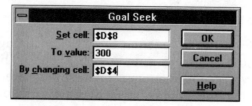

5. Click OK, and Goal Seek finds the answer. (See Figure 23.1)

Goal Seek—Case Two

You are taking a course in Biology, and you want to know what grade you have to get on the final exam in order to get a B for the course.

- There are six exams given during the course, and you have taken five of them.

- The exams scores are weighted. Exams #1, #2, #4, and #5 are each worth 10% of the final grade, exam #3 is worth 20%, and exam #6 is worth 40%.

FIGURE 23.1

Goal seek has
determined the
maximum purchase
price.

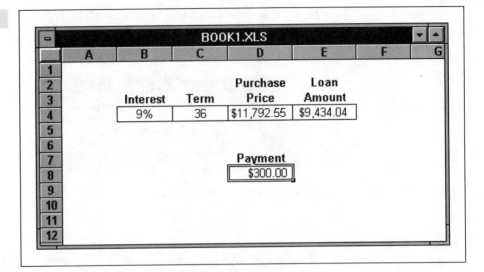

- The final score is calculated from the average of the six weighted exam scores.

Goal Seek will change an indirectly referenced value (the sixth exam score) to reach a final weighted average of 80% (which will give you a final grade of B).

1. Enter the following on a new worksheet:

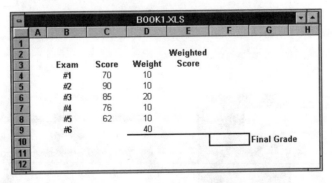

2. In cell E4, enter the formula **=C4*D4**. Then copy it down to E5:E9.

3. In cell D10, enter the formula **=SUM(D4:D9)**.

4. Copy D10 to E10.

5. In cell E10, enter the formula **=F10/D10**.

6. Select F10, then choose Tools ➤ Goal Seek. Fill in the dialog box as shown below.

7. Click OK, then Goal Seek finds the answer (Figure 23.2).

FIGURE 23.2

Goal Seek has determined the score required on the final exam in order to get a B for the course.

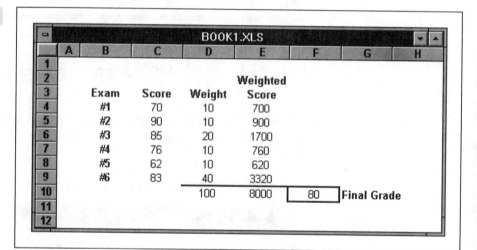

TIP

If you create a chart based on cells containing formulas, and then change a charted value by dragging a data marker, the Goal Seek dialog box is displayed. (See Chapter 14.)

If You Make a Mistake

Here are some of the error messages you'll see if you enter invalid information in the Goal Seek dialog box.

- If the cell entered in *By Changing Cell* is not referenced (directly or indirectly) by the formula in the *Set Cell*, you'll see:

- If the *By Changing Cell* contains a formula, you'll see:

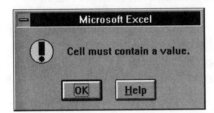

- If the cell entered in Set Cell contains a constant, you'll see:

Solving Complex Problems with Solver

Solver is used to find solutions to problems involving multiple variables and constraints—problems that are more complex than Goal Seek can handle. While Goal Seek finds a specific solution, Solver finds the best, or optimal, solution.

Solver is a complex tool, but is worth the time to learn if you must find optimal solutions to complex problems. Solver can save money and resources in your business by finding better, more efficient ways to allocate resources. It can also save you the time spent finding solutions by trial-and-error. Solver can help you to solve problems such as:

- How to find the optimal allocation of parts inventory to minimize production costs.

- How to create the most efficient personnel schedule to minimize costs while meeting business needs and individual scheduling requests.

- How to optimize allocation of funds in an investment portfolio to minimize risk and maximize return.

There may be different optimal solutions to a problem, depending on the mathematical techniques Solver uses to solve the problem. The default Solver settings are appropriate for many problems, but experimentation with the different Solver Options settings (see Figure 23.3) may yield better results.

FIGURE 23.3

In the Solver Options dialog box, you can change the allowable time and number of iterations and experiment with different mathematical techniques.

Types of Problems Solver Can Analyze

Solver can analyze and solve three types of problems:

Linear Problems A problem in which the variables are related through linear functions of the type $y = k_1x$ plus k_2 —where x and y are the variables and k_1 and k_2 are constants. If you know that your problem is linear, check the *Assume Linear Model* setting on the Solver Options dialog box (Figure 23.3) to speed up the calculation. This is especially important if the data model is large.

Non-Linear Problems A problem in which the variables cannot all be related through linear functions. Examples would include polynomials, exponential functions, and sine waves.

Integer Problems A problem in which any of the variables is constrained to an integer value. Solver takes a longer time to solve integer problems.

Business Case

Suppose you are the manager of a dairy farm, and one of your responsibilities is to determine a livestock feed mixture that meets certain protein requirements but is still cost-effective. Ingredient costs are continually changing, and as they change, you must recalculate the ingredient mix to minimize cost. Here's what you know:

- The feed mixture is composed of oats, corn, and barley.
- The final mix must have a protein content of between 9.2% and 9.5%.

Finding a solution to this kind of problem can be a lengthy trial-and-error process if you use conventional methods. Instead, Solver can find a solution for you.

First, you must understand three definitions:

- *Target cell* is the specific objective of the problem—the cell whose value Solver will set to be a minimum, maximum, or a specific value. In this problem, the target cell is the cost (which is to be minimized) of the final mix.

- *Changing cells* are cells whose values Solver will manipulate to meet the target cell objective. In this problem, the changing cells are the proportions of each ingredient in the final mix.

- *Constraints* are the limits set on the values in any of these cells—there can be constraints on changing cells, the target cell, or any cells involved in the calculations. In this problem, the constraints are:

  - The final protein concentration must be between 9.2% and 9.5%.

  - The amount of each ingredient must be at least 0 lbs. (This constraint prevents Solver from using a negative value.)

  - The total of the ingredients must equal 100%.

1. Enter the following on a new worksheet:

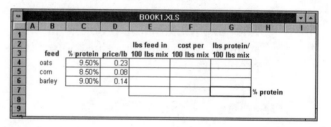

2. Enter these formulas:

CELL	FORMULA
E7	=SUM(E4:E6)
F4	=E4*D4
G4	=E4*C4

3. Copy the formulas:

   - Copy the formula in E7 to F7 and G7.
   - Copy the formula in F4 to F5 and F6.
   - Copy the formula in G4 to G5 and G6.

4. Choose Tools ➤ Solver.

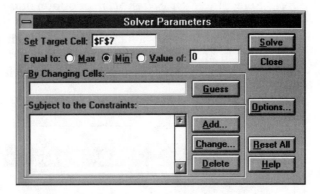

5. Enter cell F7 as the target cell, and set the *Equal To* setting to *Min*.

6. Click on the *By Changing Cells* edit box, then select cells E4:E6 (the changing cells).

7. Click the Add button to display the Add Constraint dialog box:

8. Add the following constraints. Click the Add button between each entry.

CELL	OPERATOR	CONSTRAINT
E7	=	100
G7	>=	9.2
G7	<=	9.5
E4:E6	>=	0

9. Click OK after you add the last constraint. (Verify the constraints in the Solver Parameters dialog box, and use the Add, Change, and Delete buttons to make corrections as needed—see Figure 23.4.)

10. Click the Solve button to start Solver. Figure 23.5 shows the results.

11. Select the *Keep Solver Solution* option and click the OK button to keep the new values in the worksheet. At this point, you can also save the solution as a named scenario by clicking the Save Scenario button and entering a name for the scenario in the Save Scenario dialog box. (Scenarios are covered later in this chapter.)

FIGURE 23.4

The Solver Parameters dialog box is set up to find the lowest-cost mixture of feeds within the constraints allowed.

FIGURE 23.5

Solver has found the lowest-cost mixture which meets the protein requirements.

Solver works by trying different values in the changing cells and observing the results. By default, Solver is allowed 100 seconds and 100 tries, or *iterations*, to solve the problem. Complex problems (or slower computers) may require more time or iterations to reach a solution. If Solver runs out of time before reaching a solution, a dialog box will be displayed informing you that the maximum time limit was reached.

Click the Continue button if you want to disregard the limit and continue the process.

To change the time or number of iterations allowed, click the Options button on the Solver Parameters dialog box (Figure 23.4) to display the Solver Options dialog box (Figure 23.3). Enter a new time and/or number of iterations, and click OK.

TIP

Although you can start Solver with the changing cells blank, Solver works faster if you enter some rough estimates into the changing cells.

The Solver settings are saved with the worksheet. When the price of corn changes and the feed mix must be recalculated, all you need to do is open the workbook, change the price on the worksheet, choose Tools ➤ Solver, and click the Solve button.

Solver Reports

The Solver Results dialog box provides three reports to choose from. To produce any of these reports, select the report(s) from the list (hold down Ctrl while clicking to select more than one) and click OK.

The Answer Report The Answer report (Figure 23.6) displays the starting and final values of the target and changing cells, and an analysis of the constraint cells. (Whether the constraint could be met, and how much difference, or *slack*, there is between the constraints and the final values). If a constraint is *binding*, the final value of the cell is limited by the constraint. (Notice that where a constraint is binding, the final value of the cell equals the constraint).

FIGURE 23.6

The Answer report displays an analysis of the constraints used to solve the problem.

The Sensitivity Report The Sensitivity report (Figure 23.7) tells you how much of a difference changes in the changing cells (or constraints) would make in the target cell.

FIGURE 23.7

The Sensitivity report tells you how sensitive the target value is to changes in constraints or changing values.

A different version of the Sensitivity report is created if the *Assume Linear Model* setting was checked in the Solver Options dialog box.

The Limits Report The Limits report (Figure 23.8) lists the values of the target and changing cells, and their upper and lower limits (as specified by the constraints). Essentially, this report shows the margin of variation for each changing cell.

More Facts about Solver

- Up to 200 changing cells can be specified in a single problem.
- Solver settings (parameters and options) are persistent, and are saved on the worksheet. To save different settings on the same worksheet, save the settings as a *model*. To save a model, click the Save Model button in the solver options dialog box.

FIGURE 23.8

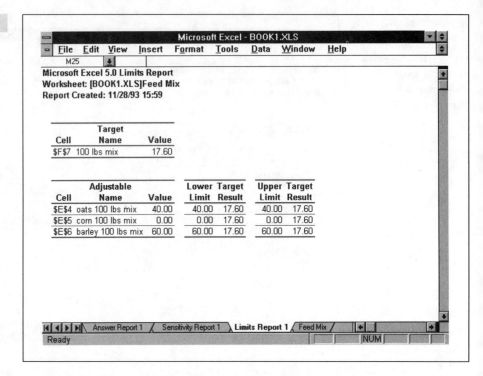

FIGURE 23.8

The Limits report shows the margin for variation in the changing cells.

- If you want to watch the values on the worksheet change as solver tries different values, check the *show iteration results* setting on the Solver Options dialog box. Each major change in values will be displayed on the worksheet, and a dialog box will ask if you want to continue the process after each change.

- Excel provides several sample solver problems in the excel\examples\solver file.

Using Scenario Manager

Scenario manager lets you create and save different sets of input values, with their results, as *scenarios*. A scenario is a group of input values (called changing cells) saved with a name. Each scenario represents a set of what-if assumptions that you can apply to a workbook model to see the effects on other parts of the model.

Use the scenario manager to:

- Create multiple scenarios with multiple sets of changing cells.
- View the results of each scenario on your worksheet.
- Create a summary report of all input values and results.

Business Case

Suppose you have been looking for a new home, and have narrowed your choices down to two: one for $200,000, the other for $300,000. The following information will apply to either home:

- The interest rate is 7%, and a 20% down payment is required.
- The term of the loan can be either 15 years or 30 years.

There are four different scenarios: Either the $300,000 house or the $200,000 house, with either the 15-year or 30-year loan. Scenario manager can help organize, manage, and summarize these scenarios.

Begin by creating a scenario for the $300,000 home, with a 15-year loan.

1. Enter the following on a new worksheet:

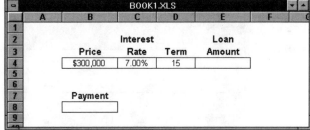

2. Name cells B3:E4 and B7:B8 using the Insert ➤ Name ➤ Create command.

3. Enter the following formulas:

CELL	FORMULA
E4	=Price*.8
B8	=PMT(Rate/12,Term*12,-Amount)

4. Choose Tools ➤ Scenarios.

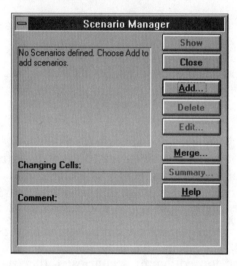

5. Click the Add button on the Scenario Manager dialog box.

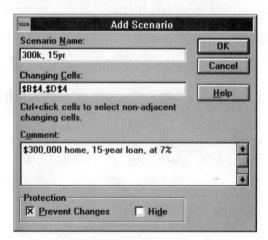

6. Type **300k, 15yr** as a scenario name.

7. Double-click the *Changing Cells* edit box (to highlight it), then:

   • Click cell B4.

   • Hold down Ctrl and click cell D4.

   • Click OK.

The Scenario Values dialog box will be displayed, with the names of the changing cells and their values.

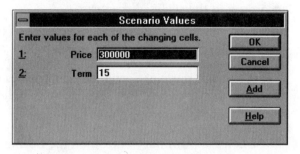

8. Since the values for the first scenario are already entered, click Add to set up the next scenario.

9. Type **300k, 30yr** to create (and name) the second scenario, and click OK.

10. In the Scenario Values dialog box, change the *Term* value to **30**.

11. Repeat steps 8, 9 and 10 to set up two more scenarios:

   - Create the scenario **200k, 15yr** with values of $200,000 and 15.
   - Create the scenario **200k, 30yr** with values of $200,000 and 30.

12. Click OK after creating the fourth scenario. The Scenario Manager dialog box now contains your list of four scenarios.

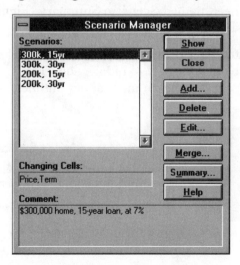

To see any single scenario displayed on the worksheet, select the name of the scenario and click the Show button. The worksheet values will change according to the selected scenario.

Scenario Summary Reports

One of the best parts of Scenario Manager lies in its ability to summarize all of the scenarios in a summary report. Follow these steps to create a summary report:

1. Click the Summary button on the Scenario Manager dialog box. The Scenario Summary dialog box will be displayed.

2. Select the *Scenario Summary* option, and be sure the *Result Cell* is $B$8 (the cell displaying the payment).

3. Click OK.

A new sheet, named Scenario Summary (Figure 23.9), will be added to the workbook.

Notice the outline symbols along the top and left side of the summary report. You can use these to hide or show levels of detail in the summary—see Chapter 22 to learn more about outlines.

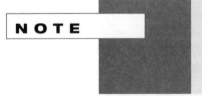

NOTE

The *Pivot Table* option on the Scenario Summary dialog box creates a pivot table based on the scenario. See Chapter 17 to learn more about pivot tables.

FIGURE 23.9

The Scenario
Summary is an
outlined report of all
the scenarios you
created.

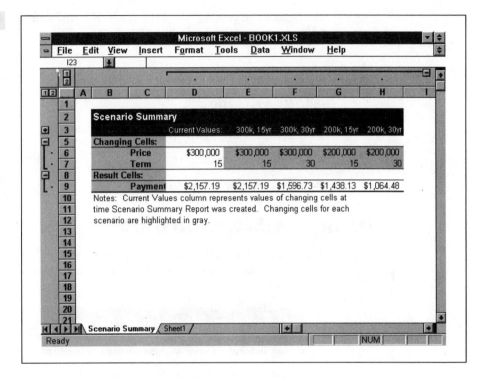

Merging Scenarios

Suppose that you have created a number of budget scenarios based on revenue forecasts, and someone else in your department has created other budget scenarios based on different assumptions. The scenarios, defined in two separate workbooks, can be merged into a single model.

Follow these steps to merge scenarios:

1. Open the workbooks that contain the scenarios you want to merge. (For example, HIS_BOOK and MY_BOOK.) Make sure the worksheet which will contain the merged scenarios is active (in this case, MY_BOOK!Sheet1).

2. Choose Tools ➤ Scenarios, and click the Merge button on the Scenarios dialog box. The Merge Scenarios dialog box will be displayed, with a list of all open workbooks and a list of the worksheets in each workbook.

3. Select the workbook (HIS_BOOK) and worksheet (Sheet1) you want to merge from, then click OK.

Deleting Scenarios

To delete a scenario:

1. Choose Tools ➤ Scenarios.

2. Select the scenario to be deleted.

3. Click the Delete button.

Using the Scenarios Tool

The Scenarios tool on the Workgroup toolbar offers an easy way to add, edit, or display scenarios is with. Until scenarios are created, the tool is an empty listbox.

To add scenarios using the Scenarios tool:

1. Enter the values you want use into the changing cells on the worksheet.

2. Select all the changing cells to be included in the scenario (hold down Ctrl while clicking to select non-adjacent cells).

3. Type a scenario name in the Scenarios tool, and click Enter.

To display a scenario using the Scenarios tool, select the scenario you want from the drop-down list.

To edit scenarios using the Scenarios tool:

1. Display the scenario to be edited.

2. Edit the values in the changing cells.

3. Select or type the scenario name in the scenarios tool. A dialog box will be displayed asking if you want to redefine the scenario based on current cell values—click Yes.

Protecting Scenarios

Scenarios can be protected by the *Prevent Changes* setting on the Add Scenario and Edit Scenario dialog boxes. By default, this setting is checked, and takes effect when the worksheet is protected.

The Tools ➤ Protection ➤ Protect Sheet dialog box also has a Scenarios setting which prevents changes to the definition of a scenario when the sheet is protected. See Chapter 11, Protecting and Auditing Your Work, to learn more about worksheet protection.

More Facts about Scenario Manager

- Up to 32 changing cells can be defined per scenario.

- Scenario Manager can be used to save scenarios created with Solver (click the Save Scenario button in the Solver Results dialog box).

- When a scenario is created or edited, the user name and date are recorded by Scenario Manager. This information is displayed in the Scenario Manager dialog box and in the first outline level of the Summary report.

CHAPTER

24

Using Excel Add-Ins

f a s t **TRACK**

● **To use special scientific, engineering, and financial functions**   **745**

Load the Analysis ToolPak add-in. Functions become available, just like built-in functions. Choose Tools ➤ Data Analysis for a dialog box that helps you build formulas.

● **To save a workbook as an add-in**   **746**

1. Open the workbook and activate a module or macro sheet.

2. Choose Tools ➤ Make Add-In.

● **Add-ins can't be modified**   **747**

Therefore, save a copy of your original workbook.

AS THE name implies, add-ins are not part of the Excel core program—they are separate components which, if designed properly, seamlessly extend the power of Excel. There are a number of add-ins that come with Excel, and you may have already used one or more of them without realizing what they were.

This chapter covers:

- *How to configure Excel to load add-ins automatically.*
- *How to use add-ins that come with Excel: AutoSave, View Manager, Report Manager, and the Analysis ToolPak.*
- *How to create your own add-ins.*

Several add-ins are discussed in other chapters. The MS Query and the ODBC add-ins are covered in Chapter 18; the Solver is covered in Chapter 23.

N O T E   Scenario Manager was an add-in under Excel 4, but is now built into the core Excel program (see Chapter 23). The Excel 4 Scenario Manager add-in is still included with Excel 5 for backwards compatibility.

Installing and Configuring Add-Ins

This section explains how to configure Excel so that the add-ins you want available all times will open automatically.

Installation Issues

When you first install Excel, there are a number of optional components that you can choose to install, many of which are add-ins. Something happens when you install add-ins that is very important to understand: in some cases, the Excel setup program not only copies the add-in to your hard disk, but also configures Excel to load the add-in automatically. (Or in some cases, a small part of the add-in is loaded automatically which, when evoked, opens the entire add-in.) If the add-ins are not used on an everyday basis, this introduces two problems:

- It takes longer to start Excel when lots of add-ins are automatically loaded.
- Add-ins consume memory.

In the following discussion, you will learn how to configure Excel to automatically load add-ins. Don't be surprised if, when you first use the add-in configuration utility, you find that a handful of add-ins are being automatically opened every time you start Excel—including some obscure ones that you may never use.

NOTE   The Excel setup program can be used to install components that were not installed when you first set up Excel on your system.

Configuring Excel to Load Add-Ins Automatically

Choose the Tools ➤ Add-Ins command to display the add-in dialog box, which is used to set which add-ins load automatically.

Using the checkboxes (in the list box), check the add-ins you want Excel to load automatically. Un-check the ones that you will never (or seldom) use.

NOTE When you un-check an add-in, it is *not* removed from your disk.

You can purchase third-party add-in products, or create your own. Click Browse to search for add-ins other than the ones that come with Excel.

TIP To use an add-in that is not setup to load automatically, use Tools ➤ Add-Ins. When done, use Tools ➤ Add-Ins to unload it.

How Add-Ins Behave

Different add-ins behave differently. Some, such as the Analysis ToolPak, are practically invisible. The ToolPak adds special worksheet functions; it does not add any commands to the Excel menu system. Other add-ins, such as View Manager and Report Manager, add one or more commands to the Excel menu system.

An add-in can be a custom application that takes over the Excel work-space, and displays a custom menu system (though none of the add-ins that come with Excel behave this way). Later in this chapter, you will learn how to save a workbook as an add-in.

Save Your Files Automatically Using AutoSave

The AutoSave add-in automatically saves your work at specified time in-tervals. Choose Tools ➤ AutoSave to display the AutoSave dialog box.

- Check the checkbox to activate AutoSave, or clear it to de-activate the feature.

- Enter the number of minutes between AutoSave.

- Specify whether you want just the active workbook saved, or all open workbooks.

- Check *Prompt Before Saving* if want the chance to confirm/cancel the save.

CAUTION Saving files automatically, without the option to confirm, can be a risky proposition. Just imagine that the save occurs right after you make a serious mistake, and just before you are about to choose the Edit ➤ Undo command.

Using View Manager

The View Manager add-in is a tool that lets you define different *views* on a worksheet, and display them with ease. A view definition consists of:

- A view name.
- A range of cells.
- Display settings such as gridlines, scroll bars, and row and column headings.
- Print settings (optional).
- Hidden row and column settings (optional).

NOTE The View Manager add-in must be loaded in order to use View Manager. This topic is discussed earlier in this chapter.

Choose the View ➤ View Manager command to display the view manager dialog box.

Adding a View

To add a new view, click the Add button on the View Manager dialog box. The *AddView* dialog box is displayed.

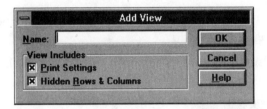

Name Behind the scenes, a hidden name is created containing the view settings. Thus, the rules for the view name are the same as those for a cell name: It has to start with a letter; no spaces allowed; it can contains only letters, numbers, periods, and underscores; it can't exceed 255 characters.

Print Settings If checked, the current print settings are stored as part of the view definition.

Hidden Rows & Columns If checked, the view tracks which rows/columns are hidden. When you add a new view, the current status of the workspace (e.g., gridlines, scroll bars) is stored as part of the view definition.

Showing and Deleting Views

Showing a View Choose View ➤ View Manager, select a view from the list, then click Show.

Deleting a View Choose View ➤ View Manager, select a view from the list, then click Delete.

Real-World Application

View Manager is a carry-over from Excel 4 and some of its functionality has been obviated by the Excel 5 workbook model. Since individual worksheets within a workbook can be formatted differently (i.e. with gridlines, row & column headings, etc.), the fact that View Manager stores such settings is only marginally useful. (View Manager does, however, allow multiple views per worksheet.)

View Manager is especially useful when it is used on an outlined worksheet. Different views can be defined for different outline levels. Try this brief exercise to get a better feel for how View Manager works.

1. On a new worksheet, select B2:D5 and choose View ➤ View Manager. Click Add.

2. Enter a name, check both settings, then click OK.

TIP

View settings are stored as a hidden name on the active worksheet.

3. Choose Tools ➤ Options, click the View tab, and uncheck the *Gridlines* and *Row & Column Headers* settings.

4. Hide column B.

5. Select D4:D9 and choose View ➤ View Manager. Click Add.

6. Enter a name, check both settings, then click OK.

Now, show the two views to see how they work:

7. Choose View ➤ View Manager, choose the view defined at step 2, and click Show.

8. Choose View ➤ View Manager, choose the view defined at step 6, and click Show.

As you show each view, the workspace is changed according to the settings at the time the view was defined.

NOTE You probably don't want to use View Manager as an aid for simple worksheet navigation. It is a large add-in, and probably not worth the load-time or memory penalties.

Using Report Manager

The Report Manager add-in lets you define custom *reports*. A report consists of:

- One or more worksheets (from the same workbook).
- Optionally, one scenario per worksheet (see Chapter 23 to learn about Scenario Manager).
- Optionally, one view per worksheet.

Here are some typical problems that can be solved with Report Manager:

- A workbook contains numerous worksheets. When you print the workbook, you want to print only three of the sheets, in a specified sequence.
- A worksheet contains three scenarios created with Scenario Manager: Optimistic, Pessimistic, and Realistic. When you print the sheet, you want to print each scenario.
- A worksheet contains two noncontiguous ranges that you want to print on the same report, using the same page number sequence. (Each range is setup as a view using View Manager.)

For every task that you perform with Report Manager (creating reports, printing reports, etc.), the first step is to activate the desired workbook, then choose the File ➤ Print Report command.

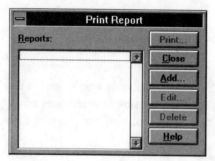

Creating a Report

To create a new report, click the Add button on the Print Report dialog box. The Add Report dialog box is displayed.

Report Name Enter a report name consisting of letters, numbers, and spaces. Special characters are not permitted.

Sheet Add sheets to the report by selecting a sheet name from the drop-down list. Then click the Add button. You can add the same sheet to the report more than once.

View You can include a view (defined by View Manager) as part of the definition for each section of the report. Only the view range will print on the page (including all of the view settings). Choose the view from the drop-down list.

Scenario A scenario (created by Scenario Manager) can be included as part of the section definition. Choose the scenario from the drop-down list.

Move Up and Move Down The sections of the reports as they display in the list box determine their print order. Use the Move Up and Move Down buttons to change the order of the sections within the list.

Delete Click Delete to remove the selected section from the report.

Use Continuous Page Numbers When checked, the entire report uses the same page number sequence.

TIP You can create more than one report per workbook.

Editing, Printing, and Deleting Reports

For each of these procedures, start by choosing File ➤ Print Report. Select a report from the list of reports. Then,

- To edit a report, click Edit. The Edit Report dialog box works the same way as the Add Report dialog box.
- To print a report, click Print.
- To delete a report, click Delete.

Analysis ToolPak

The Analysis ToolPak is different than the other add-ins discussed so far in this chapter in that it does not add commands to the Excel menu. Instead, it adds a wide variety of special worksheet functions. When the add-in is loaded, the functions are available for use just like built-in functions, such as SUM. (See how to load add-ins earlier in this chapter.)

The functions included in the ToolPak are in the following categories:

- Engineering functions
- Functions for statistical analysis
- Financial functions

Appendix B lists all of the functions included in the Analysis ToolPak.

Creating Add-Ins

As you have learned so far in this chapter, add-ins come in a variety of sizes and flavors. If you want to, though, you can also create your own. You might, for example, want to create an add-in to do any of the following:

- Add new worksheet functions, like the Analysis ToolPak.
- Add a special feature, like View Manager and Report Manager.
- Be an entire custom application, like a portfolio analysis system, or an executive information system.

Needless to say, the real work involved in creating an add-in is the process of writing the program itself. Add-ins can be written using Visual Basic, Applications Edition (VBA), and/or the old Excel macro language (XLM). Your programs will reside in a workbook, on VBA modules, or on XLM macro sheets. (Refer to Chapter 20 to get acquainted with some of the issues involved.) Follow these procedures to transform your workbook into an add-in:

1. Activate the workbook.

2. Activate any VBA module or XLM macro sheet.

3. Choose Tools ➤ Make Add-In.

4. Use the Make Add-in dialog box just as you use the File ➤ Save dialog box: enter a file name, and choose a directory. Notice the file type is set to Microsoft Excel Add-In. Click OK.

A copy of your workbook is created as an add-in, and the original workbook is left intact. It is very important that you retain the original workbook, because the add-in can not be modified.

For more information on creating add-ins, refer to the Visual Basic User's Guide that comes with Excel.

Commercial Add-Ins

There are a number of Excel add-ins that can be purchased from various software vendors. Here are some of the more notable ones.

BrainCel

A forecasting tool based on neural network technology—a non–rules-based method for analyzing data. BrainCel is available from:

Promised Land Technologies, Inc.

203-562-7335

Crystal Ball

A forecasting and risk analysis tool that creates Monte Carlo simulations. Crystal Ball is available from:

> Decisioneering
>
> 800-289-2550

Evolver

A genetic algorithm problem-solver used to provide optimal results for problems with unlimited variables. Evolver is available from:

> Axcelis, Inc.
>
> 206-632-0885

Microsoft Open EIS Pak

An Excel-based application generator that helps you develop executive information systems (EIS) and decision support systems (DSS), without having to know how to program. This product is available from:

> Microsoft Corporation
>
> 800-426-9400

@RISK

Provides advanced analysis capabilities used for forecasting and financial modeling. @RISK is available from:

> Palisades Corporation
>
> 607-277-8000

Worksheet Wizard

An add-in that helps users create common worksheet models such as income statements and balance sheets. Worksheet Wizard is available from:

> Graphitti Software Corporation
>
> 209-299-7849

CHAPTER

25

Working with Other Programs

fast TRACK

To copy information into Excel from another program   **755**

1. Activate the other program.

2. Select text/graphics and choose Edit ➤ Copy.

3. Activate Excel and choose Edit ➤ Paste.

**Object Linking and Embedding lets applications share
information**   **757**

- An embedded object "lives" in the document where it is embedded.

- A linked object updates when the source file changes.

To place an Excel OLE object into Word   **758**

1. Activate Excel and copy information (cells or graphics) using Edit ➤ Copy.

2. Activate Word and choose Edit ➤ Paste Special.

- Or, drag the Excel object from the Excel sheet to the Word document using the mouse.

**To insert an object into Excel using Excel menu
commands**   **764**

1. Choose Insert ➤ Object.

2. Select the *Create New* tab to create a new object. Select the *Create from File* tab to insert object from existing file.

To edit an OLE object 766

Double-click the object to activate the application responsible for the object.

To import a text file 767

1. Open the file using File ➤ Open.

2. If it does not have a CSV suffix, specify import options using the Text Import Wizard.

To import dBASE, Lotus 1-2-3, and QuattroPro files 773

Use the File ➤ Open command.

To export an Excel file to different format 774

Choose File ➤ Save As. Select the file type from *Save File As Type* list.

To get help if you are a Lotus 1-2-3 user 775

- Choose Help ➤ Lotus 1-2-3.

- Choose Tools ➤ Options, click the *Transition* tab, and select the Lotus 1-2-3 Help option.

No software program is an island. The ability to work with other programs—and the data created by them—is an important feature in any modern software package. Excel is an outstanding citizen in this regard. This chapter covers:

- *transferring data to and from other applications using the Clipboard*
- *sharing data with other programs using Object Linking and Embedding (OLE)*
- *importing text files*
- *importing data from other applications, such as dBASE and Lotus 1-2-3*
- *exporting data*
- *switching from Lotus 1-2-3 to Excel*

For a review of how to query external databases from Excel, refer to Chapter 18.

Exchanging Data with Other Applications Using the Clipboard

Excel has several powerful facilities for importing and exporting data, such as object linking and embedding. But for everyday manual tasks, the Clipboard is a convenient way to move information in and out of Excel. Most Windows programs are capable of using the Clipboard, and it can be used to copy text and graphics.

Copying Text into Excel

Here is an exercise that demonstrates how to copy text from Notepad into Excel:

1. Start Notepad, and enter some text.

2. Select the text with the mouse, and Choose Edit ➤ Copy. (This places the text on the Clipboard.)

3. Activate Excel, and choose Edit ➤ Paste. (This pastes the text from the Clipboard.)

The text is placed into one or more cells. It's that simple. Every other use of the Clipboard is simply a variation on the above exercise.

Copying Graphics into Excel

The procedure for copying graphics into Excel is very similar. Use a program such as Paintbrush, then use the Edit ➤ Copy command to copy a graphic to the Clipboard. Activate Excel, and choose Edit ➤ Paste. The graphic is placed on the worksheet as a graphic object, as shown in Figure 25.1.

Graphics copied into Excel can be moved, resized, and deleted just like any other graphic object. (See Chapter 12 for a review of working with graphic objects.)

Copying Data out of Excel

Copying data (text or graphics) out of Excel involves the same procedure used to copy into Excel, but in the opposite direction. Follow this exercise to copy some information from Excel into Write (the word processor that comes with Microsoft Windows).

1. Select a range of cells, and choose Edit ➤ Copy.

2. Activate Write, and choose Edit ➤ Paste.

Figure 25.2 shows a Write file where two different paste operations have occurred.

The first table of numbers in Figure 25.2 is text. The second table is a graphic (bitmap). Write can import the data in different formats, using its

FIGURE 25.1

This Canadian flag was copied from the Microsoft PowerPoint clipart library. The object is selected, and its name is displayed in the name box, just like any graphic object in Excel.

FIGURE 25.2

The same data from Excel was pasted two times, using different paste methods available in Write.

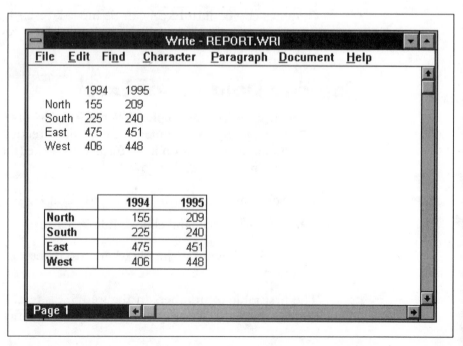

Edit ➤ Paste Special command. This illustrates an important point: the type of data that pastes into the other program is dependent on that program's capabilities. For example, Notepad is not capable of importing graphics. If you wanted to paste the data pictured in Figure 25.2 into Notepad, the only option would be to paste text.

Using Object Linking and Embedding

Object Linking and Embedding (OLE) is a Microsoft Windows technology that allows different applications to share data with one another. The term OLE is derived from the fact that a piece of data, called an *object*, which is created in one application can be *embedded* in another. And the embedded object can be *linked* to the source document.

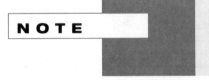

N O T E   OLE is not limited to Microsoft products. Many non-Microsoft applications support OLE, including most major word processing and graphics applications.

Unfortunately, there's a lot of jargon is necessary to explain OLE. Nevertheless, OLE is really quite simple. In this section, you will walk through a simple exercise to see how OLE works.

N O T E   Many applications, including Excel, support version two of the OLE specification. Since OLE 2 is here today, and since it is the future direction for most major Windows applications, the discussion of OLE in this chapter will focus on OLE 2.

To illustrate how OLE works, the following examples will use Excel 5 and Microsoft Word for Windows 6.

Copying an Excel Object into Word

Suppose you are writing a business plan in Word, and that you have built a worksheet (Figure 25.3) in Excel that contains supporting data. The following exercise shows you how to copy part of the worksheet to the Word document:

   1. In Excel, select the cells you want to copy. Then choose Edit ➤ Copy.

FIGURE 25.3

Supporting data for a business plan

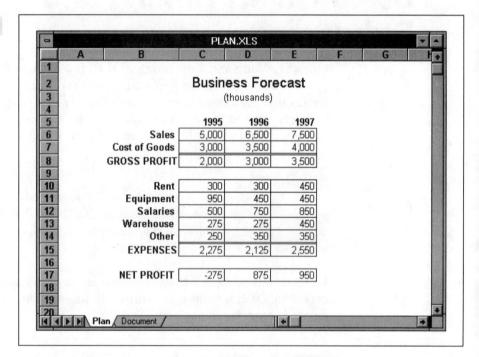

   2. Activate Word. Place the cursor at the place where you want to paste the object.

   3. In Word, choose Edit ➤ Paste Special. The dialog box in Figure 25.4 is displayed.

FIGURE 25.4

The Paste Special dialog box. As you can see from the first item in the list, Word senses that the soon-to-be pasted object is coming from Excel.

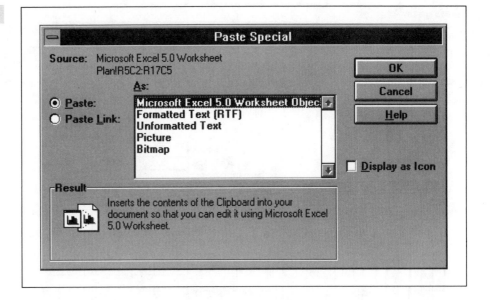

4. Select *Microsoft Excel 5.0 Worksheet Object*, and select how you want to paste:

   • *Paste* places an embedded object into Word. The Excel object then "lives" inside the Word document, with no link to the original Excel document. (You will still be able to edit the Excel object using Excel, as you will soon see.)

   • *Paste Link* links the object to the original Excel document. Changes to the original Excel document will cause the linked object to update.

5. Click OK. The Word document is shown in Figure 25.5.

Using Drag-and-Drop

Instead of using menu commands, you can drag and drop information from Excel to Word. Arrange your workspace so that you can see both applications at once. Activate Excel, and follow these steps:

1. Select the cell(s) you want to copy.

FIGURE 25.5

The Excel information is pasted into the Word document as an Excel object.

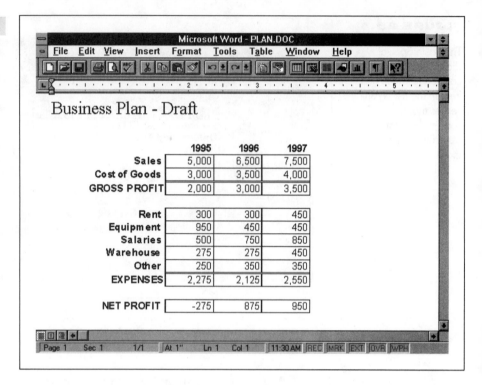

2. Click on the outermost border of the selected range, and while holding down the mouse button, drag the cells using one of these methods:

   - Drag the cells onto the Word document to *cut and paste*.
   - Hold down the Ctrl key while dragging to *copy and paste*.

TIP

You are not limited to cells when copying Excel objects to other applications. You can also copy Excel charts and other graphic objects. Just drag and drop the chart onto a Word document, for instance.

Understanding How Embedded Objects Work

Consider the dialog box in Figure 25.4. Suppose that you choose the *Paste* option. This means:

- The Excel object is *embedded* in the Word document. It is physically stored there.

- There is no link to the original Excel worksheet. A change to the original Excel worksheet has no effect on the embedded object.

- If you double-click the embedded object (in the Word document), Excel is activated and takes control—even though you do not leave the Word document (See Figure 25.6). At this point, you are using Excel, but within the context of the Word document. This is called *in-place editing*.

FIGURE 25.6

The Excel object on the Word document has been double-clicked. The Excel menu takes over, and the object becomes an editable Excel worksheet.

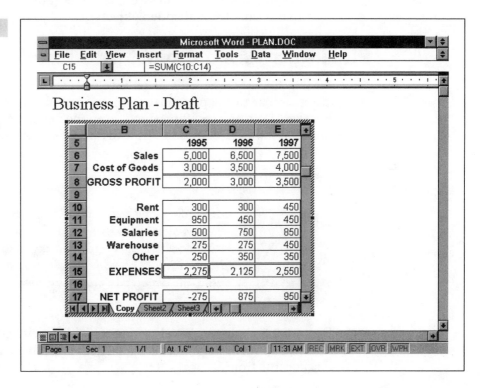

- If you edit the embedded Excel object, there is no effect on the original Excel worksheet, since there is no link.

- When you click outside the embedded object (within the Word document), Word assumes control again.

Understanding How Linked Objects Work

Suppose, on the other hand, that you choose the *Paste Link* option from the dialog box pictured in Figure 25.4. This means:

- The Excel object is *linked* to the original worksheet. The object is simply a copy of the worksheet cells.

- When the worksheet changes, the linked object changes.

- If you double-click the linked object (in the Word document), the original worksheet is loaded into Excel (unlike the in-place editing that occurs for embedded objects).

Placing a Word Object into Excel

Placing OLE objects into Excel involves identical concepts and procedures similar to the previous exercises—but in reverse. Since Word and Excel are both Microsoft products, even the dialog boxes are similar. Figure 25.7 shows Excel's Edit ➤ Paste Special dialog box.

NOTE Excel's Edit ➤ Paste Special dialog box is different, depending on the contents of the Clipboard at the time the command is chosen. If the Clipboard contains data from another application (non-Excel data), it looks like Figure 25.7. If, however, the Clipboard contains Excel data, the dialog box provides different options.

Figure 25.8 shows an Excel worksheet with an embedded Word object. Notice that when the object is selected, the formula bar shows where the object came from.

FIGURE 25.7

Excel's Edit ➤ Paste Special dialog box is similar to the Word dialog box.

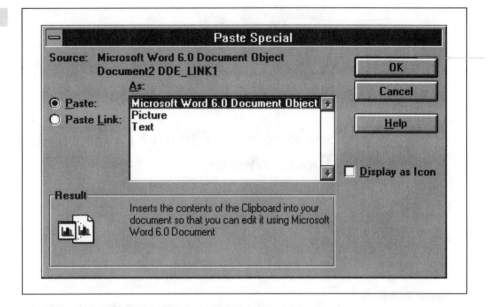

FIGURE 25.8

A Word object embedded in Excel

NOTE These examples involve using two specific OLE 2-aware applications—Excel and Word. There may be times when you try the same procedure using different OLE-aware applications.

Embedding an Object in Excel Using the Excel Menu

You have seen how to copy objects from one application to another when both applications are running. You can also insert OLE objects into Excel by starting out with a command on the Excel menu. Choose Insert ➤ Object to display the dialog box pictured in Figure 25.9.

FIGURE 25.9

The Object dialog box lets you create a new object or import one from an existing file.

```
┌─────────────────────────────────────────────────────────┐
│ ─                        Object                          │
├─────────────────────────────────────────────────────────┤
│   Create New         │    Create from File               │
│                                                          │
│  Object Type:                              ┌──────────┐   │
│  ┌──────────────────────────────────┐↑    │    OK    │   │
│  │CorelCHART! Chart                 │     └──────────┘   │
│  │CorelDRAW! Graphic                │     ┌──────────┐   │
│  │CorelPHOTO-PAINT! Picture         │     │  Cancel  │   │
│  │Equation                          │     └──────────┘   │
│  │Media Player                      │                    │
│  │Microsoft Drawing                 │                    │
│  │Microsoft Graph                   │                    │
│  │Microsoft Note-It                 │                    │
│  │Microsoft Works Chart             │     ┌──────────┐   │
│  │Microsoft Works Spreadsheet       │     │   Help   │   │
│  │MS WordArt                        │     └──────────┘   │
│  │Package                           │                    │
│  │Paintbrush Picture                │↓    □ Display as Icon│
│  └──────────────────────────────────┘                    │
│  ┌─Result─────────────────────────────────────────────┐ │
│  │        Inserts a new CorelCHART! Chart object        │ │
│  │ [icon]  into your document.                          │ │
│  │                                                      │ │
│  └──────────────────────────────────────────────────────┘ │
└─────────────────────────────────────────────────────────┘
```

Inserting a New Object The *Create New* tab (see Figure 25.9) lists the different types of OLE objects that you are able to create. Choose an object from the list, then click OK. The program that is responsible for the given object is started—when you quit the program, the object is placed on the worksheet. (The precise behavior depends on the individual program.)

Inserting an Object from an Existing File The *Create from File* tab (see Figure 25.10) lets you insert an existing file into the active worksheet. Select a file from the list of files. Check *Link to File* to link the object to the file. Check *Display as Icon* to place an icon on the worksheet representing the object.

FIGURE 25.10

Select the file you want to place on the worksheet.

Working with OLE Applets

There are several OLE mini-apps, sometimes referred to as *applets*, that are included with various Microsoft products. Some examples of these applets are *Microsoft Graph*, *Microsoft Note-It*, and *Microsoft ClipArt Gallery*. These applications cannot be run stand-alone—their sole purpose is to provide OLE services.

NOTE   The applets are stored in the MSAPPS directory, under the directory where Windows is installed.

If any of these applications are installed on your system, they will display in the Object dialog box (Figure 25.9). Try inserting a Note-It object, or an object from the ClipArt Gallery.

Working with OLE Objects in Excel

OLE objects on Excel worksheets are very similar to "normal" graphic objects.

To Set an OLE Object as Non-Printing By default, an OLE object will print when the worksheet is printed. If you don't want it to print, select the object, choose Format ➤ Object, click the Properties tab, and uncheck the *Print Object* Setting.

To Move, Resize, and Format Use the same procedures as for other graphic objects, described in Chapter 12.

To Create a Static Picture of an OLE Object Select the object, choose Edit ➤ Copy, select a cell, choose Edit ➤ Paste Special. Choose *Picture*.

To Convert the Object Type When you click on an OLE object with the right mouse button, a special command is displayed on the shortcut menu. The command text varies, based on the type of object selected, as do the commands on the sub-menu. Choose the Convert command to change the object type—use this command when you do not have the application on your system that is responsible for the object.

Importing Text Files

Since most applications are able to export data in text format, importing text files is usually fairly easy. Unfortunately, however, there are several different text file formats—something which has confounded users of earlier Excel versions. To avoid confusion, Excel 5 employs a *Text Import Wizard* to simplify the job of importing text files.

NOTE   This discussion is based on text files that contain data oriented as records, with each record containing fields of data, as opposed to random text. Random textual data can easily be copied into Excel using the Clipboard, from a text program such as Notepad.

The first step to import a text file is to choose the File ➤ Open command. Select *Text Files* from the list of file types, then open the desired file.

What happens next depends on the format of the text file.

Text Files with Delimiters

Delimiters are special characters that separate fields, allowing Excel to place each field into a new column on the worksheet. When a text file is delimited, importing it into Excel is easy. There are several delimiters that are frequently used. Perhaps the most common one is *comma delimited*, referred to as CSV (for comma separate values.) Figure 25.11 shows a CSV file which has been opened using Notepad.

If you import a certain text file on a regular basis, and have any control of the file format, use CSV format. When you open a CSV file, the data is automatically placed into rows and columns. Figure 25.12 shows the same text file opened in Excel.

When other types of delimiters are used, the Text Import Wizard verifies the delimiter before placing the data onto the worksheet.

Using the Text Import Wizard for Fixed-Width Files

If your text file does not use delimiters, then the fields will be fixed-width. This, too, is a very common format, and has historically caused users the most trouble. Figure 25.13 shows a text file with fixed-field widths, opened in Notepad.

FIGURE 25.11

This comma delimited text file contains 4 rows (records) and 5 columns (fields).

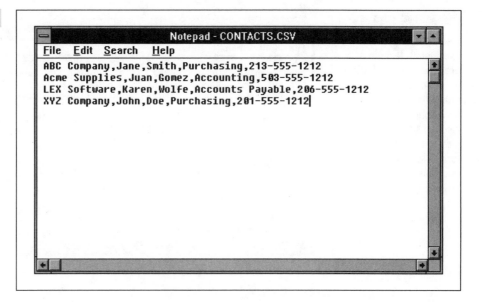

```
Notepad - CONTACTS.CSV
File   Edit   Search   Help
ABC Company,Jane,Smith,Purchasing,213-555-1212
Acme Supplies,Juan,Gomez,Accounting,503-555-1212
LEX Software,Karen,Wolfe,Accounts Payable,206-555-1212
XYZ Company,John,Doe,Purchasing,201-555-1212
```

FIGURE 25.12

When a CSV file is opened in Excel, the data is automatically placed in rows and columns without manual intervention.

CONTACTS.CSV

	A	B	C	D	E	F
1	ABC Company	Jane	Smith	Purchasing	213-555-1212	
2	Acme Supplies	Juan	Gomez	Accounting	503-555-1212	
3	LEX Software	Karen	Wolfe	Accounts Payable	206-555-1212	
4	XYZ Company	John	Doe	Purchasing	201-555-1212	
5						
6						
7						
8						
9						
10						
11						
12						
13						
14						

Sheet1

FIGURE 25.13

The fields of a fixed-width text file are typically padded with spaces. The fourth field of the third row, containing *Accounts Payable,* is the maximum width for the fourth field, and thus has no trailing spaces.

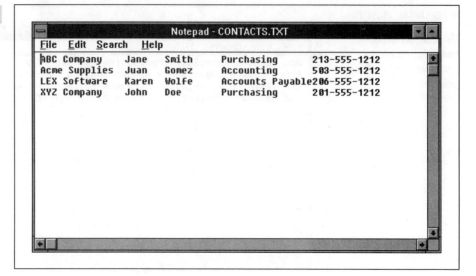

```
─                      Notepad - CONTACTS.TXT                    ▼ ▲
 File   Edit   Search   Help
 ABC Company      Jane    Smith      Purchasing          213-555-1212    ▲
 Acme Supplies    Juan    Gomez      Accounting          503-555-1212
 LEX Software     Karen   Wolfe      Accounts Payable206-555-1212
 XYZ Company      John    Doe        Purchasing          201-555-1212
                                                                        ▼
 ◄                                                                     ►
```

The Text Import Wizard makes it relatively easy to import fixed-width text files. Here are the steps required to import the text file pictured in Figure 25.13:

1. Open the File

Choose File ➤ Open, and open the file as usual. Step One of the Text Import Wizard is shown in Figure 25.14.

Original Data Type The Wizard detects that the file is fixed-width, though you can override this option if the Wizard is wrong.

Start Import at Row This lets you specify the starting row number. This setting is useful if the file contains a header row, and you don't want to import it.

File Origin There are slight differences between files originated on different platforms, i.e., the character that indicates a new row. The Wizard will usually determine this setting correctly, but you can select from the drop-down list to override the choice.

FIGURE 25.14

Step One lets you confirm the text file format.

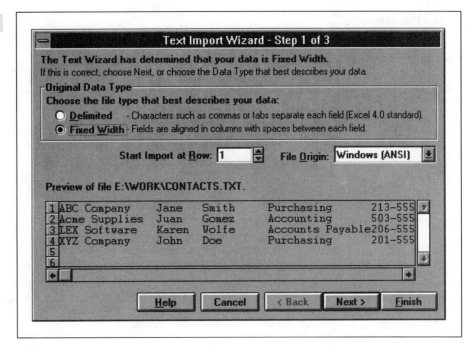

Preview Area This scrollable part of the dialog box lets you examine the file.

Click Next to move to Step Two of the Wizard.

2. Specify the Column Breaks

Step Two of the Wizard (Figure 25.15) lets you specify where the column breaks are located. The Wizard tries to determine the column breaks for you and usually does a pretty good job. But as you can see in Figure 25.15, the third row of the file has confused the Wizard—it has not detected the column break at position 48.

To correct the column breaks shown in Figure 25.15, drag the line at position 29 to position 32. Click position 48 to add a column break. If you make a mistake, double-click a column line to remove it. Click Next to proceed to Step Three of the Wizard.

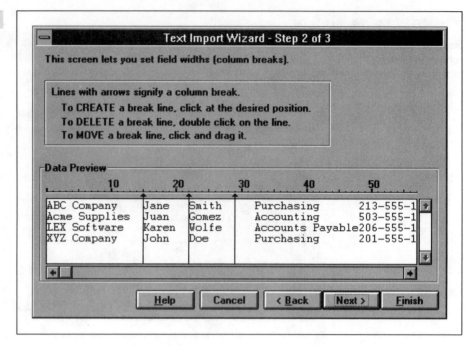

3. Format the Columns

Step Three of the Wizard (Figure 25.16) lets you format columns, or exclude them from being imported entirely.

To format a column, click on it with the mouse. Then choose the appropriate column format option.

General If a column is formatted as *General* format, Excel will automatically determine the data type.

Text Use this option when a text column contains numeric values, e.g., zip codes.

Date Use the date option (and the associated drop-down list) to format a column as a date.

Do Not Import Column Check this option to exclude the column entirely.

When you click Finish, the text file is imported onto the active worksheet into rows and columns.

FIGURE 25.16

Step Three is used to format the columns.

Suppose that you create reports each month based on a fixed-width text file that is output by a mainframe application. You can automate this task by recording a macro. (See Chapter 20 for a review.)

Importing Other File Formats

Excel is capable of importing several popular file formats using the File ➤ Open command. Here are the supported formats:

- Text (covered earlier in this chapter)
- Lotus 1-2-3 (covered below)

- QuattroPro
- Microsoft Works
- dBASE III and dBASE IV
- SYLK
- Data Interchange (DIF)
- Multiplan
- Files saved in earlier versions of Excel

Exporting Data

Excel workbooks can be saved in a variety of file formats, which are listed below. Choose the File ➤ Save As command, and choose the file format from the *Save File as Type* list.

Workbooks can be saved as:

- Template (see Chapter 10)
- Text file (space, tab, or comma delimited)
- Excel 2.1, 3.0, 4.0 worksheet
- Excel 4.0 workbook
- Lotus 1-2-3
- QuattroPro/DOS
- dBASE II, III, IV
- Data Interchange Format (DIF)
- SYLK

Switching from Lotus 1-2-3

Excel has many features to help out Lotus 1-2-3 users.

Opening 1-2-3 Files Lotus 1-2-3 spreadsheets can be opened using the File ➤ Open command, and saved using the File ➤ Save command (though Excel-specific information cannot be saved). You can build Excel models that use 1-2-3 sheets and even refer to names defined on them.

Running Macros You can run 1-2-3 macros under Excel, without having to translate them.

Getting Help The Help ➤ Lotus 1-2-3 command provides detailed help for Lotus users.

Special Transition Settings Choose Tools ➤ Options, then click the Transition tab. Select the Lotus 1-2-3 Help option. The slash key (/) will then help you write formulas using 1-2-3 syntax.

CHAPTER

26

Advanced Productivity Tips

fast TRACK

To enter an array formula   **790**

1. Select one or more contiguous cells.

2. Type the formula, and press Ctrl+Shift+Enter.

To copy/paste selected information in a dialog box   **794**

Press Ctrl+C to copy, and Ctrl+V to paste.

To perform unit-of-measure conversions   **797**

Use the CONVERT function in the Analysis ToolPak add-in.

THIS chapter covers three major topics:

- *using custom AutoFills*
- *customizing toolbars*
- *using array formulas*

You will also find several random tips and techniques to enhance your overall productivity, toward the end of the chapter.

Using Custom AutoFills

The *AutoFill* feature, covered in Chapter 7, lets you quickly fill a range of cells with months, dates, numbers, and certain text values. This section explains how to define custom lists that are recognized by AutoFill. For example, suppose your company operates in four regions (North, South, East, and West), and you are constantly typing the regions onto worksheets. A custom AutoFill will save you a lot of data-entry time.

Defining Custom Lists

Follow these steps to define a custom list:

1. Enter the list into a (contiguous) range of cells, in a row or column.

2. Select the range of cells containing the list.

3. Choose Tools ➤ Options, then select the *Custom Lists* tab (see Figure 26.1).

FIGURE 26.1

Custom lists can be
autofilled.

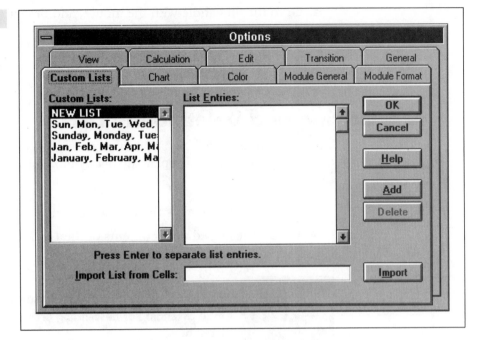

4. Click the *Import* button—the list will be displayed in the *Custom
   List* box.

5. Click OK.

You do not have to enter the list into cells first. The list
can be typed into *List Entries* (pictured in Figure 26.1),
though cells are generally easier to work with.

Once you define a custom list, it is available globally. It is not stored in a
specific workbook.

Performing a Custom AutoFill

Performing an AutoFill on a custom list is no different than on a built-in list:

1. Enter any one of the values from the list into a cell.

2. Grab the fill handle with the mouse, and drag it (in any direction).

For example, suppose you create a list consisting of regions North, South, East, and West. You can enter any of the four regions into a cell, and then perform the AutoFill.

Editing and Deleting the List

The Custom Lists dialog box, pictured in Figure 26.1, can be used to edit or delete a custom list. Display the dialog box, select a list in the *Custom Lists* box, then:

- To delete the list, click the Delete button.
- To edit the list, edit the contents of the *List Entries* box.

TIP

You can also use custom lists to sort data in other than ascending or descending order. See Chapter 16 to learn how.

Customizing Toolbars

Toolbars provide the quickest way of performing everyday tasks. In this section, you will learn how to

- create new toolbars
- modify built-in toolbars
- create your own toolfaces

NOTE

See Chapter 7 to learn how to display toolbars, hide them, and position them on the screen.

There are approximately twelve different toolbars, and if they were all displayed they would consume too much screen real estate. However, you can customize one or more toolbars to contain the tools you use most often, and you can build your own toolbars.

Adding Tools to a Toolbar

There are many tools that are not located on *any* toolbar, many of which are very useful. The following exercise shows how to add the Camera tool (covered in Chapter 12) to the Standard toolbar.

1. Click any toolbar using the right mouse button to display the toolbar shortcut menu.

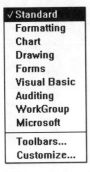

2. Select Customize from the shortcut menu to display the Customize dialog box, shown in Figure 26.2.

   - The tools are organized by category. Click a category to display a different group of tools.
   - There are tools in many of the categories that are not assigned to any toolbar.
   - When you click a tool, a brief description appears on the bottom of the dialog box.

3. Click the Utility category.

4. Click and drag the Camera tool, and drop it onto the Standard toolbar.

5. Click Close.

FIGURE 26.2

Add tools to any toolbar by dragging them from the Customize dialog box and dropping them onto the toolbar.

While the Customize dialog box is displayed, you can drag tools to and from various places to customize toolbars:

To Create a New Toolbar Drag a tool from the Customize dialog box, and drop it onto a worksheet or onto the Excel workspace.

TIP

Toolfaces, the graphic images on the tools, can be customized. With the Customize dialog box displayed, click a tool with the right mouse button and choose the Edit Button Image command from the shortcut menu.

To Remove a Tool from a Toolbar Drag the tool off the toolbar and onto a worksheet, or onto the Excel workspace.

To Move a Tool from One Toolbar to Another Drag the tool off of one toolbar, and drop it onto the other.

To Reorganize Tools on a Toolbar Drag the tool to a new position on the toolbar.

To Delete a Custom Toolbar Drag each tool onto a worksheet or onto the Excel workspace. When the last tool is removed, the toolbar is automatically deleted.

Naming Your Custom Toolbars

When you create new toolbars using drag and drop, they are automatically named Toolbar1, Toolbar2, and so on. These names cannot be changed. To create a new toolbar that you can name, follow these steps:

1. Choose View ➤ Toolbars.

2. Type a name into the Toolbar Name text box, then click New. A new, blank toolbar is created and the Customize dialog box (see Figure 26.2) is displayed.

3. Drag tools onto the toolbar.

Deleting a Custom Toolbar

Custom toolbars can be deleted by choosing View ➤ Toolbars. Select the name of the custom toolbar you want to delete, and click the Delete button. (Built-in toolbars cannot be deleted.)

TIP

At some time you may want to restore a built-in toolbar to its default state. Choose View ➤ Toolbars, select the toolbar from the list, and click Reset.

Useful Tools Not on Any Built-in Toolbar

The tools in the next four tables (Tables 26.1 through 26.4) are not available on built-in toolbars. You must add these tools to a built-in toolbar, or to a custom one, to make them available.

TABLE 26.1: Editing Tools

TOOL FACE	TOOL NAME	FUNCTION
	Set Print Area	Set selected cells as print area
	Select Current Region	Select region containing the active cell
	Insert Worksheet	Create new worksheet page
	Insert Chart Sheet	Create new chart page
	Paste Values	Paste only values
	Paste Formats	Paste only formats
	Clear Contents	Clear only formulas or values

TABLE 26.1: Editing Tools (continued)

TOOL FACE	TOOL NAME	FUNCTION
	Clear Formats	Clear only formats
	Delete	Delete selected cells
	Insert	Insert cells
	Delete Row	Delete selected row
	Insert Row	Insert blank row
	Delete Column	Delete selected column
	Insert Column	Insert blank column
	Fill Right	Copy values, formulas, and formats right or left
	Fill Down	Copy values, formulas, and formats down or up

TABLE 26.2: Formatting Tools

TOOL FACE	TOOL NAME	FUNCTION
Normal	Style	Apply/define cell style
A	Increase Font Size	Increase font size of selected text
A	Decrease Font Size	Decrease font size of selected text
	Justify Align	Justify text
	Cycle Font Color	Change text color
a b	Vertical Text	Align letters vertically
	Rotate Text Up	Rotate text sideways, reading bottom to top
	Rotate Text Down	Rotate text sideways, reading top to bottom
D	Double Underline	Double-underline selected text
	AutoFormat	Apply last table format set
	Dark Shading	Apply dark shading
	Light Shading	Apply light shading

TABLE 26.3: Miscellaneous But Important Tools

TOOL FACE	TOOL NAME	FUNCTION
	Camera	Paste picture of linked selection
	Freeze Panes	Freeze/unfreeze split in active window
	Lock Cell	Lock/unlock selected cells and objects
	Zoom In	Increase magnification
	Zoom Out	Decrease magnification
	Calculate Now	Calculate formulas
	Show Outline Symbols	Show/hide outline symbols
	Select Visible Cells	Select only visible cells within selection

TABLE 26.4: Drawing Tools

TOOL FACE	TOOL NAME	FUNCTION
	Polygon	Draw polygons
	Filled Polygon	Draw filled polygons

Using Array Formulas

Array formulas are special formulas that operate on data arrays (matrices). They have been favored by Excel power users for years and are used to perform matrix arithmetic calculations. In the following discussion, you will learn how to enter array formulas and see a couple of examples where they might be applied.

An array formula is entered into a contiguous, rectangular range of cells, even if the range consists of just one cell. The following exercise uses a primitive example intended to show the mechanics of entering array formulas:

1. Select cells B2:C3.

2. Enter: **=1**

3. Complete the formula by holding down Ctrl+Shift while pressing Enter.

The single array formula is entered into all four cells. On the formula bar, there are braces around the formula: {=1}. This formula is said to have been *array-entered*. The braces are a result of having array-entered the formula. If you were to actually type the braces, you would enter a text constant, not an array formula.

Array formulas impose several restrictions:

• You cannot change an individual cell within an array formula. If you change the formula in any cell within the array, the entire array is changed.

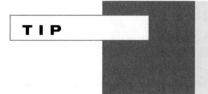

TIP

To select an entire array, select any cell within the array, choose Edit ➤ Go To, click Special, choose the Current Array option, and click OK. The keyboard shortcut is Ctrl+/.

• You cannot insert or delete cells within an array formula.

- When you edit the formula, you must terminate the entry, using Ctrl+Shift+Enter, just as when the formula was first entered.

- An array formula is limited to approximately 1600 cells.

> **NOTE** Arrays can be expressed as constants. See Chapter 8 to learn about named constants.

Putting Array Formulas to Work

Here are a few examples that illustrate the use of array formulas.

Avoiding Interim Calculations

Consider the following worksheet:

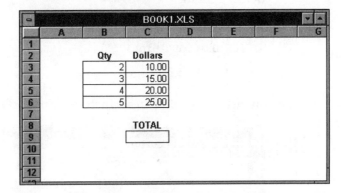

Suppose you want to know the total of Qty * Dollars. The traditional way to solve this problem is to add formulas to D3:D6 that multiply column B by column C, then add a formula that sums column D. The following array formula, entered into a single cell (C9), can perform the same calculation in one step:

```
{=SUM(B3:B6*C3:C6)}
```

Remember, the formula must be terminated with Ctrl+Shift+Enter—do not type the braces.

Performing Matrix Calculations

In the next example, an array formula entered into a range of cells performs a calculation on another range. On the following worksheet, suppose that in F5:G8 you want to display the word *High*, where the population growth exceeds 3%:

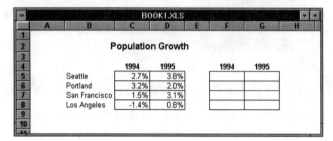

This exercise performs the calculation with one array formula:

1. Select F5:G8.

2. Type the following:

   ```
   =IF(C5:D8>0.03,"High","")
   ```

3. Press Ctrl+Shift+Enter.

The one formula calculates which cells in C5:D8 are greater than 3%.

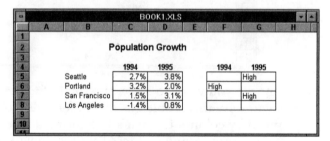

Using Array Functions

There are a number of worksheet functions that can be used to perform array calculations. The following exercise uses the MMULT function to perform matrix (array) multiplication.

On the following worksheet, suppose you want to multiply the two bordered ranges:

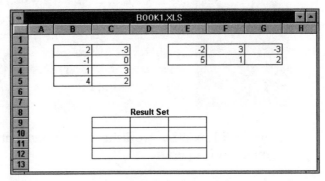

The dimensions of the resulting matrix (array) must be four rows by three columns in this case, reflecting the four rows of the left-hand multiplier and the three columns of the right-hand multiplier. The number of columns in the left multiplier must equal the number of rows in the right multiplier, which is fulfilled in this example:

1. Select C9:E12.

2. Type the following:

```
=MMULT(B2:C5,E2:G3)
```

3. Press Ctrl+Shift+Enter.

The array formula calculates as follows:

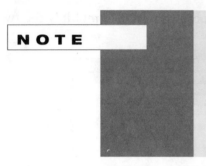

NOTE

Historically, a special syntax for array formulas has been used to conditionally sum a range of cells and to perform other types of summarization. By and large, these uses for array formulas have been obviated by pivot tables (which summarize), and the worksheet functions SUMIF and COUNTIF (covered in Chapter 8), which perform conditional calculations.

Table 26.5 lists other worksheet functions that are applicable when performing array operations.

Tips and Techniques

In this section are various tips and techniques to enhance your productivity. The tips are in random order, so you can jump around to find topics of interest.

Using the Clipboard to Transfer Data In and Out of Dialog Boxes

The Clipboard can be used to copy information into (or out of) dialog boxes. Here are two examples that illustrate the technique.

Copying Information Out of a Dialog Box

Assume that you are preparing hardcopy documentation for a workbook, and there are cell notes that you want to move to a word processing document:

1. Select the cell containing the note, and choose Insert ➤ Note.

2. Select the text in the Text Note box, using the mouse.

TABLE 26.5: Functions Used in Array Operations

FUNCTION	COMMENTS
COLUMN	Returns array when argument is a range
COLUMNS	Argument must be array or range
GROWTH	Argument can be array or range—can return an array
HLOOKUP	Argument must be array or range
INDEX	Argument must be array or range—can return array
LINEST	Always returns array
LOGEST	Always returns array
LOOKUP	Argument must be array or range
MATCH	Argument must be array or range
MDETERM	Argument must be array
MINVERSE	Always returns array
MMULT	Always returns array
ROW	Returns array when argument is a range
ROWS	Argument must be array or range
SUMPRODUCT	Argument can be array, range, or values
TRANSPOSE	Always returns array
TREND	Argument must be array or range—can return an array
VLOOKUP	Argument must be array or range

3. Press Ctrl+C to copy the selected text to the Clipboard, then close the dialog box.

4. Activate your word processor, then choose Edit ➤ Paste (or press Ctrl+V).

Pasting Information Into a Dialog Box

The following exercise will transfer data into a dialog box. Assume that you want to replace every occurrence of the name *Bach* with the name *Shostakovich*. You don't want to risk misspelling Shostakovich, so you will paste it into the dialog box from a word processing document:

1. Activate the word processing document — select the word(s) you want to copy, and choose Edit ➤ Copy (or press Ctrl+C) to copy to the Clipboard.

2. Activate Excel.

3. Choose the Edit ➤ Replace command—type Bach into *Find What,* then tab down to *Replace with:*

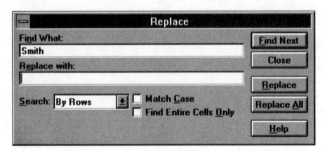

4. Press Ctrl+V to paste text into the dialog box from the Clipboard.

Remember, this technique is not specific to Excel. It can be employed in other Windows programs.

Checking Spelling in a Chart

Checking spelling in the chart is as important as in any other part of a report. To check chart spelling:

1. Activate the chart window.

2. Choose Tools ➤ Spelling (or click the Check Spelling tool).

Converting Units of Measure

To perform all kinds of unit-of-measure conversions, use the CONVERT function, found in the Analysis ToolPak. (See Chapter 24 to learn how to load the ToolPak and other add-ins.) For example, CONVERT can be used to convert from miles to kilometers, or grams to ounces.

The syntax for CONVERT is

```
CONVERT(number,from_unit,to_unit)
```

number is the quantity, measured in *from_unit*, to be converted

from_unit is a code representing the original unit of measure (case-sensitive)

to_unit is a code representing the new unit of measure (case-sensitive)

Here is an example that converts 12 teaspoons to cups (returning .25):

```
=CONVERT(12,"tsp","cup")
```

The codes for the various units of measure that can be converted are shown on the following pages.

Weight and Mass

Gram	"g"
Slug	"sg"
Pound	"lbm"
U (atomic mass unit)	"u"
Ounce	"ozm"

Distance

METER	"m"
Statute mile	"mi"
Nautical mile	"Nmi"
Inch	"in"
Foot	"ft"
Yard	"yd"
Angstrom	"ang"
Pica ($\frac{1}{72}$ in.)	"Pica"

Time

Year	"yr"
Day	"day"
Hour	"hr"
Minute	"mn"
Second	"sec"

Pressure

Pascal	"Pa"
Atmosphere	"atm"
mm of Mercury	"mmHg"

Force

Newton	"N"
Dyne	"dyn"
Pound force	"lbf"

Energy

Joule	"J"
Erg	"e"
Thermodynamic calorie	"c"
IT calorie	"cal"
Electron volt	"eV"
Horsepower-hour	"HPh"
Watt-hour	"Wh"
Foot-pound	"flb"
BTU	"BTU"

Power

| Horsepower | "HP" |
| Watt | "W" |

Magnetism

| Tesla | "T" |
| Gauss | "ga" |

Temperature

Degree Celsius	"C"
Degree Fahrenheit	"F"
Degree Kelvin	"K"

Liquid Measure

Teaspoon	"tsp"
Tablespoon	"tbs"
Fluid ounce	"oz"
Cup	"cup"
Pint	"pt"
Quart	"qt"
Gallon	"gal"
Liter	"l"

Special Prefixes

There are several prefixes that can be used as part of the **From_unit** or **To_unit** arguments that act as multipliers. For example, the prefix *k* means kilo (multiplying by 1000). As with the *from* and *to* arguments, the prefix multiplier is case-sensitive.

Here is a formula that converts 1000 yards into meters:

```
=CONVERT(1000,"yd","m")
```

Now, using the *k* prefix, the following formula converts 1000 yards to kilometers:

```
=CONVERT(1000,"yd","km")
```

Here is a list of the prefixes you can use:

PREFIX	MULTIPLIER	ABBREVIATION
exa	1000000000000000000 (1E+18)	"E"
peta	1000000000000000 (1E+15)	"P"
tera	1000000000000 (1E+12)	"T"
giga	1000000000 (1E+09)	"G"
mega	1000000 (1E+06)	"M"
kilo	1000	"k"
hecto	100	"h"

PREFIX	MULTIPLIER	ABBREVIATION
dekao	10	"e"
deci	.1	"d"
centi	.01	"c"
milli	.001	"m"
micro	.000001 (1E-06)	"u"
nano	.000000001(1E-09)	"n"
pico	.000000000001 (1E-12)	"p"
femto	.000000000000001 (1E-15)	"f"
atto	.000000000000000001 (1E-18)	"a"

Transposing Rows and Columns

Suppose you have data oriented in rows, and you want to reorient it in columns. Consider the following example:

Follow these steps to transpose the data:

1. Select cells B2:E3.
2. Choose Edit ➤ Copy.
3. Select cell B5.
4. Choose Edit ➤ Paste Special.

5. Check the *Transpose* setting, and click OK. The data is transposed from rows into columns.

	A	B	C	D	E	F
1						
2		Q1	Q2	Q3	Q4	
3		374	750	410	409	
4						
5		Q1	374			
6		Q2	750			
7		Q3	410			
8		Q4	409			
9						
10						
11						

(BOOK1.XLS)

3-D Fills

In Chapter 7 you learned how to fill data on a worksheet horizontally or vertically. Use Edit ➤ Fill ➤ Across Worksheets to fill (copy) information across multiple sheets. Create a new workbook, and try this exercise:

1. On Sheet1, enter some information into B2:C3.

2. Select B2:C3.

3. With the Ctrl key held down, select the worksheets you want to fill—in this case, Sheet2 and Sheet4.

4. Choose Edit ➤ Fill ➤ Across Worksheets—the following dialog box is displayed:

5. Select the information you want to fill—in this case All—and click OK.

The information in Sheet1!B2:C3 is copied to the same range on Sheet2 and Sheet4.

T I P

To ungroup sheets, Shift+click the tab of the active worksheet.

APPENDICES

Command Cross-Reference: Excel 4 vs. Excel 5

Cross Reference of Changed Menu Commands

EXCEL 4 COMMAND	EXCEL 5 COMMAND	REMARKS
File ➤ Links	Edit ➤ Links	
File ➤ Save Workbook	File ➤ Save	all files are workbooks in Excel 5
File ➤ Delete	File ➤ Find File	click Commands button, choose delete
Edit ➤ Paste Link	Edit ➤ Paste Special	click Paste Link button
Edit ➤ Insert	Insert ➤ Cells, Rows, Columns	
Edit ➤ Insert Object	Insert ➤ Object	
Edit ➤ Fill Right	Edit ➤ Fill ➤ Right	
Edit ➤ Fill Down	Edit ➤ Fill ➤ Down	
Formula ➤ Paste Name	Insert ➤ Name ➤ Paste	
Formula ➤ Paste Function	Insert ➤ Function	
Formula ➤ Define Name	Insert ➤ Name ➤ Define	
Formula ➤ Create Names	Insert ➤ Name ➤ Create	
Formula ➤ Apply Names	Insert ➤ Name ➤ Apply	
Formula ➤ Note	Insert ➤ Note	
Formula ➤ Goto	Edit ➤ Go To	
Formula ➤ Find	Edit ➤ Find	
Formula ➤ Replace	Edit ➤ Replace	
Formula ➤ Select Special	Edit ➤ Go To	click Special button
Formula ➤ Show Active Cell	(none)	Ctrl+backspace
Formula ➤ Outline	Data ➤ Group and Outline	

EXCEL 4 COMMAND	EXCEL 5 COMMAND	REMARKS
Formula ➤ Goal Seek	Tools ➤ Goal Seek	
Format ➤ Number	Format ➤ Cells	select Number tab
Format ➤ Alignment	Format ➤ Cells	select Alignment tab
Format ➤ Font	Format ➤ Cells	select Font tab
Format ➤ Border	Format ➤ Cells	select Border tab
Format ➤ Patterns	Format ➤ Cells	select Patterns tab
Format ➤ Cell Protection	Format ➤ Cells	select Protection tab
Format ➤ Row Height	Format ➤ Row ➤ Height	
Format ➤ Column Width	Format ➤ Column ➤ Width	
Format ➤ Justify	Format ➤ Cells	select Alignment tab
Format ➤ Bring to Front	Format ➤ Placement ➤ Bring to Front	
Format ➤ Send to Back	Format ➤ Placement ➤ Send to Back	
Format ➤ Group	Format ➤ Placement ➤ Group	
Format ➤ Object Properties	Format ➤ Object	select Properties tab
Data ➤ Find	Data ➤ Filter	
Data ➤ Extract	Data ➤ Filter ➤ Advanced Filter	
Data ➤ Delete	(none)	
Data ➤ Set Database	(none)	not required—use Insert ➤ Name ➤ Define if desired

CROSS REFERENCE OF CHANGED MENU COMMANDS

EXCEL 4 COMMAND	EXCEL 5 COMMAND	REMARKS
Data ➤ Set Criteria	(none)	not required—use Insert ➤ Name ➤ Define if desired
Data ➤ Set Extract	(none)	not required—use Insert ➤ Name ➤ Define if desired
Data ➤ Series	(none)	not required—use Autofill if desired
Data ➤ Parse	Data ➤ Text to Columns	
Options ➤ Set Print Area	File ➤ Page Setup	select Sheet tab
Options ➤ Set Print Titles	File ➤ Page Setup	select Sheet tab
Options ➤ Set Page Break	Insert ➤ Page Break	
Options ➤ Display	Tools ➤ Options	select View tab
Options ➤ Toolbars	View ➤ Toolbars	
Options ➤ Color Palette	Tools ➤ Options	select Color tab
Options ➤ Protect Document	Tools ➤ Protection	
Options ➤ Calculation	Tools ➤ Options	select Calculation tab
Options ➤ Workspace	Tools ➤ Options	select View tab
Options ➤ Add-Ins	Tools ➤ Add-Ins	
Options ➤ Spelling	Tools ➤ Spelling	
Options ➤ Group Edit	(none)	Ctrl+click sheet tabs to select multiple sheets
Macro ➤ Run	Tools ➤ Macro	
Macro ➤ Record	Tools ➤ Record Macro	

EXCEL 4 COMMAND	EXCEL 5 COMMAND	REMARKS
Macro ➤ Start Recorder	Tools ➤ Record Macro	
Macro ➤ Set Recorder	Tools ➤ Record Macro	
Macro ➤ Relative Record	Tools ➤ Record Macro ➤ Use Relative References	
Macro ➤ Assign to Object	Tools ➤ Assign Macro	
Window ➤ Zoom	View ➤ Zoom	
Help ➤ Introducing Microsoft Excel	Help ➤ Quick Preview	
Help ➤ Learning Microsoft Excel	Help ➤ Examples and Demos	

Worksheet and Analysis ToolPak Functions

Built-in Worksheet Functions

ABS(number)

absolute value of a number

ACOSH(number)

Returns the inverse hyperbolic cosine of a number

ACOS(number)

Returns the arccosine of a number

ADDRESS(DowNumber,ColumnNumber,abs_num, A3,sheet_text)

Returns a reference as text to a single cell in a worksheet

AND(logical1,logical2,...)

Returns TRUE if all arguments are TRUE, otherwise returns FALSE

AREAS(reference)

Returns the number of areas in a reference

ASINH(number)

Returns the inverse hyperbolic sine of a number

ASIN(number)

Returns the arcsine of a number

ATAN2(x_num,y_num)

Returns the arctangent from x- and y-coordinates

ATANH(number)

Returns the inverse hyperbolic tangent of a number

ATAN(number)

Returns the arctangent of a number

AVEDEV(number1,number2,...)

Returns the average of the absolute deviations of data points from their mean

AVERAGE(number1,number2,...)

Returns the average of its arguments

BETADIST(x,alpha,beta,A,B)

Returns the cumulative beta probability density function

BETAINV(probability,alpha,beta,A,B)

Returns the inverse of the cumulative beta probability density function

CEILING(number,significance)

Rounds a number to the nearest integer or to the nearest multiple of significance

CELL(info_type,reference)

Returns information about the formatting, location, or contents of a cell

CHAR(number)

Returns the character specified by the code number

CHIDIST(x,degrees_freedom)

Returns the one-tailed probability of the chi-squared distribution

CHIINV(probability,degrees_freedom)

Returns the inverse of the chi-squared distribution

CHITEST(actual_range,expected_range)

Returns the test for independence

CHOOSE(index_num,value1,value2,...)

Chooses a value from a list of values

CLEAN(text)

Removes all nonprintable characters from text

CODE(text)

Returns a numeric code for the first character in a text string

COLUMNS(array)

Returns the number of columns in a reference or array

COLUMN(reference)

Returns the column number of a reference

COMBIN(number,number_chosen)

Returns the number of combinations for a given number of objects

CONCATENATE(text1,text2,...)

Joins several text items into one text item

CONFIDENCE(alpha,standard_dev,size)

Returns a confidence interval for a population

CORREL(array1,array2)

Returns the correlation coefficient between two data sets

COSH(number)

Returns the hyperbolic cosine of a number

COS(number)

Returns the cosine of a number

COUNTA(value1,value2,...)

Counts how many values are in the list of arguments

COUNTBLANK(range)

Counts the number of blank cells within a range

COUNTIF(range,criteria)

Counts the number of nonblank cells within a range that meet the given criteria

COUNT(value1,value2,...)

Counts how many numbers are in the list of arguments

COVAR(array1,array2)

Returns covariance, the average of the products of paired deviations

CRITBINOM(trials,probability_s,alpha)

Returns smallest value for which cumulative binomial distribution is less than or equal to criterion value

DATEVALUE(date_text)

Converts a date in the form of text to a serial number

DATE(year,month,day)

Returns the serial number of a particular date

DAVERAGE(database,field,criteria)

Returns the average of selected database entries

DAYS360(start_date,end_date,method)

Calculates the number of days between two dates on the basis of a 360-day year

DAY(serial_number)

Converts a serial number to a day of the month

DB(cost,salvage,life,period,month)

Returns the depreciation of an asset for a specified period using the fixed-declining balance method

DCOUNTA(database,field,criteria)

Counts nonblank cells from a specified database using a criteria range

DCOUNT(database,field,criteria)

Counts the cells containing numbers from a specified database using a criteria range

DDB(cost,salvage,life,period,factor)

Returns the depreciation of an asset for a specified period using double-declining balance method

DEGREES(angle)

Converts radians to degrees

DEVSQ(number1,number2,...)

Returns the sum of squares of deviations

DGET(database,field,criteria)

Extracts from a database a single record that matches the specified criteria

DMAX(database,field,criteria)

Returns the maximum value from selected database entries using a criteria range

DMIN(database,field,criteria)

Returns the minimum value from selected database entries using a criteria range

DOLLAR(number,decimals)

Converts a number to text, using currency format

DPRODUCT(database,field,criteria)

Multiplies the values in a particular field of records using a criteria range

DSTDEVP(database,field,criteria)

Calculates the standard deviation on the basis of the entire population of selected database entries

DSTDEV(database,field,criteria)

Estimates the standard deviation on the basis of a sample of selected database entries

DSUM(database,field,criteria)

Adds the numbers in the field column of records in the database using a criteria range

DVARP(database,field,criteria)

Calculates variance on the basis of the entire population of selected database entries

DVAR(database,field,criteria)

Estimates variance on the basis of a sample from selected database entries

ERROR.TYPE(error_val)

Returns a number corresponding to an error type

EVEN(number)

Rounds a number up to the nearest even integer

EXACT(text1,text2)

Checks to see if two text values are identical

EXPONDIST(x,lambda,cumulative)

Returns the exponential distribution

EXP(number)

Returns e raised to the power of a given number

FACT(number)

Returns the factorial of a number

FALSE()

Returns the logical value FALSE

FDIST(x,degrees_freedom1,degrees_freedom2)

Returns the F probability distribution

FIND(find_text,within_text,start_num)

Finds one text value within another (case-sensitive)

FINV(probability,degrees_freedom1,degrees_freedom2)

Returns the inverse of the F probability distribution

FISHERINV(y)

Returns the inverse of the Fisher transformation

FISHER(x)

Returns the Fisher transformation

FIXED(number,decimals,no_commas)

Formats a number as text with a fixed number of decimals

FLOOR(number,significance)

Rounds a number down, toward zero

FORECAST(x,known_y's,known_x's)

Returns a value along a linear trend

FREQUENCY(data_array,bins_array)

Returns a frequency distribution as a vertical array

FTEST(array1,array2)

Returns the result of an F-test

FV(rate,nper,pmt,pv,type)

Returns the future value of an investment

GAMMADIST(x,alpha,beta,cumulative)

Returns the gamma distribution

GAMMAINV(probability,alpha,beta)

Returns the inverse of the gamma cumulative distribution

GAMMALN(x)

Returns the natural logarithm of the gamma function, G(x)

GEOMEAN(number1,number2,...)

Returns the geometric mean

GROWTH(known_y's,known_x's,new_x's,const)

Returns values along an exponential trend

HARMEAN(number1,number2,...)

Returns the harmonic mean

HLOOKUP(lookup_value,table_array,row_index_num, range_lookup)

Looks in the top row of an array and returns the value of the indicated cell

HOUR(serial_number)

Converts a serial number to an hour

HYPGEOMDIST(sample_s,number_sample,population_s,number_population)

Returns the hypergeometric distribution

IF(logical_test,value_if_true,value_if_false)

Specifies a logical test to perform

INDEX(array,row_num,column_num)

Uses an index to choose a value from a reference or array

INDEX(reference,row_num,column_num,area_num)

Uses an index to choose a value from a reference or array

INDIRECT(ref_text,a1)

Returns a reference indicated by a text value

INFO(type_text)

Returns information about the current operating environment

INTERCEPT(known_y's,known_x's)

Returns the intercept of the linear regression line

INT(number)

Rounds a number down to the nearest integer

IPMT(rate,per,nper,pv,fv,type)

Returns the interest payment for an investment for a given period

IRR(values,guess)

Returns the internal rate of return for a series of cash flows

ISBLANK (value)

Returns TRUE if the value is blank

ISERROR(value)

Returns TRUE if the value is any error value

ISERR(value)

Returns TRUE if the value is any error value except #N/A

ISLOGICAL(value)

Returns TRUE if the value is a logical value

ISNA (value)

Returns TRUE if the value is the #N/A error value

ISNONTEXT(value)

Returns TRUE if the value is not text

ISNUMBER(value)

Returns TRUE if the value is a number

ISREF(value)

Returns TRUE if the value is a reference

ISTEXT(value)

Returns TRUE if the value is text

KURT (number1,number2,...)

Returns the kurtosis of a data set

LARGE(array,k)

Returns the k-th largest value in a data set

LEFT(text,num_chars)

Returns the leftmost characters from a text value

LEN(text)

Returns the number of characters in a text string

LINEST(known_y's,known_x's,const,stats)

Returns the minimum value in a list of arguments

LN (number)

Returns the natural logarithm of a number

LOG10(number)

Returns the base-10 logarithm of a number

LOGEST(known_y's,known_x's,const,stats)

Returns the parameters of an exponential trend

LOGINV(probability,mean,standard_dev)

Returns the inverse of the lognormal distribution

LOGNORMDIST(x,mean,standard_dev)

Returns the cumulative lognormal distribution

LOG(number,base)

Returns the logarithm of a number to a specified base

LOOKUP(lookup_value,array)

Looks up values in a vector or array

LOOKUP(lookup_value,lookup_vector,result_vector)

Looks up values in a vector or array

LOWER(text)

Converts text to lowercase

MATCH (lookup_value,lookup_array,match_type)

Looks up values in a reference or array

MAX(number1,number2,...)

Returns the maximum value in a list of arguments

MDETERM(array)

Returns the matrix determinant of an array

MEDIAN(number1,number2,...)

Returns the median of the given numbers

MID(text,start_num,num_chars)

Returns a specific number of characters from a text string starting at the position you specify

MINUTE(serial_number)

Converts a serial number to a minute

MINVERSE(array)

Returns the matrix inverse of an array

MIN(number1,number2,...)

Returns the minimum value in a list of arguments

MIRR(values,finance_rate,reinvest_rate)

Returns the internal rate of return where positive and negative cash flows are financed at different rates

MMULT(array1,array2)

Returns the matrix product of two arrays

MODE(number1,number2,...)

Returns the most common value in a data set

MOD(number,divisor)

Returns the remainder from division

MONTH(serial_number)

Converts a serial number to a month

NA()

Returns the error value #N/A

NEGBINOMDIST(number_f,number_s,probability_s)

Returns the negative binomial distribution

NORMDIST(x,mean,standard_dev,cumulative)

Returns the normal cumulative distribution

NORMINV(probability,mean,standard_dev)

Returns the inverse of the normal cumulative distribution

NORMSDIST(z)

Returns the standard normal cumulative distribution

NORMSINV(probability)

Returns the inverse of the standard normal cumulative distribution

NOT(logical)

Reverses the logic of its argument

NOW()

Returns the serial number of the current date and time

NPER(rate,pmt,pv,fv,type)

Returns the number of periods for an investment

NPV(rate,value1,value2,...)

Returns the net present value of an investment on the basis of a series of periodic cash flows and a discount rate

N(value)

Returns a value converted to a number

ODD(number)

Rounds a number up to the nearest odd integer

OFFSET(reference,rows,cols,height,width)

Returns a reference offset from a given reference

OR(logical1,logical2,...)

Returns TRUE if any argument is TRUE

PEARSON(array1,array2)

Returns the Pearson product moment correlation coefficient

PERCENTILE(array,k)

Returns the k-th percentile of values in a range

PERCENTRANK(array,x,significance)

Returns the percentage rank of a value in a data set

PERMUT(number,number_chosen)

Returns the number of permutations for a given number of objects

PI()

Returns the value of pi.

PMT(rate,nper,pv,fv,type)

Returns the periodic payment for an annuity

POISSON(x,mean,cumulative)

Returns the Poisson distribution

POWER(number,power)

Returns the result of a number raised to a power

PPMT(rate,per,nper,pv,fv,type)

Returns the payment on the principal for an investment for a given period

PROB(x_range,prob_range,lower_limit,upper_limit)

Returns the probability that values in a range are between two limits

PRODUCT(number1,number2,...)

Multiplies its arguments

PROPER(text)

Capitalizes the first letter in each word of a text value

ALPHABETICAL LIST OF WORKSHEET FUNCTIONS

PV(rate,nper,pmt,fv,type)

Returns the present value of an investment

QUARTILE(array,quart)

Returns the quartile of a data set

RADIANS(angle)

Converts degrees to radians

RAND()

Returns a random number between 0 and 1

RANK (number,ref,order)

Returns the rank of a number in a list of numbers

RATE(nper,pmt,pv,fv,type,guess)

Returns the interest rate per period of an annuity

REGISTER.ID(module_text,procedure,type_text)

Returns the register ID of the specified dynamic link library (DLL) or code resource that has been previously registered

REPLACE(old_text,start_num,num_chars,new_text)

Replaces characters within text

REPT(text,number_times)

Repeats text a given number of times

RIGHT(text,num_chars)

Returns the rightmost characters from a text value

ROMAN(number,form)

Converts an Arabic numeral to Roman, as text

ROUNDDOWN(number,num_digits)

Rounds a number down, toward zero

ROUNDUP(number,num_digits)

Rounds a number up, away from zero

ROUND(number,num_digits)

Rounds a number to a specified number of digits

ROWS(array)

Returns the number of rows in a reference

ROW(reference)

Returns the row number of a reference

RSQ(known_y's,known_x's)

Returns the square of the Pearson product moment correlation coefficient

SEARCH(find_text,within_text,start_num)

Finds one text value within another (not case-sensitive)

SECOND(serial_number)

Converts a serial number to a second

SIGN(number)

Returns the sign of a number

SINH(number)

Returns the hyperbolic sine of a number

SIN(number)

Returns the sine of the given angle

SKEW(number1,number2,...)

Returns the skewness of a distribution

SLN(cost,salvage,life)

Returns the straight-line depreciation of an asset for one period

SLOPE(known_y's,known_x's)

Returns the slope of the linear regression line

SMALL(array,k)

Returns the k-th smallest value in a data set

SQRT(number)

Returns a positive square root

STANDARDIZE(x,mean,standard_dev)

Returns a normalized value

STDEVP(number1,number2,...)

Calculates standard deviation on the basis of the entire population

STDEV(number1,number2,...)

Returns the bond-equivalent yield for a Treasury bill

STEYX (known_y's,known_x's)

Returns the standard error of the predicted y-value for each x in the regression

SUBSTITUTE(text,old_text,new_text,instance_num)

Substitutes new text for old text in a text string

SUBTOTAL(function_num,ref)

Returns a subtotal in a list or database

SUMIF(range,criteria,sum_range)

Adds the cells specified by a given criteria

SUMPRODUCT(array1,array2,array3,...)

Returns the sum of the products of corresponding array components

SUMSQ(number1,number2,...)

Returns the sum of the squares of the arguments

SUMX2MY2(array_x,array_y)

Returns the sum of the difference of squares of corresponding values in two arrays

SUMX2PY2(array_x,array_y)

Returns the sum of the sum of squares of corresponding values in two arrays

SUM(number1,number2,...)

Adds its arguments

SUMXMY2 (array_x,array_y)

Returns the sum of squares of differences of corresponding values in two arrays

SYD(cost,salvage,life,per)

Returns the sum-of-years' digits depreciation of an asset for a specified period

TANH(number)

Returns the hyperbolic tangent of a number

TAN(number)

Returns the tangent of a number

TDIST(x,degrees_freedom,tails)

Returns the Student's t-distribution

TEXT (value,format_text)

Formats a number and converts it to text

TIMEVALUE(time_text)

Converts a time in the form of text to a serial number

TIME(hour,minute,second)

Returns the serial number of a particular time

TINV(probability,degrees_freedom)

Returns the inverse of the Student's t-distribution

TODAY()

Returns the serial number of today's date

TRANSPOSE(array)

Returns the transpose of an array

TREND(known_y's,known_x's,new_x's,const)

Returns values along a linear trend

TRIMMEAN(array,percent)

Returns the mean of the interior of a data set

TRIM(text)

Removes spaces from text

TRUE()

Returns the logical value TRUE

TRUNC(number,num_digits)

Truncates a number to an integer

TTEST(array1,array2,tails,type)

Returns the probability associated with a Student's t-Test

T(value)

Converts its arguments to text

TYPE(value)

Returns a number indicating the data type of a value

UPPER(text)

Converts text to uppercase

VALUE(text)

Converts a text argument to a number

VARP(number1,number2,...)

Calculates variance on the basis of the entire population

VAR(number1,number2,...)

Estimates variance on the basis of a sample

VDB(cost,salvage,life,start_period,end_period,factor,no_switch)

Returns the depreciation of an asset for a specified or partial period using a declining balance method

VLOOKUP(lookup_value,table_array,col_index_num,range_lookup)

Looks in the first column of an array and moves across the row to return the value of a cell

WEEKDAY(serial_number,return_type)

Converts a serial number to a day of the week

WEIBULL(x,alpha,beta,cumulative)

Returns the Weibull distribution

YEAR(serial_number)

Converts a serial number to a year

ZTEST(array,x,sigma)

Returns the two-tailed P-value of a z-test

Analysis ToolPak Functions

The following functions are contained in the Analysis ToolPak add-in (see Chapter 24).

ACCRINTM(issue,maturity,rate,par,basis)

Returns accrued interest for a security that pays interest at maturity

ACCRINT(issue,first_interest,settlement,rate,par,frequency,basis)

Returns the accrued interest for a security that pays periodic interest

AMORDEGRC(cost,purchase,first_period,salvage,period,rate, year_basis)

Returns the depreciation for each accounting period

AMORLINC(cost,purchase,first_period,salvage,period,rate, year-basis)

Returns the depreciation for each accounting period

BESSELI(x,n)

Returns the modified Bessel function In(x)

BESSELJ(x,n)

Returns the Bessel function Jn(x)

BESSELK (x,n)

Returns the modified Bessel function Kn(x)

BESSELY(x,n)

Returns the Bessel function Yn(x)

BIN2DEC(number)

Converts a binary number to decimal

BIN2HEX(number,places)

Converts a binary number to hexadecimal

BIN2OCT(number,places)

Converts a binary number to octal

BINOMDIST(number_s,trials,probability_s,cumulative)

Returns the individual term binomial distribution probability

COMPLEX(real_num,i_num,suffix)

Converts real and imaginary coefficients into a complex number

CONVERT(number,from_unit,to_unit)

Converts a number from one measurement system to another

COUPDAYBS(settlement,maturity,frequency,basis)

Returns the number of days from the beginning of the coupon period to the settlement date

COUPDAYSNC(settlement,maturity,frequency,basis)

Returns the number of days from the settlement date to the next coupon date

COUPDAYS(settlement,maturity,frequency,basis)

Returns the number of days in the coupon period that contains the settlement date

COUPNCD(settlement,maturity,frequency,basis)

Returns the next coupon date after the settlement date

COUPNUM(settlement,maturity,frequency,basis)

Returns the number of coupons payable between the settlement date and maturity date

COUPPCD(settlement,maturity,frequency,basis)

Returns the previous coupon date before the settlement date

CUMIPMT(rate,nper,pv,start_period,end_period,type)

Returns the cumulative interest paid between two periods

CUMPRINC(rate,nper,pv,start_period,end_period,type)

Returns the cumulative principal paid on a loan between two periods

DEC2BIN(number,places)

Converts a decimal number to binary

DEC2HEX (number,places)

Converts a decimal number to hexadecimal

DEC2OCT(number,places)

Converts a decimal number to octal

DELTA(number1,number2)

Tests whether two values are equal

DISC(settlement,maturity,pr,redemption,basis)

Returns the discount rate for a security

DOLLARDE(fractional_dollar,fraction)

Converts a dollar price expressed as a fraction into a dollar price expressed as a decimal number

DOLLARFR(decimal_dollar,fraction)

Converts a dollar price expressed as a decimal number into a dollar price expressed as a fraction

DURATION(settlement,maturity,coupon,yld,frequency,basis)

Returns the annual duration of a security with periodic interest payments

EDATE(start_date,months)

Returns the serial number of the date that is the indicated number of months before or after the start date

EFFECT(nominal_rate,npery)

Returns the effective annual interest rate

EOMONTH(start_date,months)

Returns the serial number of the last day of the month before or after a specified number of months

ERFC(x)

Returns the complementary error function

ERF(lower_limit,upper_limit)

Returns the error function

FACTDOUBLE(number)

Returns the double factorial of a number

FVSCHEDULE(principal,schedule)

Returns the future value of an initial principal after applying a series of compound interest rates

GCD(number1,number2,...)

Returns the greatest common divisor

GESTEP(number,step)

Tests whether a number is greater than a threshold value

HEX2BIN(number,places)

Converts a hexadecimal number to binary

HEX2DEC(number)

Converts a hexadecimal number to decimal

HEX2OCT(number,places)

Converts a hexadecimal number to octal

IMABS(inumber)

Returns the absolute value (modulus) of a complex number

IMAGINARY(inumber)

Returns the imaginary coefficient of a complex number

IMARGUMENT(inumber)

Returns the argument theta, an angle expressed in radians

IMCONJUGATE(inumber)

Returns the complex conjugate of a complex number

IMCOS(inumber)

Returns the cosine of a complex number

IMDIV(inumber1,inumber2)

Returns the quotient of two complex numbers

IMEXP(inumber)

Returns the exponential of a complex number

IMLN(inumber)

Returns the natural logarithm of a complex number

IMLOG10(inumber)

Returns the base-10 logarithm of a complex number

IMLOG2(inumber)

Returns the base-2 logarithm of a complex number

IMPOWER(inumber,number)

Returns a complex number raised to an integer power

IMPRODUCT(inumber1,inumber2)

Returns the product of two complex numbers

IMREAL(inumber)

Returns the real coefficient of a complex number

IMSIN(inumber)

Returns the sine of a complex number

IMSQRT(inumber)

Returns the square root of a complex number

IMSUB(inumber1,inumber2)

Returns the difference of two complex numbers

IMSUM(inumber1,inumber2)

Returns the sum of complex numbers

INTRATE(settlement,maturity,investment,redemption,basis)

Returns the interest rate for a fully invested security

ISEVEN(value)

Returns TRUE if the number is even

ISODD(value)

Returns TRUE if the number is odd

LCM(number1,number2,...)

Returns the least common multiple

MDURATION(settlement,maturity,coupon,yld,frequency,basis)

Returns the Macauley modified duration for a security with an assumed
par value of $100

MROUND(number,multiple)

Returns a number rounded to the desired multiple

MULTINOMIAL(number1,number2,...)

Returns the multinomial of a set of numbers

NETWORKDAYS(start_date,end_date,holidays)

Returns the number of whole workdays between two dates

NOMINAL(effect_rate,npery)

Returns the annual nominal interest rate

OCT2BIN(number,places)

Converts an octal number to binary

OCT2DEC(number)

Converts an octal number to decimal

OCT2HEX(number,places)

Converts an octal number to hexadecimal

**ODDFPRICE(settlement,maturity,issue,first_coupon,rate,yld,
redemption,frequency,basis)**

Returns the price per $100 face value of a security with an odd first period

**ODDFYIELD(settlement,maturity,issue,first_coupon,rate,pr,
redemption,frequency,basis)**

Returns the yield of a security with an odd first period

**ODDLPRICE(settlement,maturity,last_interest,rate,yld,redemption,
frequency,basis)**

Returns the price per $100 face value of a security with an odd last period

**ODDLYIELD(settlement,maturity,last_interest,rate,pr,redemption,
frequency,basis)**

Returns the yield of a security with an odd last period

PRICEDISC(settlement,maturity,discount,redemption,basis)

Returns the price per $100 face value of a discounted security

PRICEMAT(settlement,maturity,issue,rate,yld,basis)

Returns the price per $100 face value of a security that pays interest at maturity

PRICE(settlement,maturity,rate,yld,redemption,frequency,basis)

Returns the price per $100 face value of a security that pays periodic interest

QUOTIENT(numerator,denominator)

Returns the integer portion of a division

RANDBETWEEN(bottom,top)

Returns a random number between the specified numbers

RECEIVED(settlement,maturity,investment,discount,basis)

Returns the amount received at maturity for a fully invested security

SERIESSUM(x,n,m,coefficients)

Returns the sum of a power series on the basis of the formula

SQRTPI(number)

Returns the square root of (number * PI)

TBILLEQ(settlement,maturity,discount)

Returns the bond-equivalent yield for a Treasury bill

TBILLPRICE(settlement,maturity,discount)

Returns the price per $100 face value for a Treasury bill

TBILLYIELD(settlement,maturity,pr)

Returns the yield for a Treasury bill

WORKDAY(start_date,days,holidays)

Returns the serial number of the date before or after a specified number of workdays

XIRR(values,dates,guess)

Returns the internal rate of return for a schedule of cash flows

XNPV(rate,values,dates)

Returns the net present value for a schedule of cash flows

YEARFRAC(start_date,end_date,basis)

Returns the year fraction representing the number of whole days between start_date and end_date

YIELDDISC(settlement,maturity,pr,redemption,basis)

Returns the annual yield for a discounted security. For example, a treasury bill

YIELDMAT(settlement,maturity,issue,rate,pr,basis)

Returns the annual yield of a security that pays interest at maturity

YIELD(settlement,maturity,rate,pr,redemption,frequency,basis)

Returns the yield on a security that pays periodic interest

ODBC Function (Database Access)

The following function is contained in the ODBC add-in (discussed in Chapter 18).

SQL.REQUEST(connection_string,output_ref, driver_prompt, query_text, column_names_logical)

Connects with an external data source and runs a query from worksheet—returns query results as an array

APPENDIX

C

Keyboard Shortcuts

THIS appendix contains tables summarizing the usage of shortcut keys in Excel.

- Changes from Excel 4
- Entering and editing
- Command keys
- Function keys
- Moving and selecting in worksheets and workbooks
- Moving and selecting while in End mode
- Moving and selecting with Scroll Lock on
- Selecting special cells
- Formatting
- Outlining
- Print Preview mode
- Selecting chart items when chart is active
- Window commands
- Switching applications

NOTE For keyboards with only ten function keys, use Alt+F1 for F11, and use Alt+F2 for F12.

Changes from Excel 4

F4	Repeat last action
F7	Check spelling
Ctrl+F	Find
Ctrl+H	Replace
Shift+F4	Find next
Ctrl+Shift+F4	Find previous
Ctrl+N	Open new workbook
Ctrl+O	Open
Ctrl+S	Save
Ctrl+P	Print
Ctrl+Tab	Next window
Ctrl+Shift+Tab	Previous window
Ctrl+PgDn	Move to next sheet in workbook
Ctrl+PgUp	Move to previous sheet in workbook
Ctrl+A	Select all

Entering and Editing

F2	Edit active cell
Esc	Cancel entry
Backspace	Delete character to left of insertion point, or delete selection
Shift+F2	Edit cell note
F3	Paste name into formula
Shift+F3	Display Function Wizard
Ctrl+A	After typing valid function name in formula, display step 2 of Function Wizard

Ctrl+Shift+A	After typing valid function name in formula, insert argument names for the function
Alt+=	Insert AutoSum formula
Ctrl+semicolon	Enter date in cell or formula bar
Ctrl+Shift+colon	Enter time in cell or formula bar
Ctrl+D	Fill down
Ctrl+R	Fill right
Ctrl+Del	Cut text to end of line
Alt+Enter	Insert carriage return
Ctrl+Alt+Tab	Insert tab
Arrow keys	Move one character up, down, left, or right
Ctrl+Shift+"	Copy value from cell above the active cell
Ctrl+` (grave accent)	Alternate between displaying values or formulas
Ctrl+' (apostrophe)	Copy formula from cell above the active cell
Ctrl+Enter	Fill a selection of cells with current entry
Ctrl+Shift+Enter	Enter array formula
F4	Change cell reference type (absolute-relative-mixed)

Command Keys

Ctrl+N	New workbook
Ctrl+O	Open
Ctrl+S	Save
F12	Save As
Ctrl+P	Print

Alt+F4	Close Excel
Ctrl+Z (or Alt+Backspace)	Undo
F4	Repeat
Ctrl+X	Cut
Ctrl+C	Copy
Ctrl+V	Paste
Ctrl+D	Fill down
Ctrl+R	Fill right
Del	Clear contents (in worksheet); clear selected item (in chart)
Ctrl+F	Display Find dialog box
Ctrl+H	Display Replace dialog box
Shift+F4	Find next
Ctrl+Shift+F4	Find previous
F5	Go To
Ctrl+minus sign	Delete selected cells
Ctrl+Shift+plus sign	Display Insert dialog box
Shift+F11	Insert new worksheet
F11	Insert new chart sheet
Ctrl+F11	Insert new Excel 4.0 macro sheet
Ctrl+F3	Display Define Name dialog box
F3	Display Paste Name dialog box (if names are defined)
Ctrl+Shift+F3	Display Create Names dialog box
Ctrl+1	Display Format Cells dialog box
Ctrl+9	Hide rows
Ctrl+Shift+(	Unhide rows
Ctrl+0 (zero)	Hide columns

Ctrl+Shift+)	Unhide columns
Alt+' (apostrophe)	Display Style dialog box
F7	Check spelling
Ctrl+F6	Next window
Ctrl+Shift+F6	Previous window
F6	Next pane
Shift+F6	Previous pane
F1	Help Contents screen
Ctrl+7	Show or hide Standard toolbar
F9 or Ctrl+=	Calculate all open workbooks
Shift+F9	Calculate active sheet

Function Keys

F1	Help contents screen
Shift+F1	Display help pointer
F2	Activate formula bar
Shift+F2	Insert note
Ctrl+F2	Display Info window
F3	Display Paste Name dialog box (if names are defined)
Shift+F3	Display Function Wizard
Ctrl+F3	Display Define Name dialog box
Ctrl+Shift+F3	Display Create Names dialog box
F4	When editing a formula, change cell reference type (absolute-relative-mixed); when not editing a formula, repeat last action
Ctrl+F4	Close window
Alt+F4	Close Excel

F5	Go To
Ctrl+F5	Restore window size
F6	Next pane
Shift+F6	Previous pane
Ctrl+F6	Next window
Ctrl+Shift+F6	Previous window
F7	Check spelling
Ctrl+F7	Move command (document Control menu)
F8	Turn Extend mode on or off
Shift+F8	Turn Add mode on or off
Ctrl+F8	Size command (document Control menu)
F9	Calculate all sheets in all open workbooks
Shift+F9	Calculate active sheet
Ctrl+F9	Minimize workbook
F10	Activate menu bar
Shift+F10	Activate shortcut menu
Ctrl+F10	Maximize workbook
F11	Insert new chart sheet
Shift+F11	Insert new worksheet
Ctrl+F11	Insert new Excel 4.0 macro sheet
F12	Save As
Shift+F12	Save
Ctrl+F12	Open
Ctrl+Shift+F12	Print

Moving and Selecting in Worksheets and Workbooks

Enter	Move down through selected cells
Shift+Enter	Move up through selection
Tab	Move right through selection; move among unlocked cells in protected worksheet
Shift+Tab	Move left through selection
Ctrl+Backspace	Scroll to display active cell
Arrow key	Move by one cell in direction of arrow
Shift+*arrow key*	Extend selection by one cell
Ctrl+↑ or Ctrl+↓	Move up or down to edge of current data region
Ctrl+← or Ctrl+→	Move left or right to edge of current data region
Ctrl+Shift+ *arrow key*	Extend selection to edge of current data region (in direction of arrow)
Home	Move to beginning of row
Shift+Home	Extend selection to beginning of row
Ctrl+Home	Move to beginning of worksheet
Ctrl+Shift+Home	Extend selection to beginning of worksheet
Ctrl+End	Move to last cell in worksheet (lower-right corner)
Ctrl+Shift+End	Extend selection to last cell in worksheet (lower-right corner)
Ctrl+spacebar	Select entire column
Shift+spacebar	Select entire row
Ctrl+A	Select entire worksheet
Shift+Backspace	Collapse selection to active cell
PgDn	Move down one screen

PgUp	Move up one screen
Alt+PgDn	Move right one screen
Alt+PgUp	Move left one screen
Ctrl+PgDn	Move to next sheet in workbook
Ctrl+PgUp	Move to previous sheet in workbook
Shift+PgDn	Extend selection down one screen
Shift+PgUp	Extend selection up one screen
Ctrl+Shift+*	Select current region
Ctrl+Shift+ spacebar	When an object is selected, select all objects on sheet
Ctrl+6	Alternate between hiding objects, displaying objects, and displaying placeholders for objects

If Enter does not move to the next cell, choose Tools ➤ Options, then select the Edit tab and check the *Move Selection After Entry* setting.

If the selection is one column, pressing Enter and Tab both move down (Shift+Enter and Shift+Tab both move up). If the selection is one row, pressing Enter and Tab both move right (Shift+Enter and Shift+Tab both move left).

Moving and Selecting While in End Mode

End	Turn end mode on/off
End, *arrow key*	Move by one block of data within a row or column
End, Shift+ *arrow key*	Extend selection to end of data block in direction of arrow
End, Home	Move to last cell in worksheet (lower-right corner)
End, Shift+Home	Extend selection to last cell in worksheet (lower-right corner)
End, Enter	Move to last cell in current row

End, Shift+ Enter	Extend selection to last cell in current row

End, Enter and End, Shift+Enter are unavailable if you have selected the Transition Navigation Keys setting on the Transition tab in the Tools ➤ Options dialog box.

Moving and Selecting with Scroll Lock

Scroll Lock	Turn scroll lock on/off
↑ or ↓	Scroll screen up or down one row
← or →	Scroll screen left or right one column
Home	Move to upper-left cell in window
End	Move to lower-right cell in window
Shift+Home	Extend selection to upper-left cell in window
Shift+End	Extend selection to lower-right cell in window

Selecting Special Cells

Ctrl+Shift+?	Select all cells containing a note
Ctrl+Shift+*	Select rectangular range of cells around the active cell—range selected is an area enclosed by any combination of blank rows and blank columns
Ctrl+/	Select entire array, if any, to which active cell belongs
Ctrl+\	Select cells whose contents are different from the comparison cell in each row
Ctrl+Shift+¦	Select cells whose contents are different from the comparison cell in each column

Ctrl+[	Select only cells directly referred to by formulas in selection
Ctrl+Shift+{	Select all cells directly or indirectly referred to by formulas in selection
Ctrl+]	Select only cells with formulas that refer directly to active cell
Ctrl+Shift+}	Select all cells within formulas that directly or indirectly refer to active cell
Alt+semicolon	Select only visible cells in current selection

Formatting

Alt+' (apostrophe)	Display style dialog box
Ctrl+Shift+~	General number format
Ctrl+Shift+$	Currency format with two decimal places (negative numbers appear in parentheses)
Ctrl+Shift+%	Percentage format with no decimal places
Ctrl+Shift+^	Exponential number format with two decimal places
Ctrl+Shift+#	Date format with day, month, and year
Ctrl+Shift+@	Time format with hour and minute (indicate a.m. or p.m.)
Ctrl+Shift+!	Two-decimal-place format with commas
Ctrl+Shift+&	Apply outline border
Ctrl+Shift+_	Remove all borders
Ctrl+B	Apply or remove bold (toggle)
Ctrl+I	Apply or remove italic (toggle)
Ctrl+U	Apply or remove underline (toggle)

Ctrl+5	Apply or remove strikethrough (toggle)
Ctrl+9	Hide rows
Ctrl+Shift+(	Unhide rows
Ctrl+0 (zero)	Hide columns
Ctrl+Shift+)	Unhide columns

Outlining

Alt+Shift+←	Ungroup a row or column
Alt+Shift+→	Group a row or column
Ctrl+8	Display or hide outline symbols
Ctrl+9	Hide selected rows
Ctrl+Shift+(	Unhide selected rows
Ctrl+0 (zero)	Hide selected columns
Ctrl+Shift+)	Unhide selected columns

Print Preview Mode

Arrow keys	Move around page when zoomed in
↑, ↓	Move by one page when zoomed out
PgUp, PgDn	Move by one page when zoomed out; move around page when zoomed in
Ctrl+↑ or Ctrl+←	Move to first page when zoomed out
Ctrl+↓ or Ctrl+→	Move to last page when zoomed out

Selecting Chart Items When Chart Is Active

↓	Select previous group of items
↑	Select next group of items
→	Select next item within group

| ↓ | Select previous group of items |
| ← | Select previous item within group |

Window Commands

Ctrl+F4	Close window
Ctrl+F5	Restore window size
Ctrl+F6 or Ctrl+Tab	Next window
Ctrl+Shift+F6 or Ctrl+Shift+Tab	Previous window
Ctrl+F7	Move command (Control menu)
Ctrl+F8	Size command (Control menu)
Ctrl+F9	Minimize window
Ctrl+F10	Maximize window

Switching Applications

Alt+Esc	Next application
Alt+Shift+Esc	Previous application
Alt+Tab	Next Windows application
Alt+Shift+Tab	Previous Windows application
Ctrl+Esc	Display Task List dialog box

INDEX

About This Index: **Boldfaced** page numbers indicate definitions of terms and the principal discussion of topics. *Italic* page numbers indicate illustrations.

Symbols

& (ampersands)
  in file searches, 324
  for joining text, 88
' (apostrophes)
  with SQL.REQUEST, 556
  for text, 59, 188
  for worksheet references, 96
* (asterisks)
  in cell selection, 66
  in consolidating data, 690
  in criteria, 467
  in field selection, 544
  in file searches, 322, 324
  as formatting symbols, 133
  for multiplication, 86–87
  in text searches, 77, 265
@ (at signs), 134
\ (backslashes), 133
{} (braces), 790
[] (brackets), 97
^ (carets), 86–87
: (colons)
  in cell references, 56, 95
  for time, 189
, (commas)
  as array separators, 227
  in file searches, 324
  as formatting symbols, 133
  in functions, 103
  in number entry, 58
$ (dollar signs)
  for cell references, 91–94
  in number entry, 58
" (double quotes)
  in file searches, 324

as formatting symbols, 133
  with SQL.REQUEST function,
    556–557
! (exclamation points), 96–97
/ (forward slashes)
  for division, 86–87
  as formatting symbols, 133
  in Lotus 1-2-3, 775
  in number entry, 58
> (greater than signs)
  in criteria, 466–467
  in filters, 447
< (less than signs)
  in criteria, 466–467
  in filters, 447
– (minus signs)
  for collapsing outlines, 699
  in number entry, 58
  for subtraction, 86–87
(number signs)
  as formatting symbols, 133
  for number overflow, 57, 74
() parentheses
  for calculation order, 87
  in functions, 103
  in number entry, 58
  in number formats, 138
% (percent signs)
  as formatting symbols, 133
  in formulas, 86–87
. (periods)
  as formatting symbols, 133
  in number entry, 58
+ (plus signs)
  for addition, 86–87

G

Send Away for the Companion Disk

LEX Software Systems, Inc. is pleased to offer the companion disk to go along with *Mastering Excel 5 for Windows*. The example files, plus many extras, can help you get up to speed quickly. The disk includes:

- the workbooks used in all of the exercises and examples—annotated to help you out
- a completed, polished version of the application created in Chapter 21
- several extra charting examples—you can see how the pros do it
- several special templates that are not covered in the book
- extra VBA macro examples, with comments to help you put them to use

The cost of the disk is US$9.50, plus $2.50 freight and handling (within the USA). Be sure to include your return address, and allow 4 weeks for delivery. Please send your payment to:

LEX Software Systems, Inc.
Mastering Excel 5 Companion Disk
9665 Timberlane Ave.
Suite 300
Winslow, WA 98110
(206) 528-6868

(If you do *not* want a $3\frac{1}{2}''$ disk, please specify $5\frac{1}{4}''$)

Tom Chester, the author of *Mastering Excel 5*, is president of LEX Software Systems, Inc. LEX is widely recognized as one of the leading Excel consulting firms in the country. LEX offers software development and training services for Microsoft Excel, Microsoft Access, Visual Basic, and SQL Server. As a certified *Microsoft Solutions Provider*, LEX has solved problems for many of the largest corporations in the world. You are welcome to give us a call at the above telephone number to discuss your development or training needs.

These disks are made available directly by the author. SYBEX Inc. is not affiliated with Lex Software Systems, Inc., and makes no warranties concerning the materials offered here.

GET A FREE CATALOG JUST FOR EXPRESSING YOUR OPINION.

Help us improve our books and get a *FREE* full-color catalog in the bargain. Please complete this form, pull out this page and send it in today. The address is on the reverse side.

Name _____   Company _____

Address _____   City _____ State ___ Zip _____

Phone ( )_____

1. How would you rate the overall quality of this book?

❑ Excellent
❑ Very Good
❑ Good
❑ Fair
❑ Below Average
❑ Poor

2. What were the things you liked most about the book? (Check all that apply)

❑ Pace
❑ Format
❑ Writing Style
❑ Examples
❑ Table of Contents
❑ Index
❑ Price
❑ Illustrations
❑ Type Style
❑ Cover
❑ Depth of Coverage
❑ Fast Track Notes

3. What were the things you liked *least* about the book? (Check all that apply)

❑ Pace
❑ Format
❑ Writing Style
❑ Examples
❑ Table of Contents
❑ Index
❑ Price
❑ Illustrations
❑ Type Style
❑ Cover
❑ Depth of Coverage
❑ Fast Track Notes

4. Where did you buy this book?

❑ Bookstore chain
❑ Small independent bookstore
❑ Computer store
❑ Wholesale club
❑ College bookstore
❑ Technical bookstore
❑ Other _____

5. How did you decide to buy this particular book?

❑ Recommended by friend
❑ Recommended by store personnel
❑ Author's reputation
❑ Sybex's reputation
❑ Read book review in _____
❑ Other _____

6. How did you pay for this book?

❑ Used own funds
❑ Reimbursed by company
❑ Received book as a gift

7. What is your level of experience with the subject covered in this book?

❑ Beginner
❑ Intermediate
❑ Advanced

8. How long have you been using a computer?

years _____
months _____

9. Where do you most often use your computer?

❑ Home
❑ Work

❑ Both
❑ Other _____

10. What kind of computer equipment do you have? (Check all that apply)

❑ PC Compatible Desktop Computer
❑ PC Compatible Laptop Computer
❑ Apple/Mac Computer
❑ Apple/Mac Laptop Computer
❑ CD ROM
❑ Fax Modem
❑ Data Modem
❑ Scanner
❑ Sound Card
❑ Other _____

11. What other kinds of software packages do you ordinarily use?

❑ Accounting
❑ Databases
❑ Networks
❑ Apple/Mac
❑ Desktop Publishing
❑ Spreadsheets
❑ CAD
❑ Games
❑ Word Processing
❑ Communications
❑ Money Management
❑ Other _____

12. What operating systems do you ordinarily use?

❑ DOS
❑ OS/2
❑ Windows
❑ Apple/Mac
❑ Windows NT
❑ Other _____

13. On what computer-related subject(s) would you like to see more books?

_____

_____

_____

_____

14. Do you have any other comments about this book? (Please feel free to use a separate piece of paper if you need more room)

_____

_____

_____

_____

- - - - - - - - - - - - - - PLEASE FOLD, SEAL, AND MAIL TO SYBEX - - - - - - - - - - - - - -

SYBEX INC.
Department M
2021 Challenger Drive
Alameda, CA
94501

Important Toolbars in Excel 5

Standard toolbar

New Workbook · Print · Print Preview · Cut · Format Painter · Repeat · Function Wizard · Sort Ascending · Text Box · Drawing · TipWizard

Open · Save · Spelling · Copy · Paste · Undo · AutoSum · Sort Descending · ChartWizard · Zoom Control · Help

Chart toolbar

Chart Type · ChartWizard · Legend

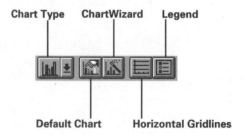

Default Chart · Horizontal Gridlines

Formatting toolbar

Font · Font Size · Bold · Underline · Center · Center Across Columns · Percent Style · Increase Decimal · Borders · Color

Arial · 10

Italic · Align Left · Align Right · Currency Style · Comma Style · Decrease Decimal · Font Color